Le Château
The lives of prisoners in Rwanda

Carina Tertsakian

ARVES
BOOKS

Published in the United Kingdom by Arves Books, 2008

PO Box 56247, London N4 2ZU

arves@rwanda-chateau.org

www.rwanda-chateau.org

A CIP catalogue record for this book is available from the British Library.

ISBN 978-0-9558215-0-9

Printed in the United Kingdom by 4edge Ltd

www.4edge.co.uk

Book design by Darryll Patterson and Carina Tertsakian

Front cover design by Karl Wood

———————

Front cover photograph: Cyangugu Central Prison, 2004 © Carina Tertsakian
Back cover photograph: Kigali Central Prison, 1995 © Hervé Deguine

Le Château

The lives of prisoners in Rwanda

Contents

"Going to paradise"   11

PREFACE

Scope of this book   16
Why Rwanda's prisons are unique   17
Recent events in Rwanda   20

CHAPTER I

Forty centimetres: space   29
    "Hell on earth": the early years (1994-1999)   34
    Improvements in prison conditions since 1999   49
    The state of prisons in 2004   51
    Health care   53
    Food   56
    Trading space   64
    A life of luxury   68
    Fashion   74

CHAPTER II

The prisoners' government: organisation   81
    The structure   85
    The *capita général*   90
    Elections   94
    Getting rich inside   98
    The prison administration   101
    Searches   111

CHAPTER III

Tomatoes, blackboards and guitars: work and leisure   115
    Work   116
    Education   125
    Entertainment   131

CHAPTER IV

God   147

CHAPTER V

"Living as sisters – a survival strategy": women in prison 159
    Conditions and organisation of the women's blocks   160
    Relations between the women   165
    Babies in prison   167
    Relations between women and men   169

CHAPTER VI

Real minors and false minors: children in prison   173
    Absolute minors   176
    Genocide minors   181
    Minors' living conditions   183
    Activities for minors   184
    Sexual abuse   186

CHAPTER VII

Families in prison   189

CHAPTER VIII

Waiting to die: the elderly in prison   195
    Lists and more lists   197
    Ill-treatment in detention   200
    The survival of the elderly in the central prisons   201
    Activities for the elderly   204
    The vulnerable among the vulnerable   208
    The memory of the family   213
    The response of the government   215

CHAPTER IX

Two armies in prison: the military prisoners 217
    Life in the civilian prisons 221
    Life in military detention 226

CHAPTER X

"You could count yourself as dead":
memories of the *cachots* and brigades 237
    Torture and killings 239
    Visits 241
    Prisoners' testimonies 244
    Improvements in conditions of detention 247

CHAPTER XI

Three minutes: prison visits 249
    Conditions of visits in the central prisons 255
    Solitude 262
    Visits: the early years 264
    The significance of visits for prisoners 267

CHAPTER XII

"The time of crying is over":
the effect of imprisonment on the family 275
    The economic burden 276
    The strain on relationships 278
    The gulf between prisoners and their families 281
    Deaths in prison 285
    The wider social circle 287

CHAPTER XIII

"Your father is a killer": the next generation 291
    Visiting parents in prison 292
    Explaining prison 294
    Children of *interahamwe* 297
    Separation 298
    The future 300

CHAPTER XIV

"It's more human inside than outside": relations between prisoners   301
    Violence and the absence of violence   302
    Ethnic relations   308
    Génocidaires and common criminals   313
    Friendships in prison   317

CHAPTER XV

"We are always in a state of maybe": attitudes to imprisonment   321
    Prison as home   322
    Hope and despair   324
    Looking back   332
    Looking forward: dreams of freedom   333
    Escaping   336

CHAPTER XVI

Talking   341

CHAPTER XVII

"Innocence can be subjective": justice   349
    The genocide trials   353
    "Buying innocence"   357
    The "big fish"   358
    Gacaca   360
    The prisoners' *gacaca*: "the real truth is in the prisons"   364
    The paralysis of the justice system   367
    Acquitted and still in prison   368
    Prisoners' views on justice   373
    Justice for RPF and RPA crimes   379

CHAPTER XVIII

"The heaviest sentence": prisoners sentenced to death   381
    The 1998 executions   382
    Life under sentence of death   388
    The abolition of the death penalty   392

CHAPTER XIX

Where the guilty are kings: confessions   395
    Propaganda, pressure and enticements   397
    The decision to confess   406
    "False confessions"   412
    "Real confessions"   415
    "The innocent"   418
    Double standards   422

CHAPTER XX

Freedom: a mirage   425
    The programme of releases   426
    Returning inside   428
    The *ingando*: "touching freedom"   434

CHAPTER XXI

Freedom: the reality   449
    The moment of release   452
    The process of readjustment   455
    Support for released prisoners   459
    Prison friendships   462

CHAPTER XXII

"I am still in that space now"   467

POSTSCRIPT

2007   475

APPENDICES

Map of Rwanda   480
Methodology   481
Glossary of terms and acronyms   484
Further reading   486

Acknowledgements   489

Index   490

"Going to paradise"

Rwanda is a tiny, fertile, densely populated country, a dot on the map of Africa. Nicknamed "the land of a thousand hills" ("*le pays des mille collines*"), it is an exceptionally beautiful country made up of layer upon layer of slopes, some steep mountains, others gentle hills. It is a country of lakes, forests, marshes, volcanoes, wide valleys and winding paths, a country of a thousand shades of green. Nearly every inch of the countryside is cultivated. Terraced crops grow up the steep slopes and across the hills: a variety of fruit and vegetables, corn, cassava, sugar-cane, coffee, rolling carpets of sparkling green tea plantations, and endless rows of banana trees, with their huge tattered leaves glinting in the sun. Herds of cows with majestic curved horns graze in the valleys and drink from the lakes. In the rainy season, heavy showers, alternating with long periods of sunshine, keep all the different shades of green alive, lush and shiny. A white mist often clings to the hilltops and hillsides throughout the mornings. It is sometimes hard to tell what is mist, what is cloud, or what is a lake in the distance.

Every visitor to Rwanda is astounded by the beauty of the country, and disturbed by the knowledge that within this environment, men and women have killed and killed and killed. In 1994, more than 500,000 people were slaughtered in a genocide carefully designed by Hutu extremists to wipe out the Tutsi minority. Hundreds of thousands of people fled the violence and remained in exile for several years, waiting for an elusive peace.

It is impossible to reconcile the beauty and the horror, and it is impossible to travel in Rwanda with a clear mind. Every hill, every marsh, every banana plantation, every village carries a memory of a massacre, an execution in cold blood, a gang rape. The knowledge is haunting and inescapable. You cannot allow your eyes to rest innocently on any part of the landscape.

When you start conversing with people, the presence of violence and suffering is even more overwhelming. Every individual has been touched by the genocide of 1994 and its violent aftermath. Almost every Rwandan has been a victim, an eye-witness or a perpetrator of violence during the genocide, and sometimes all three.

Nowhere is the contrast between the beauty and the horror more striking than in the prisons. It is as if this world of tens of thousands of people packed in like goods in containers, dehumanised, with no space to lie down, no air to breathe, amidst smells of life, disease and death, has been lifted from another place, cut out and stuck onto the map of Rwanda, like a crude surrealist experiment. In Cyangugu Central Prison, in the southwest of Rwanda near the Congolese border, the incongruity is at its most visual. An austere red brick building resembling a fortress, built on the top of a hill, the prison looms down over the breathtaking beauty of Lake Kivu and views of the Congolese town of Bukavu across the still water. The prison is surrounded by emerald hills and bushes of bright red and yellow flowers. Its own gardens, tended by the prisoners, are full of soft lawns, flowerbeds and carefully pruned shrubs. Every afternoon, at about 4pm, a group of prisoners who have the privilege of working on the gardening team can be seen lounging on the grass, at the end of their working day.

It was in one of these prison gardens overlooking the lake, in December 2004, that I interviewed a man who had spent three successive periods in prison, totalling seven and a half years. He had been accused of genocide and sentenced to life imprisonment. We sat talking on a bench which had been strategically positioned to offer the best views of the lake, like in a well-designed public park. During the first few minutes of the interview, the prisoner seemed distracted; he was trying to concentrate on my questions but couldn't help looking around him, on all sides. We then talked for around two hours. His was a complicated story which illustrated the most hopeless and dysfunctional aspects of the Rwandan justice system. It was an intense and sad conversation, concluded by a moment of rare happiness. At the end of the interview, he stood up slowly. He didn't want to tear himself away from the postcard scene of the lake and hills. As I accompanied him back to the prison gate, he told me with a broad smile: "This is the first time I am seeing the lake since 1997. Those who are sentenced to life don't get out. When I was called out to meet you, I was so happy to get some fresh air. It was like going to paradise. First I looked at the landscape on that side, and now I've looked at the lake on this side, and I've seen Bukavu." He was so happy, he could hardly contain himself; he was almost dancing. We shook hands and he walked back in through the metal gate, into the prison and the darkness inside.

Lake Kivu, seen from Cyangugu © Carina Tertsakian

Preface

Scope of this book

This book tells the story of prisoners in Rwanda from 1994 to 2004. It is an account of their experiences of imprisonment based on their personal testimonies and told, wherever possible, through their own words. Where relevant, it includes information about important developments that have taken place more recently, from 2005 to 2007.

The idea for this book was born after I visited several Rwandan prisons on behalf of an international human rights organisation soon after the genocide. In the years that followed, the images of those prisons haunted me, but my desire to speak out about the situation was prompted less by what I had seen in the prisons than by the shocking absence of public reaction. After the genocide, it was difficult to elicit any further outrage about events in Rwanda. Ordinary standards of behaviour no longer applied.

At the international level, we had the luxury of distance and the ability to see the situation for what it was, yet we failed to react. Occasional reports on the crisis in Rwanda's prisons by non-governmental organisations were generally ignored. The horror of the genocide, moral confusion and guilt defined all international reactions to Rwanda and made us blind to any other kind of suffering.

The suffering which continued silently in the prisons year after year was of a particularly inconvenient kind: these men and women dying of over-crowding, disease and ill-treatment were not the usual innocent victims. The vast majority were accused of genocide and there was little sympathy for their plight. The fact that most of them had not even been charged or tried – and that many may therefore have been innocent – did not seem to matter. Thus, over the years, the prison situation became an accepted feature of post-genocide Rwanda.

This book attempts to return some humanity to those prisoners by allowing them to speak and to inform the outside world of their daily reality. It also presents their opinions on critical questions relating to their imprisonment. There are points of view expressed in this book which I do not share, others which I do not fully understand, and many others which moved me deeply.

This book is a deliberately subjective account, presenting the perspectives of a particular group of people: Rwanda's prisoners. It is not a book about the genocide. In the many hours my colleagues and I spent talking to prisoners, we did not ask them about the crimes of which they were accused, though many of them talked about the genocide and other events willingly and liberally. In the approach to this book, there is no assumption of guilt and no assumption of innocence. Whatever they have done or not done, these individuals' stories deserve to be heard.

Why Rwanda's prisons are unique

Rwanda's prisons are unique and exceptional. They are a world unto themselves, mirroring the world outside with the kind of obsessive, disconnected realism which characterises the world of dreams.

The world of the prisons is held together by a dense web of contradictions. It is a world of extreme suffering, misery, egoism, harshness and despair. It is also a world of energy, hope, creativity, humour and inspiration. Amidst the bodies squashed up against each other, the ragged clothes, the hollow faces, the stench of sweat and dirty water, there is calm beauty and there is dignified resilience. The whole of humanity can be found there, living, breathing, thinking, remembering, acting, waiting and dying.

Those who planned the 1994 genocide made sure that responsibility for the killings was carried by as many people as possible: tens of thousands, maybe hundreds of thousands, of Hutu actively participated in the massacres. They killed their Tutsi neighbours with their own hands or delivered them to others to kill. Some killed willingly. Others killed because they were forced to kill. Some refused to kill and paid with their lives. A significant number of Hutu who were suspected of protecting Tutsi or who opposed the massacres were also killed.

All reference points were destroyed during the genocide. Families and childhood friends turned against each other, neighbours turned against neighbours. Individuals who had been known for their integrity and sense of communal responsibility turned into brutal killers overnight. Those who managed to survive and not to kill did so through a combination of immense personal courage, astuteness and chance.

The huge number of perpetrators resulting from the strategy behind the genocide meant that in the aftermath of the massacres, it became very difficult to pinpoint who had killed and who had not. Rwandans say that at the local level, everyone knows exactly who did what during the genocide, who was where, who killed whom, who saved whom and who abandoned others to their fate. But truth has sometimes been hard to find, and one of the lasting legacies of the genocide has been the destruction of trust and certainty: on the surface, any Hutu could be a killer, and any Hutu is therefore a suspect.

The uniqueness of Rwanda's prisons lies in the uniqueness of this recent history. The prisons in Rwanda are different from prisons in any other country in several fundamental ways.

First, there is the sheer number of prisoners. At the end of 2004, when I conducted the research for this book, around 85,500 people were imprisoned – more than 1% of the population of the country – the majority of them Hutu accused of genocide. At its peak, in around 1998, the prison population reached about 130,000. Almost everyone you meet in Rwanda has at least one and probably several relatives or acquaintances in prison. They may not mention this unless they are asked, not so much because of the shame but because it has become part of the normal fabric of life.

Secondly, as a result of these numbers, there is the extraordinary level of overcrowding. The Rwandan prisons are one of the most extreme experiences of mass human confinement in recent history, though they have rarely been recognised as such. Representatives of organisations who have worked in prisons in many different countries have described the conditions in Rwanda's prisons as unparalleled in any part of the world. As soon as the genocide ended, tens of thousands of people were arrested at an astonishing speed and incarcerated in prisons which had only a very limited capacity. Thousands of prisoners died as a direct result of the overcrowding and the conditions in which they were detained.

Thirdly, there is the gravity of the crimes attributed to most of these prisoners. The vast majority of them – around 90% at the end of 2004 – stand accused of genocide; a minority are accused of common crimes. But most of the prisoners have still not been tried, so their guilt or innocence remains in question.

The fourth aspect is the social composition of the prison population. In most countries, the bulk of prisoners come from disadvantaged sectors of society. They are often people with little education, who may have suffered emotional or psychological problems or developed drug or alcohol dependency; many may be repeat offenders or professional criminals. In Rwanda, this stereotypical profile is rare; it is found only among a small number of common criminals. The rest – the vast majority – are ordinary men and women from a wide range of social and professional backgrounds, most of whom had never set foot in a prison before. A whole society is living behind the prison walls, from rich government officials to poor peasants, and everything in between. While the majority of prisoners come from a rural background and have had little formal education (reflecting the make-up of the Rwandan population), an unusually high proportion are "intellectuals" – a term Rwandans use to refer to those with a good level of education.

As an illustration, the prisoners we interviewed for this book included national-level politicians, local government officials, military of various ranks, policemen, lawyers, judges, medical doctors, nurses, scores of teachers (one of the dominant professions among the educated prisoners), engineers, architects, priests, businessmen, civil servants, academics, staff of non-governmental organisations, social workers, students, and even a former prison director. At the other end of the spectrum, we found thousands of peasants and farmers, builders, carpenters, petty traders, drivers, mechanics, cooks and domestic workers. The result of this mix of backgrounds is a hugely diverse, vibrant, skilled and complex prison population.

The sense of a complete, functioning society is further accentuated by the presence of whole families who have been lifted from their homes and dropped into prison, as well as numerous groups of friends, neighbours and colleagues who knew each other long before the genocide. Family and social relationships have been transposed to the prison; all that has changed is the environment.

There are some ironic twists of fate as prisoners who had met each other in a previous life unexpectedly found themselves in the same prison. A judge joined several defendants in prison whose cases he had tried, including one he had sentenced to death. A member of the paramilitary Local Defence Force joined several prisoners whom he had been ordered to arrest, but told us with a smile: "I was never nasty to people and I never used to beat them. It was as if I knew I might end up in prison."

The final aspect in which Rwandan prisons differ from prisons in other countries is the internal organisation. Prison staff rarely penetrate the prisoners' living quarters. The prisons are almost entirely run by the prisoners themselves, reinforcing the sense of a complete and closed world.

Recent events in Rwanda[1]

The lives of prisoners in Rwanda cannot be separated from their lives outside, which have unravelled in a unique context.

Rwanda is a small country in central Africa, with a population of around 8.4 million. It is bordered to the south by Burundi, to the east by Tanzania, to the north by Uganda, and to the west by the Democratic Republic of Congo (formerly Zaire). Unlike most African countries, which have a diversity of

---

[1] This section offers only a very brief overview of recent events in Rwanda as background to the situation in the prisons. It is not intended as an exhaustive account. Details of publications on the country's recent history, political developments and human rights situation are included in "Further reading" (see Appendices).

ethnic groups and languages, Rwanda has only three ethnic groups, who share the same language, Kinyarwanda: the Hutu, who make up approximately 85% of the population; the Tutsi, who make up around 14%; and the Twa, a small minority.

Rwanda was colonised first by Germany in the late 19th century, then by Belgium from the early 20th century. In the pre-colonial era, the Tutsi had been the rulers and the elite in Rwandan society. Belgian colonial rule further entrenched Tutsi political, economic and social privileges, until the Hutu carried out a "revolution" in 1959 and seized power from the Tutsi monarchy. Suddenly, the balance was reversed. Whereas in the past, the Tutsi minority had ruled over and oppressed the Hutu majority, the Hutu were now in power and wielded that power without restraint. Tens of thousands of Tutsi were driven into exile and remained outside the country for several decades.

After Rwanda gained independence from Belgium in 1962, there were periodic massacres of Tutsi under the Hutu-led government of Grégoire Kayibanda. Heavy discrimination against the Tutsi continued and the government suppressed any dissent or challenge to its rule. In 1973, the government was overthrown by Juvénal Habyarimana, also a Hutu. Under President Habyarimana's rule, from 1973 until April 1994, political opposition was not tolerated and human rights were systematically violated.

From October 1990, the Rwandan Patriotic Front (RPF), a guerrilla group based in neighbouring Uganda, began launching cross-border attacks into Rwanda. The RPF was composed in large part of Tutsi who had fled Rwanda in the late 1950s and early 1960s and some Hutu opponents of the Habyarimana government. Between 1990 and 1994, armed conflict escalated. The RPF, backed by Uganda, attempted to invade Rwanda and was met with fierce resistance by the Rwandan army, which was receiving military support from France. The Habyarimana government, feeling increasingly threatened, cracked down further on the Tutsi inside Rwanda. Killings and arrests of Tutsi civilians intensified as the government accused them of supporting the RPF. A hardline extremist Hutu movement gathered strength, and from around 1993, a campaign of official anti-Tutsi rhetoric, expressed in explicit and unashamedly racist terms, deliberately stoked tensions in the population.

A key element of the strategy was the use of radio, the most popular form of communication in Rwanda, as in the rest of Africa. Virulent anti-Tutsi messages inciting violence were broadcast on the airwaves, notably on the private radio station Radio Mille Collines. The aim was to manipulate the Hutus' fear of the "enemy", and the strategy worked.

Eventually, in 1993, following increasing international pressure for an end to the conflict, the Rwandan government and the RPF held peace talks in Arusha, Tanzania. The talks resulted in the Arusha Accords, which set out the basis for power-sharing in a transitional government.

On 6 April 1994, an aeroplane carrying President Habyarimana and his Burundian counterpart, Cyprien Ntaryamira, was shot down over the Rwandan capital, Kigali. Both presidents were killed. To this day, no one has been able to ascertain beyond doubt who shot down the plane. Theories and speculation have abounded. To some, the RPF were the most likely culprits. Others believe the crash was organised by extremist elements within the Hutu elite, who were unhappy with Habyarimana's concessions to the RPF after the Arusha Accords and who wanted to hold onto power at any cost.

The plane crash of 6 April was the trigger for the genocide. Within hours of the crash, Hutu militia around the country – including the notorious *interahamwe* (a militia whose name means "those who attack together")[2] – started killing Tutsi. They also targeted Hutu who did not support the genocide. Over the days and weeks that followed, the massacres intensified. Tutsi were hunted down like animals, in their homes, in the banana plantations, in the marshes, in the churches where they sought safety. There was no hiding place. Roadblocks were set up every few kilometres, manned by *interahamwe* who checked the ethnicity of travellers. Hutu were allowed to pass, unless they appeared to oppose the killings of Tutsi. Tutsi were systematically taken out and slaughtered. For the most part, the perpetrators did not use modern military weapons; they hacked their victims with machetes and knives or bludgeoned them with clubs and sticks – whatever they could lay their hands on. Many of the victims died a slow and agonising death.

---

[2]   The *interahamwe* were linked to the ruling party, the *Mouvement républicain national pour la démocratie et le développement* (MRND).

In mid-April 2004, at the height of the genocide, the United Nations Security Council voted to withdraw the peacekeeping force it had stationed in Rwanda; the decision was taken after ten Belgian peacekeepers were killed. Foreigners were evacuated out of the country and the Tutsi were left to fend for themselves. The UN withdrawal was one of the most shameful episodes in recent international interventions and one which the people of Rwanda will never forget.

The genocidal massacres continued for three months. The exact number of victims has not been independently confirmed, but studies by non-governmental organisations and academics estimate that between 500,000 and one million people were killed.

Conflicts in Africa are often simplified and misrepresented in the West. The tendency to assume that they are always ethnically motivated is rarely challenged outside academic or specialist circles. The genocide in Rwanda reinforced these perceptions. There is no doubt that the killings in Rwanda were largely carried out on an ethnic basis – and explicitly so – but, as with almost every other conflict in the world, there were also more mundane factors behind the violence: this was a battle for political and economic power, land and social privileges. Ethnicity was a convenient and very effective tool with which to manipulate the population.

Meanwhile, a more classic war between the RPF troops and those of the Rwandan government, the *Forces armées rwandaises* (FAR), was taking place alongside the genocide. Following the withdrawal of UN peacekeepers, France, which had long backed the Habyarimana government both politically and militarily, sent troops to Rwanda, in the face of fierce opposition from the RPF. Known as Operation Turquoise, the French deployment, from June to August 1994, was officially intended to create a safe humanitarian zone in the southwest of the country. The operation was highly controversial, as France was accused of trying to protect its former allies and facilitating the escape of those responsible for the genocide. Nevertheless, many lives were saved through the deployment of Operation Turquoise in the final weeks of the genocide.

Genocide memorial at Nyange, Kibuye © Alison Lea

Eventually, in July 1994, the RPF overpowered the FAR and took control of most of the country. What was left of the Rwandan government and its armed forces was driven into exile. Hundreds of thousands of Hutu men and women, including many who had participated in the genocide, fled with them, in an exodus of unprecedented proportions. More than a million Rwandans fled west to Zaire, while 500,000 or more fled east to Tanzania, and between 200,000 and 300,000 fled south to Burundi. Vast refugee camps were set up in these countries. Most of the refugees stayed there for more than two years and underwent extreme hardship in exile.

The genocide stopped as soon as the RPF gained control of Rwanda. The RPF set up a new government and a semblance of calm gradually returned. However, the RPF also killed many civilians as it fought its way through the country, as well as in the immediate aftermath of the genocide. These killings have mostly been shrouded in secrecy, but testimonies indicate that tens of thousands of people, most of them Hutu, were killed by the RPF in 1994. Killings continued sporadically in 1995 and 1996.

In November 1996, the Rwandan Patriotic Army (RPA, the new Rwandan army) invaded eastern Zaire, helping Zairian rebel leader Laurent-Désiré Kabila overthrow President Mobutu Sese Seko in April 1997. Zaire was renamed the Democratic Republic of Congo (DRC) and Kabila became its new president. As the Rwandan troops invaded, they attacked the massive refugee camps near the border and killed thousands of Rwandan Hutu refugees. Thousands of other refugees fled the camps in terror and sought safety in the dense Congolese forests. Many were hunted down in the forests, hundreds of miles from the border, and killed there. The total number of victims may never be known. Others trekked for weeks or months, with nothing to eat and nowhere to go, until they died of starvation, or eventually decided to return to Rwanda out of exhaustion or desperation. Many who survived walked several thousand kilometres, some eventually reaching destinations as far away as West Africa.

The attacks on the camps also sparked a more organised mass return to Rwanda of hundreds of thousands of refugees from Zaire. Most of those who returned to their country were forced to do so; their return was at the heart of the Rwandan government's strategy in attacking the camps. In 1996, forced repatriations from Tanzania and Burundi led to the return of most of the Rwandan refugees from those countries too.

The period that followed was probably the most violent in Rwanda's post-genocide history. From late 1996 to 1998-1999, armed groups known as *infiltrés* (infiltrators), composed of members of the former Rwandan army and *interahamwe* militia who had remained in the DRC, launched cross-border attacks into Rwanda, killing Tutsi civilians. The response of the RPA was brutal. It hit back hard; the prime targets were Hutu civilians living near the borders, whom the RPA accused of collaborating with the *infiltrés*. Thousands of civilians were killed by the RPA during its counter-insurgency operations. Entire families were wiped out and entire villages destroyed.

From 1999, the violence decreased, and the situation has since become much calmer. But Rwanda remains a tense and frightened country. Not only are memories of the genocide still fresh, but the government set up by the RPF, headed by Paul Kagame, has ruled with an iron fist. It has done so skilfully. Less obviously authoritarian than its predecessors, it has used more subtle tactics to silence opposition and has embraced a rhetoric of good governance designed to impress the international community. Its success in restoring a measure of normality in the country after the genocide, with significant foreign support, has also enabled it to score high points on the international scene. But for ordinary Rwandans, the situation is desperate. While the elite is busy erecting shiny new buildings in Kigali, prices have rocketed and the majority of the population are struggling to find enough to eat. Freedom of expression is severely limited. Independent criticism has been stifled through a mixture of violent repression and a more insidious strategy of intimidation of an already traumatised population. The result has been the most effective form of silence: self-censorship.

Resentment has been building up, both among Hutu and disaffected Tutsi. Many Tutsi who initially supported the RPF subsequently felt neglected by their new leaders; those who dared to express their dissatisfaction fell out of favour with the government. Cracks began appearing in the previously tight circle of power around President Kagame. The country's stability remains extremely fragile.

It is in this context that the research for this book was carried out. Ten years after the genocide, more than 85,000 men and women remained incarcerated in Rwanda's prisons, the majority still untried. This book is about their lives in prison.

CHAPTER I

Forty centimetres:

space

Forty centimetres is the standard width of a prisoner's individual space, where he sleeps, where he eats, where he sits, where he lives. He calls it his château, his castle. It consists of one or two planks of wood placed on a metal frame. The planks are lined up next to each other, with no space in between. Sometimes there are makeshift partitions between the planks, but often there aren't. The planks are on a structure of bunk-beds, on three levels, with a wooden ladder propped up against the front to climb up to the top levels. There are no cells, just row after row of these bunk-bed structures, erected in basic buildings. Each building is a block. Several hundred prisoners are crammed into each block. Several thousand prisoners are crammed into each prison.

There are not enough châteaux for everybody – far from it. Those who get a space on these planks are the lucky ones. Others have to sleep on the ground in a tiny space underneath the lowest row of planks, on the concrete; it is so low you would not think an adult could enter it. But they do, tall men with supple bodies crawling in there like cats, their bodies bending at improbable angles. Or old men for whom the process of sliding in and out of this space is visibly painful. Once in, they can barely move. They lie there with the top of their head grazing the planks of the bunk-bed above them. They can't turn over and they can barely breathe. In Cyangugu Central Prison, these spaces under the beds are called "mines"; in Butare, they are *indake* (trenches); in Gitarama, they are *igara* (the place underneath). One prisoner told us he had spent six years sleeping in a mine, on the concrete under someone else's bed.

Other prisoners sleep on the ground in the corridors, in the gangways between the bunk-beds, where they are often trampled on or accidentally kicked. One prisoner told us that people can't complain if you walk on them, because it is obviously not done on purpose. Another prisoner who had been sleeping in a corridor for more than three years explained how he had to fold up his legs all the time so that people could pass without walking on him.

Many sleep directly on the ground. Others sleep on pieces of cardboard, or on a torn sack, or on part of a blanket, with the other part folded over them.

In one huge room in Butare Central Prison, known as the chapel, there are no metal structures and no bunk-beds. There are just rows of narrow wooden benches on the ground. Each bench is about 30 centimetres wide. One layer of prisoners sleeps on top of these benches and another underneath, in a grid-like formation. The prisoners gave us a demonstration: one person lies on the bench, on a folded sack which serves as a mattress. Three others lie underneath, on the ground between the two feet of the bench, at right angles to the one on top. The only way for those on top to get up at night is to step on the last few inches of each bench which have deliberately been left empty for this purpose. Other people sleep across all the pathways on the ground. About 400 people live in the chapel.

In Butare prison, there is another area known as Kuwait, so named by the prisoners because it is a gulf, a narrow impasse. It is dark, damp and airless, and there is an overpowering smell from the adjacent toilets and showers. Just outside Kuwait, people sleep in an area which is also used to wash, but which is distinct from the official showers. It is a narrow corridor, but less dark than Kuwait because it is in the open air. When we walk through, some of the prisoners who live there are sitting crouched up against the walls, with dirty, soapy water swilling around their feet and dripping down the walls, while others are having their shower opposite them. They have to clean the area each night before going to sleep there.

The even less fortunate sleep outside, in the yard, in the open air, exposed to the hot sun and frequent downpours of heavy rain. Some have plastic sheeting to protect them, but it is old and worn, stitched and patched up again and again until it can be patched up no longer; the rain drips in through the holes. The sheeting is rolled back during the day, unless it is raining, and brought back at night, but it doesn't cover the whole yard, so some prisoners remain exposed. Some more enterprising prisoners have erected precarious structures against the walls of the yard, made of a combination of wooden planks and pieces of sheeting; these are called *ibyari*, birds' nests. But most just sleep where they can on the ground outside, sitting against the walls, or in the middle of the yard, next to drainage channels and puddles of dirty rain.

In the annex to Butare prison, known as Rwandex, there are prisoners who sleep on top of the septic tanks located under the main path in two of the blocks, in the open air. Once or twice a month, the path has to be dug up, using metal handles, and the septic tanks emptied into the drainage channels which run through the prison and out. The job of emptying the septic tanks takes 24 hours. The team of prisoners responsible for hygiene works through the night. When the tanks are being emptied, the prisoners who live there have to move and find somewhere else to sleep. We met a prisoner who had been sleeping on the ground over the septic tanks for one year and four months: "Since arriving in Rwandex, until today, I've been sleeping over the septic tanks. The smell is very bad. They empty the tanks regularly and it stinks terribly. On the nights when they empty it, we just walk around all night. We call it *abari ku izamu* [nightwatchmen]."

Every aspect of prison life in Rwanda is defined by the overcrowding. The first hint is the noise. At Nsinda, the approach to the prison is down a quiet path dotted with small houses, one or two shops, and fruit and vegetable crops. As you draw closer to the prison, you become aware of a sound like the humming of thousands of bees coming from behind the prison walls a few yards ahead. It is the sound of prisoners talking, working, getting on with their daily lives. In other prisons, the sound is not audible from the outside, but as soon as the guards open the interior gate to let anyone in or out, the sound rises and wraps itself around you. Once you are inside, after a few seconds, you no longer even notice it.

Many of the blocks we walked through were so dark that it took some time for our eyes to adjust. We were afraid of tripping over or bumping into people as we wended our way down the narrow passageways. Some prisons have electricity, but the supply is erratic at best, and there was no lighting in the blocks we visited during the daytime. Nsinda prison has tents instead of blocks, and a larger space outside the tents in which prisoners can walk around, but inside each tent, there is the same three-tier bunk-bed structure as in the other prisons, in the same oppressive darkness, overflowing with hundreds of prisoners. In some prisons, efforts were still being made to carve out new living areas within the limited space available: in Cyangugu prison, prisoners had constructed a new place in the yard which they called *gariyamoshi* (train, in Swahili) because it is made of metal. Prisoners who live there say they live in the train. The train was covered with sacking, but within a short time, the sacking was already torn.

In Butare prison, until 2003, people were still sleeping in the showers, in the toilets and on makeshift platforms higher up above the toilets. They also used to sleep on the roof, in the open air. In 2004, the roof area – which we accessed by climbing up a long steep ladder – is still crowded but no one sleeps there anymore. It is used for classes. Groups of 15 or 20 prisoners sit clustered in front of blackboards, in the blazing sun. There is no shelter. All around them, on the rooftops, blankets have been laid out to dry on the corrugated iron roofs, placed there with long wooden poles. When you stand on the roof and look out over the prison walls, you get a clear view of the green hills all around; you can see fields and people in the distance, lots of open space, the world outside.

In Gitarama prison, the first interior courtyard, after going through the gate, is crammed full of people. It is as if they have gathered there for a purpose, awaiting a meeting or an important announcement. In fact, they are just standing there because that is where they live. It is the same thing in one of the big rooms inside, formerly used as a chapel. It is a huge room, full of people, some sitting, some standing, some lying down, again looking as if they are waiting for something. The chapel is home to 320 prisoners and, as in Butare, they sleep on benches. Further inside the prison, unpleasant smells waft in from the kitchen and swirls of acrid smoke and ashes blow into our eyes as we walk past. Prisoners are living and sleeping right next to the kitchen, with the smoke blowing straight at them. A few prisoners walk past, screwing up their eyes against the smoke, but most are just sitting there; that is where they spend their days and their nights. Inside the blocks, it is dark and extremely crowded. Many prisoners are just lying or sitting in their châteaux. Some peer out from behind improvised curtains. They don't seem surprised by our visit. Some smile and greet us. Most stare in silence. The expression in their eyes is not blank; it is a direct and piercing look, yet it is difficult to decipher its meaning. I remember, when I visited the prisons in earlier years, being met by a sea of intense stares, distrustful, defiant, even

fierce, and all of them expectant. Several years on, there is no longer any
ferocity, and no longer any expectation, just a tired resignation.

"Hell on earth": the early years (1994-1999)

Anyone who visited Rwandan prisons for the first time in 2004 would find it
difficult to imagine that conditions used to be even worse. Yet the situation
in Rwanda's prisons in the early post-genocide years, from late 1994 to 1999,
was so extreme that words fail even those who lived through it. A former
prisoner detained during that period summarised it in one sentence: "Some
prisons are prisons, and others are like hell."

Even though several years have passed since then, it is essential to
understand what prisoners lived through in those early years in order to
understand their current situation.

For any outside visitor who was allowed a glimpse into that world, however
briefly, the memory can never be erased. Visual images would go some way
towards conveying the realities, but would leave out the wealth of noises and
smells, the thickness of the air, the physical contacts, and the juxtaposition
with the outside world. There were people sitting and standing literally
everywhere; wherever you rested your eyes there were people, from the
ground right up to the makeshift shelters tenuously clinging to the walls.
People were packed in so densely, both inside and outside, that the prisoners
who showed us round had to force a path by tapping prisoners with a stick to
make way for us to step through. The mass of people then closed up again
behind us. It was like walking through thick vegetation, or through a herd of
cattle. We had to tread carefully, tiptoeing through the crowd, watching
where we put our feet to make sure we didn't trample on people or step in the
filth on the ground. There was an overwhelming smell of sweat, excrement,
urine, food and dirty water; you could smell it outside, long before entering
the prison gate. Inside, we shared an absurd intimacy with these prisoners: it
was impossible to talk to any of them or even walk past them without
touching them. We were almost pressed up against each other, feeling each
other's breath on our faces. Groups of prisoners swayed slowly, as if in a
trance, because they couldn't move. Others stood or sat still, staring, doing

nothing, waiting, they didn't know what for. Some were huddled up in sling-like contraptions they had fastened to the walls because there was no space left on the ground; they hung there like bats.

I remember a colleague asking me whether I was afraid of entering this world of genocidal killers. It had never occurred to me to be afraid. It was a frightening environment, but not a threatening one. Scanning the sea of eyes around me, the thought inevitably crossed my mind that many of these people had killed and raped in the most brutal way. But in this environment, they no longer appeared as killers. The usual labels and categorisations had lost all relevance. Whoever these people were, and whatever they may have done, the overwhelming emotions were shock and revulsion that anyone anywhere could be forced to live in such conditions. These people had lost their individual identity as human beings, yet at the same time, here was a vision of humanity at its most intense and raw, and, strangely, at its most dignified in its ability to endure and survive.

The suffering in the prisons was suffering of a different kind from the violence which had engulfed Rwanda in 1994: here, there was no blood, no guns, no machetes, but an insidious, slow and suffocating death.

It was impossible to imagine anyone coming out of those prisons alive, but amazingly, many did. Ten years on, we spoke to dozens of prisoners who had survived this period. When we asked them to describe their early experiences in the prisons, even the most articulate ones were at a loss for words. They either just shook their heads and said nothing, or came out with bland understatements like "it was a bit difficult", "we had problems", or "there were too many people". But as our conversations went on, some were able to bring back specific memories which provided a way into that world. A prisoner who had been detained for more than nine years said that before his arrest, he could never have understood how someone could spend a whole year without sleeping. That was his lasting memory of his nine years in prison. He said that sometimes, when he tried to describe the situation and the memories started flooding back, he had to stop talking.

This is the experience these prisoners have carried with them, and which will never leave them, despite the relative improvements in subsequent years.

One prisoner who was arrested in 1994 told us: "I was expecting to die at any minute. It was a cloud which blocked things out. Death hasn't meant anything to me since then."

From July 1994, the government started arresting tens of thousands of people on accusations of participation in the genocide. Within a few months, the prisons filled up to several times their capacity, until people were literally stacked on top of each other, in every square inch of the inside and outside space of the prisons. There was no room to lie down, so prisoners slept sitting between each other's knees, in tight rows. More prisoners arrived every day. Between 1994 and 1996, the prison population quadrupled, rising from around 20,000 to more than 80,000. It reached its peak in 1998 – around 130,000 – but the worst year, at least in some prisons, was 1995, before prison annexes were built, before additional buildings such as warehouses were converted into prisons, and before international humanitarian organisations could provide assistance in a systematic way.

Thousands of prisoners died during this period as a direct result of the conditions: severe overcrowding, lack of food, lack of medical treatment for illnesses and injuries sustained from torture. Diseases such as tuberculosis and dysentery spread rapidly. There were stories which sounded as if they were taken from a medieval depiction of hell, but which were all true: prisoners whose feet and legs had to be amputated because they had rotted from standing for hours on end in the filth and stagnant water; prisoners who were too weak or too sick to move and who ended up dying where they lay, trampled on by other prisoners; prisoners who were taken to be buried before they had died; and others who were taken out by soldiers and shot dead. A prisoner who worked as a nurse in Kigali Central Prison described a place where they used to stack up the corpses: "There was a whole pile of bodies there. They were not buried from Friday to Monday. We wondered why we were bothering to look after them."

Kigali Central Prison, 1995   © Hervé Deguine

Kigali Central Prison, 1995   © Hervé Deguine

Gitarama prison had one of the highest death rates. In June 1995, the non-governmental organisation Médecins sans frontières produced a report on the medical conditions there, stating that one in eight prisoners had died between September 1994 and May 1995 – in total 902 out of 7,003 prisoners, or 13% of the prison's population – as a direct result of extreme over-crowding. The report described the situation as "catastrophic" and noted that the living space of each prisoner measured less than half a square metre. It recorded the medical conditions which it found in the prison, including various diseases and infections, as well as foot wounds which caused gangrene and led to frequent amputation of the feet and legs.[1]

André Sibomana, a Rwandan priest and human rights activist who regularly visited Gitarama prison during this period, described in his book the conditions he witnessed there in 1995:

> "The living conditions are such that if you let enough time go by, the suspected killers or accomplices of the genocide will just die one by one. Whether innocent or guilty, these prisoners are gradually rotting away. When I say 'rotting away', I mean it literally. At least one UNAMIR [the UN peacekeeping force in Rwanda] officer can testify to that. When he visited Gitarama Prison and gave a nice speech to the detainees, one of them ripped his toe off and threw it in his face. After weeks of standing upright, day and night, in the mud, the prisoners' feet had started decomposing... There were three layers of prisoners: at the bottom, lying on the ground, there were the dead, rotting on the muddy floor of the prison. Just above them, crouched down, were the sick, the wounded, those whose strength had drained away. They were waiting to die. Their bodies had begun to rot and their hope of survival was reduced to a matter of days or even hours. Finally at the top, standing up, there were those who were still healthy. They were standing straight and moving from one foot to the other, half asleep... Whenever a man fell over, it was a gift to

---

[1]   Médecins sans frontières, *Report on the medical conditions at Gitarama prison*, Rwanda, June 1995.

survivors: a few extra centimetres of space. I remember a man who was standing on his shins: his feet had rotted away." [2]

For a prisoner who was detained in Gitarama from 1995, the memories were still vivid: "People were treated like animals... People got crushed and pushed in the crowd. Some died of suffocation; others were trampled... The soldiers used to take people out to question them and when they came back in, many of them died. I remember one day I counted 32 dead. The average was 20 a day, or maybe more."

A prisoner who arrived in Gitarama prison in September 1994, and was still there ten years later, described his impressions on the first day: "It was a place of death... I saw the prison fill up. It was horrible, especially at night. There were scenes which no one should see. Prisoners were brought in on trucks, piled up high. They came in all beaten up, injured, dirty. They had been held in containers and secret places of detention before being brought here."

In Butare prison, the situation was not much better. A prisoner who had spent ten years there described his first few days in 1994:

> "There were about 40 of us in what is now the infirmary... Some
> had already died there, some had been beaten and tortured. In
> the morning, when I went to the toilet, I saw the remains of about
> four putrefying bodies, dead on the ground, under the sink where
> they'd been piled up. Each night, a truck brought piles of people
> in, like logs, some alive, some dead, some old men. We looked
> out of our windows to see them arriving at night. They kicked
> them like sacks. If someone was dying, they would beat him, take
> his money, shoot into the air and shout 'he's running away!', then
> shoot the prisoner. We used to hear them dragging the bodies

---

[2]   André Sibomana, *Hope for Rwanda: Conversations with Laure Guilbert and Hervé Deguine*, transl. Carina Tertsakian, Pluto Press, 1999. André Sibomana was among the first people to intervene to try to save the lives of prisoners in Gitarama. One of the most simple and effective forms of assistance was the distribution of rubber sandals, made out of recycled tyres, which enabled prisoners to have some protection from the dirt and mud on the floor. These sandals have since become standard footwear in Rwanda's prisons.

down to the sinks. The next morning we would see men in the yard cleaning up the blood. I didn't feel much. I shut down my feelings."

Prisoners used various comparisons to describe the overcrowding in the early years: they said people were piled in like sacks of coal, like goods in a warehouse, like chickens, like cattle, or like pigs. Some compared the conditions to those of a concentration camp – an observation also made by outside visitors. One prisoner said that on his first day in prison, he felt as if the earth was opening up before him. In addition to the lack of physical space, there was the overwhelming noise of such a large number of people crowded into such a small place, all thrown in together without separate rooms or cells, and without walls or even partitions to provide some insulation from the sound. Prisoners compared the inside of the prison to a marketplace, where the market never closes. One prisoner was terrified by the noise when he first arrived: "It was deafening, all day and all night. I wondered whether my hearing would become affected. There were no hours of rest. But in the end, the body adjusts. You sleep a bit, but when you wake up, the noise is still there, even at night. It was like a chicken-coop. One person was sleeping while another was shouting. People were shouting inside all the time."

As the 40 centimetre "beds" (which at that time were more likely to measure 30 centimetres) and the spaces on the ground and in the corridors all filled up, tens of thousands of people ended up sleeping in the courtyards outside, without shelter. Even in the courtyards, it became so congested that at night, people had to sleep on their side; whenever prisoners wanted to turn over, a signal was given and everyone had to turn over at the same time. There wasn't enough space to put a plate down on the ground. People slept in the toilets, in the showers, in the kitchens full of smoke, on the roofs, on top of tables and under tables. In some prisons, prisoners took turns to sleep on alternate days: one day they stood up, the next day they sat down. Some people found nowhere to sleep at all, so they just walked around the prison all day and all night. If they paused for a few seconds, they would be shouted at to carry on walking because they were stepping on someone or standing in someone's space. Sometimes other prisoners would give up their space for them for a few hours, to enable them to sit down or catch some sleep. Then that person would walk around until it was time to return to claim back his space. This army of walkers was called *komeza*, the Kinyarwanda word for "continue". If one of them was asked in which part of the prison they lived, they would answer "I'm in *komeza*", as if it was the name or number of a particular block. Some of those who ended up in *komeza* were people who were not yet familiar with the ways of the prison. But others were wise to the strategies of survival. They were hungry and desperate, so they had voluntarily sold their space inside and joined *komeza*, because they preferred to have money to buy food.

There was a hierarchy even among the worst places to live in the prison. A prisoner who had lived in Kigali Central Prison from 1994 to 1997 ranked them as follows. *Komeza* was the worst, then came the toilets; at least those who slept in the toilets had somewhere to return to at night. The worst place after the toilets was the outside yard, followed by a place described as the hangar. The hangar was called "*chez les délinquents*" (the delinquents' area). It was covered, but people were squashed in inside. Around 1,000 or 1,500 people lived there, and no one ever cleaned it. The next level up was the entrance to the kitchen, a dark corridor. And so it went on. Each prison had its equivalent ranking of different sections. A prisoner in Cyangugu spent two months sleeping next to the drainage channel outside, but didn't feel he could complain because there were people who were even worse off than him, who slept in the toilets. Another prisoner started off sleeping inside, on the ground, next to the bucket in which prisoners defecated. After a week, he moved to a place outside, near the toilets. "Even though it wasn't in the toilets, the insects from the toilets used to crawl all over me. It was horrible. In the morning I had to shake the blanket to get rid of the insects. I tried to get a space in a mine, but I couldn't get in because I was too big."

A prisoner described his first impression of Kigali Central Prison in 1995: "There wasn't even space to reach the toilet or walk for three or four metres... I didn't think it was possible to spend a week in there without dying. People were sick and were dying just like that, piled up in a corner... If you needed to go to the toilet, you had to pull the person sleeping there off the hole, use the toilet then put him back. Some had strung up ropes above the toilets. They wrapped the ropes from wall to wall to sleep on them above the toilets."

Kigali Central Prison, 1995   © Hervé Deguine

A prisoner in Kigali Central Prison who was one of the first to become *capita général* (the "chief prisoner" responsible for all other prisoners) after the genocide took on the impossible task of organising the space for the prisoners. He had to decide who would sleep where and, crucially, how. It was like a crude puzzle: how to fit a vast number of people into a space which was obviously far too small. The fact that he was a trained architect may have helped him come up with some innovative solutions:

> "There were more than 11,700 people. I had to find them places. I lined them up... The first to arrive slept in the dormitories. The beds were called shelves [*les étagères*]. Each person had 30 centimetres. For bigger people, we tried to give them 45 or 50 centimetres. Once the shelves were full, people slept on the ground in the blocks and in the yard, in the rain and sun... At 9pm or 10pm, after the prisoners had used the toilets, we washed all the toilets and people slept there. We kept two or three free in case of accidents. Later, the Red Cross gave us planks for the toilets. We put these planks over the toilets, as shelves for people to sleep on. I also asked people to sleep in the church and in the kitchen. In the church, which was about 34 metres by 14 metres, there were benches. We made three floors with the benches: one row of people slept on the ground, a second row slept on the bench, and a third slept on a second bench on top of the first. In the kitchen, people slept in the room where they put the vats of food once they were finished. They slept on the concrete. I lined up the empty barrels and put shelves on top of the barrels. People then slept on these shelves and underneath the shelves. Almost 1,000 people slept in the kitchen, in the corridor of the kitchen and in the toilets. About 3,000 slept in the church: 1,000 on each 'floor' of benches. This was the situation from 1994 to 1998, until people were transferred to Gikondo and Kimironko prisons."

Prisoners who slept outside were given plastic sheeting by the Red Cross, but the quantity was insufficient and the protection it provided against the rain was inadequate at best. Some prisoners had blankets, but whenever it rained, the blankets got soaked. When it rained heavily, prisoners tried to find a place inside where they could shelter temporarily, then went back outside once the rain had stopped. In Gikondo prison, those who slept outside had a particularly raw deal: the blocks were closed from 6pm to 6am, so when it rained in the evening or at night, those who slept outside had nowhere to shelter.

The number of toilets and showers was dramatically inadequate, and there were serious shortages of water. Prisoners had to queue for several hours to use the toilet, to have a shower, or to collect water; it was not uncommon to queue for five or six hours, or even a whole day. One prisoner remembered having to leave his place at 6am in the hope of reaching the toilet at 11 am, but he still might not get there; it was only 20 metres away. Sometimes there were simply too many people in the way, so prisoners gave up. They couldn't fight their way through the crowds, so ended up going to the toilet where they stood. Prisoners tried not to eat very much, even when they were given food, so as not to have to go to the toilet. Some didn't even bother to get up to try to get food or water. As there were too few showers, prisoners washed in the open air, in full view of everyone, and dirty water gushed down into the places where people slept. Later, additional showers and toilets were built, and there were places where prisoners could shower privately, but they had to know where these were, and they had to pay other prisoners to use them.

It was common practice to pay other prisoners for water. Prisoners who had no money paid for their water with half their food ration. One prisoner said he used to give half his food ration to a prisoner to hold his place in the queue for the toilet and to fetch water for him. There were prisoners in charge of the taps; they used to get up at 3am to store up the water, then sell it to others during the day. Sometimes it was a question of choosing between half a ration of food and a cup of water to drink, which might have to last three or four days. In Butare prison, some prisoners who had a bit of money used to bribe the guards to take jerry cans to the truck which delivered water to the prison, or to a place up the road where water was piped in to the prison through a hole in the wall. In Kimironko prison, there was a shortage of water even as late as 1999. Some prisoners received water from their families and others were sent to fetch water from a nearby pond. A prisoner told us: "You could send someone from the water team to get water if you gave them a five-litre container. Or you could buy the water from them at 20 francs a container.[3] If lots of people went to fetch water, the price went down to 15 francs a container. Everything was a question of money."

The men's blocks were always more overcrowded than the women's, but in the early years, the women too ended up sleeping in the yard outside, in the toilets, in the showers, anywhere they could find a few centimetres. A woman who was held in Kigali Central Prison from 1995 to 1997 recalled: "We slept on the ground. We used the cardboard from the biscuits to sleep on. People slept among the plates and the dirt. Some women slept on the toilet hole. From 9pm, we couldn't use the toilets as there were women sleeping there. It was the same for the shower. There was a woman with her two- or three-year-old child who used to sleep in the shower every night. She used to lie on her back with her legs up vertically against the wall." In the first half of 1995, about 60 women slept outside, in the open air, in two parallel lines, from the door to the toilet. They were those who had arrived later, or who were "less clever", in the words of one prisoner. About 40 others slept in a building next to the kitchen, which was always full of smoke from the cooking, and was kept closed all the time.

A woman who was arrested in 1994 recalled that each day, 30 to 50 new prisoners would arrive. She was lucky to find a woman she knew, who created some space for her at the edge of her bed. The space they shared was 45 centimetres wide. To turn over, she had to get up, sit down and lie down again. In around mid-1995, a new building was opened and the women were transferred there, but one year later, it was already full; space intended for two people was used by five, and women had to start sleeping outside again.

Until 1995 or 1996, there was no civilian prison administration, so the prison staff and guards were all military. Beatings of prisoners were commonplace. A woman in Butare prison said that the military who used to run the prison were very brutal: "It was their right, almost their duty to beat us. I was beaten with a cable many times. There was no reason, and no questions were asked. I lost my teeth from the blows." A prisoner who was in Kibungo Central Prison in 1995 remembered a particular soldier who used to go round all the blocks in the prison every day, make the prisoners sit on the ground and beat them on the head, three times a day; it was like their daily

---

3   In late 2004, the rate of exchange was approximately 560 Rwandan francs to US$1.

ration. There were no registers in the prisons until around 1996, so the military, and the government, were completely unaccountable. An unknown number of prisoners disappeared.

Prison as a place of happiness

Unbelievably, a number of prisoners we spoke to described the prison as a paradise in these early years, and their first day there as a moment of intense relief and happiness – even a moment of celebration. This is a measure of the suffering they had been subjected to before arriving in the prison, in the *cachots* (local detention centres) or military detention centres where they had first been detained (see Chapters IX and X). Many had been tortured there and had seen other detainees die. They had lost all hope of surviving. A man in his sixties who spent five years in a *cachot* before being transferred to a central prison was sure that if he had stayed one week longer in the *cachot*, he would have died.

In the *cachots*, especially in the early years, prisoners received little or no food, no water, and no visits. At least in the prisons, they could wash, eat, drink and see their families, even if all these activities took place in extremely difficult conditions. Their first shower was an extraordinary moment for many of them, as they had spent weeks or even months without being able to wash at all. A prisoner remembered how happy he was when he was given a big bucket of water in the prison.

Some of those who said they were happy to arrive in the prison had not even been detained elsewhere beforehand, but were simply relieved to be alive. In the first four years after the genocide, many people were summarily executed by the army. Several prisoners we spoke to said that when they were arrested, they expected to be killed. When they found themselves in prison instead, they felt they had had a lucky escape. A man who was arrested in July 1994 said that arriving in the prison had been like a miracle for him, because so many people outside were being killed. He was one of the first to go to Kigali Central Prison after the war; he said there were only 150 prisoners there at the time, and they all congratulated themselves on escaping death. The actual moment of arrival in the prison was also significant. A prisoner who was transferred from a *cachot* to Byumba Central Prison in 1997 said he had been terrified of being killed on the way. He later learned that a group of five detainees who were due to be transferred after him were all killed in transit, on the way to the prison.

For some, the experience of arriving in prison was softened by finding familiar faces inside: there were relatives, friends and neighbours there to welcome them. In addition to the practical help which these prisoners offered them, these reunions could be moments of great joy if the newly arrived prisoner had thought some of these relatives or friends had died. A man described meeting many friends in prison on his first day: "We embraced. It was like being welcomed into a family... It made me cry because they gave me such a good welcome, despite their bad conditions."

Prisoners compared the conditions in the different prisons where they had been detained. Many prisoners had been shuffled backwards and forwards several times; it was common to have passed through at least three or four different prisons. Some transfers were intended to relieve overcrowding; others were a form of punishment for prisoners who were seen as troublemakers. Depending on their luck, and where they ended up in the pecking order, some prisoners found great relief in being transferred from one prison to another, or, on the contrary, missed their old prison after being transferred to worse conditions in another. It was often the simplest things which made the biggest difference. A prisoner living in Karubanda, the main part of Butare prison, had preferred the conditions in the annex known as Rwandex. He said it was less congested, there was more air, and, crucially, "you could stay in one place for about ten minutes without moving and without being pushed or shoved".

The Red Cross: symbol of survival

It was in large part thanks to the International Committee of the Red Cross (ICRC) that a much larger number of prisoners did not die in these early years. After delicate negotiations with an extremely prickly government, the ICRC was allowed access to all the central prisons, and eventually to the *cachots*. It was able to provide food, water, the standard cup, plate and spoon for each prisoner, blankets, soap, medical care, equipment for hygiene, and other basic necessities. In terms of the prisoners' day-to-day needs, the ICRC effectively ran the prisons. It also enabled many prisoners to get in touch with their families through a system of correspondence and tracing. It started registering prisoners and keeping records and statistics, which, at that time, were usually more accurate than those of the government. But its presence was even more important in providing oversight of what went on in the prisons. The ICRC could watch what was happening. Following its intervention, the ill-treatment and killings in the central prisons decreased significantly, and eventually stopped.

For prisoners who were arrested in 1994, their period in prison was divided into two distinct phases: a first phase before the ICRC was able to intervene, and a second phase, when the ICRC provided regular and considerable assistance. Some remembered the exact moment when the ICRC first visited the prison. In the unrelenting misery of the world in which these prisoners found themselves, the intervention of the ICRC was like a miracle and it transformed their lives. A prisoner who had been severely tortured in a military detention centre remembered the day he was transferred to the central prison: "The ICRC registered me. They gave me a card. That card was a symbol that I wouldn't be killed."

Almost every prisoner we met praised the efforts of the ICRC. Their gratitude to the organisation was very moving. Many attributed their survival directly to its intervention. They also credited the ICRC for the various improvements to their living conditions over the following years. Many prisoners still remembered by name the individual Red Cross representatives who had visited the prison where they lived in the early years. A woman recalled that when the ICRC representative who used to visit Gitarama prison was leaving, the prisoners had played music and danced to say goodbye to him and welcome the new representative.

A woman in Nsinda prison asked us to pass on a specific message to the ICRC and to other non-governmental organisations who intervened in the prisons. "I would like to thank the ICRC, Penal Reform International, and national and international human rights organisations. Please send the ICRC a message in Geneva. When I'm released, I will put money aside for them, 100 francs every month. They changed a lot for us and treated us as humans."

Improvements in prison conditions since 1999

Conditions in the prisons have improved over the years, but the word "improvement" has to be used with caution. It is all relative, and it has been painfully slow. What improvements there have been are noticeable only to the prisoners and the staff, or to people who have been inside the prisons in earlier years and have some point of comparison.

The improvements which have taken place can be attributed mainly to the efforts of the ICRC and other non-governmental organisations, such as Penal Reform International (PRI). The Rwandan prison administration has also become better organised, and, most importantly, the rate of arrests has decreased. Conditions started to stabilise from around 2000. Finally, in early 2003, the government embarked on a programme of provisional releases of several thousand prisoners. The result of these various initiatives has been a reduction in the overcrowding, improved hygiene and better organisation.

Nevertheless, when we visited the prisons in late 2004, the situation remained critical. The acute lack of space was still the dominant problem. All five prisons we visited were still filled to several times their capacity. In some of them, hundreds if not thousands of prisoners slept outside; some had been sleeping outside for several years. Others slept inside, but in extremely poor conditions. A prisoner told us that in Cyangugu prison alone, there were more than 800 people sleeping in the mines. No visitor will ever appreciate the real extent of the overcrowding: during daylight hours, a significant number of prisoners are working outside, so what we see is not even the full picture.[4]

The second most pressing problem was the inadequacy of the food, described below. Washing facilities had improved, but there was still a continuous queue for water, for the toilets and for the showers. Inside Butare prison, we passed very long queues of prisoners, some waiting for the showers, others for the

---

[4]   By the end of 2005, the prison population temporarily went down to around 70,000, following several waves of releases (see Chapter XX). Even then, around 19% of the prisons were filled to three times their capacity and more than 50% to over twice their capacity. See LIPRODHOR, *Rapport du premier trimestre 2006 sur la situation carcérale du Rwanda*, March 2006.

toilets. We asked a random sample how long they had been waiting: some said they had been waiting for the showers for more than one hour and for the toilets for about 15 minutes. There was also a long queue of prisoners waiting to collect water, holding empty buckets, jerry cans and plastic bottles of different sizes. The amount of water they collected depended on the size of their container. They were allowed to fill their containers twice, but had to queue all over again the second time.

Prisoners still could not assume that they would automatically receive even the most basic items which all prisons are supposed to provide. For example, each prisoner should be given a blanket, but there were not enough blankets to go round. A prisoner who had been sleeping outside for almost three years told us: "I can't talk about sleeping. When it rains, I get up, otherwise I would be lying in the mud. I have no blankets. We have sheeting, but when it rains in the daytime, we can't use the sheeting because at night, when we put it down to sleep on, it would go in the mud. We put pieces of sack to lie on instead. There has been no distribution of blankets since I got here. No one can lend me a blanket as each person needs his own." A disabled prisoner said all he had was a piece of sack to sit on. "When I arrived, they weren't giving blankets anymore… Later, they gave out a few blankets, but I still don't have one as there weren't enough. Another prisoner cut his own blanket in two and gave me half… I am worried about that piece of blanket. I am worried what will happen when it wears out."

When we met the Secretary General of the Ministry of Interior – the ministry responsible for running the prisons – in late 2004, he seemed unconcerned about the continuing crisis in the prisons. He told us that prisoners were very well-fed, implying that we were worrying about nothing. He acknowledged in general terms that the prisons were still overcrowded, but claimed the government had done everything it could to ease the problem and that there was a limit to what it could do. "The number of perpetrators outside is six times the prison population", he told us. "Had we had more space and means, we could have put one million people in prison."

The state of prisons in 2004

At the end of 2004, the total prison population of Rwanda, according to government statistics, was 85,550, spread across 16 prisons. Most of the local *cachots* had closed. Some of the older prisons had also closed and new ones had opened. However, even the new prisons have filled up fast. Nyagatare prison, a small prison in the northeast which opened in 2003, was full to capacity by the end of 2004. The new Mpanga prison, in Gitarama province, near the border with Butare, with a capacity of 7,005, already had 6,160 prisoners three months after it opened in June 2004.

Most prisons have a similar structure: two or three buildings, surrounded by a compound where staff offices and workshops are located and an outside courtyard where visits take place. Some of the prison buildings date back to the colonial era: for example Kigali Central Prison, an imposing red-brick building resembling a castle, with crumbling towers, is nicknamed "1930", the year it was built by the Belgians.[4] Inside the prison buildings, there are several blocks where the prisoners live and one or two interior courtyards. Each block houses several hundred prisoners; there may be ten, 20, even 40 blocks. There are no individual cells, except the punishment cells where prisoners may be locked up for a few days for indiscipline. I n prisons such as Nsinda and Kimironko, prisoners live in large tents, rather than buildings, similarly organised into blocks, with several hundred prisoners in each tent. Women are housed in a separate building, with their own blocks and interior courtyard.

Many prisons have their own gardens and fields, sometimes extensive, where prisoners work. The gardens are always well-tended, by the prisoners themselves, and the contrast between the care for the vegetation and the lack of care for the human beings inside could hardly be greater. On several visits to Kigali Central Prison, we saw a gardener – a prisoner – standing on a home-made wooden ladder, meticulously clipping the top of a rounded bush

---

[4]   Kigali Central Prison is the oldest prison. According to the Rwandan human rights organisation LIPRODHOR, five of the 16 prisons were built between 1930 and 1960, seven between 1960 and 1990 and four between 1990 and 2005. See LIPRODHOR, *Rapport du premier trimestre 2006 sur la situation carcérale du Rwanda*, March 2006.

while a colleague was crouched down pulling out the weeds beneath him. Across the yard, a potted plant had been carefully placed directly underneath a pipe which stuck out of the wall; whenever it rained, the water would gush down from the roof of the building, over the pipe which acted as a channel and straight onto the plant, ensuring that it remained well watered. In Rwandex, the annex of Butare Central Prison, there was no garden, but a prisoner who had learnt agriculture in prison and wanted to practise his new skills had taken the initiative of creating a small vegetable patch, carved out of a tiny corner of the courtyard. Emerald-green bean shoots and other vegetables brightened up the yard of this otherwise dark and dismal prison.

Cyangugu Central Prison, garden and biogas   © Carina Tertsakian

A number of prisons have piloted a system of biogas, recycling human waste from the prison into a source of fuel, thus reducing reliance on firewood. The scheme, set up with the assistance of technical experts and non-governmental organisations, was pioneered in Cyangugu prison, where a special section of the garden has been devoted to it, and prisoners have sculpted the word "Biogas" in large letters out of grass and flowers. One section of the kitchens in Cyangugu is powered by biogas, and there is considerably less smoke emanating from there than from the rest of the kitchen, which relies on conventional sources of fuel (mostly firewood). The work was carried out by the prisoners themselves, several of whom were given technical training for this purpose, and there were plans to extend the scheme to other prisons.

Health care

Each prison has its own hospital and infirmary inside, run by prisoners. Staff from the Ministry of Health visit each prison, but most of the health care is dispensed by a team of qualified doctors and nurses among the prisoners, assisted by auxiliary workers (also prisoners). Basic medicines are available in the prison hospital, many of them provided by the ICRC, and the most common diseases can be diagnosed and treated there. There are separate areas for prisoners with contagious diseases such as tuberculosis. Prisoners who develop more serious illnesses, or who require specialised treatment, are sent to the nearest hospital outside, but usually only after they reach a critical state. Each of these hospitals has a special ward for sick prisoners, and other prisoners are sent to look after them throughout their stay in hospital. The prison is supposed to pay for the cost of transport to the hospital, but prisoners complained that they sometimes had to find the money themselves. Treatment for chronic illnesses such as diabetes and asthma is not available in the prison, so prisoners are dependent on their families to bring them their medication.

The ICRC used to provide 100% of medical treatment to the prisons until 1998 or 1999, but has gradually decreased its assistance in an attempt to push the government into taking on its responsibilities. It stopped providing medical supplies completely in January 2007. Similarly, until April 2004, the ICRC provided 100% of hygiene products and equipment used in the prisons, including brooms, brushes, buckets, chlorine and disinfectants, but subsequently reduced its contribution to 50%; by the end of 2005, it was supplying only soap and chlorine.

A prisoner in Cyangugu who was a trained nurse had started working in the prison infirmary soon after he arrived in the prison in May 1997:

> "When I arrived here, there was a doctor who had been the director in the hospital where I used to work. After talking to him,

I started working in the infirmary. We used to talk about our lives since 1994. I'm still doing that job. I like it. I talk with the sick and care for them… We don't have enough materials. If someone is sent to the hospital, the family has to pay the hospital fees, so we do what we can in the prison infirmary…

For prisoners with serious illnesses like malaria, tuberculosis and Aids, we treat them as much as we can, then they are transferred to hospital. In other cases, we diagnose them and treat them every day as best we can. We have ordinary surgeries twice a week, and emergencies at any time. Theoretically, our work is confidential, but because of space restrictions, people always know what's going on. We insisted on a calm space in the infirmary so that the sick can get some rest. Other prisoners can visit their sick friends at any time."

The most common causes of death in the prisons are a combination of Aids and tuberculosis, malaria, dysentery and various other illnesses, including chronic illnesses which probably would not have been fatal had the patients not been in prison and had access to appropriate medication. There is a high rate of HIV-Aids in the prisons. Prisoners and non-governmental organisations run special classes and campaigns in the prison to raise awareness of the disease. The ICRC has trained educators among the prisoners so that they can continue the information sessions on an ongoing basis.

The prisoners' own Red Cross association assists with health education for prisoners. When we visited the women's block in Butare prison, the coordinators of the women prisoners' Red Cross association were carrying out a health information session in the interior courtyard and invited us to join them. A group of around 30 women were sitting on the ground listening to a lecture on reproductive health, their eyes glued to a makeshift blackboard with drawings of the male and female reproductive organs, which looked as if they had been carefully copied from a textbook.

Prisoners' access to treatment for HIV-Aids is very limited, as it is in Rwanda more generally, where approximately 13% of the population is thought to be infected by the virus. The doctor in charge of the prison hospital in Kigali Central Prison (himself a prisoner) complained about the lack of treatment:

> "Aids patients in prison don't get treatment. From a sample of 600 taken by a non-governmental organisation, about 17% were HIV positive. They're just here, waiting for their death. When we ask for medicines to treat them, we're told that even the genocide survivors don't have these medicines, so how can we expect to have them as prisoners? This is said by the [prison] director, on the radio, even in the hospital. CHK [*Centre hospitalier de Kigali*, the main hospital in Kigali] doesn't have anti-retrovirals. In CHK, when they see a prisoner has Aids, they comfort him a bit then send him back to the prison. We get treatment for tuberculosis, but about 80% of tuberculosis patients are HIV positive so the tuberculosis medicines are not sufficient."

In some prisons, prisoners have taken the initiative of setting up a *mutuelle de santé*, their own health insurance scheme to supplement the treatment they receive in the prison. Prisoners who want to join the *mutuelle* pay a certain amount of money into the fund and can then benefit from health care if they fall ill. These funds are sometimes also used to provide health care to sick prisoners who are too poor to afford medical treatment. Most of the prisoners who talked about this system thought it was a good idea, but one prisoner objected to it strongly, on the grounds that the state should be providing health care for the prisoners, not the prisoners themselves.

In each prison, there are also prisoners suffering from mental illness, in many cases brought about by the genocide and their experiences in detention; some may also have suffered from these illnesses before their arrest. The only treatment available for them is tranquilisers. The *capita* (chief prisoner) of the women in Butare prison told us that the burden for looking after them fell to the other prisoners. She knew of eight or nine women in Butare prison who had serious mental health problems. Three of them had been ill before the war, and five or six had developed these problems since their arrest:

> "They were beaten on their heads, which caused the illness. They were traumatised when they were arrested... The trauma shows

in their behaviour. For example, they shout a lot. They stay in bed, hiding completely under the covers and not talking to anybody. They don't get up all day. We have a system among ourselves to call by their bed every two hours and talk to them a little, to persuade them to look out. Then they go back under their covers. Then we do the same thing two hours later. This helps the women to let out their distress. Many of these traumatised women think about their dead children. They cry and cry all night."

Of the five prisons we visited, only one, Nsinda, kept a separate record of the number of mentally ill prisoners: in December 2004, it had counted 41 (39 men and two women) out of a total prison population of more than 12,000. These were probably only the most serious and noticeable cases. There is no separate area for them; they live with the other prisoners. A prisoner in Kigali Central Prison estimated that about 90% of the male prisoners there suffered from some kind of trauma or were psychologically disturbed by their experiences, but there was no support available for them. He said the trauma of these prisoners would remain one of his strongest memories of his eight years in prison.

Food

One of the main complaints of the prisoners we spoke to was the inadequacy of the food. In the prisons we visited, food was distributed to prisoners once a day. This ration had to last them the whole day. It usually consisted of one cup of maize, one cup of peas or beans, and one cup of porridge made of sorghum. They received the same food every single day. There was no alternative, no variety, and no provision for people whose health conditions may have required a different diet.[6] As we made our way around the prisons, the sight and smell of this food became very familiar to us: wherever we looked, there were bowls of half-eaten lumpy dry hash dotted with small pieces of yellow corn and thick grey-pink porridge which exuded a

---

[6]   Prisoners who have specific health problems can apply for an authorisation from the government for their families to bring them food on a daily basis, but not all families have the means to do this.

distinctive and unpleasant smell. Several prisoners described it as "survival food", which they ate just so as not to die.

Everyone received the same amount, except pregnant women and those with babies, who received a double ration. Prisoners complained not only about the poor quality and the monotony of the food, but the insufficient quantity and the frequent shortages. For one prisoner, the prison cup would always remain a powerful symbol of his life there. He said if he was ever released, he would buy a prison cup to keep in his house, just so that he could look at it: "It's a cup of food that couldn't even satisfy a baby."

There were days when prisoners were not given any food at all, sometimes for several successive days. According to the prison authorities, this was due to shortages of food, late deliveries, or a shortage of firewood. A prisoner in Cyangugu had counted 164 days when they had not received any food between December 1999 and December 2004. On some days, food was distributed but in reduced rations: for example prisoners were given either maize or beans, but not both. Prisoners had a special jargon for these situations: "the wild cat has fallen into the kitchen" meant that there was a shortage of food, while "it's going to rain" meant that food was finally on its way after a period of shortage.

Serious food shortages started occurring only once the ICRC began pulling out. Until 1998 or 1999, the ICRC had provided 100% of the food for the prisons. From 2000, they and the government were each responsible for 50%. As part of a strategy to try to persuade the government to take on full responsibility for feeding the prisoners, the ICRC gradually decreased its contribution further, as with the provision of medical assistance. For a while, an arrangement was set up whereby the ICRC and the government each provided food to the prisons alternately for three months at a time. The prisoners all commented that there were no problems during the three months that the ICRC was in charge but that there were always shortages when it was the government's turn to feed them; they were apprehensive about what would happen when the ICRC pulled out altogether. By the end of 2004, the ICRC was providing just 15% of the food; by the end of 2005, it had stopped completely.

Prisoners receiving food, Kigali Central Prison, 1995
© Malcolm Linton/Getty Images

Each prison has one, or sometimes two, large kitchens where the food is cooked in huge black vats and distributed to the prisoners. The preparation, cooking and distribution of the food are done entirely by prisoners; there are no kitchen staff. The kitchens are usually located outside, or in a kind of open hangar from which the smoke billows out, but in some prisons, the kitchens are still inside, close to prisoners' living quarters. In some prisons, such as Nsinda and Gitarama, there is a separate kitchen in the women's block, but in other prisons, the food is cooked by the male prisoners. In prisons such as Butare, the cooked food is brought to the women's blocks in big barrels; the women distribute the food, then wash the barrels before they are returned to the kitchen.

A group of prisoners first have to carry the food from the delivery point in the outside yard to the kitchen. The sacks they load onto their shoulders are so heavy that even the strongest men among them look as if they will collapse under the weight as they stagger across the yard. In the kitchen, a special team of prisoners is responsible for cooking the food and dishing it out to the prisoners. In Nsinda prison, for example, the kitchen team is composed of 110 prisoners, for a total population of around 12,000; in Butare prison, there is a team of around 200 for a population of around 10,700. It is a complex and large-scale operation, but extremely well-organised and efficient. The kitchen team works around the clock; there is a day shift and a night shift. Huge piles of wood are stacked up by the side of the kitchen and prisoners replenish the supply at regular intervals. The kitchens churn out the same food every day, but in Cyangugu prison, we were introduced to a prisoner who was a baker, and who worked from a small oven next to the kitchen. Later that day, we were able to sample some of his wonderful fresh rolls, straight from the oven. But the bread is not given to the prisoners. It is sold in the prison shop.

In each prison, there is a fixed routine. For example in Gitarama prison, the kitchen starts distributing the food at 7.30am. From 7.30am to 9.30 or 10am, prisoners go to the kitchen with their plates to collect their ration, then return to their block. The ration has to last the whole day: 300 grams of corn, 250 grams of peas, 100 grams of porridge, but the full amounts are not dispensed every day.

The cooking and the distribution of food are supervised by the prisoner in charge of the kitchens (the kitchen *capita*) and his assistants. These are much-coveted positions. The *capitas* of the kitchen are among the richest prisoners. It is difficult to get onto the kitchen team. Not only are the prisoners responsible for the kitchen accorded all the same privileges as other prisoners in positions of responsibility, including double rations, but they also spend almost their entire day outdoors, and, crucially, have unrestricted access to one of the most precious commodities of all: food.

Food rations are a whole currency in themselves. They are bought and sold and used to grant or repay favours. Some people prefer to use them as money rather than as food. One prisoner told us that the "bosses" (the rich prisoners) never ate the prison food; they ate food brought to them by their families, then sold their rations to other prisoners. With 200 francs (about US$0.35), a poorer prisoner could buy rations off the "bosses" to last him a whole month.

The position of kitchen *capita* is especially open to corruption. The prison directors not only turn a blind eye, but connive in the scams. Whenever there were shortages of food, prisoners rarely believed the official explanations provided. They told us that these alleged shortages were a lie, and that in reality the prison director, as well as some of the prisoners responsible for running the kitchens, were diverting the food or the firewood for their own ends. Firewood destined for the prison would mysteriously disappear; it was sold off before it even reached the prison. The rations of food for that day were not kept and served up the next day: in the words of one prisoner, "they were as good as eaten". A prisoner said that in 1997-1998, the *capita* of the kitchen in Gikondo prison used to keep back a whole barrel of food which he used to sell, and only distributed what was left over. Prisoners were made to pay 20 or 50 francs for a ration.

Most of the prisoners we spoke to who worked in the kitchens denied that they took advantage of their position. They told us: "the people in the team have to have good conduct and not steal", or, even more categorically, "it is not possible to steal food". But a few admitted that they regularly took food away, usually for the purpose of selling it, rather than eating it. A prisoner who was in charge of the management of stocks in Nyanza prison said his task was to make sure that all prisoners had enough to eat, and any surplus automatically went to the prison director. A prisoner who had been detained in Kigali Central Prison told us that the *capita* of the kitchen would distribute a smaller quantity of food than he was supposed to and sell the rest. It was a deal hatched between the *capita* of the kitchen, the *capita général* and the prison director, "to get the most out of the food". The prison director decided officially to reduce the food, and the *capita général* had to sign for the quantity of food coming in to the prison, so the three of them controlled the whole process. Another former prisoner confirmed that the *capita* of the kitchen used to be very influential with the prison director, and that the director paid him to keep quiet while he diverted trucks of food or reduced the quantity of oil and siphoned off the rest. The prison guards sometimes also demanded food for themselves, from the prisoners' rations.

A prisoner who was first in charge of the wood supply and then in charge of the kitchen when he was in Kigali Central Prison said he had enjoyed this work. There were many advantages, and his popularity had increased. He boasted that he could find a friend in every prison in Rwanda because of the work he had done in the kitchen. However, once, it got him into trouble. "When they brought the wood, I had to measure it according to the director's orders and confirm the quantity. One day, the director of prisons [from the Ministry of Interior] came on a visit. She checked the quantity of wood and accused me of lying about it and of being a thief. I was sent to the punishment cell for one day. The following morning, the prison director released me because he understood that if I had lied, it wasn't my fault."

Separately from the official distribution of food rations, there is a parallel informal trade in food which prisoners receive from their families or ask other people to fetch for them from outside, then sell on to their colleagues. Almost any kind of food can be obtained for a price, and prisoners who have money or whose families visit them regularly can enjoy a varied and healthy diet. A prisoner explained the system:

> "You can arrange to buy everything you need: sweet potatoes, bananas, bread, potatoes… It's not allowed, but it happens. You have to give a commission. You can either give money to a friend who is going outside and ask him to bring you something back. Or you can go out with money to buy quite a large quantity of something outside, then pay a tariff to the guard. You pay for the goods and you pay a 'customs fee' to the guard. Everyone profits from it. There's no fixed percentage. Some guards ask for double or more. They're the bad ones. But others don't want to penalise us and accept a small amount. If you pay 300 francs for something, you may give 50 francs to the guard. The director says if he catches us doing this, both the prisoners and the guards will be punished. But the guards have a very small salary and are willing to take the risk."

A woman in Kigali Central Prison used to bring in special meals to order, for example at Christmas. Prisoners could order whatever they wanted from her, until a guard found out about her trade, and she was made to stop.

A prisoner in Cyangugu gave a few examples of the things which could typically be bought on the black market inside: "Some people have a thermos inside. You can also buy water from the kitchen. They have a sort of cafeteria. A cup of tea with soya milk costs 80 francs. Tea without milk is 40 francs. People also sell things like avocados and meat. They buy it from people who get visits and sell it for a profit. An avocado costs between 30 and 50 francs. When there's a shortage of food, like now, the price goes up: an avocado currently costs 100 francs. The rich people buy them. A small piece of meat costs 70 francs." A similar market existed in Nsinda: "You pay 10 francs for a portion of vegetables, or 40 francs for a handful of tomatoes. There are big businessmen who sell a lot of things inside. They have little shops selling sugar. A block of soap costs 40 francs. Bread is 50 or 100 francs, depending on the size. There are cafes where you can drink tea or milk. A cup of tea with two spoonfuls of sugar costs 25 francs." A prisoner in Butare told us that goods could be bartered, "but people prefer money. It's the best merchandise."

Sugar is one of the most popular items, both because it adds taste to the extremely bland prison food and because it does not go off. A prisoner explained that sugar is the prisoner's dollar, and that prisoners calculate the value of other items in terms of their equivalent value in sugar. One kilogram of sugar is equal to 450 francs (around US$0.80) and lasts two weeks, and so is considered more valuable than perishable food, which has to be eaten immediately.

Prisoners have also set up their own private cooking facilities, which they described as "clandestine", even though everyone seemed to know about them. They have their own supply of firewood inside, separate from the kitchen, and use it to cook raw food brought to them by their families.

Very occasionally, prisoners were allowed to indulge in a special feast. A prisoner who had worked in the team responsible for nutrition in Kigali Central Prison had recorded in his diary that on 9 July 2000, the Pope had sent large quantities of rice to all the prisoners in Rwanda for a celebration: "Everyone had enough rice. We were all very happy. But this only happened once." An even more extraordinary event took place in around 1996, when the director of Kigali Central Prison arranged for a whole cow to be brought into the prison and invited friends for the celebration. The prisoners cooked the meat, then distributed it and everyone ate some. Those who could afford to paid 500 francs for the privilege; some of the male prisoners paid for the women to be able to take part. The incident created a storm, with newspapers reporting that the *interahamwe* were feasting and celebrating. The director was fired soon afterwards.

Tobacco and alcohol are strictly forbidden in the prisons, but still manage to find their way inside. In Nsinda, one cigarette costs 20 francs and loose tobacco leaves 100 francs. Some prison directors have recently tried to crack down on the use of tobacco and the trade in cigarettes on health grounds, with only limited success. Prisoners make their own beer; in Nsinda prison, a one litre bottle of banana beer costs 200 francs. A former *capita général* in Kigali Central Prison told us how he had been disgraced in 1995 after turning a blind eye to this activity: "Once some prisoners started making beer and I didn't stop it. There was a search around Christmas time and they found the beer. I knew the prisoners were making it. At Christmas, everyone drank, including me." As a punishment, the prison director fired him from his position of *capita*, put some of those who had made the beer in the punishment cells for eight days and transferred others to other prisons.

Aside from the black market, each prison has a little shop within its compound, run by prisoners, where prisoners and visitors can buy basic items, such as bags of sugar and soft drinks. Non-food items, such as toiletries, pens and paper, are also sold. The prisoner who was the coordinator of the shop in Butare prison said the most popular items were soap, toothpaste, skin cream, toilet paper, razors, sugar, milk powder and tinned sardines. The shopkeeper's job is an enviable one, as he is able to spend the whole day outside. We did not hear as many stories of corruption about the shops as we did about the kitchens, but undoubtedly, a similar system operates there too. The shop is located in the outside courtyard, in the prison compound, so the shopkeeper is able to meet prisoners' relatives there and receive money from visitors.

In theory, prisoners are not supposed to buy items directly from the prison shop, as they are not allowed to keep cash. Any money they are given, for example by their families, is supposed to be entrusted to the prison *social* (social worker) and the prisoners then place specific requests for the *social* to buy the items they need from the shop. In practice, however, very little of the money which finds its way into the prison goes anywhere near the *social*. The coordinator of the shop in Butare prison explained: "When the *social* has the money, he'll use it in the meantime to buy things for himself, or else he just tells you to come back later, so you can't get what you want when you want it. So prisoners try to keep their money to buy their own things directly... Because prisoners staff the shop, and when the director is not there, we can arrange things with the guards. After a while, we get to know each other. We arrange times with the guards when we can go to the shop and buy directly as prisoners."

Trading space

Like so much else inside the prisons, the system of allocating spaces to prisoners is entirely run by the prisoners themselves. Prison staff are not involved in the process at all, except on rare occasions when they may recommend a vulnerable prisoner or a newcomer who is known to them. The allocation is overseen by the *capita général* and implemented by the *capitas* of the blocks. In theory, it's first come, first served, so the prisoners who have been in prison the longest should have a space inside, while those who came later end up sleeping outside. There is also supposed to be a waiting list for prisoners who sleep outside for them to be gradually moved inside whenever spaces are vacated through releases. In practice, it is a different story, and who ends up where is determined by money and by an elaborate system of favouritism.

Money is officially prohibited, yet it is everywhere and it defines the economic and social structure of the prisons. Without money, and without influential contacts among the *capitas*, prisoners drop to the bottom of the pile, regardless of how many years they have spent there. A prisoner who had spent almost nine years sleeping outside told us: "I have slept outside until today... To get a place inside, you have to have money or be well-known. For us, the poor, it's difficult. The places are given to those in positions of responsibility. Newcomers can get places before us. It depends on money. First you have to know who wants to give up his space. But if you have money, it's easy."

Different châteaux go for different prices, depending on their location, on the estimated wealth or desperation of the buyer, and on their negotiating skills.

Beds are sold, and half-beds are sold. The places on the bottom floor attract the highest prices, whereas those on the top floor are usually considered less desirable because of the heat; they are nicknamed *ikarayi* (large cooking-pot). However, one prisoner who had occupied a space on the top floor said he had preferred it there because he was tall; at least he didn't hit his head on the floor above him. Minor hazards such as prisoners on the higher floors spilling water over those on the lower floors also have to be taken into consideration. It is not only the spaces in the bunk-beds which are sold; prisoners have to pay for a space in the mines, in the corridors, and even outside. A place in the mine, on the concrete underneath someone else's bed, can cost as much as 1,000 or 2,000 francs (about US$1.7 to 3.5). A space outside can go for around 200 francs, and prisoners sometimes also have to pay for a share of the sheeting. One prisoner said that when it rained, he and other prisoners who slept outside used to pick up their things and squash up next to those who had some sheeting, in order to shelter; but if they decided to stay permanently under someone's sheeting, they had to pay, as the people they found under the sheeting had bought it to begin with.

The *capitas* and the *chefs de bloc* (the prisoners in charge of individual blocks) operate a ruthless system. They exploit prisoners' vulnerability while pretending to assist them, and allow thousands to sleep outside in order to make a fatter profit on the places inside. One prisoner, who gave us a breakdown of the tariffs for different kinds of places, said: "Everything is sold. There is no pity. Life is hard here." Another said: "We gave money to the *chefs de bloc*. We don't know how they shared it. I didn't want to know. I just wanted a space... When you're forced to live in a hard place, you learn how to survive."

Newly arrived prisoners were particularly vulnerable to extortion and inflated prices. A former prisoner said there was a whole business network inside: "Some people buy up all the empty spaces and re-sell them... They charge a big amount to new prisoners who don't know how much it should cost and may have more money on them... Good spaces were kept for the purpose of selling them. They were not given out even to the people sleeping outside. There were different prices for different places. In the blocks, it was difficult to breathe, so it was more expensive to be near the door. The door was left open to let some air in. The places at the far end were cheaper. There were three floors... I was on the ground floor. The advantages were that I could sit with my feet on the ground and chat to people." He had to pay 10,000 francs for his space (about US$18). Another prisoner who arrived in the same prison at around the same time had had to pay 15,000 francs (about US$26) for a space one metre wide which he had to share with two other people. It was normal for several prisoners to share a space intended for one person. One prisoner remembered the first space he bought, which was the size of a single mattress: five people shared it.

Tariffs vary from prison to prison. In Gikondo prison, the prisoners in positions of responsibility were particularly merciless in their extortion, and some of the guards were also involved. One prisoner who was there from 1997 to 1998 had had to pay 58,000 francs (about US$103) for a standard 40 centimetre space. The money went to the *capita* but the *surveillant chef* (chief guard) was the intermediary because he knew how much money the prisoner's family had given him. Another had to pay 30,000 francs (about US$53). In other prisons, the rate for a standard space rarely seemed to rise above 5,000 or 10,000 francs (US$8 to 17).

Prisoners may change places as they gather up enough money. Each time they move, they have to pay again. A prisoner was sleeping in the mine when he first arrived in the prison, but after three days, he couldn't stand it so he decided to go outside, where he spent the next nine months. He didn't pay for the place outside, but he bought a mattress for 500 francs. It was a standard mattress which the prisoners make themselves: two sacks stitched together, with woodchip or straw inside. (Foam mattresses are usually forbidden in the prisons because they take up too much space.) The wood-chip cost him 300 francs and the sacks 100 francs each. He borrowed the money from friends and had to pay them back later. He remembered the exact date when he finally managed to get 5,000 francs together to buy a bed inside. "To get a bed, you have to negotiate for a long time. I had to start negotiating even before I had the money. Sometimes we use an 'agent' who knows how to negotiate well. If he finds you a bed, you give him 200 francs to buy himself some tea."

Prisoners who have been transferred from one prison to another, several times over, have had to pay for a place every time, in each prison. For example, the prisoner who had to pay 58,000 francs for a place in Gikondo then had to pay 5,000 francs when he was transferred to Kimironko prison a year later, and a further 5,000 francs when he was transferred to Kigali Central Prison three years later. Whenever there were large-scale transfers or a big influx of new prisoners, there were windfall profits for the *capitas*. The *capitas* also made a killing from the waves of releases, as all the spaces which had been freed up could be sold to other prisoners.

Occasionally, the guards would try to intervene, if they smelled a good business opportunity. On one occasion, this caused a revolt. When Byumba prison was closed, many prisoners there were transferred to Nsinda. The *surveillant chef* in Nsinda tried to sell places to these new prisoners at 80,000 francs each. The prisoners refused and occupied one of the blocks by force. However, only those who were quick and strong were able to help themselves to a bed. One of the prisoners who was not forceful enough ended up sleeping in the corridor: "I could have had one of the beds but I wasn't strong enough. Now, dust falls on me as other prisoners pass by. I'm right next to the entrance, so I'm the first to get dirty. Rain also falls on me… People have to climb over me to get to their beds. I sleep in front of another person's entrance to his bed, but he never complains."

If places were traded between friends – directly, without going through the *capita* – it was sometimes possible to get a place for free. But even then, it depended on why the friends were vacating the place and where they were going. Many prisoners told us how friends had offered them their places when they were about to be transferred to another prison, but still asked them for money as they knew that they would have to buy a new place in the prison they were going to.

What prisoners spend their money on varies from person to person, but for many, buying a decent place to sleep is one of the top priorities. One prisoner described the system he had used for saving up: "At first, the Red Cross used to give us biscuits. Of the 20 biscuits we were given, I used to eat 10. I kept the other 10 and continued keeping them until I had 300 francs worth. For 300 or 500 francs, you could buy a place to sleep. Until I had saved up 300 francs, I slept outside in the yard. I spent three months out there. Then I bought a place on the top floor. The middle floor is better but more expensive. I stayed at the top so as not to waste money. You had to pay the *capita*. It was called 'giving tea to the *capita*', as a way of thanking him."

A life of luxury

The simplest way to gauge a prisoner's place in the prison hierarchy is to look at the space where he lives. Prisoners with money can buy luxury châteaux, with ample space – several times the size of a standard château – and facilities ranging from real mattresses to electric lamps. Those who can afford such luxury are those with money or status. They include those who were rich before being imprisoned and the nouveaux riches: those who got rich inside, for example the *capitas* and other prisoners who were given positions of responsibility. The contrast between their living conditions and those of the masses is astounding. It is not only a question of space: the privileges extend to other facilities too. For example, when prisoners queue to go to the toilet or to collect water, the first prisoners in the queue are not necessarily the first to use the toilet or to receive water. The important people go first. A prisoner who had been detained in Kibungo Central Prison, where the overcrowding was so severe that prisoners had set fixed times for washing, told us: "We could wash until 6pm only. After this, only *les grands* [the big men] could wash."

Even in the early days, prisoners with status were treated differently. A former prisoner told us about a block in Kigali Central Prison known as Block 00, which used to be reserved for prisoners who had dysentery, but later became the block for the dignitaries. There was also Block Texas, located near the *capita*'s office. A prisoner explained: "Block Texas is for those who live well, like in the USA. It is for rich people." [7] In the women's blocks, the same principles applied, and spaces were miraculously found for certain prisoners. A former prisoner in Kigali told us that when two nuns were arrested, there was no space left but somehow "we found a way, and we arranged for them to have mattresses". Even in Gitarama prison in 1995, prisoners found a way of accommodating important arrivals. A Rwandan

---

[7]   A former prisoner in Kigali gave a different explanation: according to him, the area was called Texas because the ground there was unpaved and stony, "like a desert".

Kigali Central Prison   © Hervé Deguine

journalist who visited the prison when conditions there were at their worst discovered a special cell for the "bosses": former local government officials, teachers and others.

On our tour of Nsinda prison, the *capita général*, a young man, showed us his château. I crawled into it to get a sense of his little world from the inside, although as *capita*, he would be spending most of his time circulating around the prison rather than sitting in his château. His château was like a small box, not especially grand but large enough to sit or lie down in comfortably. It had a padlock on the door. Inside, he had a mattress, a mosquito net, a collection of books and other objects, including two large radios, neatly arranged on a shelf. I asked him why he had two radios. He told me that it was because he was rich, and he was the *capita*.

Some wealthy prisoners have taken the initiative of building their own space, rather than inheriting someone else's. One prisoner told us how he had had a new shack (an *icyari*) constructed for himself and his brother; he had bought both the space and the materials. When he was released, he gave it to two other prisoners. Some prisoners preferred these shacks to the châteaux inside, as they provided an opportunity to escape the airless blocks.

Those with status had to pay for their space too, but when they first arrived in the prison, some were given a better space for free, simply because of who they were. They included former politicians, government officials, priests, lawyers, big businessmen and other well-known individuals who had commanded respect in their former life or who came from well-established families. A prisoner who had occupied a senior position in the army had not had to pay for his comfortable space in the prison when he arrived there in 2004: "Here, I have an alcove. It is like a small container. I can close it with a little door. I am alone in there. I am spoilt. They gave it to me as I was well-known." A lawyer said that when he arrived in prison, "the reception was automatic. They made me a special place. I have an individual space, with a table and a light. It is exceptional. I still have it now."

This type of preferential treatment seems to be an instinctive reaction to seeing prominent individuals arrive in the prison. It is a social reflex transposed directly from the world outside. As a prisoner told us, "people are no more equal inside than outside". However, the social rules from outside are not imported wholesale into the prison. There are subtle but important distinctions. For example, being a former government authority does not automatically buy respect in the eyes of prisoners. Some prisoners who had held positions of responsibility at local government level under the previous regime said that on the contrary, they were not well-perceived at first, because other prisoners blamed them for getting them arrested and leading people into committing crimes during the genocide. They had to work to establish their credibility and earn the trust of the prisoners.

Some former local government officials were singled out for ill-treatment not by their fellow prisoners but by prison officials. A prisoner who had been a *conseiller de secteur* (local government official) in Kigali said that the prison director in Gikondo had personally ensured that he and other former local government authorities enjoyed none of the advantages usually associated with their status: "As a former authority, I didn't have any privileges. On the contrary. The director accused us of leading people into killings... I was called by the director in person. He asked the guards to beat me. I spent one month in hospital."

In Gitarama prison, we met a priest accused of genocide who had been in prison for almost ten years. A relaxed and genial man, he had a large château, which he called his lounge, in which he received people. When he first arrived in the prison, the prisoners immediately welcomed him, found him an airy space, collected blankets for him, made him a bed and gave him food and plates. As early as March 1995, he had set up an arrangement with a boy (another prisoner) who cooked food for him. He was in a privileged position: not only was he accorded respect by the prisoners themselves, but he received significant support from the Roman Catholic Church. He gave the impression that he received almost more financial and material assistance than he needed, but he shared it with other prisoners. In exchange for the welcome prisoners gave him, he helped them both materially and spiritually: "If you can get money, you can live well in prison. Even as a priest, I did this. I collaborated with people outside for them to send 5,000 or 10,000 francs so that I could live reasonably and help others. I was with some very unfortunate people and I was in a position to help them."

He told us how he had arranged his current living space: "I built a little house with sheeting. I sleep on the top floor. I have a lounge where prisoners can visit me. I paid a carpenter to make me a bed. It cost 50,000 francs. I have a little table. Now two people share this space with me... We have a minor who is our housekeeper. He prepares our food and eats with us, but he sleeps in the minors' block. We found a polite boy who wasn't a thief. I've tried to instal electricity because I like to read or write in the evenings. I have a little library: books on theology and spiritual matters. I can prepare lessons from these books. I've made shelves from cardboard boxes. The house is made of sheeting but it's just like my room in my parish. Prisoners come here to discuss their problems... My evenings are always free. People see my light on at night. We have electricians here who fit the appliances. You place your order with the *capita général* and the electrician will instal what we need. Other times we use batteries."

Most of the *capitas* also have enough space to "receive" prisoners for discussions and chats. One of the *capitas* of Cyangugu prison told me he had an 80-centimetre place on the second floor "because I'm an authority. I can receive the population." A prisoner who was seen as close to the current government described being "invited to dinner" by the *capita* of the block on his first night in the prison. The *capita général* in Kigali Central Prison said his space measured 120 centimetres: "Now I can go in standing up. Before, I had to bend down to go in." The *capitas* and their team also have their own office, known as the *capitariat*, furnished with a wooden table, one or two chairs, and some space for papers and other documents.

It is common practice for prisoners who have money, even just a little money, to pay other prisoners to do their chores for them: basic tasks such as preparing food, washing their clothes or cleaning their space, in exchange for a few hundred francs or some food. It is seen not only as a mark of status, but as a way of helping out less fortunate prisoners. A prisoner who was not particularly rich nevertheless employed another prisoner to wash his plate and his clothes: "That way, I'm respected and the other prisoner is happy to be eating." He said they had become close friends and looked after each other when they were sick. He paid 10 francs to the prisoner to wash his jeans, 5 francs to wash a shirt or trousers, and 30 francs for a blanket, because it required more water. In Ruhengeri prison, some prisoners paid younger prisoners to fan them with a piece of paper when the weather was too hot.

Some of the wealthier prisoners, like the priest in Gitarama, were willing to help their less fortunate colleagues to find a better sleeping space than they would otherwise have been able to afford. A young prisoner in Kigali Central Prison said that when he first arrived there in 1995, he was completely overwhelmed by the situation. He spent the first few days sleeping in the yard. Then, luckily, he met a prisoner he knew, a wealthy former politician, who was prepared to move the suitcase he kept under his bed to allow his young friend to sleep there, without making him pay. The space was 40 to 45 centimetres high. He stayed there for two years. His benefactor was prepared to pay to find him a better place, but there were no other places available.

Some prisoners are not necessarily in the top social class but have found ways and means of making their living quarters more homely, or less miserable. In Butare central prison, we passed a row of châteaux which resembled box-like cubicles, near the main entrance. Some prisoners had a whole box to themselves, others shared it with one other prisoner. We noticed one fairly comfortable-looking cubicle, which had two shelves, some artificial flowers, a radio cassette player, a light bulb, pictures on the walls and clean blankets. In another smaller château in the passageway, a prisoner had decorated his walls with coloured pictures cut out of sweet packets and the covers of notebooks.

At the very top of the social ladder, but so high that they are outside the normal league, are one or two prisoners who are given individual cells.[8] In 2002, President Pasteur Bizimungu and minister Charles Ntakirutinka were arrested on a number of charges, including endangering state security, and detained in Kigali Central Prison. The president and the minister were held in two separate, individual cells, located in the courtyard outside the main prison building. One of these cells had previously been occupied by another VIP, the Archbishop of Gikongoro, Augustin Misago.[9] We did not meet the

---

[8]   A former prisoner told us that in the past, these "VIP cells" were reserved for foreigners accused of common crimes.

[9]   Augustin Misago was one of the most prominent individuals accused of genocide in Rwanda. Arrested in 1999, he was tried, acquitted and released in 2000. He has since resumed his functions as Archbishop of Gikongoro.

president or the minister, but other prisoners described their living conditions to us. "The minister is in a cell under the lookout. Bizimungu is in a room to the left of the main entrance. They built him a special corridor so that he can walk about inside. When his wife goes to visit him, she goes in with a policeman, a special intelligence agent and a guard. It is the same for the minister, but he doesn't have an exercise area. At 6am every day, he is taken to the courtroom [within the prison] to exercise." Soon after his arrest, the president went into the main prison building to receive a massage for his bad back. Prisoners jeered at him, so from then on, he was given massages in his own private room. The president has a special prisoner attached to him, living with him at all times. Other prisoners joked about this spy who pretended to be a prisoner: "He watches how the president sleeps, how he dreams."

Fashion

The most distinctive feature of Rwandan prisoners is their uniform. Men and women are all dressed in pale pink. Huge rolls of this pink fabric are supplied to the prisons, and tailors among the prisoners cut it and sew it into an astonishing variety of styles: shirts and three-quarter-length shorts for the men, and dresses or blouses and skirts for the women. Prisoners are obliged to wear their uniform whenever they step out of the interior building, even just to work in the yard or meet a visitor within the prison compound.

This particular shade of pink has become so immediately recognisable to anyone who has visited a prison or who has seen groups of prisoners working outside that it has become forever associated with prison. Few Rwandans living outside would now choose to wear a pink shirt or a pink dress unless there was no alternative. On the rare occasions when you see someone walking down the street wearing pink, there is an immediate reflex that the person must be a prisoner, even if they are clearly not.[10]

There is a whole system of corruption and theft of uniform fabric, as there is with every other item in the prisons. In Nsinda prison, there was a rumour

---

[10]   In 2007, a new orange uniform, without a collar or buttons, was introduced for prisoners who had been convicted and had exhausted all possibilities of appeal.

that pink fabric sold by the prison directors had ended up in Uganda, where schoolchildren wore it. We were told about a staff member in Kigali Central Prison who had appropriated some of the pink fabric and had had curtains made out of it for his own home.

In the first few months after the genocide, the prisons, like the rest of the country, were in such a state of disorganisation that there were no uniforms. Prisoners wore whatever clothes they happened to be wearing at the time of their arrest, and any others which their families were able to bring them. The *capita général* of Kigali Central Prison told us that before 1994, the prison uniforms used to be black. He was pleased that they had changed the colour; he felt pink was more human. To European eyes, it seems an odd choice of colour – a kind of pastel shade associated with little girls' clothes, which looks incongruous on full-grown men. The fact that the men are all wearing shorts adds a certain pathos to their appearance, especially in the case of the older men; shorts are not normally worn by adults in Rwanda. But none of the prisoners complained about the colour or the style of their uniform.

Only one prisoner of all those we spoke to objected to having to wear a uniform as a matter of principle. A deputy *capita*, he said he wore it only because he was a "leader". For him, his uniform signified his bondage, and he was ashamed of it. He felt it was fundamentally wrong for a person who had not even been tried or found guilty to have to wear a prisoner's uniform for eight years.

All prisoners are supposed to receive a uniform when they first arrive, but as with every other commodity in the prison, there are the haves and the have-nots. Uniforms are supposed to be free. Sometimes they are, but sometimes they're not. There is a trade in uniforms and in tailoring services, such as sewing them to specific designs or adjusting them to the right size. In Kigali Central Prison, a male prisoner's uniform goes for between 1,000 and 2,500 francs (US$1.7 to 4.4). Some prisoners don't have a uniform at all, and have to borrow one from another prisoner if they are called outside. One prisoner was wearing a uniform which he described as "communal": three people shared it, and whoever was called outside wore it. Others can only afford half a uniform, for example just a shirt, which will cost a few hundred francs. But others have several uniforms, in different styles.

Some of the women's styles are especially elaborate: there are dresses with big bows, frills, fancy buttons, puff sleeves and different necklines. Women are not allowed to wear trousers, but any other style is permitted, except mini-skirts or high slits. The men's range is less varied, but there is still room for taste and a sense of style, with different types of breast pockets and collars, including some Mao-style collarless shirts. A prisoner had had a special collar made on his shirt, with a kind of gold braiding; it made him look like a priest or a military officer. Another prisoner had a label, like a brand-name, sewn onto the front pocket of his shirt. In the early days, some prisoners wore full-length pink trousers, but the uniform was later changed to shorts, in order to save on the fabric. Some of the *capitas* have been allowed to keep their long trousers, but any new uniforms now have to be made into shorts.

In addition to paying for their uniforms, prisoners can pay for a range of related services, such as washing, ironing and pressing. The washing and ironing can cost 100 or 200 francs; the ironing alone 5 francs a piece. Even though most prisoners have only one uniform, most of them look remarkably smart and always clean. When prisoners came out to talk to us, we were struck by the almost miraculous contrast between their crisp, immaculate, pressed uniforms and the squalor and deprivation from which they had emerged. Ironing is a favourite activity inside the prison, among the men as well as the women; we saw many prisoners ironing away inside, using heavy old-fashioned coal-irons. In Cyangugu prison, a team of prisoners had set up their ironing service in the garden, and were conscientiously pressing uniforms and folding them into neat piles while we interviewed their colleagues in a hut nearby.

Some prisoners, however, cannot afford such luxuries. If they were lucky enough to receive a uniform when they first arrived, that uniform may now be in a such a poor state eight or nine years on that it is barely recognisable. Prisoners endlessly repair and patch up their worn or torn clothes. Inside the blocks and in the interior courtyard, where they are not obliged to wear their uniforms, prisoners sitting or crouching, bent over with a needle and thread, are one of the most common sights. Most are repairing their clothes, some are repairing their blankets; even if they are in shreds, they are still worth repairing. The poor prisoners are easily identifiable: their uniforms are faded, ragged, and have been repaired so often that they look like a kind of patchwork. Others are wearing a uniform which is obviously the wrong size, because it belongs to someone else. It is rarer to see women in tattered uniforms than men, perhaps because their uniforms become less worn as they are not allowed to work outside, or because they take better care of them.

Prisoners wear their own shoes and any style is permitted. For prisoners who have taste, or wealth, or both, shoes are one of the best forms of self-expression. The women wear shoes with heels, open-toed sandals or smart, closed shoes. The men wear a variety of styles ranging from trendy white trainers to black, polished shoes which would normally be worn with a suit. Often these types of shoes are worn with socks, of a variety of colours, which, combined with the three-quarter length shorts, create an unusual effect; some of these socks are made by the prisoners themselves. Shoe polish is sold in the prison shop, and some prisoners clearly make use of it. The poor prisoners, however, cannot indulge in fancy or shiny footwear. Inside the prison blocks, the vast majority wear plastic flip-flops or the more common and longer-lasting version made of recycled tyres, which have almost become a uniform for the masses inside; they are usually made by the prisoners themselves and can be bought for around 250 or 300 francs. There is a vibrant shoe-repair business inside, with skilled cobblers willing to repair any kind of shoe. Even the flip-flops are repaired, for around 20 francs, until they can literally no longer be worn.

The sea of pink is also interrupted by a flash of colour from the scarves which some women, and even some men, wear draped around their neck or shoulders; some of the women also wear woolly hats. In the carpentry workshop in Cyangugu prison, we met a priest who ran the workshop, who wore a bright blue woollen scarf around his neck, over his pink uniform, as if he was about to go to a football match. Some of the women wear jewellery and occasionally make-up. Many of the men wear watches, and some also have gold chains or bracelets. Prisoners make and sell their own jewellery inside, including a range of engraved rings and bracelets. In Butare prison, we saw a man sitting in the interior courtyard mending watches. Men and women sport a surprising variety of styles of glasses too, some hanging on chains around their necks. The *capita général* in Butare had two pairs of glasses, one the latest style of thin wire-rimmed rectangular glasses, the other a more ordinary pair. Prisoners who spend most of their time outdoors often wear an extra garment of their own to protect them against the cold or the rain. The *capita* of Butare prison usually wore a green anorak over his uniform, while one of his acolytes wore a woolly multi-coloured cardigan over his. The shopkeeper in Cyangugu prison wore a bright royal-blue padded ski-jacket which contrasted nicely with his pink shorts and could be spotted from a distance even when he stood inside his little shop.

Male and female prisoners are required to shave their heads as soon as they enter the prison and to keep them shaven for the duration of their detention, apparently to avoid the spread of lice. It is common to see prisoners shaving each other's heads with hand-held clippers, inside the prison or sitting in the yard outside.

Prisoners who work on designated teams are sometimes given special clothes to protect them from the rain, the mud or the dirt. Members of the hygiene team are given black wellington boots. Some of those who work outside also wear these boots, as well as yellow macs to protect them from the rain. Members of the hygiene and security teams wear special caps – usually made of green, yellow or blue cloth – which give them an air of officialdom and enable other prisoners to spot them at a distance. In some prisons, the caps of those responsible for these teams have "R" or "RA" embroidered on them: *responsable*, or *responsable adjoint* (deputy). Members of the prisoners' Red Cross society wear a red and white cap.

Inside the blocks, in their own châteaux and in the interior yard, those who have their own clothes can shed their uniforms. Again, there are the rich and there are the poor. Some prisoners have several sets of their own clothes. They can buy more through outside visitors, or even inside, where there is a market in secondhand clothes. A woman who was detained in Kigali Central Prison said that from the end of 1996, this market started flourishing after many refugees were arrested and came into the prisons. They had been used to doing trade in the refugee camps, so they just continued trading in the prison. They asked their families to bring them all types of items, particularly clothes, so that they could sell them to other prisoners. In the women's block, there was a room called "the international market". It was especially active on Fridays. One woman spotted a gap in the market and started selling bras and knickers to her fellow prisoners. Every Friday, she would ask visitors to bring her more. By Saturday, they were all sold.

Many prisoners, however, have no choice but to keep their uniform on all the time, because they have nothing else to wear. They may have to borrow a shirt or a pair of trousers from a friend while they wash their uniform. Washing clothes is a constant activity inside, and at any given time, there are thousands of pieces of clothing dripping down from makeshift washing lines, or hanging off nails or the corners of beds. This was a source of irritation to one of the "intellectual" prisoners, who complained that there was nowhere to study, and that other prisoners' washing was always dripping onto his books.

Some prisoners have just one set of their own clothes, which they have had since their arrest, but which have become so old and worn that they can no longer wear them. Many men inside are bare-chested; others wear vests or T-shirts full of holes. People wear whatever they have, or whatever they're given. In the interior courtyard in Butare prison, we saw a young prisoner wearing a T-shirt with the picture of President Kagame – these T-shirts were distributed around Rwanda in the pre-election period in 2003. The prisoner had been wearing it at the time of his arrest, so he was still wearing it one year on.

CHAPTER II

The prisoners' government:

organisation

In Rwanda, the prisons are run by the prisoners. Every aspect of prison life –
the reception of new prisoners, the allocation of space, the distribution of
food and water, hygiene, medical care, security, discipline, the dissemination
of information, legal advice, work, education, leisure, religion – is taken care
of by the prisoners, with astounding efficiency. The prisoners run such a
tight ship that the staff, including the prison director and the guards, hardly
ever set foot inside the main building. Their role in the day-to-day running
of the prison is kept to an absolute minimum. A prisoner told us: "Inside, it's
the prisoners who direct. Outside, the director directs. In practice, there are
two different direction systems. For me, it's the inside system which counts,
as that's the one I see."

In their structure, hierarchy, organisation and discipline, prisoners have
replicated the world outside. Rwandan society is highly stratified and
hierarchical, and successive governments have managed to keep the
population under tight control through a system of local government where
the smallest administrative unit is a group of just ten households. This was
one of the factors which facilitated the organisation of the genocide and
enabled the authorities to manipulate the population down to the lowest
level.

The administration which prisoners have put in place has many of the same
characteristics. It has a well-defined and multi-layered structure, from the
capita général at the top of the ladder down to the individual *capitas de bloc* at
the "local" levels, and a multitude of other prisoners in charge of specific
teams and duties. Like real politicians, many of these leaders not only control
and rule, but manipulate and extort. And like all good Rwandan politicians,
they know everything that is going on in their country: who is who, who
lives where, and who does what – not an easy task when the population of a
single prison exceeds 8,000 or 10,000.

These structures within the prisons existed in Rwanda before the genocide, in a less elaborate form; indeed, variations on the same theme – self-organisation by prisoners – can be found in many countries around the world. But the prison crisis which followed the genocide in Rwanda gave rise to a completely new situation. As the number of prisoners kept rising and the authorities showed little interest in taking control of the situation, prisoners had to take control themselves. Initially, the proliferation of organisational structures within the prison was a survival mechanism on the part of prisoners, to prevent their world from slipping into total chaos. The emphasis was on practical organisation. Efficiency was a necessity, not a luxury. In the first few months after the genocide, there were no prison directors or civilian staff at all: all the guards were military, who routinely ill-treated the prisoners, so it was even more important for prisoners to divide up responsibilities among themselves, for their own protection.

A prisoner described the evolution of the structures and organisation in Kigali Central Prison since 1994:

> "The leader was chosen by all of us, and he then chose the others. To begin with, there was just a team for cooking, but when no wood was delivered, we went out ourselves to collect wood. These were the first two teams: those responsible for the cooking and for fetching the wood. Other teams were set up later... The people who were given responsibility inside had held positions of responsibility outside. They were the same kind of people, who knew how to organise. As the numbers grew, we had a *capita* for each block... The director didn't start until October 1994. He came after the *capita général*... The director was a good man. But the *capita général* was a prisoner like us, while the director was not. We had no relations with the director. It was all through the *capita général*.
>
> Since 1994, I have worked for the hygiene team. Things were very dirty at the beginning. People never washed and the place was never washed. Spontaneously, four of us started cleaning the prison. We fetched branches as brooms and we had one wheel-barrow... Later the Red Cross saw us working and started a bigger

team. It grew from four to 16. Now we're 140. One group works in the outside yard, one in the inside yard, and one near the kitchen. I work near the kitchen. I weed the area and I unblock the toilets."

An academic who had been in Butare Central Prison since 1994 was among a small number of "intellectuals" who took it upon themselves to introduce organisational procedures in the prison in the early days. He was proud of their achievements:

"I was in Block 10, which was legendary. We were like dignitaries. We didn't have any privileges except we could introduce changes to the way the prison was organised. For example, the guards used to beat people at night. We bribed the guards or talked to them in a friendly way. In return, they let us organise life inside the prison. Before, the custom was that prison life was organised by the hardened criminals...

When the first civilian director came in 1995, he gave us permission to organise the prison internally. First we organised the system for visits, then the general order. Every block had two or three security people. We had a system for hygiene, cleaning the toilets and the corridors. Before, the hygiene work was done voluntarily, so there were many deaths from epidemics. We set aside a secluded place for those who needed medical treatment. Before, they would just lie on the ground in the dirt, without water, and the rain drenching them. We established a hospital. Volunteers staffed it, and one qualified nurse."

As the years have passed, the situation in the prisons has gradually stabilised. Yet an inordinately large number of prisoners still hold positions of responsibility in each prison. Those who occupy these positions have no intention of giving them up, because with responsibility comes status, and with status comes money.

The obsessive organisation which goes on in the prisons is also an extremely effective form of escapism. The busier a prisoner, and the higher his position in the pecking order, the easier it is for him to forget that he is in prison.

The structure

The big chief – the head of all the prisoners – is the *capita général*. The men and the women each have their own *capita général*, and there is also a *capita* for the minors' block. The *capita général* has a team, usually composed of one or two deputies, a private secretary, and various other assistants. This team, and the office they occupy inside the prison, is the *capitariat*. The composition of the *capitariat* and the responsibilities allocated to its members vary slightly from prison to prison. In Gitarama Central Prison, the team includes a prisoner in charge of public relations – the public being the prisoners, not the general public outside. The women in Cyangugu Central Prison have their own protocol officer.

The *capita général* has an army of other *capitas* beneath him. The prisons are divided into blocks, and each block has its own *capita*, responsible for several hundred prisoners. In some prisons, the blocks are further sub-divided into zones or groups, each with their own *capita* too.

Then there are the *capitas* in charge of different teams. One of the most important is the security team. The *capita* in charge of security is called the *brigadier chef* or *commissaire*. His team members are sometimes called policemen, or security guards. The members of the security team far out-number the guards in the prison: for example in Nsinda, for a prison population of around 11,800, there are about 200 members of the security team (all prisoners) and just 89 prison guards. The security team is responsible for maintaining law and order inside the prison and its members patrol throughout the day, zigzagging through the blocks, wearing their distinctive yellow caps. Their main role is to make sure prisoners are not infringing any rules and that there are no incidents of violence. They try to mediate when there are disputes and, in more serious cases of indiscipline, they have the authority to punish troublemakers by sending them off to the punishment cells, where they may spend several days, or even weeks. The prison director is called upon to intervene only if the matter is exceptionally serious, and if neither the security team nor the *capita général* is able to resolve it.

The *capitas* of the blocks have to settle disputes which occur within their area of jurisdiction. The causes of these disputes are sometimes trivial but they have the potential to escalate fast in this overcrowded environment. A former *capita* of a block said a typical problem he used to have to sort out was "people who were sleeping in a way which annoyed their neighbours, such as taking up too much space".

In Cyangugu prison, the head of the security team happened to be a former military man, though he claimed that he, like others, had been chosen for his personal qualities rather than his professional experience. "I organise the policemen and the general security inside", he told us. "There are 70 policemen. I was appointed by the director and I appoint the policemen. If there is a serious security problem, I refer it to the director. Tobacco, alcohol and traditional medicines without authorisation are not allowed. I am not paid, but I can stay outside (in the courtyard) all day, to liaise with the director. I can see whoever I like. I work mainly at night. In the day, I can rest and walk around." The *commissaire* responsible for security in Rwandex (the annex to Butare Central Prison) liked his work too, but found it difficult as he had to argue with prisoners: "I'm halfway between the prisoners and the director. I can't satisfy everyone. I have to be impartial."

The women have their own security teams. The head of this team in Butare prison explained how they were organised: "There are 17 of us in the team. This includes one at the gate, two in the toilets and showers, especially when there isn't enough water, two to help distribute the food and two who patrol at night. Everyone is supposed to be in bed by 10pm and all the radios should be switched off by 11pm, until 5am the next morning. The night guards keep the place quiet and make sure everyone is in their beds." Sometimes there were problems when women didn't want to obey the security team: "The women don't always accept the responsibility of the security guards... There are nasty words and some of the women are jealous... Those who have been tried and sentenced are among the most difficult. When we try to discipline them, they say: 'I've been sentenced to death, or five years, so what can you do to me?' Those who are still waiting for justice are better behaved."

There are many other teams, each with their own *capita* and deputy *capita*. They include a team responsible for hygiene – usually one of the largest teams – for water, for the kitchens, for health care (running the prison hospital), for maintenance and logistics, and for the work teams.   Other teams and committees are headed by prisoners who are referred to as *responsables*, rather than *capitas*, but their role is similar.   The term *responsables* is often used by prisoners as a catch-all phrase to refer to any or all prisoners who have some position of coordination or responsibility over others.   Thus there are *responsables* heading the information team and the legal team – a special team set up to advise prisoners on the law, on their rights, and sometimes on their individual case-files.   In Kigali Central Prison, a prisoner had recently been appointed to a new post heading the prisoners' national reconciliation team, presumably modelled on the National Unity and Reconciliation Commission set up by the government.

Prisoners have also formed their own societies and clubs: they have their own Red Cross association, their own Scouts, and their own Mouvement Xaveri, a church-inspired welfare group.   These associations are active in the social and cultural life of the prison, but tend to operate at the grassroots and are not normally viewed as part of the prisoners' administration.   They are the prison equivalent of the voluntary sector.

In Butare prison, the group formed by the nine prisoners in the most senior positions of responsibility – a kind of cabinet – is called *nyobozi*, a Kinyarwanda term which usually refers to local government authorities; the prisoners use this term to differentiate their own leaders from *la direction* (the prison management).   The *capitas* themselves often refer to the rank-and-file prisoners as "the population" or "the people" – the ones they govern. A former prisoner had developed his own terminology for the leaders, based on the model of a national government and the corresponding local government structures:[1]

> "In the prison, it was like another government… I thought of the prison organisation like this. The *capita général* is the president of the government of prisoners. The deputy *capita* is the prime minister. His secretary is the principal private secretary. The heads of department are the ministers. The prison is a country: a whole organisation. There were various departments. Medical and hygiene were the ministry of health; security was the army; the social department was the ministry of local administration and social affairs; the kitchen was the ministry of food, which was the most coveted.
>
> They held meetings, like government meetings. The prisoners imprisoned other prisoners. There was a brigadier chef and his deputy who were like the ministry of defence. If that ministry hadn't existed, we wouldn't have survived. They kept the 'roads' clear. There were people from the security department every ten metres to keep the roads open so that people could walk up and down. They were like the traffic police.
>
> The *capitas* of the blocks were the provincial leaders. The block was like the province… It was the same structure in each block: a *capita*, a deputy, a security department, a food department, etc. Each block was divided into zones, like districts or *secteurs*, with people responsible for each area."

The women operate the same system as the men, but their regime seems to be less rigid. The *capita générale* of Butare prison told us that there were eight people in her team: "We sit down and find the person who can best manage the job. We all know each other. It's a democracy. Two people can share a role; for example in the hospital, there are two different areas, but only one

---

[1]   At the time, Rwanda was divided into 12 provinces (formerly *préfectures*) which were divided into districts. Districts were divided into *secteurs* (sectors) which were further divided into *cellules* (cells). Each province, district, *secteur* and *cellule* had its own administrative structures.

person is officially the head. It's just like life outside. The eight of us have a team meeting every Saturday. We discuss food, health, security and life in the prison, then we organise our programme." She was satisfied with her team: "My authority is respected. I have a good team but a lot to organise. My main concern is that everyone should be safe, calm and without problems."

Overall, prisoners seemed happy to live under this kind of regime, or happier than if the prison were run by staff. The advantages of this extremely efficient organisation seemed to outweigh any feelings of resentment, and the sense of order and discipline has enabled prisoners to feel relatively safe. There were also benefits to being ruled by prisoners who shared their plight – even though the leaders' privileged status took the edge off the harshness of their own imprisonment; the *capitas* were unlikely to beat or physically mistreat new arrivals, even if they exploited them in other ways.

In most prisons, prisoners have set up a reception committee, whose duty is to receive new prisoners on their first day, once the guards have pushed them through the prison gate. A prisoner who arrived in Kigali Central Prison in 2002 told us: "I've never seen a better organised entity than that prison... They assign you to a block and book you in and take you there. They send someone to orientate you. My fear evaporated. People greeted us and welcomed us."

In addition to these formal structures, individual prisoners have used their own initiative to improve the general conditions. One prisoner decided to import cats into Kigali Central Prison to get rid of the rats. He asked a guard to get two kittens from outside. The cats then set to work and, within a short time, had got rid of all the rats. They would wander around the prison then return to their owner's château to eat and sleep. The cats were very popular with the prisoners, who fed them regularly, despite the fact that they barely had enough to feed themselves. Once a prisoner who accidentally stepped on one of the cats was almost lynched by the other prisoners. Within less than two years, the cats had multiplied. Two were later transferred to Kibungo and Gitarama prisons.

The prison directors and other staff are content to let prisoners manage the prisons, as it makes their own jobs considerably less onerous. They can afford to run the prisons in this remote way because they know that by and large, prisoners obey the *capitas* and comply with the system in place. It is in the prisoners' interest to do so if they want a decent quality of life. As a former prisoner told us, "if the *capita* doesn't want you to do something, you don't do it". In theory, if prisoners are not happy with their leaders' performance, they can complain to the prison director, or to the *capita* himself. In some prisons we noticed wooden suggestion boxes, where prisoners could submit complaints. But we were told that the *capita général* was the one who opened the box, so if the complaint concerned his performance, there was no guarantee it would be acted upon.

The *capita général*

The *capita général* is a big fish in a small pond. Sometimes nicknamed "*le chef suprême*", "*le président*", or simply "*général*", he is effectively responsible for several thousand prisoners and oversees all activities in the prison. He is the main representative of the prisoners, but also reports directly to the prison director. A former *capita général* explained: "I had two roles as *capita*: the role of a prisoner and the role of government agent."

The *capita général* is busy 24 hours a day, overseeing, supervising, issuing orders, coordinating, liaising with the director. In many ways, he is not like a prisoner at all. He is able to walk in and out of the main prison building at any time, without special permission, and ends up spending a large part of his day in the outside courtyard of the prison, rather than in the stifling atmosphere inside. However, he rarely goes outside the prison compound. One of the *capitas* told us: "The *capita* stays inside… I accept I'm a prisoner and must stay here. I don't see the need to go out… The main privilege as a *capita* is being able to move around in the prison and to get out of the inside building."

We met the *capita général* and other *responsables* in all the prisons we visited. They were a strange cast of characters, who behaved, almost literally, as if they were acting a scripted part in a play. The *capita général*, in particular, seemed to have a dual personality. Most of them were charming and obliging, yet were clearly figures of power within the prison, and did not hesitate to display that power. Their tone and behaviour towards other prisoners, and the prisoners' response to them, left no doubt as to who was the boss. The *capitas* often had an exaggerated sense of their own importance, reinforced by the readiness of other prisoners to pander to them. Whenever a *capita général* issued an instruction, prisoners would immediately rush off to carry out the order, then rush back to report on the outcome, literally running across the prison yard with a great sense of urgency, regardless of the importance of the request. But in the way they related to the prison director, and even to us, the *capitas* came across as subservient and slightly ingratiating. They were like children trying to do the right thing to please their schoolteacher – an impression accentuated by the fact that they often walked around carrying a file of papers. One of them even got a little notebook out of his pocket and started taking notes at the beginning of our interview. We noticed that some of the *capitas* effortlessly switched backwards and forwards between their two roles – the "leader" and the "star pupil" – while others, who may have been less experienced, tried hard to stick to one or the other, but occasionally lapsed into a third mode, that of their natural, and often quite different, personality.

The *capitas* spoke a double language. During the first part of our interviews, most were careful to stick to the official line. They spoke confidently and authoritatively about life in the prison. However, as our interviews progressed, they began to talk more freely. Our conversations with the *capitas* were illuminating, not because of the information they revealed but because of the multitude of contradictions in their discourse, and the contrast between what they thought they should be telling us and what they really wanted to talk about. One of them, in particular, felt obliged to lavish praise on the government at several points during our conversation, but was also one of its harshest critics. He was both formal and very warm towards us, and seemed to be struggling with a strong desire to tell us things he knew he should not be telling us.

All the *capitas* we met, and almost all other prisoners in positions of responsibility, were accused of genocide; prisoners accused of common crimes are rarely appointed to these positions. Most of them were men and women with a high level of education – typically teachers, who spoke excellent French. For the post of *capita général*, a minimum level of education is required, including a command of either French or English in order to be able to receive outside visitors. As a result, almost all of them are "intellectuals". Being a *génocidaire* [2] is sometimes equated with having a certain level of education. An elderly woman told us: "Those accused of genocide are in positions of responsibility because they are the most intelligent. I can't have any responsibilities because I can't read or write." However, the *responsables* do include people with lower levels of education. The lower the position in the hierarchy, the fewer formal qualifications are required. However, in all these positions, integrity and honesty are deemed essential, both by the prisoners and by the prison management.

Almost all the *capitas* seemed to take pride in what they did, and their eagerness to perform their duties satisfactorily gave them a sense of purpose. They were especially proud of their privileged relationship with the director and of the trust which the director placed in them. They enjoyed their work, even though it could be demanding. The *capita* of Kigali Central Prison told us: "I get pride out of being busy. People respect us… I can come out into the yard and supervise prisoners and talk to office staff. Even just knowing the director is a good feeling. People can't just push me about." Even some of the lower level *capitas* shared this feeling. A prisoner who had been *capita* of a block for two years described it as "an honour. It was the third rank in the prison hierarchy."

The exception was one of the women who had been elected *capita générale*. She had not been happy to be appointed and she found her position stressful. She said it was difficult to manage the women prisoners and complained that other women badmouthed her behind her back because they were jealous. I asked her why she had accepted the position. She said no one could really refuse. She wanted to stop at the end of her six-month term and said she would continue only if the director specifically asked her to.

The *capitas* gave us well-rehearsed speeches on the importance and difficulty of their job and their achievements during their tenure. They denied receiving

---

[2]   "*Génocidaire*" is the term commonly used in Rwanda to refer to someone who has participated or has been accused of participating in the genocide.

any payment or reward in exchange for their hard work, other than an extra ration of food, longer family visits and an open door to the prison director's office. The *capita général* of Gitarama prison stressed that even though the *capitas* received slightly larger food rations than other prisoners, in Gitarama these were not double rations, as was the practice in some other prisons: "Here we are very democratic. If the prisoners are not happy with us, they complain to the director." The *capitas* all claimed they did the work out of the goodness of their hearts, because they wanted to serve their colleagues. The *capita* of Cyangugu prison stated: "I am motivated by working for others. I like doing this work because I like people. I'm proud when people have no problems." This myth was perpetuated by the prison management. The deputy director of Gitarama prison told us with a big smile: "The *capita* is not paid. There are no benefits. He does it out of devotion. He works for his brothers." In reality, a well-organised system of extortion and "taxation" ensures that the *capitas* and other *responsables* receive the equivalent of a healthy salary.

The appointment of a good *capita général* is as important to the prison director as it is to the prisoners; it will determine the ease with which he can do his job. If the *capita* is conscientious, efficient and popular, the director will not have to do very much at all. In addition, he will benefit financially by creaming off some profits. The smooth running of the prison depends in large part on this relationship.

In most of the prisons we visited, the *capita général* submits a report to the director every morning, sometimes verbally but usually in writing. These reports, based on the contributions of all the *capitas* of the blocks and other *responsables*, describe the situation inside and note any particular problems. The reporting system ensures that the director is always kept up to date, without having to make much effort himself. The *capita général* of Gitarama prison described the procedure:

> "There is a book for daily reports. I collect reports from all those responsible for the different departments. There may be a special report if something unusual has happened. I go with the reports to propose solutions. We also have regular meetings: the *capitariat* meets once a week, we meet with the *chefs de service* [heads of

department] every two weeks and with the *chefs de blocs* twice a month. There is a schedule for each block. Each block has meetings and its own systems. I forward the opinions and proposals from these meetings, not my personal opinion. We do written or oral reports, but my daily reports are in writing."

The *capita général* in Cyangugu prison reported to the director at 6am each day. After his meeting with the director, he would take a rest between 12 and 2pm, then resume his work with the prison population in the afternoon.

"I walk around the blocks and see how things are. I have good relations with the prison population. After all, they elected me. Some are not happy but they can come and talk to me. You can't please 100% of people. I like to live in harmony with colleagues, to change their ideas and provide good security and a good atmosphere.

There are times when prisoners leave and others arrive. When there's a changeover, ideas which are not good can come in from outside. I can also lose good people who I've trained up. I have to start all over again. You can get 100 people coming in who are recalcitrants. I have to make sure they don't continue in their bad ways. I have security who follow me around if I need help, but there haven't been any incidents."

Elections

In most prisons, there are elections for the *capita général*, as well as the *capitas* of the blocks. Elections are conducted according to carefully laid-out procedures. There are usually several candidates for each post. Individual prisoners who are felt to have suitable qualities are sometimes approached to stand for these elections, by other prisoners or by the director. We met a few prisoners who had turned down the offer to stand as *capita* because they didn't want the burden of responsibility and feared it would drag them into complicated political situations. But most of those who were approached rushed to take up the offer, especially if they had been singled out by the director.

Capitas are usually elected for a six-month period, which is renewable if they perform well. Different voting procedures are used in different prisons. Some have written ballot papers; in others, prisoners line up behind the candidate of their choice; in others, they gather in meetings and shout out their approval or disapproval of particular candidates. The *capita générale* of the women in Butare prison described how she had been elected: "The director came to visit the women's block. He had a list of intellectuals. When he suggested my name, everybody clapped. If there's a lot of clapping, you're chosen, and the director announces the choice." In theory, the final choice should reflect popular opinion, but the winner for the position of *capita général* has to be approved by the prison director before he or she can assume office.

In Cyangugu prison, there are two *capitas* for the men: one for the prisoners who have confessed to their crimes and another for those who haven't (see Chapter XIX). Since October 2004, the two groups have lived in separate blocks. The contrast between the two *capitas'* personalities was interesting. The *capita* of the "confessed" was in his early thirties and was still a student when he was arrested; he was conscientious, keen to please, and careful not to step out of line. He seemed slightly nervous when I interviewed him; his eyes were darting and he became edgy when the prison director walked past. He had been in post for almost a year and had just been re-elected when we met him. In contrast, the *capita* of those who had not confessed was a teacher in his mid-forties, who had been politically active at the local level under the former government. He exuded confidence and was clearly at ease in his role of leader. He had been *capita* for five years and used to be *capita général* of the whole prison until the two groups were split into separate blocks. Although his burden had been reduced since the creation of the second *capita* position, he was still responsible for about four-fifths of the prison population – around 4,000 prisoners.

The *capita* of those who had not confessed described the election procedure:

> "Each year, voting takes place. The last elections were on 25 October 2004. We use buckets with lids on for the ballot papers. The prison authorities give everyone a piece of paper stamped by the *direction* [prison management] and pens. Before giving out the papers, we put up a list of all the candidates. There were eight of us last time. The prisoners choose a name from the list, write it on the paper, put the paper in the bucket, and we collect the buckets in the yards... They're counted by the administrative and management staff. We start at about 8am and finish at about 3pm. The *direction* announces the result.
>
> I had to write an official letter to be a candidate. It's like a CV. You state your objectives, examples of what you've achieved, your hopes for the future, plans for security. It's about one page. You give it to the *direction*. The director selects the candidates who he thinks are capable.
>
> When we hold elections, the kitchen staff continue to work. They have their own bucket in the kitchen to vote. For the other prisoners, it's like a day's holiday. Everything comes to a standstill No one goes outside their block. People clap when the result is announced. We have a microphone. I give a little speech. I say: 'I'm happy to have been elected and I'll do my best to serve you.' The next day, I oversee elections for the *capitas* of the blocks and the *capita* of security. Those take place every six to 12 months. We ask the prisoners for their opinions. They can choose how they vote, whether by raising their hands or by writing. The candidates are isolated after they've been shown to the population. Then the elections take place. I announce the results."

The *capita* of the prisoners who had confessed had won the election in a contest against three other candidates:

> "Voting is voluntary... I got 950 votes out of 1,500. The second candidate got about 200 votes, the third about 120, and the fourth

about 95. January 2004 was the first time for me. The term is six months but it was extended to around October. I was re-elected last time as I am a bit honest.

For the elections for the *capitas* of the blocks, two prisoners who organise the election stand at the entrance of the block. There are two to four candidates. They call out: 'Who wants to vote for X?' The people come out. Then: 'Who wants to vote for Y?' etc. Each group is counted.

We don't do election campaigns as it could cause problems. We announce the elections only at 6pm for the following day. It's very orderly."

We came across different views on the credibility of these elections. The *capitas*, and a number of other prisoners, gave the impression that the final choice reflected the wishes of most prisoners. But a former prisoner in Kigali Central Prison said that only the lower-level *capitas* were genuinely elected, while the top leaders were imposed by the director: "They were not elected. The *capita général* was appointed by the *direction*, as well as his deputy and his private secretary. Other *responsables* were proposed by the *capita général* to the director. The director accepted or rejected them." This view was confirmed by some of the prison directors themselves. When we asked the deputy director of Kigali Central Prison how they could be sure that their choice of *capita* would be popular with the prisoners, he said: "We judge their qualities on behalf of the prisoners… We talk to them… They must have good morality and good behaviour. They must be well-accepted." The *capita général* of Kigali Central Prison himself, who had been elected only two weeks before we met him, confirmed that the director appointed the *capita général* and other *responsables*, but only after consulting "the high-up officials inside".

In some prisons, such as Nsinda, there are no elections at all. The deputy *capita* there told us his name was one of eight put forward to the director who approved them on the basis of their good behaviour. The director first talked to the director of Byumba Central Prison, where the prisoner had been detained before, to obtain a reference, then simply approved his appointment. The absence of elections seemed to have a direct consequence on the quality of the leadership. A prisoner in Nsinda complained: "The administration here is mediocre. They are all appointed by the director. They don't listen and they don't care."

Getting rich inside

Many *capitas* and other *responsables* have become very rich off the backs of poorer prisoners. Even though they deny receiving payment for their work, it is an open secret that all of them do. As a colleague told me: "The *capita* is not paid but he gets money." The system is so institutionalised that no one even thinks of challenging it. Prisoners have to cooperate with the system in order to survive, and the better they cooperate, the higher the chance of receiving kickbacks or other favours themselves. The *capita général* will take a cut of every transaction and every activity which goes on in the prison, sometimes directly, sometimes through intermediaries such as the *capitas* of the blocks, who also take their share. Unlike other prisoners, the *capita général* will not be harassed as he goes in and out of the gate and is able to carry on with his daily business without hindrance. A prisoner who had been a deputy *capita* admitted: "One of the advantages is that our goods don't get searched after visits. I used to arrange to take money for other people from their wives when they visited, and I used to take a cut."

Every position of responsibility in the prison brings some financial or material advantage; if it is not money, it may be extra rations of food, water, soap, new uniforms or blankets. As a result, the creation of an ever-growing bureaucracy of prisoners has become an end in itself. A prisoner in Nsinda estimated that by 2004, almost half the population of the prison had some kind of job or responsibility; this may have been an exaggeration, but the number of prisoners holding positions of responsibility certainly seemed out of proportion with the real needs. This situation was having a direct impact on the rest of the population: "They [the *responsables*] all get an extra ration, which reduces the rations for the rest of us. When the Red Cross comes and counts prisoners who have a job, people give a lower number as they don't dare tell the Red Cross that so many of them have jobs. To have a job, you have to pay... The *capitas* often fire people from their jobs so that they can get more money from a new person."

All the *responsables* receive some kind of reward, but the *capita général* and the *capitas* of some specific departments, such as the kitchens, take the lion's share. We heard many stories about *capitas* amassing so much money that they had had several large houses built outside while they were in prison, either for their families or in preparation for their eventual release. Some of these people may have been wealthy before their arrest, but others started saving in earnest after their arrest. A prisoner in Cyangugu pointed to another prisoner, the head of the hygiene team, who seemed to spend all his time strolling around in the garden, enjoying the fresh air: "That man is very rich. He's built a house outside and has cows. The *capita général* also has a house and cows. The *capita* of the kitchen too. A *capita* who was released recently had 150,000 francs in cash (around US$267). He had a very thick double mattress. He had had a house built outside. Some prisoners have hi-fi systems. Some have their own TV, apart from the communal ones."

The *capita général* pays the prison director to become *capita*. The cost of becoming a *capita* can reach 300,000 or 500,000 francs in some prisons (approximately US$ 535 or 890); it is usually highest in urban areas. It is a large sum but a sound investment as the *capita* knows he will make it up through income from other prisoners within a short time. The lower-level *capitas* and other *responsables* also pay for the privilege. They pay the *capita général*, who can use the money from these appointments to start recouping some of what he has spent to buy his own position. In Gikondo in 1997-1998, a prisoner would pay around 15,000 francs (US$26) to be *capita* of security and about 20,000 (US$35) to be *capita* of a block.

The sources of revenue are numerous and varied. The most easy and lucrative is the allocation of space. Each new prisoner who arrives in the prison, and each prisoner who decides to move within the prison, has to buy his space, sometimes directly from the *capita général*, or the *capita* of the block, sometimes from another prisoner, but usually with the blessing of the *capita général* who takes a share of the profit. Money is also made from the sale of food, water, clothes, and every legal or illegal commodity which makes its way through the prison gates. A former prisoner told us: "There are shops inside, like a marketplace. You pay to have a shop. A percentage goes to the *capita général* and a percentage to the *capita* responsible for security." Another prisoner told us: "They [the *capitas* and *responsables*] sell everything. They take cooking oil, soap and clothes which they conceal under the rubbish in the wheelbarrows and take them outside to sell them. Uniform material should be free but we have to buy it... I've never got anything for free in my one year here."

The prisoners in charge of the teams which work outside (see Chapter III) also operate a racket: prisoners have to pay the *capita* for the privilege of joining the work teams. As one prisoner described it, "even the air outside is bought". Another prisoner explained how the system worked: "Each member of the work team has to give the *capita général* 500 francs every time they go out to work. It goes through his subordinates, who give a report to the *capita général*. They say, for example: 'Today, 2,000 people went outside. They gave X amount of money.' The *capita général* takes the money and pays the tax collectors, his subordinates." A one-off payment was usually not sufficient. A prisoner told us: "Once you'd paid, it was supposed to be valid until the *capita* changed, but the *capita* could change his mind and ask for more. To stay in the team, you had to keep good relations with the *capita*."

The relationship between the *capita général* and the prison director could also be very lucrative – for both parties. Profits were shared between the two. A prisoner explained: "One of the responsibilities of the *capita* is to collect money for the *direction*. It is the same in all the prisons." A former prisoner in Kigali Central Prison told us how on one occasion, the *capita général* had gathered the prisoners inside and told them the prison director urgently needed a large sum of money, around 400,000 francs (about US$714). Within a short time, he had collected the money from the prisoners: "To give the money to the director, the *capita général* first used his own money, then got it back from the prisoners. For a while after that, everything else became more expensive for us inside."

The prison administration

In comparison to the complex and intricate world of the prisoners' organisation, the structure of the prison staff seems one-dimensional, and the role they play somewhat peripheral to the realities inside. The staff typically includes a director, two deputy directors, one or two secretaries, an accountant, a registrar, one or two social workers, and a team of guards. In total, at the end of 2004 when the total prison population was around 85,500, the prison staff for the whole country numbered around 1,000, of whom around 800 were guards.[3] The number of staff in each prison rarely exceeded 100, even in the larger prisons where the prison population could exceed 10,000. In Butare central prison, for example, there were 64 guards and 12 office staff for more than 10,700 prisoners. Working in the prison service is not a very prestigious profession, and none of the staff earns big salaries, so they are always on the lookout for ways of making extra money on the side.

Overall responsibility for the administration of the prisons rests with the Ministry of Interior, and all the prison staff are employees of the Ministry of Interior. Following a number of reforms aimed at decentralising the system of government, the budget for the prison service is set by the Ministry of Interior but disbursed by the individual provinces. Each prison director draws up a proposed budget for his prison and submits it to the authorities. Requests for materials follow the same procedure.

Training for prison staff is organised by the Ministry of Interior but often delivered by other organisations and individuals. Academics and specialists from non-governmental organisations are brought in, as appropriate, to conduct sessions on specific topics, including administration, management, international law, human rights, welfare of prisoners, hygiene and health. The International Committee of the Red Cross (ICRC) has played an important role in staff training, as has Penal Reform International (PRI), which conducted a comprehensive training programme for prison staff across Rwanda until 2004.

---

[3]   As a point of comparison, in 2007 the Prison Service in England and Wales had 47,747 staff (of whom 33,263 were operational staff) for 71,362 prisoners. See HM Prison Service, *Annual Report, April 2006 to March 2007*.

All the prison staff work from offices located within the prison compound, but outside the main prison building. As a result, they seem both physically and emotionally removed from events inside. They only venture inside when there is a specific reason for doing so: to hold a meeting with prisoners, to check up on a particular problem, or occasionally to carry out searches. The rest of the time, they stay outside, walking around the compound or sitting in their offices. Nevertheless, the directors and their deputies we met had a fairly good understanding of prisoners' needs and views, and the gulf between them and the prisoners was not as great as might be expected. When the first prison directors were appointed after the genocide, in late 1994 or early 1995, many of them were former military or individuals close to the ruling Rwandan Patriotic Front (RPF), and they treated prisoners very badly. The more recent appointments still include individuals who are close to the government, but they tend to be more sympathetic to the needs of prisoners. Several of the directors and deputy directors we met had a background in teaching rather than in the security forces.

Prison directors and their deputies

The prison director and his deputy are a kind of double act. In each prison we visited, the personality and demeanour of these two individuals were in stark contrast with each other. As a general rule, one was francophone and the other anglophone.[4] The directors came across as slightly aloof and detached from the day-to-day running of the prison, while their deputies were the friendly face of the prison administration and the hands-on managers. The directors all sat in big offices, behind big desks, on which a few sheets of paper were scattered, awaiting their signature. On the wall was a big blackboard with the statistics of the prison population updated daily in white chalk. The deputies sat in smaller offices, surrounded by messy piles of paper and shelves full of files. The directors were often absent, as outside meetings seemed to take up a large proportion of their time; the deputies were more often on site.

---

[4]   As a former Belgian colony, Rwanda's colonial language was French, until the RPF took power in July 1994. Many of the leaders of the RPF and of the new government had grown up in Uganda, so they spoke English rather than French. They have since made English one of Rwanda's three official languages, alongside French and Kinyarwanda.

For our research in the prisons to succeed, we needed to get a measure of the directors' and deputy directors' personalities and disposition so that we could find the quickest way of securing their cooperation. Overall, this was relatively easy, and none of the directors refused us access, although we first had to go through a particular ritual. On our first visit to each prison, we started off by meeting the director to explain the purpose of our research and to ask for his permission to interview prisoners privately. There were a few minutes of suspense while he listened to us, without giving anything away in his facial expressions, then he paused, asked a few questions, read our letter of authorisation from the ministry two or three times, very slowly, then just put the letter down and agreed to virtually all our requests. In every prison, it was the same routine, a futile exercise of authority whose sole purpose was to remind us of the director's power to obstruct us, should he so desire. But none of them did, and some turned out to be much more interested in our research and concerned for the well-being of the prisoners than they first appeared.

Only the director of Butare prison was slightly guarded, but even he did not hinder our work. He seemed to rule in a more authoritarian way than some other directors, and his personality had rubbed off on some of the other staff, who were less forthcoming too. The usual routine on our visits was for us to jot down a list of names of the prisoners we wanted to speak to and submit it to the director. He would then sign the list and authorise the named prisoners to come out to talk to us. The director of Butare prison scrutinised this list more closely than other directors. Once he had signed it, the list was handed to the *capita général*, who sent for the prisoners to come and talk to us. We worked in Butare prison for several consecutive days. After a few days, we needed to add some names to the list, but the director was not there to sign off on the new names. Initially, this caused some concern to the *capita général*, who was not sure he could fetch these additional prisoners without the director's authorisation. But after a bit of persuasion, he agreed, and we simply added the new names onto the same list, above the director's signature. For the remaining days, this list – a small scrap of paper to which the *capita* had added his own scribbles – remained with one of the *capita*'s assistants, a messenger who was given the task of fetching the prisoners for us one by one. The list lived in the messenger's pocket, and he ticked off the names conscientiously as we worked our way through the list. Later, the director returned and saw that we were talking to prisoners whose exit he had not authorised, but he did not seem perturbed.

The directors and their deputies each had their distinctive characteristics, which we learned to recognise and appreciate on our repeated visits to the prisons. The deputy director in Cyangugu prison rode to and from work on a large motorbike, which he parked in the prison yard. We were there during the rainy season, and there were huge downpours of rain almost every day. Whenever it rained, a prisoner who had been given the special responsibility of looking after the bike would wheel it into one of the rooms and lean it against the wall, then wheel it out again when the rain stopped. This was a regular routine, several times a day, and the prisoner treated the motorbike with great tenderness, as if it were a horse which had to be groomed and protected from the elements.

In most prisons, we were able to walk straight into the director's office if he was there, but in Kigali Central Prison, we had to go through his secretary, an older man with an athletic build who always wore a baseball cap and jeans, greeted us without smiling but with a firm handshake, then strode off to check whether the director was available to see us, with military efficiency. This secretary worked in a large, cavernous room with one or two female members of staff, each sitting behind ancient manual typewriters, but rarely typing. Two or three computers sat silently in the corner, permanently switched off. In the reception area outside the secretaries' office, there were disorderly piles of files falling all over the wooden shelves and gathering dust; as far as we could judge from the labels, some of them may have contained prisoners' case details. The reception area was always empty. No one seemed to be looking after these files or worrying about their security.

In Gitarama prison, the atmosphere seemed particularly relaxed, and we understood why as soon as we met the deputy director. He was a tall man with a huge smile, very relaxed and welcoming. He gave us unlimited access to the prison, answered all our questions, and was happy for us to spend as long as we wanted in the prison, even beyond the normal closing time, after he had gone home. He liked his work and saw it as his mission to help the prisoners. He clearly had a good relationship with the prisoners. The director was a very different type of person. He also received us with a smile and gave us the access we needed, but yawned throughout our conversation and did not take any interest in what we were doing. His job didn't seem to inspire him. He was rarely there when we visited, and a colleague who had visited the prison frequently in the previous months told me he had never seen him before.

The directors and their deputies rotate regularly between prisons. We asked some of them how they compared the different prisons in which they had worked. Generally, they preferred working in more rural areas, where the prison population was apparently more compliant. Those who had worked in prisons with a high proportion of "intellectuals", such as Kigali Central Prison, had found the work there more demanding as the prisoners tended to have their own ideas about how things should be done.

The personalities of the director and his deputy have a direct influence on the atmosphere in the prison, even though they rarely step inside. Prisoners compared the various directors who had succeeded each other during their many years in detention. A prisoner who had spent seven years in Kigali Central Prison had seen several directors come and go: "Some directors are nasty and brutal and this can change the atmosphere. Some assume that all prisoners are killers. Others, like the current one, are very relaxed with everyone. They all follow government policy, but their personal character makes a difference."

In the earlier years, some of the prison directors had been much harsher and had treated prisoners with contempt and even brutality. A former prisoner remembered an incident during a search in Kigali Central Prison in 1998 or 1999: "The prison director intervened in person to tighten up the searches. He asked everyone to take off their shoes to search them. What shocked me was the way he often hit the prisoners, even those who hadn't done anything wrong. He hit them on their heads, with their sandals, and some of them started bleeding." One young prisoner was caught with a letter and a photograph of a young girl. " 'Who is this girl, you idiot?', the director muttered. 'She's a friend, sir'. 'A friend or a fiancée? Say she's your fiancée and I'll show you here and now that a *mabuso* [a Swahili word used to refer to prisoners] is not allowed to have a fiancée'. He had already ripped up the photo and hit the young man."

A prisoner in Cyangugu remembered that under previous directors, prisoners who were caught doing something wrong were made to lie down on the stones in the courtyard and were beaten before being sent to the punishment cells. But this practice had since stopped, and in the last two years, punishments had become "lighter and more educational".

Overall, the situation seems to have evolved positively and, by 2004, most prisoners did not judge their current directors too harshly. Their main criticisms related to corruption, but this was offset by positive reforms which directors had introduced into some of the prisons. For example in Cyangugu prison, the director's approval of two television sets for the interior courtyard was extremely popular, as was his permission for the prisoners to play football in the sports stadium outside, once a week. Prison directors who cracked down on smoking were also popular with some, though not all, prisoners. One former prisoner was full of praise for a director who had encouraged cultural activities and attended some of the prisoners' theatre and music shows himself. The directors and their deputies had also all perfected the art of turning a blind eye to activities which were officially forbidden, particularly the possession of cash in the prison. When we toured the inside of Cyangugu prison, we came across a noisy section of the interior courtyard where a group of prisoners were counting out big piles of coins on a table. We were told that this was old currency, which the prisoners were going to exchange for new currency. Where and how they were planning to exchange the money and for what purpose was not explained to us. The deputy director, who was standing beside us, stood watching the prisoners counting out the money. "It's forbidden," he stated calmly, then moved on.

The more political prisoners remained critical of the directors simply because they were government employees and were therefore bound to toe the government line. When directors held general meetings with the prisoners, some prisoners boycotted them on the grounds that they were just an exercise in propaganda. Others attended because they felt obliged to and had nothing else to do, but did not expect to learn anything new. In Cyangugu, I was halfway through an interview with a prisoner when I realised that the director was holding a meeting with prisoners inside. I asked the prisoner whether he wanted to take a break from our conversation to attend the meeting. He dismissed the suggestion with contempt: "He doesn't often hold meetings and when he does, there are usually no results. People may express themselves but they're fearful. I'm not interested in going to meetings with the director. We can't give our opinions, so there's no point. Those people [the directors] have disappointed me." However, some prisoners appreciated the meetings called by the directors because they discouraged rumour-mongering and enabled them to keep up to date with developments relating to the justice system, in particular.

The guards

The guards are the official public face of the prison. At the entrance to each prison, at street level, there is a small post where one or two guards sit all day long. There is little for them to do there, except let visitors in and out and watch the general coming and going. They are occasionally joined by other colleagues for a chat. Otherwise they just sit there, listening to the radio or dozing. Kigali Central Prison was the only prison where the guards asked us to leave our mobile phones at the entrance, but our bags were not searched, and had we not declared our phones, we could have walked straight in with them. They also asked us for our passports, but only in order to identify us as the owners of the phones. None of the other prisons we visited had any kind of security measures, and no one searched our bags. Our letter of authorisation to visit the prisons specified that we were not allowed to take photographs or recordings, but the guards never checked whether we were carrying cameras or tape-recorders. They read the letter and simply waved us through.

In the prison courtyard, the guards are slightly more active, though there too, the majority seem to be hanging around doing nothing. There is usually a group of three or four guards standing in front of the gate which leads into the prison building, or sitting on a wooden bench, and a few others strolling around the yard or the gardens and fields surrounding the prison. The guards are noticeable from a distance, with their distinctive blue uniforms: sky blue shirt, navy blue trousers tucked into black military-style boots, and black cap. Many of them wear shades, especially the younger ones, and smoke cigarettes – a luxury forbidden to prisoners. All of them carry a gun slung across their shoulder. The guards work around the clock, on day shifts and night shifts. They live in housing provided by the prison, usually basic

huts in the fields behind the prison buildings. They also have their own little
office in the front of the prison compound, but don't have much cause to
use it unless they want to shelter from the rain or sit down for a rest. In
Kigali Central Prison, the guards lent us their office for our interviews.
Occasionally, one of the older guards would come in, shuffle some papers
around, glance at us disapprovingly, then walk out. The rest of the time, they
left us alone, until around 3.30pm, when the working day officially ended and
we were expected to leave.

The guards are an eclectic group of individuals. Some are stern, others are
relaxed. They include men and women, some young, some old. With a few
exceptions, most of them do not have a high level of formal education and do
not speak more than a few words of French or English. Theirs is a fairly low-
status job; they earn about 18,000 francs a month (approximately US$32).
Many of them are former soldiers who joined the prison service straight from
the army, or, in the early days, straight from the RPF. An exceptionally
charming and helpful guard in Kigali Central Prison told us he had joined
the RPF at the age of 11, when it was still a guerrilla movement. He was now
25 and had been working as a prison guard for seven years; he preferred the
life of a guard to the life of a soldier. We chatted to him on our numerous
visits to the prison; it was hard to believe that such a gentle man had ever
been a fighter or a soldier. Those who had been in the army were not given
any kind of special training before becoming guards. Training was only
provided for those who had not been soldiers.

The guards' boss is the *surveillant chef* (chief guard). Within the broader
hierarchy of the prison, the *surveillant chef* seems to occupy a place halfway
between the prison director and the *capita général* and acts in some ways as
an intermediary between the two. He is responsible for supervising his team
of guards and for any extra tasks which the prison director sees fit to delegate
to him. The *surveillant chef* in Kigali Central Prison was a polite and friendly
man, who spoke a little English. Once we had befriended him, he tried to
teach us to play *igisoro*, the traditional game which prisoners and many other
people in Rwanda love to play (see Chapter III). He excelled at it, and we
often saw him playing with other guards in the prison courtyard.

Guard standing outside Kigali Central Prison   © Carina Tertsakian

The guards' attitudes towards the prisoners and towards their job varied enormously. This was apparent from prisoners' anecdotes as well as from watching the guards at work and talking to them. Some were abrupt with the prisoners, did not hesitate to manhandle them during searches or visits and enjoyed asserting their authority over them; others treated them with respect, even as equals. Some prisoners claimed that the guards, most of whom are Tutsi, tended to grant favours to Tutsi prisoners, but no one dared complain.

In Cyangugu prison, we sought out a particular guard whom several prisoners had talked about in glowing terms. He was the prisoners' hero, a kind and straightforward man who was not only sympathetic to prisoners' problems but went out of his way to help them within his limited means. A 15-year-old girl told us that he had paid for her and another prisoner who didn't have any money to join the prisoners' health insurance scheme. A prisoner who was otherwise very critical of the prison staff, especially the guards, also praised him: "He is very human. But other guards are fanatical. Clemency is bought. He is the only one to treat us kindly without being paid. Some released prisoners have helped him in return."

In Butare prison, we chatted with one of the few guards who spoke good French. Like many of his colleagues, he used to be in the RPF. He had worked in the prison service for a year and a half but didn't like his job. He felt frustrated because he wanted to study instead. He seemed to get on well with the prisoners and said he did what he could to help them. Then he corrected himself: "In fact, we help each other. We give them cigarettes and pass on other items, either for money or for free. The only things which are not allowed are drugs and alcohol, although alcohol does get in. All the guards help prisoners like this." He did not believe that guards should be nasty to prisoners: "If you do that, it will backfire and make the situation worse. We should treat them like human beings."

The fact that guards receive a low salary and that many are not very motivated by their job has turned into an advantage for prisoners. A two-way relationship based on mutual interest has developed. Guards are always on the lookout for ways of topping up their salary, and opportunities for doing so abound in the prison. In turn, their cooperation can significantly accept payment is what keeps life going inside." In the prison jargon, the guards are sometimes called *rujigo* (customs officer), and *amahoro* (customs taxes) is the money they collect from prisoners. The prison gate, where the guards are posted and where many of these negotiations take place, is called the customs post.

Prisoners – and their families – who have money can pay a guard to do almost anything. Guards will willingly offer their services to extend family visits, to smuggle money, letters or goods in and out of the prison, and to turn a blind eye to other activities which are prohibited. We heard stories of guards allowing prisoners to have sex with their wives while they were working outside, and in some cases, facilitating this by providing a quiet place for them (sometimes their own house), away from prying eyes.

Many prisoners have forged close relations with guards over the many years they have spent in prison, and have come to consider individual guards as "their" guards, those they would approach in the first instance if they needed a favour. These relationships could be expensive, but they were almost always worth it. The situation has evolved significantly, as in the first few years after the genocide, guards systematically ill-treated and humiliated prisoners, and it would have been almost inconceivable for prisoners to develop relations resembling friendships with any of the guards. Now, the guards' attempts to assert their authority over prisoners were little more than symbolic. A prisoner told us: "The guards are just like us." When we asked the *capita général* of Butare prison about the relationship between prisoners and guards, he gave us a big smile: "Guards and prisoners are like brothers. Relations are good. Even if there are problems, we reconcile quickly. Once the director said that the guards and prisoners are the same."

Searches

Periodically, rumours of weapons in the prisons have led to large-scale searches. One such search in Kigali Central Prison, in 1998, was memorable, as it was far more extensive and thorough than any other. This was during the time of the insurgency in the northwest of Rwanda, so the climate was tense. The military had been brought in to conduct the search, and together with the prison authorities, had emptied the entire prison, thrown out all prisoners' possessions and destroyed many of their makeshift beds. They had found money and other objects, but apparently no weapons. Guards had helped themselves to any valuable objects, while other belongings, such as blankets, clothes and even cups and plates, were burnt. Prisoners had returned to their châteaux with nothing. Several prisoners we spoke to cited this search as the most important event which had taken place during the years they had spent in prison. They had found it traumatic, even though, objectively, they had probably been through many more painful experiences.

A former prisoner remembered that some of the belongings which were taken during the search found their way back into the prison several weeks later:

> "Trucks had transported the belongings taken during the search to a depot about 20 kilometres away. The guards could sift through any objects of value, which they then re-sold to their real owners in the prison at a relatively low price. That was how two weeks later, I bought back my own pair of shoes which had been taken by a guard, who then sent them back to the prison in search of a customer. So I paid four thousand francs to get back at least one of my possessions thrown out during the search. Some of my colleagues managed to get their radios back in the same way. None of us ever forgot that search. From then on, it became a threat every time the director didn't like the way we were behaving."

For several months after this search, families visiting prisoners in Kigali Central Prison were not allowed to bring food in containers, but only in plastic carrier-bags, on the pretext that they might otherwise conceal subversive messages in the food. On one or possibly several occasions, all the visitors were made to pour the food they had brought into big barrels, regardless of what the food consisted of. That evening, all the prisoners were served their daily ration from the barrels, where all the food which visitors had brought – vegetables, corn, meat, fish, fruit – had been mixed up. The same former prisoner recalled: "Even those prisoners who never received any visits were fed that day and could 'take advantage', exceptionally. The director had commented with irony: 'Visits are being rationalised.'"

There were at least two other general searches in Kigali Central Prison, during which the châteaux of the more political prisoners were searched particularly thoroughly. Prisoners believed these later searches, which took place in 2002 or 2003, in the run-up to the elections, may have been prompted by rumours that some prisoners were writing pamphlets against the government and that some had mobile phones. But there were no reports of weapons found in the prison.

The threat of impending searches remains real for prisoners. A number of "intellectuals" who were writing diaries or other accounts in prison had got into the habit of smuggling their manuscripts out through their families for fear that the authorities might one day seize them.

Piles of prisoners' belongings thrown out in 1998 prison search, Kigali Central Prison
© Trish Hiddleston

CHAPTER III

Tomatoes, blackboards and guitars:

work and leisure

Work

With the assistance of international organisations, a work programme was put in place in the prisons.[1] The main purpose was to enable prisoners to get some fresh air and exercise and to receive a token reward for their work. The results of their work were also intended to benefit the prison as a whole, either directly – for example if they carried out maintenance work in the prison – or indirectly: the prison administration would sell crops grown by the prisoners or objects they had manufactured, and the profits were supposed to be fed back into the prison budget.

Over the years, the work programme has grown from just two or three teams sent out to fetch wood or water to a plethora of well-organised and specialised teams composed of several hundred prisoners, who work on a daily basis and provide a range of commercially competitive services to clients outside. Joining a work team can transform a prisoner's life, simply by giving some respite and distraction from the suffocating atmosphere inside.

Working inside

Some of the work is carried out within the prison compound, so even though prisoners leave their blocks, they do not venture into the world outside. Prisoners work in the prison gardens, grow crops in the prison fields, and rear ducks, hens, rabbits or pigs. Other prisoners do cleaning and maintenance work in the staff offices and around the prison compound. The prison management sometimes makes use of the specific skills of prisoners who may be better educated and more qualified than the staff: a former prisoner who was a trained statistician was asked to organise some of the office systems and

---

[1]   Penal Reform International was the main organisation which facilitated this programme in the central prisons, while Dignité en Détention set up work projects for detainees in some of the *cachots*.

office systems and information for the director. A prisoner who used to work as an accountant in the university was given several different responsibilities, including assisting the prison accountant, submitting six-monthly financial reports on all the activities of the different work teams and keeping the accounts of the prison shop.

The prisons we visited all had large sewing and carpentry workshops within their premises. At any one time, scores of male and female prisoners sat behind old black Singer treadle sewing machines, making prison uniforms or clothes for sale outside. In Cyangugu Central Prison, prisoners held up for us several professionally tailored dresses and jackets to which they were adding the finishing touches; others were hanging on the wall, waiting to be collected by customers. In the carpentry workshops, which are surprisingly spacious and well-equipped, a large team of men saw and carve away all day long, making everything from religious artefacts and sculptures to tables, chairs, wardrobes, beds and upholstered three-piece suites. Furniture is made to order; prisoners in Cyangugu showed us a glossy catalogue of the designs on offer, with pictures, descriptions and prices. In Rwandex (the annex to Butare Central Prison), a prisoner who used to be a carpenter had designed and made his own machine with a crank handle for turning wood on a lathe. Most prisons have a blacksmith with a welding team, making a variety of tools and other metal objects, a garage with a team of mechanics and a maintenance team.

Prisoners who make smaller objects which require less specialised equipment can work within the prison blocks. Walking around the main interior courtyard in Butare prison, we came across a huge range of artistic talent. A whole team of prisoners was making beautifully carved artefacts: boxes in the shape of birds or pineapples, magnificent sculptures of crocodiles and cows, candlesticks, trays and dishes, maps of Rwanda, religious panels and tabernacles, all made of pale wood, some painted and varnished in bright colours. Others made large framed paintings, often with a religious theme, or small greetings cards. Some of these objects are sold in the prison shop; others are made to order for individual clients outside. A young prisoner in Gitarama Central Prison had learnt to draw in prison and was trying to turn his new skill to commercial advantage: "We draw illustrations, posters for theatre shows and notices. I like doing this. I never used to do it outside, but

I saw others doing it here, so I started. There are lots of things I've seen in here for the first time: people making bouquets of flowers, sculptures, baskets, bags and other things… I sell my drawings to organisations inside the prison. I earn a bit of money this way. Sometimes other prisoners buy my drawings to send to their families. I can get 100 or 200 francs. It helps, but there's not much profit as I have to buy the paper."

Wooden bird and crocodile made by prisoners in Butare prison   © Karl Wood

In parallel with the organised work teams, there is a whole black market of workers, making and selling all kinds of objects and services directly to their prisoner friends, without going through the prison administration. These transactions depend on prisoners' individual skills and ingenuity and are not part of a formal system, although the practice is so widespread that it appears to be even more established than the official work teams. There is such a broad range of skills and creativity in the prison that virtually every product or service is available, some more or less prohibited than others. A former prisoner in Kigali Central Prison was amazed to find prisoners making everything from tools and jewellery – chain bracelets, bangles and rings engraved with a razor blade – to gold and copper teeth, "but you have to be there for around three months before they let you see these things. Some tools are not allowed inside. Sometimes there are spot checks and they confiscate them. Then within a week, the prisoners have made the tools again themselves."

In the women's blocks, basketry and weaving are the main activities. All over the courtyard, there are women making baskets, sitting on pieces of cloth on the ground. The traditional Rwandan tightly woven cream-coloured baskets with splashes of colour, in a great variety of shapes and sizes, are sold to customers outside, through the prison shop, as well as to individuals within the prison, but there are so many women making them that the supply tends to outweigh the demand. For the women, it is primarily a way of keeping themselves occupied. They have to buy their own materials, so those with no money, who are most in need of this income, are unable to work. Women also sew, knit and embroider: clothes, tablecloths, bedspreads and other articles. A young woman told us she had managed to save up enough money from selling the articles she embroidered and knitted to pay for her sister's school materials for the duration of her studies. But she was one of the lucky ones. Not all the women found these activities so lucrative. Some gave away the articles they made in exchange for favours. One woman made baby clothes for the female guards when they were pregnant, in exchange for being allowed longer visits. The guards supplied the materials and she sewed the clothes. She told us proudly: "I never learned sewing at school or in prison. It's a gift from God."

Working outside

The work outside the prison compound is strictly for the men. Women are not allowed to work outside.[2] Even among the men, not all prisoners are allowed to work. Certain categories are excluded by the prison management as it is thought they are more likely to try to escape once they find themselves outside. These include prisoners accused of common crimes, prisoners sentenced to death or to life imprisonment, prominent prisoners suspected of having played a leading role in the genocide, military prisoners, prisoners who have committed acts of indiscipline, prisoners who have been released and re-arrested, and, more recently, prisoners who have not confessed to their crimes (see Chapter XIX). Getting a place on the work teams quickly became a matter of competition, as only a limited number of places were

---

[2]   The only exception was Miyove prison, until it turned into an all-male prison.

available. Inevitably, the exclusion of the above categories has created resentment and jealousy among prisoners.

Each work team has its own team leader, who supervises and organises the work. He chooses the members of his team and submits the list of workers to the prison director who has to approve it before they can go out. A prisoner can make a request to join a work team by writing to the *capita* of the team or the *capita général*, but there is no guarantee that he will be accepted. Prisoners who have technical skills – for example builders or mechanics – are more likely to be invited to join certain teams, but work such as agriculture is, at least in theory, open to almost anyone. In practice, it depends on who the prisoners are, how much money they have (every prisoner has to pay the *capita* to join the work team), and on their relationship with the *capita* and other prisoners. As there are always more prisoners wanting to work than places on the teams, any excuse is good enough to get someone excluded. One prisoner told us: "If you say something bad, it will stop you from working outside. If you don't want someone to work outside, you can just accuse them of trying to escape."

The work outside is mostly manual labour. It includes agriculture, construction work (building houses for individuals, or larger commercial projects for businesses; prison labour has also been used to build new prisons), making bricks and tiles, car repairs, and cleaning and other menial duties in local government offices. The system has been set up so that the prison can bid for almost any type of contract, and, as its manpower is often considerably cheaper than that of commercial companies, it is fairly easy for the prisons to secure contracts. Prisoners in Kigali have set up their own construction company: *PCK Entreprise de Construction*. Armies of men in pink working on building sites in the middle of town or in fields in the countryside have become a common sight. In the early days, passers-by would stop and stare as trucks carrying groups of prisoners drove past, but now, they are just part of the normal landscape of Rwanda.

Prisoners working in a brick-making factory, Butare, 2003
© Per-Anders Pettersson/Getty Images

Prisoners are supposed to receive 10% of the payment for their work, while
20% is paid into the prison budget and 70% goes to the Ministry of Interior.
The 10% is paid in kind, as prisoners are not allowed to keep cash. In some
prisons, payment takes the form of sugar or soap. In others, the prisoner can
choose to invest it in an account or to buy food, clothes or other items of
necessity. In practice, very few prisoners ever get to see their 10%. They may
even end up out of pocket, as they have to pay to join the work team and may
receive nothing in return. Some prisoners felt cheated by the system, but for
most, the financial reward was less important than the chance to breathe
fresh air and see a little bit of the world outside. Those who went outside also
had the opportunity to buy things which they could not find inside, which
they either consumed themselves or, more often, sold on to other prisoners
for a profit. A prisoner who had been the leader of a team working on a land
drainage project about one kilometre away from the prison said: "I was very
interested to see all the people outside the prison and to have a quick look in
the shops. I had the freedom to buy my own food. I bought little fish,
cassava flour and vegetables. We cooked it and ate it outside." In addition,
these work expeditions offered prisoners a unique opportunity to see their
family in a more relaxed environment and to talk to them for long periods

without interruption. Many prisoners tried to get onto the teams for this reason only and barely did any work once they got outside (see Chapter XI).

Prisoners who had money, a bit of education and initiative could go even further afield on the pretext of working outside. One former prisoner used the opportunity to check the progress of his case-file in person: "I asked the *capita* in charge of work teams to put me on his team, so that I could go to the prosecutor's office or the court and ask them some questions. The first day I went out to work, I couldn't see the officials there. I told my wife to take 50 bags of potatoes to the secretary of the president of the tribunal. The second time I went outside, I saw the president of the tribunal. He looked for my case-file but said I didn't have one. The assistant prosecutor was told to make up a case-file. Two weeks later, when I went on the work team again, I went to the prosecutor's office to read my case-file. Each time, I had to negotiate with the head of the work team and I had to pay 500 francs."

In a practice which seems perverse in view of the regular shortages and monotony of prison food, the vegetables and fruit grown by the prisoners are normally destined for sale outside, not for consumption by the prisoners themselves. Prisoners grow beautiful vegetables and fruit, yet inside, they still get only one meal a day, which never varies. On our first visit to Butare prison, we saw a display of large green cabbages just outside the prison gate. Two prisoners were guarding them, one clutching a bunch of banknotes in his hand. The cabbages, grown by the prisoners, had been strategically laid out on the ground to tempt visitors and passers-by. While we were standing at the gate, two young women walked past and stopped to check out the cabbages. They bought several, selecting them carefully in the way they would in an ordinary market.

Occasionally, prisoners are allowed to bring in a few of the vegetables they have grown, but it is at the guards' discretion. Sometimes, the vegetables just go to waste. A prisoner who didn't work outside told us: "I can sometimes eat vegetables brought in by the teams who work outside. But the guards may refuse to let them bring the vegetables in. They throw them on the ground. They get dirty and damaged and have to be thrown away. The guards ask for money to allow the vegetables in. Some prisoners prefer not to pay the money, and just throw the vegetables out."

In Nsinda prison, one of our visits coincided with a hive of activity by a team of prisoners who were packing freshly picked tomatoes into bright green plastic bags. Each bag contained 20 kilos of tomatoes, harvested by the prisoners themselves. The prisoners lined up the bags of tomatoes in the prison yard, then tied each one tightly with a bundle of straw to form a handle. The tomatoes were not for the prisoners; they were for sale to visitors, to people like us. My colleague bought one bag, and we saw several bags being put aside for other customers. The same day, the floor of a nearby office where we interviewed prisoners was covered with mounds of beautiful, bright red tomatoes, waiting to be packed. It was like a photograph from a tourist brochure advertising holidays to Italy. The deputy director of the prison was worried that the smell would disturb us during our work, yet this was the only office available on that day. He took me by the hand into the office so that I could check the smell, and be sure I could work there among the tomatoes. It was both touching and absurd in view of the multitude of unbearable stenches elsewhere in the prison, in which prisoners had to live day after day. That day, I interviewed prisoners with the sweet, pungent smell of tomatoes wafting over me.

Not working outside

In view of the living conditions in the prisons, I had assumed that every prisoner who was physically able would want to join one of the work teams. A former prisoner had told me: "If you don't get visits and you're not on a work team, you stay in. People used to climb on the walls to look out." But not everyone felt such a strong attraction to the world outside. We came across a surprising number of prisoners who said they were not interested in working outside and deliberately chose not to do so. They gave a variety of reasons. Some objected to having to pay to join a work team. Many more simply didn't have the money to pay. Some didn't even own a uniform, which was compulsory for working outside. Others said that their occupations inside the prison were sufficient for them and they didn't have time to work outside. Some said they felt physically too weak to work. Even some of the young, strong-looking men said that they felt their strength ebbing away because they weren't getting enough to eat in prison.

For some of the better-educated prisoners, it was a matter of pride: they didn't believe in working for nothing and equated the work with slave labour. An older, well-educated prisoner told us: "My attitude wouldn't allow me to work for no pay. I thought it was degrading to spend two to three months working for nothing. It was inhumane treatment. Those who wanted to work had to ask, and I didn't ask." A former prisoner had been asked to carry bricks to a building site but he refused: "I said I would stay inside until I was released or until I died, but I would not build other people's houses." Another prisoner, who had had a successful professional career before his arrest, categorically ruled out the possibility of manual work: "Work? No. I want something more intellectual, not physical labour."

It seemed that some of these prisoners were hiding behind these explanations, and that there were other, deeper reasons for their reluctance to go outside. The world outside had become an object of fear, especially for some of the "intellectuals". They were frightened not only of seeing it but of finding themselves in it physically, without being able to be a part of it. A highly educated and professionally successful man who had been detained for seven years said: "I don't want to work outside. It doesn't interest me. I find it depressing to see what other people are achieving when I've achieved nothing. If I were going out for good, that would be OK, but otherwise I'm not interested." A man who had been in prison for nine years and was suffering from depression since the death of his wife said he just sat around inside doing nothing all day, but he still didn't want to work: "I'll wait till I'm released. I don't want to go out before then." Another prisoner offered some wise words of advice: "If you think you're likely to be released, it is good to familiarise yourself with the situation outside. But if you don't think you'll be released soon, I wouldn't advise it as it can make you want to go out."

Other prisoners were afraid of being seen, or being recognised by people they knew, of being humiliated or insulted, or even killed. Especially in the early days, going outside the prison was considered dangerous. There have been surprisingly few attacks on prisoners working outside. However, when we were in Kibuye in November 2004, we learned of an incident which had occurred two days earlier in which a man had thrown three grenades at a group of prisoners who were working in the town, rebuilding the courtroom. Two prisoners were killed and 12 were seriously injured. We were told that the man had thrown the grenades after recognising one of the prisoners as the killer of one of his relatives during the genocide.

For most prisoners, however, the feeling of humiliation is often stronger than the fear of being attacked. A prisoner in his sixties told us: "I don't want to be seen outside. It increases people's hatred… Once I accompanied a prisoner to hospital. I met a woman from my neighbourhood who insulted me. Even though I had never done anything to her, just because she saw this uniform, she automatically said I was a *génocidaire*. It hurts me a lot to be accused of this crime when I'm innocent."

Education

Thanks to the large proportion of teachers and well-educated professionals among the prisoners, a whole system of education has flourished inside. Most of these classes are taught by the "intellectuals", including students who were arrested before they had completed their studies. But others are taught by prisoners accomplished in manual or technical professions: builders, mechanics, carpenters or welders. As almost every profession is represented inside, so almost every subject and trade is taught, and prisoners have the opportunity to learn new skills which they may never have had the chance to acquire outside. The subjects include literacy (reading and writing in Kinyarwanda), foreign languages (French, English, Swahili, Lingala, German, Italian, Spanish, Arabic), maths, physics, accountancy, economics, electronics, computing (the theory only, as there are no computers on which to practise), health education, religion, music, agriculture, building, mechanics and the highway code. Prisoners have the chance to work as apprentices in the prison workshops. Lessons are for prisoners of all ages, whether old or young. In Kigali Central Prison, a prisoner told us that even some of the guards were being taught by the prisoners, following a request from the staff.

The teaching is taken seriously, with the teachers setting exams and students receiving diplomas upon successful completion of their course. Classes take place every day, at fixed times, usually in an improvised space in the interior courtyards, in the open air. Only in Cyangugu did we come across a lesson taking place in the prison garden, overlooking the lake. In all the prisons we visited, we saw several groups of 20, 30, 40 or more students, some young, some old, sitting cross-legged on the ground in front of a blackboard, studying with varying degrees of concentration. Some listened avidly with a notebook in their lap, others gazed absently at the teacher or the blackboard. The teachers use large blackboards on wooden easels. In the men's block in Butare prison, we came across two different classes, sitting face to face with the blackboard standing in between them: one class was being taught one subject from one side of the blackboard, and the other another subject on the other side. When no blackboards are available, the teachers write in chalk on the metal doors or on the concrete floor.

One of the most memorable sights during our prison visits was a class in *hôtellerie* (hotel management) in Kigali Central Prison. The teacher, an older, lean man wearing a cap, was demonstrating to a group of prisoners, with great seriousness and intensity, the correct way to carry a tray of drinks and to pour from a bottle without dripping the liquid. He was like an actor completely immersed in his role, leaning forward with his tray balanced on the palm of his hand and speaking emphatically to make sure his students understood the precise techniques involved. Behind him, on the blackboard, the word "*hôtellerie*" had been written in capital letters and there was a drawing of a tray with a bottle and glasses on it. By the side of it, various drinks were listed – port, Martini, Cinzano – names which can have meant little or nothing to most of his students. Whenever we approached other classes in the prisons, the teachers stopped to welcome us and explain what they were teaching. Not the *hôtellerie* teacher, who was so absorbed that he did not even notice us standing at the back of the class. His passion, combined with the slightly preposterous nature of the skills he was teaching the prisoners, was both poignant and comical. It was as if he, and the picture he was evoking of luxury hotels, immaculately dressed waiters and expensive European drinks, had been lifted out of another universe and dropped accidentally into this world of grime, deprivation and confinement.

One of the main frustrations for both teachers and students was the lack of materials. A prisoner who taught the principles of electricity said prisoners were very interested in learning practical skills "like how to mend a light or make an electric current work" but they lacked the materials for demonstrations. Teachers found it difficult to teach properly without basic textbooks and a regular supply of stationery. Paper and pens could be bought in the prison shop, but not everyone could afford to buy them regularly, so students often ran out halfway through a course and had to drop out. Nevertheless, when we wandered through the prison blocks, we noticed a large number of prisoners sitting in their châteaux or in the courtyards conscientiously reading or writing notes in exercise books. Paper is precious, so not a centimetre of space is wasted in the exercise books. Pens are used until the last drop of ink has run out. We saw prisoners repairing not only pens, but refills for biros which were leaking. Others were making notebooks out of recycled paper, bound with blue ribbons.

There is no formal system of payment for the teachers, but prisoners who attend the classes are expected to make a financial contribution of around 100 or 200 francs. In some prisons, prisoners who can't afford to pay don't bother to go to the classes, but in others, the teachers are happy to teach people for free. Some prisoners prefer to teach private lessons rather than an organised class. The teachers may charge for these private lessons or make some other arrangement with the student. The private lessons take place in a prisoner's château or in a corner of the courtyard. In Rwandex, we came across a prisoner learning to read and write on a small, hand-held blackboard, with a piece of chalk. He was sitting on his bed with his friend who was teaching him. He had started learning only two days before.

Attitudes to learning varied among the prisoners. Many were keen to make use of their time and took their studies seriously, not only to keep themselves busy but in order to acquire new skills which might increase their chances of finding work after their release. Even well-educated prisoners attended classes. Academics took the opportunity to learn manual skills and vice versa. One former "intellectual" prisoner was amazed by the number of other "intellectuals" and academics he found in the prison: "I was a member of an English club. We organised classes in English in our specific fields. A prisoner who had studied in the USA was the chairman of the club. I studied economics and mechanics and I learned to play the guitar." Another highly educated prisoner, who had been sentenced to life imprisonment and so had little reason to feel motivated to learn, was nevertheless enthusiastic about the classes: "You can spend a whole day as if you've spent a day working, then you feel tired. I'm learning English now. I follow the news in English on my radio and I have English books."

But for some, enthusiasm for learning went in fits and starts. A man who had been in prison for seven years attended classes in maths and languages, but only when he was in the right state of mind: "When I get discouraged, I stop, as I wonder what I will do with all that. Then I pick it up again later, when I am in the mood." A man in his mid-forties had spent four of his ten years in prison learning to read and write. He had found it difficult at first, but grew to like it and had succeeded in obtaining a certificate. But since then, he had lost his motivation: "I dropped it because of the many thoughts I have: I wonder will I die here? Will I ever get out? I'm waiting, waiting, waiting… I got discouraged."

Others attended classes half-heartedly, just as a way of passing the time. And a significant number didn't attend at all, either because they couldn't afford it, or because the experience of imprisonment had sapped them of all their energy. Many told us they had lost the appetite for learning.

In Kigali Central Prison, we met a prisoner who positively delighted in teaching his friends inside. A highly intelligent young man with graceful features and a calm and patient manner, he seemed ideally suited to teaching, even though he had not yet finished his own studies when he was arrested in 1995. Now aged 30, he had more than made up for it during his nine years in prison. He had learnt English – one of the most popular subjects – and a variety of other subjects, and spent several hours a day teaching literacy and English to other prisoners:

> "Every year I have a class and start a new course. I teach two classes every morning, one for minors and one for the young adults (18-24). I like teaching the young prisoners… Lessons for minors are obligatory. The team responsible for security rounds them up. Some learn well, but others don't. There is a special programme for people who haven't finished primary school…

> Those who learn pay 100 francs for three or four months. Sometimes a person can pay for the whole class, so that people

who can't afford to pay can still attend. Those who live in the
place where we hold the school are given priority for free lessons."

Despite his positive attitude towards teaching and learning, he admitted that
he was worried about completing his own studies outside. His concern was
shared by many young prisoners who didn't know whether, when or how
they would ever be able to complete their studies. A prisoner, who was just
finishing his second year at university when he was arrested, had asked his
brother to bring his books and university notes to the prison so that he could
try not to fall behind. He told me he was reading books on philosophy,
history and economics.

There is a huge thirst for books among the more educated prisoners. Any
book which is donated to the prison or to a prisoner will be avidly read, re-
read and passed around, regardless of the subject matter. A prisoner who
was a former local government official told me he was reading *A Brief
History of Canada*, in English: "It's very interesting." A prisoner who was an
academic said he used to have a shelf of about 20 books of his own in his
château, including five Bibles (one in English, one in French, one in Swahili,
one in Luganda and one in Lingala) but after a number of searches inside the
prison, he decided to give most of them to his family in case they were
confiscated. A member of the former Rwandan army had been inspired by a
book he had read while he was detained in a military camp: "It was called
The 25th Hour. The character in it escapes execution. I am also hoping for
my 25th hour."

Some of the prisons, especially those in the larger towns, used to have a
library, but over the years, the stock has become depleted and the libraries
barely function anymore. The libraries were run by a prisoner, under the
supervision of the *social*. There was a catalogue from which prisoners
requested books, and they could keep them for about a week. A former
prisoner – a young man who was a secondary school student when he was
arrested – had made good use of the library in Kigali Central Prison. "There
used to be more than 10,000 books. They were mainly textbooks. I used to
make a list of difficult words and look them up in the dictionary... I read
Martin Luther King and Angolan and Cameroonian books. They were all in
French. I made a list of the books I read. Most were novels. I used to read a

lot. There were English and German books there too. I put a small electric lamp in my château so as not to disturb others. I used to like reading in prison. Now, since I've been released, I'm running after life all the time. I have no time to read, but I hope to resume one day."

A few newspapers are also available in the prisons: *Kinyamateka* (the newspaper of the Catholic Church), *Imvaho* (the government newspaper), a newsletter published by the Ministry of Justice, and occasionally the French magazine *Jeune Afrique*. Newspapers deemed too political or too critical are not allowed. Even though most prisoners are very well-informed, a prisoner remembered an occasion when he saw two prisoners arguing over a page of a newspaper which had photos of President Kagame and minister Patrick Mazimhaka: "They were disagreeing over which was which, which photo was Kagame and which photo was Mazimhaka. I was amazed they were so ill-informed."

The well-educated prisoners also used their time in prison to write: diaries, accounts of prison life, histories of Rwanda, personal reflections, the story of their life. Some of these works were long and detailed, and the process of writing them very laborious. It was not always clear whether their authors were hoping to publish them one day, or whether they were writing simply for themselves. Either way, attention to detail and concern for the historical record were hugely important to them.

For the older prisoners – teachers, lecturers, former politicians – writing was a way of getting things off their chest. An academic prisoner had written reams of paper about the history of Rwanda – his own version, as he was dissatisfied with the official version. He had smuggled out the first part of his text to his family, as officially, prisoners are not allowed to write such things in prison. When we met him, he was writing the next instalment. Once completed, his tome was likely to number several hundred pages. Another "intellectual", a former local government official who had written and published books before the genocide, had started writing another book in prison, entitled "The Rwandan people and their cowardice".

For the younger prisoners, writing was a way of keeping their mental faculties alive and experimenting with different forms of expression. A former prisoner who was only 14 when he was arrested wrote prolifically during his seven and a half years in prison: plays, novels and poems. He entered writing competitions at the provincial level and won several times, but was not allowed to receive the prize money because he was a prisoner. Once when he won the third prize in a competition, the prison director just bought him some biscuits; the real prize money should have been around 50,000 francs (about US$ 89). He was one of several prisoners in Butare whose composition for a national anthem won a nationwide competition: "Five of us wrote the words. Five others wrote the music. We won the competition. The jury didn't know it was written by prisoners. It was a big profit for the prison... Eventually we got 10% of the prize. The rest went to the prison. Each person who had contributed got about 50,000 francs. I used my share to write."

A former university student in his twenties was writing a testimony on life in the prison, based in part on his own experience and observations, and in part on interviews with other prisoners. He was very enthusiastic about this work, and his interviews with prisoners provided him with the kind of satisfaction he might have derived from writing a sociological dissertation. When I met him, he had been doing this work for six months and had written 60 pages. He told me he was about halfway through, and when it was finished, he was planning to send it home to be typed up. He wasn't sure what he would do with it after that.

Entertainment

Music

Not all the activities in prison require hard work or concentration. Prisoners organise a range of cultural and leisure activities to keep themselves entertained and, as one of them told us, "to chase away our despair". There are many talented artists and musicians in the prisons, and prisoners can enjoy theatre, music, songs, dance and traditional story-telling. Many of the plays and songs are written by the prisoners themselves. Prisoners make their own musical instruments. In Butare, we saw prisoners at work in the courtyard, making guitars. For the strings, they used wire from inside car cables; the metal parts were made by the prison blacksmith.

A wide range of musical styles can be heard inside the prison. At one end of the spectrum, there are the large prison choirs. Hundreds of prisoners are members of these choirs, which perform to a high, professional standard. Each of the main religions has its own choir, with its own choirmaster. Some of these prisoners had sung for years in choirs before their arrest and had taught, and continued to teach, choral music; one prisoner we met specialised in Gregorian chants. The choirs are taken more seriously than any other kind of music, and there are frequent practice sessions, rehearsals and services. Each choir has its designated time and day. During a visit to Butare prison several years ago, I happened to hear one of the choirs practising. The sound of several hundred male voices, all singing perfectly in tune in unwavering, strong voices resonated against the high walls of the large room in one of the blocks. The power and beauty of the singing was over-whelming. It was like a real church.

At the other end of the spectrum, younger prisoners play Western-influenced music. On one of our visits to Gitarama prison, we just missed a performance by a band which had a whole range of sophisticated instruments and equipment: drums, electric guitars, amplifiers and speakers. I stopped one of the musicians as he was walking back into the prison building and asked him about the band. He grinned and informed me proudly, in English, that they were the Gitarama Jail Band. I was later told that some of these modern instruments were donated by the Church, but that on other occasions, technicians among the prisoners adapted accoustic instruments for electric use.

There are other forms of music too, many of them traditional. Prisoners play for themselves, for small groups of friends, or as part of organised concerts inside. Prisoners who can afford to pay a token amount to attend these concerts. A prisoner in Cyangugu said there were three different musical groups in the prison, each specialising in a different genre. The group he coordinated had three guitarists, three singers, one drummer and eight dancers. He was a guitarist and a singer. Another prisoner had made his guitar for him, for 4,000 francs.

There are formal music lessons in the prisons. In Butare, we came across a studious young prisoner learning to read music. He showed us his exercise book and sang a few lines for us from the hymn he was revising. In another part of the prison, we found four prisoners huddled together with their guitars, practising basic techniques. Older prisoners teach younger prisoners how to play traditional instruments.

Prisoner playing a guitar in a local detention centre, Gikongoro, 2003
© Per-Anders Pettersson/Getty Images

We were treated to some of the music and dancing on our tours of the prisons, particularly in Butare, where we met three very different and equally captivating musicians. The first was in the large room called the chapel. The man was sitting at one end of the room, bare-chested, with a guitar on his knees. He played a song for us, which he had composed himself. It was a simple, expressive song in several verses, with a strong melody. He was a well-built, muscular man in his forties, with rippling biceps, yet his voice was sweet and he sang with passion, closing his eyes as he launched into each new verse. His voice rose effortlessly over the crowded darkness of the room. He sang about his nostalgia: when would he be released, when would he see his mother again, when would he see his friend, when would he see his wife. (Apparently, his wife had died several years before.) We exchanged a few words with him after the song. He told us that he used to earn his living as a woodcutter and that he had been in prison for ten years, accused of genocide.

In Rwandex, the annex of Butare prison, we noticed a traditional instrument hanging on a wall in the interior courtyard as we walked through. We stopped to ask whether the prisoner who owned it would give us a demonstration. The owner was a tall, dignified man, probably in his late fifties, wearing an old pale-coloured shirt with a feminine floral pattern. He agreed to play for us, but had to prepare himself, so we agreed that we would come back at the end of our tour. By the time we returned, he was ready. The instrument, known as *umuduri*, was made of a long wooden bow with a string and two gourds attached, one at the top, the other in the middle. He played it with two sticks tied to each other, with a small rattle. He sang a traditional song for us, surrounded by other prisoners who listened excitedly. This was a humorous song, a song with a moral, about a woman who went into a bar, had too much to drink, and got into trouble. We didn't get a full translation, but the song provoked much laughter and appreciation among the prisoners who had gathered around. For most of the song, the man stood upright, singing with his head tilted slightly backwards. Then for the final verse, he launched into a little dance, energetically turning and stamping his feet in a circle, just there where he stood, in his cramped corner of the courtyard. Everyone cheered and clapped. The musician told us he had learnt to play when he was about twenty years old. He had been in prison for ten years, accused of genocide. No one ever visited him in prison.

The third musician looked even older. He was a small, thin man with a lined face and a cheerful smile, wearing faded and tattered uniform shorts and a dirty red sweatshirt. He played a basic thumb-piano, known as *icyembe*, which he had made himself. For this performance, we were invited to sit down in one of the little offices, like a proper audience. He sang two traditional songs, and probably would have sung many more had we had more time. The first was a welcome song, especially for us; the second was a tale about a frog, a flea and a bachelor. He was a true performer, with a very expressive face and voice. He played with great gusto, moving rhythmically as he sang, plucking his instrument with his small hands. He told us he had learnt to play as a child. He loved playing, as it took his mind off things and lose all sense of time. He played in the evenings in the prison; it helped cheer up the other prisoners.

Dance and theatre

In Cyangugu prison, our tour of the blocks coincided with the rehearsal of a dance troupe. About 15 male dancers, all of them prisoners, some young, some old, most stripped to the waist and barefoot, were performing a kind of warrior dance in one of the interior courtyards. Each dancer had his own style, his own movement, his own voice and expressions. Some of the older dancers were the most elegant and lithe. The dance was perfectly synchronised. They stamped their feet, jangling the big metal bells tied around their ankles, and brandished their bows and arrows, swirling from side to side, with resonant war-cries and beaming smiles. My Rwandan colleague picked up a small drum and began beating it in time with the dancers' rhythms. The performance was riveting, not only in its choreography and its rich sounds, but in the sheer variety of physical and facial expression among the dancers. There was a potent contrast between the exuberance and passion with which these men threw themselves into their dance and the misery and humility of their daily existence and the physical environment in which they were performing.

Prisoners also write and perform plays, and narrate traditional tales and stories. For performances and concerts, men and women are allowed to mix. Most of these activities take place in the men's blocks, but the women organise their own events too. A woman in Gitarama prison explained to us: "We do theatre shows and some women write plays. The men also do shows and we can put on plays with them. We might do a story about the genocide, or about love outside the prison, or about friendship. People like to watch the plays. About 80 men can watch our plays in the women's block. About 40 to 50 women can watch the plays in the men's block."

Television

Television was still a fairly recent addition to prison life in 2004 and one which was not yet taken for granted. The prisons we visited had one or two communal televisions. In Gitarama prison, there was only one, for around

8,800 prisoners. They watched in shifts, whenever there was electricity. In Cyangugu prison, there were two, located in the interior courtyards; one of them sat in a wooden box with retracting doors, made by the prisoners. Both sets were located in the men's block, but once or twice a week, one of them was taken into the women's block. Prisoners had clubbed together to buy the television – 100 francs each for those who could afford it – and the director had also made a contribution. When the television first arrived, all the prisoners wanted to watch it, so the prisoners drew up a rota, with specific viewing times for each block. The *capita* told us about the different channels and programmes:

> "We have Canal Plus [a French channel], but the reception is bad; Raga TV [a Congolese channel]; Rwandan TV, but the reception is bad; and TV5 Afrique et Asie [a French channel]. We used to like TVR, the national Rwandan station, because it's our country and we could see the situation. There are special times to gather and watch TV: from 4.30pm to 11pm, or later if there is a good film. When there is a good programme, the yard is completely full. For example on Sunday evenings, there is a programme on Canal Plus on tourism and animals. This is good. For some people, it is the first time they are seeing lions, crocodiles and hippos. TVR was good as it was in Kinyarwanda. Many people don't understand English or French, but it is still interesting to see the pictures as they have probably already heard the news on the radio, for example Rwanda sending troops to Darfur."

In Nsinda prison, the television set stayed in the men's blocks for five days a week and came to the women's block two days a week. A woman there told us: "We watch TVR, and sometimes the European news. We followed the US elections, Tony Blair, the Middle East and other things. Sometimes TVR has images from CNN or TV5. We can't change the channels."

Sport

There is also leisure in the form of physical exercise, at least for the men. Volleyball and football are the favourite sports, and the larger prisons each have several teams. In Cyangugu, about 100 prisoners get to play football once a week. They have a team leader and a trainer. Some of the teams are named after European teams and the players take on the names of their favourite celebrities, such as David Beckham. A prisoner who organised the football for the younger prisoners told us: "Our team usually wins. If you win the competition, the team gets 5 kilos of sugar as a prize. The members share it out." In Butare prison, there are three volleyball teams: one is named the Public Team (for "the general population"), another the Tigers. The guards also play the prisoners, but they are unevenly matched and the prisoners always win. Sports are usually played in the interior courtyards; spaces where prisoners normally sleep are temporarily vacated for this purpose. In Kigali Central Prison, the interior courtyard where the prisoners used to play sports was called Stade Agahinda, the stadium of sorrow. A former prisoner explained: "That is where you go to get some relief when you have sorrow in your heart." In Cyangugu, prisoners are taken outside the prison, once a week, to play football or to run. Prisoners in Butare used to be allowed to play outside too, but the director put a stop to this after a prisoner escaped during one of the matches. For the women, physical exercise is limited. Some are able to walk or occasionally run in the interior courtyard, but beyond that, there are few possibilities.

Passing the time

Alongside these organised activities, individual prisoners find their own ways of whiling away the time. One of the favourite pastimes, among the men, is *igisoro*, a traditional game found across many parts of Africa. It is a simple game for two people, played on a small wooden board in two halves, with stones or beans as pieces. All over the interior courtyards and all around the blocks, prisoners sit facing each other over an *igisoro* board. The game is especially popular among the older men. As an alternative, some play draughts, with bottle-tops or corks as pieces. A few have packs of old and battered playing cards. The boards – whether for *igisoro* or for draughts – are often made by the prisoners themselves, out of pieces of wood or cardboard. The sight and sound of *igisoro* – with the soft clinking of the beans on the wood – has become an intrinsic part of the daily lives of prisoners, especially those with little education. It also provides a form of social contact. The prisoners in Rwandex had *igisoro* teams and competitions, but as they couldn't get any prizes, "we just shake hands with the winner". The prisoners we spoke to who didn't have the physical or mental strength to work or to study still found enough enthusiasm to play *igisoro*. It was part of the daily routine, alongside washing, eating, praying and sleeping. The minority of prisoners who didn't enjoy *igisoro* – and didn't work or study either – spent their days doing literally nothing. We asked one such prisoner, who had been detained for eight years, how he spent his time. He replied: "I just cross my arms and wait."

Prisoners playing cards, Kigali Central Prison, 1995   © Hervé Deguine

Some tried to relieve their boredom by chatting to other prisoners, but the physical conditions and the monotony of their existence meant that these conversations were not always uplifting. A prisoner summarised the situation as follows: "If you want to have a chat with a friend, you have to go to his 40 centimetres and sit on his bed and fold your legs up so that you can fit in there with him. The conversation is always the same: 'When will we get out of prison?'"

Radio: going round the world

The radio is the prisoners' main link with the outside world. Initially, in the period immediately after the genocide, radios were forbidden in the prisons, but prisoners managed to smuggle them in anyway. After the prohibition was lifted, radios started proliferating. Listening to the radio has now become such an accepted part of prison life that it is difficult to imagine that it was ever otherwise. Radio is the most popular mass medium in Rwanda, as in the rest of Africa, and in towns and villages across the country, it is common to see people walking down the street with a radio held to their ear, or gathered round a radio in small groups. In the prisons, it is exactly the same. Many prisoners have their own hand-held radio sets; those who don't crowd round their friends' sets and avidly listen in, or wait for their friends to tell them the main items of news. There are also communal wind-up radios dotted around the prisons. Radios are among prisoners' most treasured possessions. If a radio stops working, every effort will be made to repair it. If someone is obliged to sell a radio, for example to buy medicines, it is a big loss.

In Rwanda, radio has a particular resonance because of the way in which it was used by those who planned the genocide. In 1993 and 1994, the private station Radio Télévision Mille Collines broadcast speeches of ethnic propaganda and hatred, exhorting Hutu to kill Tutsi. It was a powerful tool of mobilisation, as it reached people not only in the urban towns and centres but deep into the countryside.

Ten years on, the government which replaced the genocidal regime has kept a tight control over the airwaves and exercises strict censorship over the local and national media. As a result, most prisoners prefer to listen to foreign or international stations as they are perceived as more objective than the government-controlled Radio Rwanda. The routine of a woman in Nsinda prison, who had her own radio, was typical: "I listen to all the foreign service broadcasts in the early morning: Voice of America Kinyarwanda news, BBC and Radio France Internationale... I go to bed at 8pm after listening to the BBC, VOA and RFI again. I go round the world."

Prisoners are extremely well-informed about events outside, often better informed than people outside, even about basic things like the price of food. A prisoner in Kigali Central Prison boasted: "We are the best informed – up to the minute. This is the prison of intellectuals." A former prisoner there said: "The government's cabinet meetings end at 3pm. By 5pm, prisoners know the outcome. They used to inform visitors of events before they happened. We were always ahead of events." It is largely thanks to their radios that prisoners manage to keep up to date with events. Some also have extensive networks of contacts outside, and news can be transmitted, very quickly and succinctly, during family visits. In addition, every new prisoner will be pumped for information on his first day, as soon as he arrives. Prisoners who have been released and re-arrested are often the best sources of information, as they share the same language and frames of reference as the prisoners, and know instinctively what needs to be known.

On their radios, prisoners naturally follow the domestic news especially closely. Over the ten years that many of them have spent in prison, there have been many dramatic events and significant changes in the country. The 1996 and 1998 wars in Congo, the attacks by members of the ex-FAR (the former Rwandan army) and *interahamwe* militia on western Rwanda between 1996 and 1998, the first executions of prisoners accused of genocide in 1998, the trials of the leaders of the genocide by the International Criminal Tribunal for Rwanda in Arusha, the 2003 elections which returned President Kagame to power, the start of *gacaca*[3] – all these and many other events have become milestones for the prisoners. They listen especially attentively to announcements by the government, or about the government, and monitor every shift in the political scene, positioning themselves in relation to these events.

The 2003 elections – Rwanda's first general elections since the genocide – were an important event for the prisoners, even though they could not vote. In the days leading up to the elections, prisoners obsessively followed developments on the radio. The authorities kept a close eye on the prisoners during this period, particularly on their interactions during visits. In Kigali Central Prison, the authorities suspended visits for one or two months before the elections as they suspected prisoners of organising a campaign for the opposition presidential candidate, Faustin Twagiramungu. A former prisoner told us: "They used to say that if a prisoner scratched his head [during a visit], it would mean 'vote for Twagiramungu', because he is bald." In any case, whether real or imagined, attempts by prisoners to influence their families would have been futile, as President Kagame was re-elected with a sweeping

---

[3]   *Gacaca* is a system of local justice based on community participation, introduced to try genocide cases (see Chapter XVII).

victory, following an election campaign marred by fraud, intimidation and muzzling of the opposition. A prisoner who had carried out an improvised survey of prisoners' opinions noted in a written summary of prisoners' attitudes towards the elections: "Many of them, about three-quarters, supported Twagiramungu because they said he would release the prisoners and relieve their wives of their cooking pots [a reference to families' burden of bringing food to their prisoners]. And he was a Hutu too. All the prisoners were glued to their radios until midnight when they announced the results. When they heard that Paul Kagame had been elected, everyone felt ill for two days and they concluded that he had cheated or stolen the votes."

The annual commemoration of the genocide was another landmark in the prisons. "Every year, we are marked by the mourning period in April," a prisoner told us. 'It affects us psychologically. Prisoners listen to the radio. They cry and sing songs of mourning. People remember. Every April, I see prisoners becoming traumatised, whether they have confessed or not [to participating in the genocide]. They're afraid, I don't know of what. People talk about it inside. Those who killed remember what they did and what they saw and you can see the fear in their behaviour. Some of them say: 'I don't want to listen to this. Turn the radio off.' Those who didn't kill just listen to the radio for the sake of listening, then it passes."

The news prisoners pick up on the radio ranges from the sublime to the ridiculous. A prisoner we spoke to in Butare asked us lots of questions at the end of our interview. Among other things, he had heard on the radio that it was now illegal to spit in the street in Kigali, and that if you were caught spitting and couldn't pay the fine, you could be sent to prison; he wanted to know if this was true. He had also heard that men were no longer allowed to beat their wives, and seemed very concerned about this, even though he wasn't married.

Prisoners also have extensive, animated discussions on current affairs and have opinions on most major world developments, including the war in Iraq and other events in the Middle East, in other parts of Africa, and in Europe. During the 2004 US elections, prisoners in Butare held their own elections, voting for either George Bush or John Kerry. Bush won, simply because he was not a Democrat: according to the prisoners, the Democrats, under Bill

Clinton, had supported Kagame's government in the aftermath of the genocide and therefore did not deserve their votes.

The prisoners' internal radio

Not content with listening to external radio broadcasts, prisoners have set up their own "radio". The prisoners' radio is not a real radio service, but a system of disseminating information among the thousands of prisoners. Like a real radio station, it follows a strict schedule and is run by a dedicated team, "*le service radio*". The members of this team listen to news broadcasts on the radio every day, take notes, and produce an edited digest of the main items, which they then broadcast to prisoners, reading their summaries out on a loudspeaker as they walk round the blocks every evening. They also make their own announcements and broadcast other relevant information, including any developments which took place in the prison during the day. In Kigali Central Prison, the internal radio was run by prisoners who belonged to the Mouvement Xaveri, an organisation linked to the Catholic Church; the radio there was known as Radio MX or RMX.

The internal radio is an effective way of communicating with such a large number of people and can be a powerful tool to inform and mobilise. The content of its broadcasts is checked by the prison director, but – strangely only after it has been broadcast. The head of the team is usually one of the high *responsables* among the leadership of the prison, and the directors trust him not to broadcast subversive information. A former prisoner explained: "Sometimes the director used to check that they were not criticising the government too much. If so, they could suspend the radio, then re-negotiate if they promised not to do it again. But in the written version which they showed the director, it was more diplomatically worded. Some of the people who prepared the information were more educated than the directors."

I met the editor-in-chief of the prisoners' radio service in Butare, which was called Radio Urumi (The Light). He was an enthusiastic young man who had studied literature. He started off interviewing me about the purpose of my visit, taking detailed notes as I talked. He was intending to include this information in his evening broadcast, so that all prisoners – not just those we interviewed – would be informed about our visit. Then he talked about the work of the radio team:

"We listen to the radio. We start with information on Rwanda, then on Congo and neighbouring countries, then we end with information from the US, Iraq etc – for example recently, there was information about Côte d'Ivoire and Fallujah. We write down the news and broadcast it. Then we talk about events in our prison: information about visits, the Red Cross, etc. We will broadcast information about your visit today…

We have a team of seven, composed of three groups of two, who collect the information. I am the editor-in-chief. One team does it one day, the next team the next day, and the third team the day after. The aim is to inform prisoners, especially the illiterate ones. We have a technical room, which is the editorial office. The teams bring the information, we sit and discuss and decide what to broadcast.

We broadcast the information with a loudspeaker when there is electricity, as it is a very big space. Otherwise, I use my own voice. There are four sites for broadcasting. When there is no electricity, it is difficult. When there is electricity, we start at 4pm. Each site takes about 20 minutes. The whole thing lasts one and a half hours. We read out the information… There is lots of reaction and discussion. Prisoners like some but not all of the information. They like hearing information on releases, or that trials will start soon… When US soldiers were captured in Iraq, people said the US didn't know how to fight. They said the US was being defeated, unlike France which was strong. They like France more than the US.[4] They are happy about the French troops in Côte d'Ivoire. They like Yasser Arafat. They were saying recently: 'Why are they trying to bury him when he's still alive?' " [Our visit coincided with the death of Yasser Arafat.]

---

[4]   France had supported the former government of Rwanda and would therefore be more popular among those prisoners who had sympathies with the Habyarimana regime or who may have participated in the genocide.

When the radio service was first set up, it was extremely popular with the prisoners. A former prisoner in Kigali Central Prison told us: "The Radio Mouvement Xaveri used to come to each block, at about 8pm or 9pm. They even went to the yard outside. They got an extra cup of food for this service. If they broadcast it through a microphone, you could hear it even from outside the prison. Even those who slept outside woke up to listen, especially if there were interesting stories, for example information from Arusha [the International Criminal Tribunal for Rwanda]." One of the original purposes of the radio was to discourage rumours. Some of the wild rumours flying around Kigali Central Prison in the early days included a rumour that a "big general" was coming to release all the prisoners, and another that the government was plotting to kill all prisoners.

There were different opinions about the quality and objectivity of the information. Some said the summaries were faithful to the real news broadcasts. A former prisoner in Kigali Central Prison, who was himself very well-informed, told us: "MX were very careful and usually accurate. They tried not to appear biased or as if they were trying to exert influence. They quoted their sources and were very professional. Some were journalists by training." But other prisoners complained that the information was distorted and the selection of news items influenced by political considerations. A former prisoner in Kigali claimed that the internal radio tended to favour channels or news items which were critical of the Rwandan government, because the prisoners were assumed to be "against the government": "They concentrated on stories which showed the Rwandan government in a bad light. They wanted to hear information saying the government was no good."

The period when the insurgents known as *infiltrés* stepped up their attacks on northwestern Rwanda in 1997 and 1998 put the radio teams' impartiality to the test. Prisoners followed the news about these events particularly closely as they felt the outcome of the conflict would affect them directly. A former prisoner claimed that the information about these attacks was not conveyed accurately and that the prisoners' broadcasts became politically partisan, in favour of the insurgents: "They did not communicate the information faithfully. For example when they talked about the attacks in the northwest, they used to say: 'We're going to take revenge'. They claimed they were doing this to quell rumours, but it was more like encouraging hatred. I didn't like it, but it was entertaining… Some prisoners felt they would never get out and therefore that imminent war was the only solution. They would celebrate when they heard on the radio that there were attacks by the *infiltrés*. Some of them used to say: 'They [the *infiltrés*] should come and free us and give us arms so that we can fight too.' "

Even in the *cachots*, detainees had their internal radio service, though it was less sophisticated than in the central prisons. A former prisoner who spent several years in a *cachot* described the system there. Two prisoners were responsible for the dissemination of information through a daily bulletin of news. The information they broadcast usually related to developments in and around the *cachot*, rather than external news items, as real radios were less widely available in the *cachots* than in the prisons. The prisoners in charge of this service had a duty to share information on a daily basis, even when there was no information to share. The news was often put together on the basis of fragments of events glimpsed through the window of the *cachot*:

> "One person used to watch through the hole that was the window and another person used to tell us the news. He was called 'the journalist'. He would report to us even when there was nothing special to say. He would say, for example: 'This morning we got up. We prayed. We went to the toilet. Then there was a big meeting outside. I don't know what it was about but some genocide survivors appeared to be arguing. Then visitors came to bring food and were beaten', and other things like that. They did this every day."

However, during a certain period in the *cachot*, the authorities had blocked the windows, so "the journalist" had had to suspend his service. For a while, the prisoners were briefly deprived of even this tenuous link to the outside world.

This obsession with observing and relaying events has been a constant feature of life in Rwandan prisons since 1994. The discipline with which prisoners record even the most trivial developments inspires a certain admiration, even though its immediate usefulness for the prisoners may sometimes seem obscure. Even more striking is the irony of this dedication to bearing witness to each and every event in the world outside on the part of a population that has been ignored and forgotten by that same world.

CHAPTER IV

God

*"We have a special God who protects us in prison.
That is how we survive."*

Religion is the heart of prison life. From day to day, from hour to hour, it occupies the prisoners, it comforts them, it encourages them, it makes sense of their misery, it justifies their survival and gives them an irrational hope that everything will turn out fine. Religion has taken the place of reality.

In Rwanda, religion occupies a central place in the lives of many men and women. In prison, it has taken over completely. People who were already religious before being arrested have become twice as fervent; their faith has been enhanced by the experience of imprisonment. People who were not especially religious or who were sceptical about religion have found God in prison, and religion has become their new raison d'être.

A multitude of religions are practised in the prisons. Catholics, Protestants, Muslims, Pentecostalists, Seventh Day Adventists, Jehovah's Witnesses, all live and pray side by side in the congested blocks and courtyards. Many prisoners wear long rosaries of cream-coloured beads around their necks and a large cross over their pink shirts. There are numerous conversions from one religion to another, and prisoners who have converted have thrown themselves into their new faith with heightened intensity. There are priests, pastors and nuns among the prisoners, and others from outside who visit the prisons. All day long, prisoners pray, they preach, they sing, they read their Bibles, they talk about God.

"There are prayers every day, every hour," a prisoner told me. "It's very important. Religion is a pillar for people to lean on." An older prisoner commented with a touch of sarcasm: "Everyone prays. It's a speciality here, even among those who don't believe."

Almost all the prisoners we spoke to – the young and the old, the men and the women, the educated and the illiterate, the rich and the poor – described praying as their main activity, and in some cases, their only activity. Praying is as basic and vital in prison as eating and sleeping. "A life without prayer is like a fish without water," one prisoner told us.

In the prisons, God is the answer to everything. When we asked prisoners how they managed not to despair after so many years of hardship, or how they coped in moments of despair, the standard answer was that their faith in God kept them going. It was a simple remedy, a kind of tranquiliser. "When I lose hope," said an elderly prisoner, "I give someone a Bible to read to me so that I can calm down." Even those who seemed to have abandoned hope clung on to the notion that God might still get them out of there, one day. After all, he had got them out of worse situations before.

A prisoner who had spent almost eight years in prison said: "I trust in God but I don't trust in people. With that trust, I'm sure I'll get out. I don't lose hope. The only ones who lose hope are those who don't pray." "Religion is a way of reflecting," said another. "It is a refuge when you see so many innocent people in prison. It provides moral consolation. I wonder why I have been in prison for seven years. No one has the answer except God."

For the majority of prisoners, God has become a substitute for a justice system which has failed them and which they profoundly distrust. The phrase "God will be the judge", which we heard many times over, took on a new, literal meaning. Instead of waiting for a reply from the government or the judicial authorities, prisoners were waiting for a reply from God. A prisoner spoke for many when he said: "I'm waiting for *gacaca*,[1] but I prefer to trust myself to God."

Prisoners' families often have the same attitude. Most of them have given up on the justice system, and a divine intervention seems a more likely prospect than a trial. The attitude of the wife of a prisoner who had been detained for seven years typified the response of many families: "We're waiting for a miracle of God for my husband to be released." The wife of another prisoner told us she was waiting for her husband to return "like I wait for the return of Christ".

---

[1]   The *gacaca* system of justice is described in Chapter XVII.

Religion, like every other activity in the prisons, is highly organised. Special timetables are drawn up for services for each religion and each denomination. Prayers and other activities continue outside the fixed times for formal prayers. Prisoners engage in informal and spontaneous discussions about religion. On our tour of Cyangugu Central Prison, we came across a Muslim and a Christian prisoner sitting in the interior courtyard side by side, engaged in an animated conversation, comparing passages of the Qur'an and the Bible. Prisoners respect each other's religious beliefs and there are no obvious tensions between different religions, although the high number of conversions from one religion to another implies a certain level of criticism. One prisoner told us: "In prison, my main activity is prayer, all day. I used to be a Catholic, but since being in prison, I've become a Protestant. My whole family is Catholic, but in prison the Catholics have disgusted me. They don't pray enough." This was a surprising comment as the Catholics seemed to be among the most active in the prisons. Some prisoners also reported internal splits and factionalism within some denominations.

Designated areas of the prison blocks and the interior courtyard are given over to sermons, prayers and singing. At other times, these double up as meeting areas. Prisoners who normally live in these areas vacate them at specified times. These spaces are called the church, the chapel or the mosque, and when prayers are in full swing, they feel exactly like places of worship outside. For the more popular religions, thousands of prisoners attend the services. A prisoner in Kigali Central Prison, who had been sentenced to death, was one of those in charge of the "grassroots Catholic community" among the prisoners. He told us there were 2,806 Catholics in the prison, more than a third of the total population of the prison: "There are 22 prayer groups. Each has its specific prayer time. There is also a morning prayer session for everybody, in the church, and a service every Sunday. A vicar and other priests come from outside to do confessions and other things… The peace which reigns inside [the prison] depends on those who pray. Often everyone is praying. It's very good."

Prayers are often led by prisoners who used to be priests or pastors and continued preaching in the prisons. In other cases, prisoners who had studied religion, who had led choirs outside, or who were seen as natural leaders took on the role of religious leaders. These religious leaders, as well as the religious welfare and other organisations set up by the prisoners, also play an important social role in the prison. Beyond praying and preaching, they support, encourage and advise prisoners. Especially in the early days after the genocide, when many prisoners expected to die in prison, these religious leaders – some of whom are inspiring and charismatic figures – succeeded in lifting their spirits and giving them the will to live. They also instituted a culture of charity, encouraging prisoners to share what little food or material possessions they had with their less fortunate colleagues.

In Gitarama Central Prison, we met a striking man in his late fifties, who had started preaching when he first arrived in the prison in 1995. He was a Seventh Day Adventist. Other prisoners who shared his religion looked up to him as a source of encouragement and guidance. He had been in prison for more than nine years, accused of genocide, and was still awaiting trial, but never got discouraged: "I know everything is possible with God." He was a calm and resilient man, who showed enormous compassion towards other prisoners. Even though he had suffered greatly himself, the seemingly endless reserves of internal strength he derived from his faith enabled him to rise above that suffering.

He recounted with great precision and clarity every stage of his own imprisonment, and still remembered the exact words of the *bourgmestre* (mayor) soon after his arrest: "He told me that Tutsi were killed innocently, so Hutu should also be killed even if they are innocent. He said to me: 'You know Mandela? Well you should also go to prison even if you are innocent and spend years in prison like Mandela, then you can be released later.' He talked about Israel. He said Hitler wanted to kill the Jews but didn't exterminate them all. He said to me: 'You Hutu wanted to kill all Tutsi but you didn't succeed. Even if no one has accused you, I'll find people to accuse you.' " After a month of detention in a *cachot*, he was transferred to Gitarama prison. He described how prisoners used to disappear or were abducted from the prison in 1995, but he was always protected by God. "There, I started teaching prayers. I prayed and taught people to share and not to have a wild mentality. I taught the *capita général* first. I just started teaching what was in my head. A woman from the Red Cross gave us about 50 Bibles." He had continued leading and teaching prayers in the prison ever since and had earned the respect and trust of many prisoners.

When he talked about the injustices he and others had suffered, he was both forgiving and slightly defiant towards those in power: "We've been told about *gacaca*. I don't think it will ever happen. This government lies. It's been ten years now. I just put myself in the hands of God. There is nothing else I can do." He described the imprisonment of so many innocent people as "vengeance" by one ethnic group against the other, but didn't bear grudges against anyone "as I know Satan is strong".

In Gitarama prison, we also met a Catholic priest who had continued with his functions ever since he was arrested in 1995. He had been accused of genocide, tried and sentenced to life imprisonment in 2001. He had appealed against his conviction, and when we met him, he was still waiting for his appeal to be heard. A relaxed and friendly man, he seemed to know everyone in the prison and was so completely at home in his role of priest that it was easy to forget that he was a prisoner himself. He told us he had recently circulated a questionnaire among the prisoners entitled "Ten years in prison with a priest". He talked to us about his years in prison and told us how he had immediately slipped into his natural role:

> "The first day, I started preaching and everyone took this as a sign of hope. The first evening, I led a group in prayer. There was an old Bible there. I explained the readings. I insisted on hope. I told them a day would come when all this would end. 'Take courage from this. You will be free one day.' People were surprised. It was the first time they'd heard this kind of message.
>
> I set up a choir. People began to think life would be better. I didn't only work with the Catholics. I organised with other religions through all the blocks. We set up an association of solidarity for all Christian religions in the prison. The chapel was full of people but they tried to move to other blocks while we held our service. It was like going to Mass. During the week, we had the choirs. We worked together, but I also did separate services for the Catholics... I used to go from block to block, from Monday to Saturday. It was a new parish for me, only in prison. The Catholic religion started to grow after I arrived...

I think my presence helps. In the women's block, the children call me 'Papa'. I see them especially at Christmas. I take them sugar and sweets. I can talk to the women. I'm called there sometimes. I give teachings once a week. I help some guards who want to regularise their marriages. They come to me too. Sometimes I can advise the guards and they change their behaviour. They all think I'm rich, but it's a spiritual role. I don't get paid. I may give them a Bible, a rosary or a book. After I've given them advice, we have good relations. I sometimes bring important visitors, such as the bishop, to meet other people.

I'm an optimist... One day, I will be free. Anyway, my prison is just like my parish to me. I've got lots of things to do. I would regard my release more as a change of place than freedom... Even if I leave here, my heart will always be in prison. All those who are in prison will remain in my head. Even if my sentence is confirmed, I will continue to visit my 'parish' here."

Religious organisations from outside also visit the prisons. They conduct services for prisoners and provide them with moral, spiritual and material support, donating food and clothes to those who are destitute. Some organisations also encourage repentance and confessions (see Chapter XIX). A former chaplain from an evangelical organisation which regularly visited the prisons said a kind of competition had developed between the different religions, who all saw the prisons as fertile recruiting ground. He talked about the work of his ministry, which was also involved in reconciliation programmes between released prisoners and survivors of the genocide:

"We trained people from different churches in skills such as reconciliation, to prepare prisoners to live with genocide survivors after their release. We gave a message on repentance... We did discipleships and taught verses of the Bible... We had a choir and instruments. We did open-air preaching. We keep contact with prisoners after their release, when they join churches. Some become religious teachers through local churches outside.

We offer counselling. We know some of the prisoners. They come and explain their problems to us. They pass messages to us secretly. We go and see their wife or family about their problems.

There is no professional counselling. I do it myself in my personal capacity for a few people. I can't counsel prisoners directly, only indirectly through the families. We can counsel genocide victims openly, but the government does not allow counselling in the prisons. The government is always watching. Religious ministries have asked to do counselling but the government refuses categorically as they think we will discuss other issues. We can never speak to prisoners privately, only in groups.

We go in as a registered organisation and they give us a card. We speak in the name of the organisation. The organisation has to tell the authorities in advance what they will do and say in the prisons. There are many negotiations with the ministries of interior and justice. They have to give their agreement at national level, then discuss with the director of each prison. Sometimes the directors ask for Bibles in exchange."

Muslims are a small minority in Rwanda, but their numbers have increased since 1994. There have been many conversions to Islam, especially from Catholicism. The reputation of the Catholic Church was irreparably damaged by the role it played during the genocide. A number of Catholic priests participated directly or indirectly in the killings; others failed to intervene to protect people at risk. The hierarchy of the Catholic Church also failed to use its influence to try to stop the genocide. On the other hand, a number of priests showed extraordinary courage in opposing the genocide and saved many people.[2] A former prisoner told us: "Some prisoners who were disgusted with the role of the Catholic Church in the genocide became Muslims as they thought no Muslims had participated in the genocide: 'I'm a Muslim, therefore I'm innocent.' "

---

[2]   See André Sibomana, *Hope for Rwanda: Conversations with Laure Guilbert and Hervé Deguine*, transl. Carina Tertsakian, Pluto Press, 1999.

In Butare Central Prison, we met one of the two deputy imams, a tall softly-spoken man with an easy smile, who wore a green cap; he had been in prison since 1994. Before his arrest, he used to work as a driver and mechanic for the Scouts. He told us that in 1994, there were eight Muslim men and two women in the prison. Now, there were 234 Muslim men in Karubanda (the main prison), 64 in Rwandex (the all-male annex), and 12 Muslim women; 28 other Muslim women had been released in 2003. All those who had converted to Islam had been Catholics. He described how Muslim prisoners organised their activities:

> "There is a special place to pray in the men's block. There is space for 29 people. We pray in shifts. Others pray in their own space. Tomorrow, for the end of Ramadan, men, women and children and those from Rwandex will all pray together.
>
> Every year there is an election for the imam. There is one imam and two deputy imams, one for Karubanda and another one for Rwandex. There is also an imam for the mosque, one for the women and one for the minors."

We spoke to him again the following day, when Muslims were celebrating the end of Ramadan. A large group of male Muslim prisoners wearing their best clothes and caps were gathered outside in the prison yard. On our way to the prison on that day, we had also met groups of families and other visitors on the road outside.

> "Today our families brought food and clothes. We like to eat meat and rice. Last year, the whole family was allowed to visit inside the prison. We had lots of food. There were 230 of us and about 50 visitors. It was lovely. But this year, the families are too poor. We wrote to the Muslim association in Kigali to ask for help. For example we asked for clothes for 100 men and 50 women. We also ask for prayer mats. The imam's mother helped us get things for the end of Ramadan."

For many prisoners, religious activities have become their main form of social contact with other prisoners. Religion has enabled prisoners to break down social and ethnic barriers, as well as personal animosities. A prisoner accused of genocide explained: "Religious groups are helpful in getting prisoners to speak to each other and gain self-respect. We discuss ideas and we feel free. Everyone talks to each other, both *génocidaires* and common criminals. The common criminals realise we are not animals. From outside, they thought we were all *interahamwe*." Even those who seemed isolated and lonely had found one or two friends among their congregation, and these were the ones who usually helped them out in times of need and to whom they would turn for comfort. The strong bonds which prisoners developed with members of their religious community also meant that people were sometimes prepared to grant favours to each other without expecting payment in return.

Of all the prisoners we spoke to, only one said explicitly that for him, religion was unimportant. He was an older, well-educated man, a former politician who had not yet been tried but knew he stood little chance of being released as he was classed in Category 1 (the category of those accused of playing a leading role in the genocide). He recognised the positive role religion could play for prisoners, but was critical of the way many of them passively and unquestioningly put their fate in the hands of God: "There has been an increase in religion, especially after the war. There were lots of conversions, but not from a deep understanding. People abandon their physical and moral capacity and just say: 'God looks after everything'. It is difficult to persuade people that God will not help you prepare your defence in a trial. I judge religion from the outside, not from inside. Religion is important for society but there are too many superstitions over reason. It is not good to rely on God for everything. Religion is not important for me. What keeps me going is experience. I accept it. I'm OK here."

He went on to talk about some of the more extreme superstitions among prisoners: "Some people despair. Some have gone crazy and are seeing apparitions of the Virgin. They believe she will open the doors of the prison and release them. One prisoner keeps saying that the Virgin said they would be released in February. He prays frantically. When it doesn't happen, he says it's because they haven't prayed enough. There is constant praying. It gives them hope, but when it doesn't happen, they go mad."

The only other person who expressed reservations about the way religion was practised in prison was a former prisoner who was sceptical of the sudden increase in religiosity he encountered among his fellow inmates: "I didn't practise religion in the prison. Some prisoners tried to drag me along. I felt it was better to pray when things were going well. You shouldn't only pray when you are suffering misfortune."

CHAPTER V

"Living as sisters - a survival strategy":

women in prison

Many women, as well as men, participated in the genocide, and thousands were arrested, but like the men, the majority are still awaiting trial. There are also women prisoners accused of common crimes, such as murder, poisoning and infanticide. Many of these are teenagers or women in their twenties. Girls under the age of 18 live with the women, in contrast to the male minors who, in theory, live separately from the men.

Most of the prisons house men and women.[1] The proportions vary from prison to prison. Among the prisons we visited, Kigali Central Prison had the highest proportion of women – over 10%, or 785 out of a prison population of just over 6,000. In other prisons, the proportion was lower: in Gitarama Central Prison, for example, there were 200 women out of a total of more than 8,880 prisoners.[2] In Cyangugu Central Prison, only 52 of the 5,640 prisoners were women. By early 2006, women accounted for around 3.5% of the total prison population,

Conditions and organisation of the women's blocks

The women have their own separate building within the prison compounds. The layout inside is similar to the men's: several dark blocks, with bunk-beds on three floors, an interior courtyard, and a special room given over to the infirmary. In some prisons, the women have their own cooking area and

[1]   There are a few exceptions, such as Kimironko, an all-male prison in Kigali, and Miyove, in Byumba province, which was an all-women prison until 2003.

[2]   The number of women in Gitarama prison, as in several other prisons, has remained stable for the past eight years. According to the prison's end-of-year statistics from 1996 to 2004, the number of women had fluctuated only between 200 and 229, whereas the number of men had risen from over 6,200 in 1996 to over 9,300 in 2003.

sewing workshop. Inside the women's block in Kigali Central Prison, we were shown a special section for Muslim women, separated from the main section by a thin curtain.

Although the structure and facilities in the men's and women's blocks are similar, the women's living conditions are less extreme. Their space is considerably less congested as the number of prisoners is much smaller. Even though the bed space allocated to each woman is the same size as the men's – the standard 40 centimetres – by 2004, most women had their own bed, or at least a space indoors which they could call their own. None was sleeping outside or even in the corridors. As a result, the air can circulate more easily in the blocks and it is possible to walk down the passageways without bumping into people. The strong smell of so many human beings packed into one place, which characterises the men's blocks, is absent in the women's. The women's châteaux are all very basic but look quite clean. I tested out one of the beds in Cyangugu prison. Like most prison beds – for those who are lucky enough to have such a thing – it was an improvised mattress, a sack stuffed with straw, but it was surprisingly comfortable, and the château felt almost cosy. As in the men's blocks, there are clothes, blankets and implements hanging all around, over the beds and in the corridors, but overall, it is tidier and neater. The brightly coloured cloths hanging in the blocks and around the courtyard create a sense of decor, in contrast with the bleakness of the men's blocks. The women's showers and toilets are generally clean and, when we visited, there were no queues. After we had spent so much time in the men's blocks, some of the women's blocks seemed comparatively empty.

This has not always been the case. Even though their conditions have never been as acute as the men's, the women also suffered from severe over-crowding and very poor facilities until around 2000.

The exception was Miyove prison, in the north of Rwanda. Miyove was a special prison. Until 2003, it housed only women. Women who had been imprisoned in Miyove had positive memories of their time there. Their testimonies provided an idea of what life in prison could be, with a bit of will and imagination – even in the difficult circumstances which prevailed after the genocide. A 70-year-old woman told us that living in Miyove was almost like being free. The conditions were significantly better than in any of the other prisons. There was more space, better food, which they could cook themselves, and running water. They were given mattresses, blankets and clothes. It was the only prison where women were allowed to work outside the prison compound, and they were paid for their work. A woman who had been detained there had tried out her skills in a number of different areas: "All women could participate in the work if they wanted to, depending on their age. I sewed with a sewing machine, then I reared hens, then I did embroidery, then I did building work: we built houses for the cows and the hens. Then I did agriculture. It really helped us make money, keep busy and get physical exercise."

Despite improvements in the women's living conditions in most of the prisons by 2004, the women's blocks would still be judged extremely crowded by any other standard. When the women spill out into the courtyard in the daytime, the open space fills up quickly.

The women have created an atmosphere which is quite different from that in the men's blocks. Largely as a result of the smaller number of people, it is more relaxed, and women go about their business at their own pace, without jostling each other. Even visually, the first impression of the women's block is not one normally associated with a prison. Women sit against the walls of the courtyard, sometimes on a piece of cloth they have laid out on the ground, sewing, making baskets and chatting. Few women wear their uniforms inside their blocks or in their courtyard. "Inside, we wear our own clothes," one woman told us, "it gives us a better status. We can forget we're prisoners." Indeed, the fact that women are wearing clothes which they would wear outside, in a variety of colours, creates a feeling of normality and restores these women's individuality. Only their shaven heads give the game away.

The women prisoners seem more sociable than the men: all around the courtyard, there is the sound of conversation, gossiping and laughter. There are few prisoners sitting alone in corners. We asked some of the women what they usually talked about among themselves: they talked about their life in prison, their families, and most of all about God. It appeared from our conversations that there was a certain spontaneous solidarity among the prisoners and that the women helped each other more readily than the men, although there were, of course, quarrels and disputes too. Many of the women commented on the friendships they had developed in prison. "We live as sisters," one of them told us, "it's a survival strategy." Some were welcomed by former friends or neighbours in prison, but also developed new friendships quickly. In some respects, the women seemed to have adapted to life in prison better than the men. They showed a certain resilience which helped them fight off their despair.

Women in Kigali Central Prison, 1998   © Carina Tertsakian

When we went round the women's blocks in the different prisons, the women welcomed us warmly, with big smiles, and showed us round their quarters as if they were showing us round their own homes. In Butare prison, we were given a special welcome. In the interior courtyard, the women's Red Cross society was giving a class in health education. As we approached to watch, the leader of the group invited us to join the class. The women – 20 or 30 of them – spontaneously launched into a welcome song for us, moving and clapping to the rhythm. Most of them didn't even know who we were or why we were visiting the prison, but this was their traditional way of welcoming visitors. When the song ended, we all clapped, we thanked them, and they continued with their lesson as we drifted away.

The internal administrative structure in the women's blocks is the same as that of the men's: they have their own *capita générale*, deputy *capita*, and other *responsables* in charge of security, hygiene and other areas. There is a clear hierarchy, but it seems to be less pronounced in terms of social relations, with the *capita* and others in positions of responsibility mingling with the masses on an equal basis, at least superficially. In the early days, however, there were tensions between the *capita* and the other prisoners. A former prisoner who was among the first women to arrive in Kigali Central Prison recalled: "The first *capita* used to just look after her own interests. This caused lots of problems. The prisoners she didn't like were at risk. Later, we had better *capitas* and we could talk to them. The first *capita* was chosen by a soldier who liked her. The second time, there were two candidates and we voted."

One of the first prisoners we met in Gitarama prison was the *capita générale* of the women, a friendly, lively woman who wore a green woolly hat on days when it was raining or when there was a breeze. She was constantly busy and always running around, so much so that we never got the opportunity to interview her properly. She seemed to enjoy a good relationship with other prisoners and did not speak to them in an authoritarian way. I chatted to her briefly in the courtyard on the first day. Her name was Joyeuse. My colleague told her that with a name like that, she had no choice but to be cheerful. She smiled, and smiled again every time we saw her, racing around the courtyard, attending to her business.

There are fewer organised activities for the women than for the men, perhaps because the proportion of educated women is smaller. Classes are infrequent and irregular, and the range of subjects on offer is limited. Prisoners are hampered by the lack of basic materials for studying, such as exercise books and pens, and classes sometimes stop completely because of the absence of materials. There are a few literacy and language classes, as well as more practical education and awareness classes, in particular on health and first aid. A young woman in Cyangugu prison taught English and nursing to a group of around ten women, but she had to teach from memory because she didn't have any books.

Women do not have much opportunity to play sports or to exercise, other than walking around the courtyard. They are prohibited from working outside. Some work in the tailoring workshops, others in the infirmary, but they do not benefit from the wide range of work offered to the men. For women, the main activities are making baskets, sewing, knitting or embroidering. Some play card games and take part in songs, dances and plays. The rest of the time, they chat, they sit, they pray, or they sing in choirs. There is little to keep their minds stimulated. One woman, despite being well-educated, told us she just spent her time knitting and reading her Bible. A 60-year-old woman giggled when we asked her how she spent her time: "I sit on the ground," she told us. "I am a cobbler, so I make sandals. I knit. I don't sew because of my poor eyesight. I have lots of friends here, and we chat and laugh." Her sociable nature seemed to be the key to her survival in the prison; she told us she had never had any arguments with other women. Apart from these conversations with other prisoners, she had little to cheer her up. Her four children had all been killed in the war and her husband had died many years earlier. Only her godmother, who was even older than her, visited her, once every three months.

Relations between the women

Overall, there seemed to be a certain social cohesion in the women's blocks. The more educated women sometimes complained about the behaviour of some of the uneducated women, but most of the women we spoke to described the relations between prisoners as harmonious. However, quarrels between individuals could sometimes turn nasty, especially in the earlier years, when the conditions were harsher. There were physical fights, as well as arguments, over places in the queues for food, for water and for the showers, with women trying to steal food or pieces of soap, or fighting for access to the very few radios. Rumours and gossip were also frequently causes of tension. Most of the women we spoke to attributed these problems to jealousy, especially on the part of the common criminals or less-educated women, who were often labelled as troublemakers. A number of these were former prostitutes, who, according to one of the women we spoke to, "were very rude and used to talk loudly". One woman told us that if someone had a nice wrapper (a piece of fabric traditionally used as clothing), another woman might burn it, just out of spite. "Or if one woman gets family visits but another woman doesn't, they may be nasty to you. Those who don't get visits are the most difficult."

"Unhappiness can turn people nasty," one former prisoner told us. "For example there was a woman who used to soak our biscuits deliberately so that we couldn't sell them. When they stopped Saturday visits in Gitarama prison, some poorer prisoners were pleased as it meant the richer prisoners wouldn't get visits or extra supplies of food. Again, it was jealousy." Prisoners did not always show much sympathy towards those who were ill. The same woman told us: "Those with Aids were marginalised, except by the Red Cross. Other women would say to them: 'You've got Aids, you're going to die.' Some of the women who were sick were also very nasty. I remember especially one prostitute who thought she had Aids. She deliberately used to throw up in other people's food. She died five years later, in prison."

Tensions could also surface between women who had known each other before and were already enemies before they came into the prison. We met a 20-year-old woman accused of infanticide, whose baby was only three days old when it died in 2004. She claimed that her aunt had taken it away while she was sleeping and killed it. Her aunt initially admitted killing the baby, then changed her story and accused her niece instead. They were both arrested and taken to the central prison. When they were allocated a place to sleep, the niece wanted to be as far away as possible from her aunt: "I said I didn't want to be next to her. I was very angry with her. She had done something very serious which I'll never forget. Still now, we don't talk. I only say hello to her... My aunt stays with her friends and I stay with mine, in separate corners."

A 72-year-old woman found herself in prison with one of her husband's relatives who had been accused of poisoning and had implicated her by accusing her of manufacturing the poison. There were serious tensions between the two women, which exploded one day when her husband's relative told one of the guards she was a poisoner, and the guard beat her on the head with the butt of his gun. The injury left her unconscious for five days. When she recovered, she was given a different place in the block, separate from the other woman. Both women were tried in around 1998 and sentenced to death. The woman we spoke to was still awaiting the outcome of her appeal when we met her. The two women were no longer on speaking terms.

Babies in prison

Some women have their babies with them in prison. Mothers who give birth in prison, or whose children were very young at the time of their arrest, are allowed to keep their babies with them, up to the age of three. Then, the children are sent to stay with their families outside. If there are no relatives to look after them, they may be sent to an orphanage. The *capita* of the women in Butare told us about the case of a little boy who had nowhere to go. At the age of four, he was still in the prison with his mother. Eventually, one of the prison guards gave him a home. But such situations are rare. Usually a member of the extended family, or even a neighbour, agrees to look after the child. Most women receive occasional news of their children through family members who visit them, but some have lost all contact with their children, as the relatives who were looking after the children have never visited them in prison.

In all the prisons we visited, there were a few babies, living in the women's block. For example in Kigali Central Prison, there were 18; in Gitarama and Butare, there were 11. The women in Gitarama told us that all 11 had come in with their mothers; none had been born in prison. The youngest was just two weeks old. The babies we saw seemed fairly well-looked after, not only by their mothers but by many other women prisoners who were happy to help. Their presence seemed to bring the women together and created a family-like atmosphere in some of the blocks. In the main courtyard in Butare prison, there was a little shack which the prisoners had turned into a creche, with drawings and toys which had been donated for the children. Mothers with babies are given additional or special food, and in Kigali Central Prison, the babies, but not the adults, were given eggs from the ducks kept in the prison yard. A woman whose baby was two months old when she was arrested recalled being given "special vegetables", biscuits, hen's eggs and chicken when she was first transferred to Gitarama prison. "I had a basin to wash the baby and the Red Cross gave me soap. All the mothers got on well together… My son was sent home when he was three years and two months old. My mother-in-law came to take him home. It wasn't difficult to give him up because he went with her, and is still with her. He goes to school now and is trying hard to study."

Women prisoners with babies, 1995   © Hervé Deguine

A number of women gave birth while they were in prison, and in the early years, the conditions were especially hard. Some gave birth in the prison hospital, but others gave birth just wherever they happened to be in the prison. A former prisoner told us: "Women gave birth and there were miscarriages. It was very sad. They were already pregnant when they arrived in the prison. Some women gave birth inside, especially at night, where they slept, because the guards didn't open the doors fast enough." Only in rare cases were the women transferred to hospitals outside. We were told about one woman whose baby was born prematurely and who had to be transferred to a private hospital as it was the only hospital with an incubator. She stayed there for one week; she and her baby both survived.

We spoke to another woman who was eight months pregnant when she was arrested in 1994. As she was ill and had medical complications, she was also sent to a hospital outside for the birth. "Before leaving home, I had packed some things for my baby as I knew it might be born early. I gave them to a colleague to keep for me. But her husband was killed in the genocide so she changed her attitude. She didn't like the fact that I was a prisoner accused of genocide. When I asked someone from the hospital to collect the baby's things, the woman said she had given them all away as she thought I had been killed. She never visited me after that. I had no clothes for the baby. A white person at the hospital helped me and found me some clothes. A woman from the prisoners' Red Cross came to see me in hospital. She brought me three wrappers." By the time we met her, her child was no longer with her in the prison, but was being looked after by a neighbour's family as the few members of her own family who were still alive lived too far away.

Relations between women and men

The women's and men's living quarters are completely separate, but there are occasions when male and female prisoners meet, in particular during church services and religious celebrations. The only areas large enough to accommodate gatherings of several thousand prisoners are in the men's block, so the women join the men there for these organised prayers. The same applies to general meetings called by the prison director and to the prisoners' internal *gacaca* sessions, which men and women usually attend together.[3] Occasionally, men and women attend theatre performances together. Their only other opportunities to mingle may be on their way to or from family visits (although the visits themselves are segregated), in the infirmary (women who are qualified nurses may work in the men's block and vice versa) or in the outside courtyard, for those whose privileged status allows them to wander outside their blocks.

In addition to these times when men and women can meet openly, there are unofficial contacts between the men and the women. These may have been more common in the early days after the genocide, when the overcrowding was so extreme and the prison administration so overwhelmed that it was

---

[3] For further information about *gacaca*, see Chapter XVII. In Kigali Central Prison, the women hold their own *gacaca* sessions. They attend the main *gacaca* meeting with the men, usually in the morning, then hold their own session, for about 30 minutes, in the afternoon.

difficult to control every movement. Now, these contacts have become less visible, but prisoners still form social and even physical relationships.

A former prisoner who had spent time in Kigali and Gitarama prisons between 1994 and 1998 talked about these relationships and the problem of sexual solitude:

> "In both prisons, there were lots of relations between male and female prisoners. About 60% of them communicated with each other. Sometimes they had sexual relations, but not always.

> Male and female prisoners communicated and exchanged gifts. These were relationships based on self-interest: the women used to get given things by the men who went outside. The young and beautiful women got the most attention. The women chose the "high up" male prisoners. If a man was out of favour – for example if he was put in the punishment cell for indiscipline – the woman would abandon him. In Kigali, there was a man who obliged his family to bring food to his girlfriend who was in prison. The presents were just a show of affection, to avoid solitude. Sometimes people exchanged underwear. The men would take a woman's underwear to masturbate. Even women who had a husband outside could have a relationship inside. The *capita* of the men could be more wealthy and therefore more interesting than a woman's husband. Some women fought over male prisoners, especially if they were rich. The more friendly they were with the *capita*'s group, the prouder they were. The older women were mostly interested for economic reasons, so they tended to look at the *capita* and wealthier prisoners. Younger women could be interested in ordinary prisoners if they found them nice or attractive. It was the same among the men."

Some women mysteriously got pregnant in prison, causing intense speculation among the prisoners. We were told of two cases in Kigali Central Prison, between 1995 and 1997. Both women had been made pregnant by prisoners, one by a prisoner in the hospital, the other by a prisoner who was working, or pretending to work, as a technician in the women's block. The women who told us about these cases did not know the full details of the stories, or whether these relations had been voluntary or not. In Nsinda prison, we were told that there were six children there who were born as a result of relations between prisoners; these relations had been voluntary, and the prisoners had paid the guards to allow them to meet. A woman who had been detained in Byumba Central Prison said relationships between male and female prisoners were easy there, as the men had to pass through the women's block to get to their blocks.

Reports of rape of female detainees by prison guards were common in the *cachots*, but in the central prisons, they are rare. Some women had relationships with guards, apparently voluntarily, but even these were not very common. A former prisoner explained:

> "At the start, guards tried to have relations with women prisoners, but it was limited as everyone would find out. At the beginning, soldiers who guarded the prison had relations with women. It was not by force. The women did it out of self-interest. Some women wanted to sleep with soldiers for reasons of credibility, because they [the soldiers] had liberated the country. Once a woman reported that a soldier was sleeping with women. It created a scandal. The soldier made all the women come out and asked who had dared say that... His superior from the brigade intervened. The woman who had spread the rumour was put in the punishment cell, just to end the story."

A former *capita* in Kibungo Central Prison became unpopular after she tried to stop women from having sexual relations with guards.

> "There was no fence. We had close contacts with the guards. The director was not very vigilant about the relations between the women and the guards. The women could go to the guards' houses to cook and clean, and to have sex... I asked for a fence to be put up and for relations with the guards to stop. I had to give up my position of responsibility because I wanted to end the women's relations with the guards. The women didn't understand. They used to get sick and have unwanted pregnancies. The guards

gave them alcohol and wrappers [clothes]. I couldn't stand to see this."

The women we interviewed were more open with us than the men about the nature of relationships between male and female prisoners. While the men were reluctant to be drawn on the subject at all, some of the women seemed keen to let us into this secret world and even share intimate details of the emotional and sexual life of the prison. It is an aspect of prison life which remains invisible to those outside and one where, once again, prisoners have woven a complex, fragile replica of relationships in the outside world.

CHAPTER VI

Real minors and false minors:

children in prison

At the end of 2004, there were about 800 boys and girls under the age of 18 living in Rwandan prisons. The number varied from a few dozen in some prisons to over 100 in others. The vast majority were boys. Male minors are held in a separate block from the adults. Female minors live with the women in the women's block.

The Rwandan justice and prison system divide minors into two categories: "genocide minors" (*mineurs du génocide*) and "absolute minors" (*mineurs absolus*). The genocide minors are those who were under the age of 18 in 1994, at the time their alleged crime was committed. Some of them are still in prison and are now adults. Absolute minors are boys and girls who are currently under the age of 18. They are accused of common crimes committed since the genocide.

In practical terms, there is a great confusion between these two categories. The male genocide minors and absolute minors are detained together, in the minors' block, even though a significant proportion of them are now in their mid-twenties and therefore no longer minors. Prison and even judicial authorities often lump the two categories together and cite misleading statistics which do not differentiate between the two. Official figures referring to the number of minors in prison often – but not always – include the genocide minors who are now adults. For example in Gitarama Central Prison, the statistics in the director's office indicated that there were 316 minors (309 boys and seven girls), but during a conversation with the deputy director of the prison, it transpired that only 41 of these were absolute minors, aged under 18. The rest were minors at the time of their alleged crime. The consequences of this confusion are serious, not only in legal terms but also in terms of how these prisoners live. Most prisons have a separate block for minors, in a bid to conform to international guidelines, but the principle of protection which motivates this separation is undermined by the fact that many of the so-called minors who live in this special block are actually adults. In fact, in many prisons, these "false minors", as some people call them, outnumber the real minors.

In the mass arrests which took place immediately after the genocide, hundreds of children were rounded up across the country. Some were arrested with their parents, and ended up in prison with them, but many others were picked up alone. Children as young as eight or nine found themselves accused of participation in the genocide and were thrown into prison without going through any form of procedure. Some were accused of killing, others of leading the killers to places where Tutsi were hiding, others were not even accused of a specific offence, just "genocide". At that time, there were no separate arrangements for minors in the prisons, so these young children found themselves living side by side with thousands of adults, in extremely harsh conditions. Many of the younger ones did not know what they were doing there or why they had been arrested. I remember the expressions of incomprehension and helplessness on the faces of some of these children when I visited several prisons in Rwanda in 1996.

A former prisoner who was 21 when he was arrested recalled:

> "One day, they brought a six-year-old. He was transferred to the women's block. I remember two eight-year-olds. Most were between 13 and 17. They were all accused of genocide. They had no case-file, they were just picked up like that. They [the authorities] used to just write 'genocide' on the paper and that was it…
>
> I was in charge of distributing the food, including to the minors. Sometimes the ICRC gave special rations for the children. Unicef also helped a bit. Sometimes the children were given meat, once a year. A special medical assistant [a prisoner] looked after the minors.
>
> The minors didn't understand why they were in prison. They used to ask why they were there."

After international organisations intervened on their behalf, several hundred children were transferred to the Gitagata re-education centre, outside Kigali, and remained there for some time. Even though Gitagata was not technically a prison, the children were not free to leave and were effectively in a detention centre by another name. From 1998 onwards, the government announced, on repeated occasions, that children under the age of 18 would be released. In the period that followed, gradually, many were released, from the prisons as well as from Gitagata. Under pressure from international non-governmental organisations, the authorities also started moving the absolute minors that were left in the prisons into separate blocks. In 2004, several of these organisations were assisting with the construction of these new blocks.

By the end of 2004, the only absolute minors left in the prisons were those accused of common crimes; they were between the ages of 14 and 18. But a significant number of genocide minors remained in prison as the release programme had not been completed.

Absolute minors

Most of the absolute minors – boys and girls accused of common crimes – are from poor backgrounds and have a low level of education. Some of them have been tried, others are still awaiting trial. Most of those we spoke to had spent between one and three years in prison, so had not endured the even more extreme conditions which the genocide minors were subjected to in the earlier years. Nevertheless, their lives in prison were empty and bleak, and the tone in which most of them told their story was devoid of hope. Their answers to our questions tended to be brief and somewhat vague. The experience of arrest and imprisonment appeared to have alienated them from their environment. The long delays in the justice system affected minors just as they affected adults, although those accused of common crimes tended to be tried more quickly than those accused of genocide. Even a question apparently as basic as their age seemed to take an eternity to resolve. The *capita* of the minors in Butare Central Prison told us about four minors accused of common crimes whose cases had been brought to the attention of the prison director, because some may have been just under the age of 14 at the time of the crime (according to Rwandan law, children under the age of 14 at the time of their alleged crime should not be prosecuted). The director had referred their cases to the prosecutor's office who said they would question the four and check their dates of birth. They had been waiting for the answer for a whole year. In another typical case, officials in the prosecutor's office in Cyangugu had recorded a girl's age as 16, even though she was only 14 or 15 at the time.[1]

Many of these children were accused of serious crimes, including murder. A surprisingly high number were accused of rape – girls as well as boys. In Butare prison, 62 of the 69 common criminals among the male minors were facing charges of rape. Of the remaining seven, four were accused of theft, one of murder, and two of insulting the assistant prosecutor.

Accusations of rape have proliferated in Rwanda over the last few years, with a pattern of domestic workers being accused by their employers of raping young children or even babies within the family. According to many Rwandans inside and outside the prisons, these accusations are often unsubstantiated. The absence of a clear definition of rape has compounded the problem. Many people suspect these accusations are used to settle scores or provide an easy excuse to get rid of the young workers without paying them. The government's declared intention to crack down hard on rape, particularly against children, may have unwittingly emboldened people to make these kinds of accusations. Many of the girls and boys imprisoned on the basis of such accusations find themselves totally cut off from their family and friends once they are in prison: in many cases, the place where they were working as servants was far from their home, and their families cannot afford the cost of the journey to visit them.

One of those accused of rape was a 16-year-old orphan. He had left school at primary level and had been working as domestic help – cooking, washing and fetching water – for one month when he was arrested. We met him three months after his arrest:

> "I was accused of raping a neighbour's child. The girl was eight.
> The child's mother accused me. She called me and locked me in a
> room. She beat me and accused me of raping her daughter. She

---

[1]   The question of a prisoner's age is often the subject of dispute. Especially among the rural population, people do not always know their exact age and may not have official documents to prove it.

called my boss. They took us to the hospital for tests but instead of going to the hospital, they took me to the brigade and detained me there...

I stayed in the brigade for five weeks. I'm an orphan so no one could visit me. I never knew my father. My mother died of illness two years ago. I have two older sisters but they didn't know I'd been arrested. We were 58 detainees in the brigade, in one room, including three minors... The prisoners who got visits shared their food with me...

I was questioned twice. I denied the charges. The *parquet* [prosecutor's office] also questioned me twice. Then I went to meet the judges. They asked the same questions. I denied it. They said I should be held in preventive detention. They said they couldn't release me as it would obstruct the investigations... Three days later, I was brought here to the prison... I'm still waiting. They said if I'm found guilty, I will get a two-year sentence...

I had to wait for another prisoner from my area to receive a visit to pass a message to my sisters. My sister visited last Tuesday. She's about 25. I was very happy. She brought cassava and beans. I hadn't eaten that for ages. She said she would try to come back.

I live in the minors' block. I sleep on the ground and I put pieces of sack down to sleep on. I don't have a clean blanket. Someone lent me one. I was also lent this uniform for this visit. I have one set of my own clothes. I get on well with other minors. We play cards and *igisoro*. Some do sports but I'm not interested. I learn to read and write. There are lessons in our block. Adults teach us. I like it but some of the minors don't want to study...

I hope I'll be released as I know I haven't done anything wrong. The first thing I'll do is go home. I could live with my sister. I won't go to work for people who can do nasty things. I don't know why they accused me. We didn't have any problems. I didn't even know the girl. I used to play with her brother. My boss never came to see me. He never paid me."

A 15-year-old boy had adapted less well to life in the minors' block. He had been bullied by some of the older prisoners and was living in a state of semi-permanent fear. He had been in prison for around five months, accused of murder. He described it as an "involuntary killing", claiming that the victim had provoked him.

> "Since I've been here, no one has questioned me. My mother comes once a month. Only my mother visits. I have three younger sisters but they don't visit as they are too young... My mother is melancholic towards me. She said I should understand the gravity of what I did...
>
> In the minors' block, I am vulnerable as I am the smallest and the youngest. I have to be like a sheep. If I try to rival them, there will be trouble. The stronger ones can get aggressive towards me. Once I was laughing with another boy, who was about 17. He turned round and said: 'We're not in an orphanage here' and slapped me. He wasn't punished. He hit me and laughed at me for not even complaining. This was soon after I arrived. I have to be careful... The minors are all as strong as each other, except for me. When there is no electricity and it's dark, some cause trouble but they're controlled by the security. The security are adults but were minors when they were arrested.
>
> I can never go out of the block. I don't dare as I'm afraid I'll be beaten. How could I go among 7,000 people? I'm so small I could be trampled on. I can only come out when there are visits.
>
> I have some friends who are older than me. The friendship is just sharing food from our families. There are no games. I haven't gone to lessons yet. The conditions here are very different from outside. There are no materials. They are not really lessons. There are no pens or chalk. I don't do anything. I wash my clothes. I left my clothes at home so I just have this T-shirt and

trousers. I also have these uniform trousers which I bought from a released prisoner for 300 francs…

I can't think about my release. I haven't even been tried yet. I expect to be here for a long time. I don't know what sentence I'll get…

I'd like to play to ease my suffering, but there's nothing to do here. Only a few can go and play volleyball… It's always the same team. Not everyone can play. Those who play are adults but live with the minors. They wouldn't allow me to play. I haven't tried asking as I'm afraid of being attacked. Once I met the *social* and told him about my problem. He just said this was prison, not leisure. I asked him how I could study. He said there was a shortage of materials. My mother couldn't find materials for me to study."

We also spoke to a 15-year-old girl who had been working for a family as a domestic worker when her employer accused her of raping her two-year-old child. Her employer beat her severely and called a neighbour over who beat and kicked her too. They told her that if she didn't confess to raping the child, they would kill her. She confessed, and the next day, she was arrested and taken to prison. Two years later, she was tried and sentenced to 20 years' imprisonment.

"The mother of the child wasn't present at the trial. There were no witnesses. It was just me, the officials from the *parquet*, and the judges. The trial lasted one hour. I didn't say much in my defence. I admitted and I asked for forgiveness. I couldn't answer their questions. I felt very intimidated before all these people in black robes… They sentenced me to 20 years. I thought I might get five years, or at most ten years as I had admitted and asked for forgiveness. When they said 20 years, I felt as if lightning had struck me. I wrote to the president of the appeal court to file an appeal. Since then, I'm waiting. The *assistante sociale* helped me write the letter as I didn't know what to write. I didn't know the procedures… I'm hopeful the appeal court will reduce my sentence. I wish someone could accompany me to the trial, even if it's not a lawyer, just someone who knows a bit about the procedures."

She never received any visits in prison: "Even my mother has abandoned me. I sent a message through other prisoners who get visits, so I think she knows I'm here. I've never known my father. I'm all alone here. If my grandmother was younger, she would visit me, but she's 80 now and can't visit. I don't know why my mother doesn't come. Even if she's poor, she could still come without bringing anything." However, the women prisoners looked after her and made her feel at home: "The women welcomed me. For three weeks, I was given a bed normally used for sick prisoners. The nurse gave me tablets to reduce my swelling from the beatings, on my arms and legs. A woman rubbed me with salt water. She was very nice to me… After three weeks, I got a bed on the first floor, for one month. When I had completely recovered, I was put on the top floor. Because I'm young, it's easier for me to climb up. I wasn't asked for any money." She had learnt to read and write in prison, and proudly showed us her notebook, in which she had written in Kinyarwanda "I can read and write". She told us she had never been to school before. She said she would like to learn embroidery but didn't have any money to buy the materials. She spent most of her time chatting with the other women, especially the younger ones.

Genocide minors

The genocide minors include a higher proportion of educated prisoners. Partly as a result of this, and of their greater maturity, they were more forthcoming during our conversations. Our interviews with them were not significantly different from those with the younger adults from the men's blocks, but inevitably, the impact of their imprisonment on their lives, on their psychological development and on their thoughts and expectations had been different. Some had spent all of their adolescence and their early years of adulthood in prison, with no certainty as to when they might be released.

The minors' blocks have their own internal structure and administration, like the adults. There is a minors' *capita*, who is usually a genocide minor, therefore not a minor at all. The utter confusion was illustrated by the explanation of the *capita* of the adults in Butare prison: "The minors have a *capita* who is a minor himself. He is a genocide minor who is now about 26." Then he added, in an attempt to clarify: "Adults can't go into the minors' block."

We later met the *capita* of the minors, a young man aged 25 who was 16 when he was arrested in 1995, and only 15 at the time of the genocide. "I was coming back from a refugee camp in Burundi where I had been living for one year, with my family. I came back before them, on my own... After three days, the soldiers arrested me. The head soldier said I was a killer." One year later, his family returned from Burundi, and in 1999, his father was also arrested and joined his son in the *cachot* where he was detained. They had since both been transferred to the central prison.

In Gitarama, we met a 28-year-old prisoner who was 18 at the time of the genocide, and 19 at the time of his arrest. He had been appointed coordinator (the equivalent of *capita*) of the minors' block from 2002 to 2003. He told us that in November 2003, there were 436 prisoners in the block: 334 of them were accused of genocide. Two of them were only 12 years old at the time of the genocide, about 15 of them were 14 years old and the rest were slightly older. All were adults now but still lived in the minors' block.

For many of the genocide minors still awaiting trial, the number of years they had spent in prison already exceeded the length of their supposed sentence, had they been tried and found guilty. Others had been tried and received heavy sentences, even though the law specifies that children who were under 14 at the time of the crimes of which they are accused cannot be prosecuted, but should be placed in rehabilitation centres or solidarity camps instead. In Kigali Central Prison, we met a middle-aged man who had been charged and tried along with two other people: a man and his son, who was only 16 at the time of the genocide. The two men were sentenced to life imprisonment and the boy was sentenced to 20 years. The father appealed against his own sentence but later died. His son didn't appeal. According to his co-accused, the situation was beyond him. He was later transferred to Kimironko prison, where he was serving his sentence.

Minors' living conditions

The minors' blocks we visited were less crowded than the men's blocks, but just as gloomy. In Butare prison, the minors' block is a large, empty and very dark room, with rows of bunk-beds along the walls. Even when the door is open, the daylight barely finds its way inside. Eyes peered out at us from the shadows when we walked in. Some of the boys were sitting on the ground or on their beds – or rather, planks, as few of them seemed to have anything resembling a bed, but most were standing around idly, in clusters, or alone. They looked bored, restless and isolated. Even our visit didn't excite them much. There was little conversation to be had there, and the boys were barely even talking to each other.

In Kigali Central Prison, the minors' block was more crowded and the mood different. As we entered, a group of boys surged forward to see who these strange visitors were. Some were curious; others sniggered; others looked down at us from their perches on the bunk-beds in a defiant and slightly threatening way. A couple of boys were pulled out from the crowd for us, as a sample, before we embarked on our more detailed interviews. They were 15, 16, 17, most of them accused of rape. These boys came across as more typical "delinquents", as the older prisoners often like to call them. We asked a few questions to one teenage boy, accused of rape. He stared at us blankly through half-closed, bloodshot eyes. His answers were monosyllabic and harsh. He looked as if he was in another world.

The girls live in better conditions, among the women, although there is little to occupy them there. We assumed, from the way the older women talked about them, that the adult women tried to look after them, but there were no special facilities for the girls. In Gitarama prison, during our tour of the women's block, we were introduced to a young girl, who, according to the *capita*, was 18, but looked several years younger. She was accused of infanticide – a common accusation against young women – of killing her own baby as soon as it was born. She seemed traumatised and almost unable to speak. It was hard to tell whether she was just very shy or mentally disturbed. She was small and frail, and kept her head down throughout our brief conversation. The *capita* gently made her look up, but even when she did, her eyes didn't give anything away. She looked as if she didn't even know where she was, or what was going on around her. We cut short the conversation, as we were worried that we were frightening her. I asked the *capita* about her afterwards. She told me she was always like that, but would speak sometimes. She didn't provide any other explanation and we never found out anything more about her.

Activities for minors

The most striking aspect of the minors' lives in prison is the emptiness. Few provisions are made for the fact that they are still children. "Minors live like the rest of us," a young adult prisoner told us.

Minors can attend classes, like the adults, and some prisons have a special programme of classes for the minors. However, most of the minors we met were not especially enthusiastic about attending, probably because they had never been through a formal education system, or had left school at an early age. Teachers among the prisoners commented that many of the minors were easily distracted or discouraged. The exceptions were those who had been in the middle of their studies when they were arrested. They were anxious not to fall behind and keen to learn new subjects. A former prisoner who was 15 when he was arrested told us he had learnt English, Spanish, Italian, Swahili and Lingala during his eight years in prison. Another boy who was still studying at school when he was arrested told us he had got used to life in prison, but his school was what he missed the most. Since his arrest in March 2003, only two of his friends had visited him, just twice. I asked him what they had talked about during those visits. He said they just told him which chapter they had reached in their textbook at school.

In some prisons, the adult prisoners make attendance at the classes compulsory for the minors, with some success. The literacy classes, in particular, had enabled a few minors to learn to read and write in prison. A well-educated, middle-aged prisoner in Butare had been in charge of teaching minors from 1999 to 2002:

> "The minors are often very poor children. I gave them books and tried to instil values and knowledge and teach them to read and

write. At a higher level, they learned French and Swahili. In 1999
we started teaching English. The minors were at different levels of
education. Some had never been to school. Each was a type of
his own. Most had left school at the primary stage and were
traumatised. Those who had been to school had fewer problems.
Some had learning difficulties… We have a good programme for
the minors and some do well. One minor, a common criminal,
was with us for a year. He had left school in the fourth grade.
After his release, he qualified at the sixth grade and succeeded in
entering secondary school. He and others have come back to visit
me. Sometimes, after they leave the prison, they make a leap and
progress outside. We also helped students who had given up halfway through secondary school. Then the former director stopped
the programme. He said to the minors: 'You're not here to study,
you're here to plead guilty and go home.' "

Minors attending a class in Kigali Central Prison, 1995   © Ladislas Niyongira

In terms of leisure and physical exercise, there seems to be a paucity of
activities for minors. In theory, the boys can take part in sports alongside the
men, and in some cases, have their separate team, but there didn't seem to be
any other special activities for them, with the result that many of them spend
their whole days inside their miserable, dark blocks. The option of using

work as an opportunity to get fresh air and physical exercise is also closed off to them, as minors are not allowed to work outside. They have the opportunity to learn practical skills such as carpentry or mechanics, but only inside the prison. In Butare prison, there was a large, well-equipped carpentry workshop. We chatted to the prisoner who was in charge of teaching woodwork. He told us that disappointingly, few minors came to learn these skills, as they were too weak and had difficulties concentrating.

Sexual abuse

As a consequence of detaining minors and adults together, there are numerous cases of male rape and sexual abuse in the prisons, which have contributed to the spread of Aids. Even where minors live in a separate block, this block is often adjacent to the adults' blocks, and may even be in the same building. The adult prisoners were more willing to talk about this problem than the minors themselves, who either evaded the question or answered it vaguely with statements like "it used to happen, but not so much now".

The prisoners described the practice as "homosexuality", not rape. They were not always explicit about the degree of coercion involved. Adult prisoners often paid the minors for sexual favours, with money, food or other items. Sometimes they developed ongoing relationships with these boys, sustained by the constant supply of favours. "For the minors, the sex was not voluntary," said a former prisoner. "They were hungry. The older prisoners gave them food. Even after they created the separate block, the children got out and continued having sex with the adults as that had become their way of behaving." The prisoners in Butare had a special name for the adults who paid for sexual favours. An adult prisoner there told us: "We call them *imbyeyi*: rich but kind men. Literally, it means the cow who feeds the calf with her milk. It has come to mean an adult who has homosexual relations with minors... You can spot the minors who are involved in homosexual activity. They have a nice gold watch, new shoes, sunglasses or a nice radio. Or they act like girls. Some are very pretty."

A former prisoner accused of genocide, who was 15 when he was arrested and spent eight years in prison, was one of the few (former) minors we spoke to who was more open about the sexual relations between minors and adults: "It was difficult being with adults. Some took minors as wives. They got ill. They hurt us. Adults used to corrupt minors and offer them food and other things. They used to say: 'You don't get any visits, here, have some food'... Some prisoners were violent. We were afraid. We had to be very careful... Some adults took children into their own châteaux. We used to see it happening."

Prisoners caught engaging in such acts are disciplined and sent to the punishment cell. Homosexuality is not accepted in Rwandan society, so the primary offence here was the homosexual act itself, rather than rape, sexual abuse or exploitation. The boy, as well as the adult, would be punished. In Gitarama prison, the adult could be sent to the punishment cell for 30 days and the boy for two weeks. When two minors were caught having sex together, they would both be punished. A prisoner in his fifties in Kigali Central Prison told us: "Homosexuality is becoming common... If they're caught, they're punished. Their place is taken and they become marginalised. They can ask for forgiveness. If the same person does it again and again, he can spend ten to 15 days in the cell. During that time, we try to speak to them to reform their ways. The minors are now kept separate so there are fewer cases, but if they're caught, they're punished too. The social workers are not doing much to help us." Some adult prisoners were trying to educate these prisoners rather than just punishing them, especially on the dangers of Aids.

CHAPTER VII

Families in prison

It is common to find several members of the same family in prison, sometimes three, four or five: a husband and wife, brothers, sisters, sons and daughters, cousins, usually all accused of genocide, and sometimes facing the same charges. They may be living in the same prison, or many miles away, in different prisons.

In the first few years after the genocide, when prison conditions were at their worst, finding a close relative in prison was a godsend for any prisoner. That relative could help the new prisoner by welcoming him, finding him a place to sleep or something to eat, and giving him a crash course in how to survive the terrifying new environment. In some cases, finding relatives in prison was like a long-awaited reunion. One man was relieved to find several of his relatives in the prison when he first arrived there, including his uncle, five nephews and his godfather. He told us: "I thought even if I died soon after, at least I had seen my family again."

In the *cachots*, however, conditions were so harsh that even close relatives could do little to help each other. In Gitarama Central Prison, we met a young man who was 18 when he was arrested in 1995. His father, who was 59, was arrested one day later and they were held together in a *cachot*, where they were both beaten. After four days, they were transferred to Gitarama prison. There, both the son and his father slept outside, sitting all day and all night because they couldn't find a place to lie down. The father was so weak and ill from the beatings that he couldn't even fight his way through the crowds to reach the dispensary in the prison. He died as a consequence of his injuries one month later.

Another prisoner, who was only 16 when he was arrested on accusations of genocide, spent six years in a *cachot* in Butare, where he was joined by his 64-year-old father. When we met them, they had been transferred to Butare Central Prison: the son was in Karubanda (the main part of the prison) and the father was in Rwandex (the annex). They saw each other once a month. Several of their cousins and other relatives were in the same prison. Being in prison with his father, especially in the *cachot*, had marked the son deeply. He said it was the one thing he would never forget. Likewise, for the father, seeing his son imprisoned at such a young age had caused him great sorrow. He had tried to comfort him in the *cachot* by sharing his food with him and giving him advice and encouragement.

In the early days after the genocide, relatives who visited prisoners or inquired after their cases could find themselves arrested arbitrarily. A man who had spent nine years in prison saw his mother and then his brother arrested in such circumstances, in 1995. Once when his mother visited him in the brigade (the local detention centre) where he was first detained, she asked the soldiers why her son was detained there and how he could be accused of killings in that area when he hadn't been there during the war. A soldier told her to wait; he said her son would be able to go home with her. She waited, but after two hours, she too was arrested. Soon after their transfer to the central prison, the man's brother went to ask the authorities why he and his mother were being held there, because it was far from their family home. The brother was then also arrested. He was released after one year; the mother was released more than seven years later, on the grounds of her age: she was 74. The prisoner we spoke to, however, remained in prison at the end of 2004.

Families split across several different prisons never get to see each other. They can only receive news through relatives who visit them separately, or through the broader network of other prisoners and their visitors. Occasionally, they are able to send each other letters, but writing from one prison to another can be a complicated process and cannot be relied upon as a channel of regular news. One woman was arrested three months after her husband in 1997. They both spent seven years in prison, but were moved around several times. For a while, they were in the same prison. Their children visited them there but they couldn't meet all together. The parents used to divide up the questions they wanted to ask the children, to make the most of the limited time allowed for visits (see Chapter XI): "Three questions for him, four questions for me." Since her husband had been transferred to another prison, she had received only one written message from him.

For those who are held in the same prison, a special day is allocated for family meetings once a month. These meetings are only for relatives who are in prison; relatives outside do not join in. A prisoner responsible for supervising these meetings in Butare told us that about 400 individuals took part, including 70 couples (husbands and wives). A family meeting happened to be taking place while we were there. It was a calmer and more sedate affair than the visits from the general public. Benches were set out on a raised space in the prison yard and the prisoners trooped out. The men sat on one bench, the women on another. They talked for about 15 minutes. The conversations seemed intense but quiet. Not a second of that time was wasted.

A prisoner whose wife was arrested two years after him, and ended up in the same prison, said they both took part in the monthly family meetings in the prison. "We sit with all the other people and the guards, so it's not private… If I see my wife by chance in the prison, I can't greet her properly or stop and talk to her. We pass notes secretly, to tell each other about things like the children being sick or problems with school fees, because ten minutes is not enough to discuss these sorts of things." Other prisoners had gone beyond the stage where they had anything useful to say to each other. A young woman whose elderly parents were also in prison met them once a month, during the family meetings, but their conversations seemed aimless: "We just talk about how we are, whether we're ill, how to keep well, how to behave well. We don't talk about our case-files. I'm sad to see my parents in here."

Members of the same family who are of the same sex can see each other more frequently if they wander around the blocks inside, but they don't always make the effort. After a few years, the proximity is taken for granted. A typical example was a man who was in the same prison as his brother-in-law: "I see him sometimes, but not often if there is nothing special to say. It's just normal."

Members of the same family who are detained together do not always face the same accusations or share a case-file. They could be imprisoned for different durations, and, even if they were tried together, receive different sentences.

A woman accused of a common crime found herself imprisoned with her four children, the youngest of whom was only 14. Her husband had hanged himself in 1999. She and her children were accused of killing him and pretending he had committed suicide – a charge which they denied. During the first few days of their detention in a *cachot*, friends brought her food but she didn't want to eat or drink and just gave the food to her children. She felt desperate: "I had become a widow, I hadn't been allowed to bury my husband, I was accused of killing him myself and my children were being accused of parricide. It was unbearable." After a month, they were all transferred to the central prison, then a few months later, they were provisionally released. The trial took place about a year later. It lasted just one day. The children were sentenced to six months each, but as they had already spent more than six months in prison, they were not re-arrested. The mother was sentenced to death and sent back to prison. She appealed against the verdict, but two years later, the appeal court confirmed her death sentence. Her children had continued visiting her in prison since their release. The older ones were working in the fields to try to earn some money and help the younger ones study. Their mother spent sleepless nights in prison worrying about them, and cried throughout our interview.

A 61-year-old man was arrested along with his wife, who was already in poor health. They spent two months in a brigade, in very bad conditions. He was able to see her about once a week because, as a qualified nurse, he was allowed to visit the women's block to treat the sick. He was worried that the stress of prison life would aggravate her health problems. Two months later, they were transferred to the central prison together. There, he was also able to see her regularly as he continued his nursing work in the prison. They also took part in the monthly meetings for families in prison. Their relationship suffered while they were in prison – "relations between a husband and wife in prison are reduced to the level of a friendship" – but he said they were so used to suffering that "we didn't make a big thing of our problems in prison". His wife was released in 2000. Her release was a cause of celebration for him, but also one of sadness, as he did not know whether he would ever see her again. She tried to visit him once a month until her health deteriorated further, and eventually she became almost paralysed. When we met him, he had not seen her for several years. He had asked for a provisional release to look after her on humanitarian grounds, but his request had been refused.

He had a photo of his wife, which he kept by his side in the prison. He told us: "Sadly, I don't think I'll see my wife alive. She's very ill. What pains me even more is to think of her dying in such poverty. Every time a visitor comes, I wait for the bad news about her. I live with this worry."

CHAPTER VIII

Waiting to die:

the elderly in prison

Among the crowds in the prison blocks, corridors and courtyards, there are old men and old women, some in their late seventies, grandparents and great-grandparents, struggling to survive, or waiting to die. They are among the most vulnerable prisoners. By the end of 2004, some had spent more than ten years in detention without trial, in conditions which would break even the hardiest person.

We spoke to about 20 men and women between the ages of 65 and 79 and collected additional information on the plight of the elderly from other prisoners and from prison staff. Most of the elderly prisoners we spoke to had grown up in rural areas; they were peasants, farmers or cattle herders. With a few exceptions, they had had little formal education; some had never set foot in a school. Most were accused of genocide, a minority of other offences. Some were frail and in ill-health, weakened not only by age but by prolonged ill-treatment in the *cachots*, limited access to medical care, insufficient food, and the epidemics and disease which ravaged the prisons in the first few years after the genocide. Some had been able to rely on their family for support and received occasional visits from their elderly spouses or from their children or grandchildren. Some found themselves in the same prison as their wife, husband, sons or daughters – a proximity which, on the one hand, brought comfort and, on the other, increased the humiliation and despair. Others, who had lost all contact with their families, ended up in prison alone, dependent for survival on the generosity of fellow prisoners and church organisations. Some told us how their relatives had been killed during or after the genocide. Others had lost their husbands or wives to disease, poverty and old age.

The elderly prisoners all spoke candidly about their experiences, with a clarity and acuity which was often lacking from the discourse of their younger colleagues. They told their stories straight, apparently without exaggeration, and reflected on the justice system and the political situation with remarkable objectivity.

Lists and more lists

From around 1998, the government announced that it would provisionally release the elderly and the very sick. A trickle were released over the following years, including some of the oldest. When I visited the prisons in Rwanda before 1999, I remember meeting men and women in their eighties or even older, including a blind woman in her nineties in Kigali Central Prison, who didn't even know where her home was or what she was doing in prison. Most of these prisoners, including the elderly blind woman, have since been released; others, presumably, have died. On 1 January 2003, the government announced again that the elderly and the very sick were candidates for release. Lists were made, over and over again, of the names of prisoners who qualified for release on the grounds of their advanced age. Some were released, but many were not.

When we visited the prisons at the end of 2004, there were still scores of prisoners over the age of 70, especially among the men. Few prisons keep reliable statistics on the number of elderly prisoners or a precise breakdown by age. Most statistics just refer to two age brackets: adults and minors. Of the prisons we visited, only the directors in Butare Central Prison and Nsinda prison were able to give us the precise number of prisoners aged over 70: there were 139 in Butare (133 men and six women) and 102 in Nsinda (97 men and five women). In Kigali Central Prison, representatives of the elderly prisoners told us that there were still around 40 male prisoners over the age of 70 there, the oldest of whom was 84. Representatives of the women gave us a list of 28 names of women over the age of 70 with their dates of birth; the oldest was 79. In Gitarama Central Prison, an elderly prisoner estimated that there were at least 75 male prisoners over the age of 70.

The hopes of elderly prisoners have been raised and dashed again and again, after government and judicial authorities have repeatedly visited the prisons compiling lists of the elderly and promising to release them after verifying their ages. A 72-year-old prisoner who had been detained for more than seven years told us his name had been on these lists seven times. A 73-year-old man who had spent eight years in prison had had a similar experience: "Three times I was on the list of people to be released because of old age. Three times I came out and stood in the prison yard, and three times I was taken back in again. I wasn't given any explanation. I'm on the most recent list again. I don't think a lot about my release. I could only think about it if I knew either the length of my sentence or that my case was progressing. But I'm just here waiting, with nothing."

A 70-year-old man apparently qualified for release on the grounds of both his age and his ill-health, but was still waiting: "They're lying… I've waited in vain. I think my problems will be resolved by God. I'll die and that's the only solution."

Contradictory messages from different authorities have also confused prisoners. A 72-year-old man who had spent ten years in prison without any form of judicial procedure remembered that in around 2002, the prosecutor visited the prison and said that, contrary to earlier indications, the elderly could not be released, because even if they were old, some were guilty. Almost two years later, other officials – he couldn't remember who – came to the prison and called the elderly prisoners again, by name. "They checked we were here, then they went away. We're still waiting."

Like other categories of prisoners, some of the elderly who have been released have been re-arrested. A 76-year-old man, married with eight children and many grandchildren, was arrested in 1996 after a neighbour accused him of killing a woman during the genocide. He denied this charge, claiming, on the contrary, that he had saved her. In 1998, he was released on account of his age. He was free for just ten days, then was re-arrested. He claimed that the neighbour who had initially accused him was not happy at seeing him released and paid the *parquet* (the prosecutor's office) to re-arrest him. When he was re-arrested and taken to the *parquet*, the *substitut* (assistant prosecutor) asked him for money too and threatened to send him back to prison if he didn't pay. The old man didn't pay and returned to prison, on the same accusations as the first time. He told us that during his ten days of freedom, he was so afraid that he didn't dare go out at all and didn't even see his children. Since his second arrest, his children had only been able to visit him twice over a period of six years. His wife had not been able to visit him at all as she was too old:

> "I despair, living separately from my wife... When the children visit, they have a long journey, so they arrive late and are in a hurry to get back home... The children visit me together some-times. I don't really have time to talk to them all. Some leave without talking to me. There are just too many people during the visits... None of my grandchildren have come. When they're asked if they want to come and see their grandfather, they say they're afraid of prison."

Towards the end of 2002, about four years after his re-arrest, his name was once again on a list of elderly prisoners who were supposed to be released. "I went out in the prison yard. The prosecutor was there and he intervened. He said I should be put back in prison because I hadn't confessed. He personally ensured I went back in... But I have nothing to confess."[1] When we met him at the end of 2004, his name had been included on yet another list of elderly prisoners. Despite his repeated disappointments, he had not given up hope: "I wait for my last moments. I have great hope that I will be able to finish my days at home, I'm convinced of this. I spend a lot of time thinking about my home and my family and I pray for them."

A 71-year-old nurse and father of nine was arrested in 1994, detained for about four years, then provisionally released. One week later, he was re-arrested, told his release had been a mistake and sent back to prison. When we met him, he had spent around another five years there. His spirit had been broken. He spoke so quietly it was difficult to hear him at times, and his answer to many questions was simply a sad silence and a hopeless stare. His wife visited him once a week. He said he didn't have many friends and spent most of his time praying. As a trained nurse, he assisted with the care of the sick inside the prison. He stressed that many were worse off than him: "There are lots of old people who have absolutely nothing: no visitors, no family. My wife receives my pension. It's very little but we are luckier than some. Some have nothing. We help them with medicines, food, clothes and

---

[1]   As explained in Chapter XIX, prisoners who confess to crimes committed during the genocide are given priority for an early release.

money." He said that old people eventually got used to life inside and that those who had no family were perhaps better off in prison. Finally, we talked about the prospects of release and his thoughts about resuming life outside. The question was visibly painful for him. He felt his entire life had been destroyed. He asked whether we realised how difficult life was in Rwanda, not just in prison, but also outside. "I don't know if I can imagine life outside. It's hard. There's no money. I had 12 cows but they're all dead. Everything was confiscated. I lost everything. I don't like to think about my life before." Towards the end of the interview, he stated simply: "You can die in prison or you can die outside prison. I would prefer to die outside because I would be free and I could visit friends and I could live. I'm waiting to die."

Ill-treatment in detention

The elderly were not spared from ill-treatment in the *cachots* and other detention centres where they were held for months, sometimes years, before being transferred to the central prisons. Many were badly beaten and some were tortured with the aim of extracting confessions. An unknown number died in detention during the first few years after the genocide. Those who survived still bear the physical and emotional scars of their ill-treatment.

A 73-year-old man was beaten by soldiers at the time of his arrest in 1996 and tortured in a local detention centre. Soldiers tied his testicles and pierced them with needles. After the Red Cross intervened, he was taken to hospital and stayed there for one and a half months. Eight years later, he still suffered from headaches, chest pains and back pains. A 68-year-old man who was beaten every day during the 13 days he spent in a *cachot* showed us the scars on his forearm where his bones had been broken. His kneecap had been beaten out of place; for a while he was unable to walk and trailed his leg on the ground. Other detainees had to hold him up.

Elderly women also suffered serious ill-treatment. A 79-year-old peasant woman, who was detained in a *cachot* in 1995, told us how soldiers had kicked her on the jaw with the soles of their boots, causing her back teeth to fall out, and knocked her to the ground by hitting her on the head with a stick.

Some prisoners died in transit while being transferred to the central prisons. Weakened by ill-treatment and the conditions in the *cachots*, they didn't survive the journey. A former prisoner told us how an old man died from lack of oxygen during a two-hour journey from a *cachot* to a central prison, in around 1996; he was one of 120 detainees transported in a closed container similar to a truck used for carrying merchandise.

Once prisoners were moved to the central prisons, the ill-treatment usually stopped, except in the early days, when the prisons, like the *cachots*, were run and guarded by the military. A man in his late sixties who was arrested in 1994 described how soldiers guarding the prison continued beating and humiliating detainees, including the elderly: "They used to come inside the prison to beat us. They made us lie on our backs and they sat on our chests. They made us lie on our stomachs and told us to scream, as if to imitate a cat, a dog, or a pig, to humiliate us. I remember they told one old man to imitate a cat. I can't tell you everything that they did." He remembered being beaten on the head with a rope when he went out to see his family who had come to visit him; he said he felt as if he was going mad and his head was spinning as he walked back inside. That day, he was unable to eat the food which his family had brought him; another prisoner collected it and kept it for him, until he was in a state to eat it two days later.

The survival of the elderly in the central prisons

In the three or four years after the genocide, when the overcrowding was at its peak, the old, like the young, were stuffed into the prisons with no regard for their age or fragile health. It was a cut-throat environment in which every prisoner had to look after himself if he was to stand any chance of surviving. The elderly were less equipped than others to withstand these conditions. A man who was in his late sixties when he was arrested in 1996 said that in the initial period, "we were on the edge of death".

A man in his early seventies described his first impressions of Gitarama prison in 1994:

"It was a terrible place. Lots of people died from these conditions. I could have died too. Only God saved me. At the start, I was sleeping in the cellar. There were about 30 of us. We were sleeping on the concrete, without any blankets. I spent about 15 days in there. There were old and young prisoners there. Most of them died from beatings, injuries, and lack of medical treatment: for example, I remember two young men and one old man who died. The military forced us to go into the cellar. I remember one of them who was especially nasty, who had only one eye… We couldn't go outside even to go to the toilet.

The *capita général* found me sleeping on the ground. He recognised me and found me a more comfortable place. He made me climb out of the cellar and put me in front of his château. He said to me: 'Come and die here because otherwise, you're likely to die down there.' I stayed there in the new place for one year. He asked me if I knew some of the other old prisoners and I met another old man. When the extension was built, I moved to another place, with better conditions. I have my own bed now, on the ground floor. I had to pay 500 francs to the *capita* who ran the block. I am still there now.

We still live in difficult conditions, especially those of us who are old. To wash, it is the law of the jungle. People jostle each other, especially the young ones… These conditions are not for everybody. I have had to plead for water for a shower. You can spend five or six days without having a shower because you can't get water. You have to beg for it."

Despite ten years of suffering, and no progress at all on his case-file, he remained optimistic about his release, amidst moments of gloom: "Often I sit here and I think and I don't find solutions, so I become resigned. I wonder why I'm here… But after living so many difficult moments, I won't die now."

The health of a 70-year-old prisoner had been seriously affected by ill-treatment and conditions of detention. While he was talking to us, he suffered an asthma attack. He explained that he used to suffer from asthma before his arrest but that it had never been serious until he went to prison. Now, he had an asthma attack every two or three days. He had spent his first nine months in the prison sleeping in the yard, in the open air.

> "When it rained, I was given a piece of sheeting to hold over my head, but my feet were in the water. In the morning, I'd be covered in mud. I stayed all day in the sun. I had no choice. I could walk about in the day, but not at night because there were too many people sleeping everywhere. To go to the toilet, we had to walk through mud and water… My health suffered. I had malaria frequently, and I used to shake. I had flu and skin rashes. I was looked after in the infirmary but there weren't many medicines. They did what they could to care for us.
>
> Later, I got a place inside, when they built the metal beds with planks. I was given a place on the middle floor, but it was too hard for me to climb up. So I got a place underneath the lowest bed on the ground floor. I could tuck my legs inside but my torso stuck out into the corridor. There was a space for people to walk around me and they tried not to walk on me. When they did walk on me, it was by accident. I still sleep there, but I prefer it because I don't have to climb up. I had a blanket which is now worn. I don't have another one. I had to sell my other clothes to buy medicines, so I only have what I'm wearing now."

His two sons were in the same prison, but like him, were very poor and didn't have the means to help their father. They simply spent time together in the prison and talked about their situation. The only help he received was from a Catholic organisation which occasionally gave him 200 francs for his medicines.

The situation of the elderly in the central prisons has gradually improved, especially since 2003. Nevertheless, very basic problems remain, relating mostly to overcrowding, lack of food and poverty.

In Rwanda, where average life expectancy is around 44, the elderly are usually accorded a place of respect in society. Prison is no exception. Once conditions had slightly improved, younger prisoners started helping the elderly; they now give them priority in the long queues for food or water, and assist those who are sick or too frail to look after themselves. A younger woman told us: "If old women have a problem, they ask us and we try to help them. We wash their clothes for them. We treat them like our mothers." The *social* (social worker) is supposed to assist vulnerable prisoners, including the elderly. In practice, however, these prisoners derive most of their support and assistance from other prisoners, as the staff seem either unable to help them or uninterested in doing so. In several prisons, the prisoners have appointed their own *social*, a prisoner, to assist their vulnerable colleagues.

Activities for the elderly

In some prisons, the elderly prisoners have organised themselves more formally and coordinate special activities. These include daily walks around the prison compound and other forms of physical exercise. Some of those who are still physically able can join the teams which work outside the prison.

Working

In Butare and Cyangugu central prisons, teams of elderly prisoners work in the fields, in the coffee and banana plantations. Those in Kigali Central Prison have special permission to work in the prison gardens and fields, from 7am to 10am. They grow tomatoes, onions and lettuces and are allowed to bring some in for themselves.

A 68-year-old man who had been in prison for more than ten years told us how he had recently started going out with the group of elderly prisoners:

> "I like it but I don't do it every day. Sometimes I choose not to go out because I want to do my religious activities inside… We collect straw for the coffee plantations, weed the cornfields and water the potatoes. There are about 150 of us in the team. We work from 7 to 12 each morning. There aren't any other special advantages to

going out, but you feel better and you don't go blind. You can see for miles."

For some, the work routine turned out to be too strenuous. A 72-year-old man told me he had gone outside twice, with the team that made bricks, but it was physically too hard for him. "I had asked to go outside out of curiosity and to get some exercise. It was painful and I couldn't stand it, so I gave up. You're forced to work hard. I can't work from 8 to 12 without rest. You have to work all the time. I wanted to change to cultivation, but my fingers were not strong enough."

Walking

On our tour of Cyangugu prison, we came across a group of about 40 elderly prisoners taking a stroll on the stony path around the prison building, within the prison compound. They walked in a compact and disciplined group, reminiscent of a slow-motion military formation, all dressed in pink shirts and shorts, armed with walking sticks, silent and docile. They stopped to talk to us. Their leaders – prisoners like the others – told us that any prisoner who was elderly, vulnerable or sick could take part in the walk and that there was no specific age requirement. Two of those we spoke to were in their seventies. However, there were several much younger prisoners in the group, who appeared weak and in ill-health. In contrast, some of the older men, despite their lined faces and grey beards, looked strong and healthy and clearly enjoyed their brisk physical routine.

Later we interviewed the 70-year-old former primary schoolteacher who was the leader of this group. He said they walked around the prison grounds four times a week, from 8am to noon: "We're not accompanied by a guard. I'm responsible for the group. We're not allowed to go beyond the boundaries of the prison. It helps us relax, see the world outside and get some fresh air."

A 76-year-old man told us he usually joined the group for walks on Mondays or Wednesdays: "I go on the walk once a week. I can stretch my limbs. The coordinator is given a list of names from the infirmary with notes on who has rheumatism or other problems. The director gives permission for us to go on the walk. The walk is a good time to talk to people. We talk about our detention, when we might be released, when it will end." A 69-year-old man said the walks enabled him to see the world outside – Cyangugu prison offers spectacular views of the lake and hills, even from within the prison compound – but he was aware that it was out of his reach: "The outside world is a foreign land. The prison is where I am."

A 73-year-old man who was detained in Byumba Central Prison for around eight years had been the leader of the elderly prisoners there. "I used to take them to walk outside. We were about 70 in the group; we went walking, with our sticks. We were allowed to walk outside the prison. We went to look at the cows, the rabbits and the carpentry workshop. We could stretch our legs. It was good." In a remark typical of the pride many prisoners take in the discipline and structure of their lives, he added: "After the walk, we went back inside in an orderly way." When Byumba prison closed, he was transferred, with many others, to Nsinda prison. He complained that there, there were no walks or special activities for old people. Nevertheless, he had bought a walking stick inside, for 20 francs.

A number of prisoners felt frustrated at not being able to take part in these walks, either because they were not old enough to qualify or for other reasons. A man who suffered from rheumatism said he would have liked to join the group but was not allowed to do so because he was sentenced to death. A 73-year-old man said he used to participate in the walks around the prison, but the leader of the group had stopped him "because he says I'm lazy... Since then, my strength has diminished and my eyes have got worse because there isn't enough light inside the prison."

Ageki

Kigali Central Prison typically showed the highest level of organisation among the elderly. Elderly prisoners there have formed their own organisation, known as Ageki, the acronym for the Kinyarwanda name *Ishyirahamwe ry'Abasaza bo muri Gereza Nkuru ya Kigali* (Organisation of Elderly People in Kigali Central Prison). We had a meeting with three male representatives of Ageki, including its president and vice-president. It was a slightly formal but friendly meeting. All three were extremely courteous, helpful and disciplined, each speaking in turn, answering our questions precisely and – unlike some of the individual interviews – never straying into the realms of emotion or politics. The tone of the meeting was constructive and upbeat. They described the main purpose of their organisation as ensuring the survival of the elderly in prison. After listing all the activities for the elderly, one of the Ageki representatives concluded with a smile: "Life doesn't end just because we're in difficulty."

Ageki was set up by the prisoners in Kigali Central Prison in May 1999. At the end of 2004, it had 238 members among the men and 133 among the women, but the total number of elderly prisoners is higher, as membership of the organisation is voluntary and not all elderly prisoners have joined. The women's branch of Ageki has its own coordinator. To qualify for membership, prisoners must be over 55.

The Ageki representatives identified the three most acute problems facing the elderly as finding a place to sleep, lack of medical treatment, and poverty. They estimated that between one and three elderly prisoners died every quarter, as a result of illness, the prohibitive cost of obtaining adequate medical treatment, and the cumulative effect of the strain of prison life. In agreement with the prison director and prisoners in charge of organising the blocks and the kitchen, Ageki tries to ensure that older prisoners are given priority, for example by asking the *capitas* of the blocks to find places for them to sleep, ensuring that they are served first in the long queues for food and water and that they go out first to meet their relatives on visit days.

Ageki also performs a social function and encourages the older prisoners to take part in cultural activities and entertainment. They try to keep their spirits up, through reassurance and solidarity and through involvement in a variety of activities:

> "We tell them we are not the only ones in this situation. We ask them to participate in celebrations, for example to mark the anniversary of our organisation, and debates with the younger prisoners. They share their knowledge with the younger prisoners and talk about history. The old prisoners are very active in all the religious events. They pray three or four times a day and listen to evangelisation, which keeps them busy most of the day. Some

give speeches, tell stories, and play traditional or cultural games. Some old people make and play traditional instruments. Young prisoners have been learning to play traditional instruments, such as harps, and are learning oral story-telling from their ancestors. A youth organisation organises a day of theatre. The old ones go and watch. We try to bring some happiness into our lives."

A woman in her late sixties told us how much she enjoyed watching plays written by younger women. "The plays are about love, about engagements, about street children. I like watching them. We forget our troubles and it helps us put up with prison life. If we didn't have this, we would die of solitude."

The vulnerable among the vulnerable

These activities may give the impression that the lives of the elderly in prison are tolerable, but those who are physically or mentally too frail to participate end up isolated or lost. The *capita* of the female prisoners in Butare spoke to us about the vulnerability of the elderly women there:

"There are six old women here. The oldest is 73. She walks with a stick. I am worried people could push past her and she could fall over. She is fragile. Three of them don't receive any visits at all. One of them is seriously traumatised. All her children were massacred in 1994, except one surviving daughter who is here in prison with her. The mother has gone mad. She clings to the daughter's skirt and doesn't want to let her go. Her husband is also in prison. There are two other old women who either have no children, or their children have fled to Zaire and they don't have any news. Some visitors bring food especially for the elderly. We share this out. At Easter, people bring clothes and we give these out first to the most needy."

We spoke to the daughter and the husband of the old woman who had lost all her other children in 1994. All three were in Butare prison. The father, aged 68, was arrested in 1994, the mother, aged 70, was arrested in 1995, and the daughter, aged 37, was arrested in 1996. All three were accused of genocide.

We did not speak to the mother herself as we were told that she had lost the capacity to hold a conversation. She was entirely dependent on her daughter for all her needs. The daughter was widowed: her husband, and several other relatives, had been killed by the RPF in 1994. She had one son, aged about eight, who was living with his grandparents; she had not seen him since her arrest in 1996. Despite her desperate situation, the daughter was very calm when she talked to us, and smiled sweetly throughout the conversation. She was gentle, almost saintly in her patience.

Despite her advanced age, the mother had been so badly beaten in the *cachot* where she was first detained that by the time she was transferred to Butare prison, she was unable to move. When her daughter first visited her two months later, she noticed that her mother's mental state had also deteriorated: "She recognised me when she saw me, but she had changed. She had lost her awareness. Now, as the years pass, she is not normal. She told me she'd been hit and kicked, especially on the head." Since the daughter joined her in prison in 1996, she had spent most of her time caring for her mother. Another prisoner, who knew the mother and daughter well, told us that the mother often woke in the middle of the night and checked to see if her daughter was still there; that she followed her daughter to the toilet and to the shower; and that even while we were talking to the daughter, the mother was standing at the gate, waiting. The daughter told us: "I'm especially sad when my mother needs something and I can't get it for her because I'm in here too. I will always look after my mother until she dies. I will do everything for her. She knows she's in prison, but she always thinks she's going to be killed. She doesn't remember the past. She has lost her mind."

The father, mother and daughter were able to meet all together occasionally, on the days designated for meetings of families in prison. For the father, these meetings didn't bring any joy at all. He asked us: "Is there any reason to be happy? It's no comfort for us to meet. It's no use." His ten years in prison had made him bitter, and he didn't even pretend to look forward to his release: "If I'm released, I've got no one to join at home. To start rebuilding my life at my age would not be easy. I would need help from friends. But are they really friends, those who don't visit me in prison? We used to share a beer when we were outside, but they've forgotten me since I've been in prison. My houses and fields have all been destroyed. I've lost my wife, my child and my cows. I've lost hope, so I'm not afraid of death."

Even in less extreme cases, the life of the elderly in prison is often miserable and empty. A 73-year-old prisoner, who didn't have enough clothes to wear, told us he ate only every other day, so that he could keep his food rations and sell them until he had enough money to buy clothes. A 65-year-old man who suffered from a series of illnesses in prison spent his first two months in prison sleeping outside, next to an open drain, then spent three years in and out of the prison infirmary, where he received basic but insufficient medical treatment. Other prisoners didn't want to sleep next to him because he had abscesses which had burst and smelled bad. He was told he needed an operation but didn't have enough money to pay for it. His relatives visited him occasionally, but these visits had decreased because his wife and children didn't have the means to support him. He never dared complain about the shortage of food and clothes or about his illness in front of his family, so as not to upset them. The clothes he was wearing when he first went to prison, more than five years earlier, were now in rags, and his wife couldn't afford to buy him new ones. He had a pair of sandals which had been repaired several times, and a blanket from the time when he was arrested, which was so worn you could see through it. We asked him how he spent his days in prison: "I can't do anything. I stay lying down. I can't even sit to play *igisoro* as my abscesses hurt when I sit. I spend whole days in bed. I think a lot about my situation. It makes me despair. Sometimes I wonder if I'll live much longer… I could die in prison. It would be a way of getting out of here."

A 73-year-old man said he too spent most of his time just sitting or lying in bed. "I don't know how to play any games. When my eyes were better, I used to read the Bible. I talk to people, but only to the old men. I can't talk to the young men. They're different. They know how to play games, they know more about the world. I like to talk to the old men, about past times and about our future. I miss my family. I think of them often. I see their absence. I have too many thoughts. When I get these thoughts, I pray."

The attitudes of the elderly to their life in prison varied enormously. One of our most inspiring encounters was with a very small, 79-year-old woman, who came out to greet us with her walking stick and hugged us for a long time before saying anything. She held onto us tightly as if we were long-lost relatives, before even knowing who we were or why we wanted to talk to her. Despite her age, and the nine years she had spent in prison with little or nothing to sustain her, she was strong and courageous, smiled a lot, and was grateful for the support she received from other prisoners. She was a peasant, a widow and mother of five children, four of whom had died during the war. She was arrested in 1995 along with her only remaining son, aged 27. She told us she was accused of killing a man during the genocide, but that she was "not at all afraid, because I knew I was innocent. Anyway I wouldn't have had enough strength to kill that man."

When she first arrived in Kigali Central Prison, she said she thought she would die there, but after meeting many other women prisoners, some of whom had been her neighbours, she felt reassured. She told us how she survived:

> "The first day, I slept on the ground, inside. Because of my age, I was put inside. The deputy *capita* gave me the space I have now. I didn't have to pay for it. They gave me one uniform, a blanket, a plate and a spoon. We were given food once a day, in the evening. It was not enough, but what could we do? Should we commit suicide? A prisoner is a prisoner. Some prisoners gave me a few spoonfuls of sugar, or money. There was a lot of solidarity between prisoners. The women got on well.

> I used to spend all day just sitting. Other women made baskets because their families brought them materials. Even now, I'm still sitting all day with nothing to do because I have no materials to keep me busy.

> I've spent ten years in prison. Sometimes I think I'll go mad. I wait for the days to pass. No one visits me. I live through the goodwill of God and the generosity of others, because I have no family. I'm not a sickly person. If I am ill, I get treatment at the dispensary. Other women encourage me to walk about a bit to avoid rheumatism.

My son was transferred to Kigali Central Prison at the same time as me. I saw him just once: he asked for permission to meet me, to tell me he was to be transferred to Gikondo prison and wouldn't be able to see me again. I was happy to see him. I'd love to see him again. It was a joy. At least we were close to each other. Since then, I learned he was moved to Kimironko prison because Gikondo closed. He's still there."

Like a number of other women in Kigali Central Prison, she was transferred to Miyove prison, in Byumba province, for three years, before being returned to Kigali in around 2000. She had been happier in Miyove. The conditions were better there and there was more solidarity; she complained that the prisoners in Kigali were too "individualist".

"When I came back here [to Kigali], I missed Miyove... Here I took back my old space, on the ground floor. I have enough space but I don't have a mattress now. I put a blanket on the planks and I have another blanket to cover me. Both are old blankets. I have a small basin to wash in and a container which holds five litres of water. I have nothing else except one plate which I've had for ten years. Someone stole my spoon, so I don't have one. I have another old wrapper [cloth]. My only other possession is God.

I never went to school. I can't read or write. I tried the prison classes but I think I'm too old and my eyes are not good. So I stay sitting or sleeping all day. Mostly I stay in my bed. Other women make things in the yard, but I live like this, and at night, I go to sleep again. I join them to talk, sometimes outside in the yard. I go to see them when I can't sleep any more, to distract myself.

There has been no progress with my case-file. I was only ever questioned once. They promised to make inquiries but there's been nothing since. They made another list of old people to be released, about a month ago. I'm on that list. They're always making lists... My son sent me a message telling me not to lose hope and that people are speaking up for me, saying that I am innocent...

If I go home, what will I do? I can't make any plans. I don't know if my house is still there, but I just want to go home to die at home."

The memory of the family

The loss or infrequency of contact with their families is one of the aspects of imprisonment which affects elderly prisoners most acutely as it increases their sense of isolation. Support from other prisoners is important, but can never be a substitute for relationships with the family.

A 70-year-old widow and mother of 12 children, one of whom was also in prison, told us that her separation from her family was what upset her the most, even though her relatives had continued visiting her during her seven and a half years in prison. She told us that when they visited her, "they asked me if I was living in peace. I said it was all right. I was happy to see them alive, but I could see they were sad. They had tears in their eyes when they asked me questions. It was as if their mother had already died, even though I was still alive." Frustrated with the short time allocated to family visits, she had once asked another prisoner to help her write a message to her youngest daughter. She hid it in a bag in her pocket, in preparation for her daughter's visit, but a guard found it during a search and tore it up into little pieces. During the years she had spent in prison, several of her children had got married and moved away. "I feel like I have no family now. My children are all scattered and I don't have any friends. I don't know what to hold onto. If I am released, I won't lead the same life as before, but at least I'll live at home. I'm old and I've lived my life. I want to die in my own house. We feel forgotten, but when we're called out to see people like you, or when we're given a piece of soap or when we're helped, then we feel like we exist again."

In many cases, the husbands or wives of elderly prisoners are themselves too old to visit, so prisoners can spend years without seeing them, with no guarantee that they will ever see them again. A typical example was a 73-year-old man who had not seen his wife for eight years, since his arrest in 1996. Nine of his 12 children were killed by the RPF in 1994. Only one daughter and four grandchildren remained in Rwanda. The two other children who survived the war had fled to Tanzania or Uganda; he had lost all contact with them. Since his arrest, his wife was living with her one remaining daughter and her grandchildren. She had not been able to visit him in any of the three locations where he had been detained as she was too old to make the journey. He had waited for her when he was transferred to Nsinda prison, as it was closer to her home, but she hadn't come. He explained this without resentment: he knew she was old and unwell. He occasionally received news of her through neighbours who visited other prisoners. He worried about his wife a lot, especially as he had never been able to comfort her about the deaths of their children, and he was not there to look after her in her old age. Even before his arrest, his wife had been traumatised by the death of her children and had begun to lose her mind. He believed that his imprisonment had been the final straw for her.

Even his daughter could not visit him frequently, because she was too poor. When she did visit, the visits seemed to cause him more pain than pleasure:

> "When she came, she said she had nothing, and they don't have enough to eat outside, and I believe her... When I see my daughter, I remember lots of things and I feel very sad. I see how she's become. She is very thin. The last time, I said to her: 'Be careful you don't get Aids, because if you get Aids, you'll abandon your mother.' She laughed. Other prisoners laughed at me too; they heard what I said because you can't say things privately.
>
> I have four grandchildren in Rwanda. I don't know them. One of them came recently with my daughter. He was very young when I was arrested. He looked at me and cried. I also had tears in my eyes. He is about 13 now... If I could spend just one year outside before dying, at least I could be with my grandchildren and find them a house. If I'm released, I won't be much use, but at least my grandchildren will be able to see me."

Like so many other prisoners, he had been on a list of old people to be released. All but three of those on the list were released. He and two others were transferred to another prison without any explanation. Nevertheless, he held onto the hope that he would eventually be released. He believed that those who lost all hope were those who had something on their conscience. Unlike some of the other prisoners, he did not begrudge the fact that he had been arrested, even though he swore he was innocent, but deplored the way he and others had been left to languish in prison for so many years without trial. He became more angry when he talked about killings by the RPF and the impunity which protected the perpetrators. In addition to his own children, scores of other members of his family had been killed by the RPF in 1994. He felt it was impossible to ask anyone for an explanation of the death of his children. "All I ask for is peace," he told us, "but justice has collapsed around us."

The response of the government

Many countries which have faced the task of bringing to justice people accused of grave crimes such as genocide, war crimes or crimes against humanity have struggled with the question of how to deal with suspects who are very old, sick or physically or mentally frail. There is a widely held view that someone's advanced age does not exonerate them from responsibility for the crimes they may have committed. On the contrary, in the case of Rwanda, many people believe that the elderly bear a particular responsibility for encouraging and inciting younger people to kill during the genocide. But the extreme prison conditions in Rwanda, which have a far more significant impact on the elderly than the young, give the question a greater degree of urgency, as does the inability of the government to set a date by which their cases will be resolved. These circumstances mean that many of these prisoners are unlikely to be tried before they die.

We raised concerns about the plight of elderly prisoners in our meetings with Rwandan government officials at the end of 2004. The officials claimed that the majority of prisoners over 70 had been released and that if any remained in prison, it was only a small number – a claim disproved by the evidence we collected in the prisons. They justified their continued detention on the grounds that some prisoners lied about their age or that it had been difficult to verify their age. The Secretary General of the Ministry of Interior told us that some elderly prisoners had refused to be released as they had no family at home and that some had insisted that they shouldn't be released because they had killed so many people. Some government officials, in particular the then Attorney General, justified the detention of the elderly by linking them with crimes perpetrated against Tutsi many years earlier, in 1959. They associated the elderly prisoners with those events simply by virtue of their age and ethnicity, even though they were facing a completely different set of charges.

It is certainly true that people of all ages, including the elderly, participated in the genocide in 1994. However, the fact that the government decided to consider the elderly for early release indicates some acceptance of the argument for releasing them on humanitarian grounds. Yet by the end of 2004, these promises had been only partly fulfilled. In the meantime, many elderly prisoners have died in prison without even having had a chance to appear before a court.

———————

Some of the elderly prisoners we met in 2004 have since been released.

CHAPTER IX

Two armies in prison:

the military prisoners

The military form a distinct category among the prisoners in Rwanda. Whether accused of genocide or of other crimes, their life in prison has followed a different course.

Until around 2003, military suspects were held in military prisons and detention centres. With a few exceptions, most of these sites were out of bounds for visitors, including detainees' relatives and human rights organisations. The army also used other, secret locations to detain people, especially in the period immediately after the genocide. Torture and ill-treatment were rife there and an unknown number of detainees were killed secretly. These sites were closed off to visitors altogether and families often didn't even know that their relatives were detained there.

There were also civilians held in military custody. In theory, only those accused of complicity with military suspects were supposed to be detained there. In practice, many other civilians, whose alleged offences had nothing to do with the military, were held in military detention. In particular during the period of insurgency and counter-insurgency in 1997 and 1998, large numbers of civilians were arrested and held in military detention, suspected of collaboration with the insurgents. Many have since been released.

By the end of 2004, most military prisoners had been transferred to the central, civilian prisons in order for them to be closer to the scene of their alleged crimes and to be tried by the jurisdiction in the appropriate location.[1] Previously, all military suspects and their civilian accomplices were to be tried by military courts, but following changes in the law, military detainees accused of genocide, like their civilian counterparts, are to be tried by the *gacaca* jurisdiction of their own area (see Chapter XVII). Only those classed

---

[1]   The human rights organisation LIPRODHOR reported that there were 572 military prisoners in civilian prisons in early 2006. See LIPRODHOR, *Rapport du premier trimestre 2006 sur la situation carcérale au Rwanda*, March 2006.

in Category 1 (such as those accused of playing a leading role in the genocide) or whose cases were already before the military courts would be tried by the military justice system.

As a result of these transfers, we were able to speak to a number of military prisoners in the central prisons, as well as to several civilians who had been held in military custody.

There is something disarming about seeing and talking to a soldier in prison, especially in a country such as Rwanda which, despite appearances to the contrary, is still ruled by the gun and where soldiers still have the power to terrorise civilians. These prisoners had been stripped of that power, stripped of their AK-47s, and stripped of their authority. The pink uniform had replaced the camouflage, and they had become human beings again.

The testimonies of military prisoners were different both in quality and content from those of civilian prisoners. Their attitudes towards their own imprisonment and the tone in which they recounted their stories were also different. Some seemed more accepting of their situation than the civilians, or less obviously indignant at the treatment to which they had been subjected, as if their experience in the army had taught them to put up with such hardships. With a certain macho bravery, some dismissed practices such as beatings as "normal" or insignificant; yet they complained vociferously about other seemingly less serious problems, such as the monotony of the food.

The military in prison include members of the former army of Rwanda, the *Forces armées rwandaises* (known as ex-FAR) – which had been the national army under President Habyarimana and until the end of the genocide – and members of the current army, the Rwandan Patriotic Army (RPA) which ousted the FAR in July 1994.[2] Most of the ex-FAR are Hutu and most of the RPA are Tutsi, but there are enough exceptions to invalidate any simplistic distinction on ethnic grounds.

---

[2]   The RPA was later renamed Rwandan Defence Forces.

The ex-FAR prisoners

The ex-FAR were prime candidates for arrest as they had played a central role in the implementation of the genocide. Some ex-FAR were arrested immediately after the genocide, in 1994 and 1995. Many more were arrested in late 1996 and 1997, following the return of hundreds of thousands of refugees from Congo. A large number of ex-FAR and their families were among these returnees and were thrown into jail as soon as they came back; others were killed soon after their return to Rwanda.

After the genocide, some ex-FAR soldiers volunteered to join the new army, the RPA, and were encouraged to do so, to boost its ranks. Some of these ex-FAR were among those arrested, after they had been retrained and integrated into the RPA. One ex-FAR we spoke to was arrested on the very day he and others were celebrating the completion of their training.

The RPA prisoners

More surprisingly, a number of RPA soldiers were also accused of genocide and found themselves incarcerated alongside their counterparts from the ex-FAR. Some are Hutu, others are Tutsi. Documentation of the genocide has shown that the perpetrators included a small number of Tutsi and that some of these Tutsi even excelled in hunting down and killing members of their own ethnic group, for fear of being killed themselves or seeing their families killed if they did not participate.

Other members of the RPA have found themselves in prison accused of a variety of common crimes not connected to the genocide. They form the bulk of RPA soldiers in prison.

Very few RPA soldiers are in prison in connection with the killings and other abuses they carried out themselves as their forces took over the country after the genocide and in the years that followed (see Chapter XVII). A small number were arrested but most were released after a short period. A prisoner who spent eight years in military detention had mingled with ex-FAR and RPA detainees in various military prisons. He said most of the RPA soldiers in prison were accused of murder, armed robbery and other common crimes.

He had met some who were arrested for killings during or after the genocide – he remembered one soldier accused of killing 36 people in 1994 – but said they had all been released without trial.

Life in the civilian prisons

Once transferred to the central prisons, the military prisoners lived side by side with the civilians. They were not assigned separate quarters. Some developed friendships with civilian prisoners, but most, especially the RPA soldiers, tended to stick with their former colleagues. An RPA soldier who was one of around 70 military prisoners transferred from Mulindi military prison to Gitarama Central Prison in mid-2003 said he and most of his military colleagues lived in the same block. Some of them had managed to bring in their mattresses from Mulindi. The mattresses came in handy as the room in which they lived had no bunkbeds and they slept on the ground. He shared a mattress which belonged to a friend: "We have an internal system. Sharing a mattress is almost obligatory. If he refuses, he would have to fold the mattress in half to make space for me. I don't pay for it. I contribute by bringing blankets and other things."

Several of the military prisoners we spoke to seemed to find life in the civilian prisons harder than life in the military prisons, especially in terms of the atmosphere and relationships between prisoners. They commented on the lack of solidarity in the civilian prisons and missed the spirit of cooperation which characterised the military prisons. One of them stated: "There is a big difference between military and civilian prisons. The military collaborate more and help each other. In the civilian prison, people don't help each other." He complained that he had to pay for everything, including a place to sleep, which had cost him 5,000 francs (around US$9), and a prison uniform. A former RPA soldier complained that the civilians were "too civilian… They're just different. For example, they're afraid of the guards during visits. I'm a military so I'm not afraid of the guards. The guards are like civilians to me."

Many complained about the physical conditions in the civilian prisons, particularly the overcrowding, which they had not experienced in the same way in the military prisons. They complained about the shortage of food, water and clothes, the restrictions on the possessions that they were allowed to bring into the prison, and the fact that military prisoners were not allowed to work outside. Surprisingly, they spoke as if their life in the military prison had been one of relative luxury. A prisoner who had been transferred to Gitarama prison after about six years in Mulindi was almost nostalgic about his time there: "There is no comparison between Mulindi and Gitarama. In Mulindi, it was much better. It was less crowded, and the prison had many facilities." Another prisoner who had been physically active and used to take part in sports in Mulindi stopped all these activities when he was transferred to Nsinda prison: "Here, I pray. The rest of the time, I just walk around. There are sports here too, but I don't like going any more as it requires strength and I don't get enough food."

Despite these complaints, the military prisoners found ways of making their day-to-day routine bearable and were as ingenious as their civilian colleagues in terms of survival tactics inside. Every opportunity was seized and nothing went to waste. An RPA prisoner told us how he and his colleagues made sheets out of the pink uniform fabric: "We bleach it. We heat water, put chlorine in and dip the fabric until it is white. We are preparing for an eventual transfer to another prison, or for our release. If the sheets are pink, we would immediately be stopped outside as people would recognise the fabric. If they are white, we can take them out. It is not easy to find chlorine. The hygiene teams have it. If we are friendly with someone in the hygiene team, we can take five spoonfuls of chlorine."

Relations in the civilian prisons

Most of the ex-FAR fitted into life in the civilian prisons without much difficulty. They found themselves cohabiting with thousands of other Hutu who, like them, were accused of genocide. In this context, the distinction between military and civilian soon became irrelevant. One ex-FAR summed up the situation bluntly: "Here, I'm together with all the civilian prisoners because we're all Hutu and we're all accused of the same thing. We share the sin. One race is in prison. The other race is in government."

For RPA soldiers, the process of adjustment in the central prisons was more complicated. They did not blend in with the rest of the prison population. Prisoners greeted them with suspicion; they viewed them either as agents of the government, or, if they were Hutu, as traitors. Tutsi RPA soldiers found themselves in a particularly unenviable position, surrounded by thousands of Hutu prisoners accused of genocide. Some felt acutely threatened, especially in the initial period. As time passed, most of them gradually got used to the situation and realised that expressions of hostility from other prisoners rarely went beyond words. The verbal taunts usually stopped after a few days if they didn't respond aggressively or if they learned to dismiss insults with humour. In some cases, the accusation of genocide became a kind of equaliser – as in Nsinda prison, where there were about 70 RPA soldiers accused of genocide. One of them told us that when he first arrived there, prisoners who sympathised with the former government saw him as someone who had fought with the regime which conquered them, but their suspicions were laid to rest when they discovered that he too was accused of genocide: "If you're accused of genocide, even if you're a Tutsi, you're not a Tutsi anymore. You become a Hutu."

In Gitarama prison, we met an RPA soldier who had worked in the intelligence services – the Directorate of Military Intelligence (DMI) – and was then accused of genocide and arrested in 1997. The first time I saw him, he was standing in the prison compound, outside the metal gate, a tall, thin man with dark skin and a bony face, standing very straight, with an air of quiet authority. Unlike many other prisoners who greeted us as they walked past, he did not make eye contact until I walked up to him and started talking. I knew nothing about him at this stage, but something about his appearance and his composure intrigued me. He spoke softly. He told me his name, that he had been in Gitarama prison for one year and seven months, and that he was accused of genocide. Later, my colleague interviewed him and found out his full story. During our first, informal encounter in the yard, he had been courteous and gentle but had not smiled much. After speaking with my colleague for two hours, he was transformed, and came out with a broad smile. Thereafter, he always smiled and welcomed us whenever we visited. On several subsequent visits to Gitarama prison, I spotted him from a distance in the prison yard; he was immediately recognisable among the sea of pink uniforms and shaved heads. He had an unusual way of walking, straight, almost wooden. He looked different from the others. For reasons I cannot explain, he did not look like a prisoner.

Two of his brothers had been killed in the genocide and he himself had narrowly escaped death. It had therefore never occurred to him that he could be arrested: "I thought it was a case of mistaken identity as I was involved in the security services and had access to many secrets and confidential documents. I was so convinced it was a mistake that I didn't believe I would spend long in prison." By the time we met him, he had spent more than seven years in prison, most of them in Mulindi.

He had not found it difficult to adjust to life in a civilian prison. He was one of the rare Tutsi RPA prisoners who had been given a position of responsibility within the civilian prisoners' administration: he had been made deputy *capita*. Perhaps as a result of this privileged position, he had a positive attitude towards other prisoners. He claimed that ethnic differences were only ever expressed in a lighthearted way, or in the form of jokes, for example when some prisoners blamed their suffering on the fact that the Tutsi were in power.

However, another RPA soldier in Gitarama said that some civilian prisoners still insulted RPA prisoners. They shouted at him: "There's the Tutsi going past!" (even though he was a Hutu), called him and other RPA prisoners "*inyenzi*" (cockroaches, the term used by extremist Hutu to designate Tutsi before and during the genocide) and accused them of "being at work" – spying on the Hutu prisoners. But he was not afraid of them, and believed that, on the contrary, they were more afraid of him. He spent most of his time with his friends (other soldiers who had been detained with him in Mulindi prison) and said that they felt safe together.

One former RPA soldier detained in Gitarama for just over a year still felt ill at ease with the civilian prisoners. He had joined the RPA in 1998, at a time when it was recruiting people to fight in Congo and in the northwest of Rwanda; he decided to leave the army in 2003. After his demobilisation, he was arrested for illegal possession of arms. When he first arrived in Gitarama, prisoners accused of genocide were aggressive towards him because he had been in the RPA. They said to him: "You fought for the *inyenzi*, and now you've come in here. What are you doing here?" The insults decreased as time went on, but he still felt nervous when tensions broke out among prisoners. He complained of a more general discrimination against military prisoners, with the military treated as second-class citizens by the internal prison administration. He claimed that the *capitas* put them in a separate section of the prison, in a corner, and that when spaces became available, they were automatically allocated to civilian, not military, prisoners.

A small minority of Tutsi RPA prisoners never built up the confidence to tread the delicate ethnic and political balance of (predominantly Hutu) civilian prison life. They could not become accustomed to living side by side with those they saw, collectively and even individually, as the killers of their relatives, and who still treated them as the enemy. One RPA soldier felt so isolated that, more than a year after his transfer to the civilian prison, he was unable to mingle with other prisoners, or even converse with them on a superficial level. He was a Tutsi who was almost killed during the genocide and was then accused of genocide himself. He was arrested in 1995 and spent eight years in Mulindi prison. In 2003, he was transferred to Butare Central Prison. Throughout our conversation, he seemed nervous and frightened:

> "I don't have any friends here. When I came, people accused me and talked about me. They said I was from the RPA and they had been imprisoned by the RPA, therefore they didn't like me as I was from the regime. I can't set foot outside as the prisoners accuse me of wanting to escape. The leaders of the prisoners stop me. They give reports. I still feel threatened, verbally not physically. They throw bad words at me. I never go out. Because of this, I would prefer to be very far from here, even though my home area is near here.
>
> In the genocide, I was threatened and almost killed by people from my *commune* [district] who are now in Karubanda [the main part of Butare prison]. So I preferred to be in Rwandex [the annex]. It is an ethnic question too. I was lucky that the truck from Mulindi dropped us in Rwandex. They wanted me to go to

Karubanda to be with the people from my *commune*. I talked to the director who said I could stay in Rwandex.

I live alone here. I have no contact with others. I would rather die. I just pray; there are no problems in the prayer group. I have an English Bible. I learned English in Mulindi. I was lucky, but I can't study here because of these problems.

My wife visits me less often now. She has come only three times in one and a half years. I have spent too long in prison and she's desperate. She is also a survivor of the genocide."

One of the few civilian prisoners whom he seemed to trust confirmed to me that the soldier felt so frightened that he never even went out into the prison yard. When he first arrived in the prison, the prisoners responsible for the internal radio had broadcast hostile messages about him. He had complained to the prison director, who calmed the situation down and told the prisoners to stop broadcasting these messages.

Life in military detention

We did not set out to document in detail life in the military prisons and detention centres, but the sample of testimonies we gathered from military prisoners gave us a glimpse of the world from which these prisoners had emerged. In my previous work in Rwanda – several years before the research for this book – I had already spoken to people who had been held in military custody. Memories of their stories of torture and summary killings of prisoners between 1995 and 1998 made me apprehensive when I sat down to talk to military prisoners this time around. In the end, many of their testimonies were less harrowing than those of some of the civilians we spoke to, but I had the underlying feeling that a lot remained unsaid. Perhaps they preferred not to relive these profoundly humiliating experiences and found it easier to talk about the mundane problems of day-to-day life.

Most of the soldiers we spoke to had been detained either in Mulindi or in Kibungo – the two main military prisons in Rwanda – and some in both.

Others had been detained in Rilima prison, which housed both civilian and military prisoners in the initial post-genocide period, or in military camps such as Camp Kami or Camp Ngoma. Some had been held in other, smaller detention centres in the days or weeks following their arrest, usually for short periods of intense suffering.

The living conditions and treatment of prisoners in these different locations varied enormously. At the top end of the range, prisoners in Mulindi (at certain periods) enjoyed sufficient space, lengthy family visits and leisure facilities. Some who had been arrested while they were still serving in the army continued receiving their salaries. In Kibungo prison, an RPA soldier was given his salary in cash in the prison, for three months; on market days, he could go out and buy food, accompanied by the guards. At the other end of the spectrum, those held in unacknowledged military detention centres were locked up in tiny dark cells or containers, never saw the natural daylight and were subjected to brutal torture. Many did not survive.

Relations between ex-FAR and RPA prisoners

Members of the ex-FAR and the RPA – two armies which had fought such a brutal war in 1994 – were thrown together in the military prisons. Prisoners gave different accounts of the relations between the two groups. An RPA prisoner detained in Mulindi for about six years estimated that there were around 400 ex-FAR and around 300 RPA. He claimed there was no serious friction between them: "Some RPA used to say to the ex-FAR: 'we beat you, we won the war', but it was like a joke. If it got too serious, other people calmed it down." Another RPA soldier also said that relations between the two groups were good: "When you're all in prison, you're conditioned to live together. Everyone just has his eyes on the exit door."

In Rilima prison, the ex-FAR were also in the majority. There were disagreements between them and the RPA and they sometimes insulted each other, but they didn't resort to physical violence. Ex-FAR and RPA also mixed in some of the military camps used as detention centres. An RPA soldier detained in Camp Ngoma said the RPA and ex-FAR there were held in two separate cells, but they could have contact with each other and used to chat freely. He said being in prison acted as an equaliser between the two groups.

However, in Kibungo military prison, tensions between the ex-FAR and the RPA prisoners were so serious that they exploded into violence, culminating in the death of an ex-FAR major at the hands of RPA prisoners in January 1998. There were about 700 or 800 prisoners in Kibungo military prison at that time. The majority – around 600 – were RPA. The ex-FAR and the RPA lived together, but the officers (of both armies) were in a separate room from the lower-ranking soldiers. There were often arguments between the ex-FAR and the RPA, and grudges: for example the RPA soldiers still received their salaries, but the ex-FAR didn't. As in most of the military prisons, the RPA prisoners were given preferential treatment as the prison guards were their colleagues. They were allowed to bring in various types of food, as well as alcohol. Sometimes they got drunk, and this could lead to fights. There were, of course, ethnic tensions too, as most of the ex-FAR were Hutu, while most of the RPA were Tutsi. An ex-FAR who was held in Kibungo military prison for one year said that on his first day there, an ex-FAR prisoner was almost beaten to death by an RPA prisoner who accused him of killing his own family. "The RPA guards used to allow this kind of thing to happen. Sometimes instead of trying to reconcile us, they would incite disagreements. I was lucky as I had an RPA friend [a prisoner] who protected me."

Later, he personally witnessed the incident in which the major – also a prisoner – was killed: "They strangled an ex-FAR major, Rugambaje Lambert. It happened inside. I saw it and I testified during investigations by the military prosecutor, but there was no trial. The major was the highest-ranking FAR in the prison. He was on the government's list of Category 1 suspects.[3] The RPA soldiers didn't like him. They killed him the day the list was published." According to another prisoner, some RPA prisoners invited Major Rugambaje to their cell one night and gave him alcohol. He got drunk, and when he went out to go back to the officers' cell, he was ambushed and strangled. The next day, prisoners found his body in the yard outside, lying in a drain full of water.

---

[3]   The government published a list of people accused of playing a leading role in the genocide, referred to as Category 1 suspects (see Chapter XVII).

The murder of the ex-FAR major caused the authorities to separate the two groups. On the day he was killed, all the ex-FAR prisoners were immediately transferred from Kibungo to Mulindi.

In addition to tensions between the ex-FAR and the RPA, the RPA prisoners in Kibungo military prison were themselves divided: there were those accused of genocide (who tended to be closer to the ex-FAR) and those accused of common crimes, who were in the majority. An RPA prisoner accused of genocide explained that those accused of common crimes had the upper hand.[4] "The common criminals were allowed to go out. They used to get different food... There were also political problems. Once, the common criminals demanded to meet the chief of staff and organised a revolt for about a week. One of their complaints was that they didn't want to be held with *interahamwe* or people who had killed their families. They closed the doors and nothing and no one could come in, not even the prison authorities. They made lots of noise by banging metal objects. The rest of us didn't want this action as we were hungry and they were stopping food from coming in. We almost started fighting. The chief of staff came and it calmed down."

Mulindi

Mulindi was the prison in which most military detainees spent the longest period – often several years, until the government's policy to transfer them all to the central civilian prisons took effect, from 2003. Located on the out-skirts of Kigali, Mulindi was originally a factory which was turned into a prison after the genocide. The number of prisoners there fluctuated between around 700 and 1,000; none of the prisoners we spoke to described it as overcrowded.

Between 1995 and 1997, conditions in Mulindi were bad: there was a shortage of food and water, detainees were not allowed to go outside or receive visits, and were regularly beaten and humiliated. Conditions improved significantly from mid-1997 after the ICRC intervened. Most prisoners gave a fairly positive account of life in Mulindi from 1997 onwards. A rare measure of

---

4   This is the reverse of the situation in the civilian prisons, where prisoners accused of genocide form the majority and have the upper hand (see Chapter XIV).

luxury – according to one prisoner who was comparing Mulindi with the civilian prisons – was that prisoners not only had mattresses, but space between the mattresses.   Food was provided twice a day, and there was a greater variety than in the civilian prisons.   A room where no one slept had been allocated for showers.   Visits took place in a big tent.   In around 1997, they lasted about 15 minutes.[5] By 2003, visitors could stay for a whole hour, and sometimes longer, and could chat with the prisoners privately, in a relaxed environment.   Visitors were allowed to bring almost anything to the detainees, including money; only substances such as alcohol and drugs were prohibited.

Some prisoners had the opportunity to work outside the prison.   Food and other commodities such as soap were the standard form of payment.   A team of prisoners who made uniforms for military prisoners and for a private security company were paid in sugar, rice or soap: about 10 kilos of sugar for two months of work.   Inside, there were sports and games.   There was also television in the prison – as many as eight sets, according to one prisoner, paid for by the military authorities.   Some prisoners were allowed to have laptop computers.

The internal organisation in Mulindi was similar to that in the central, civilian prisons.   A demobilised RPA soldier boasted: "Civilians can't be better organised than the military." The military prisoners, like the civilians, ran their own affairs, with a *capita général*, prisoners responsible for each block (called SA Major, rather than *capita de bloc*), and prisoners responsible for security, who, according to one prisoner, were always RPA, never ex-FAR. Those in positions of responsibility were not necessarily those who had occupied high-ranking positions in the army.   They just had to earn the respect of other prisoners.   The military police from the Kanombe military camp nearby came to Mulindi prison to organise elections for these posts.

In 1998, the treatment of prisoners in Mulindi took a turn for the worse. This period coincided with the rise in armed conflict in the northwest of Rwanda and with the arrest of people suspected of being *infiltrés* – Rwandan insurgents who carried out incursions into Rwanda from neighbouring

---

5   This is in stark contrast to the three minutes allocated for visits in civilian prisons, as described in Chapter XI.

Congo – or collaborators of *infiltrés*. The *infiltrés* were detained in a separate section of the prison and were treated very harshly. An ex-FAR prisoner painted a bleak picture of the situation in 1998:

> "During the war with the *infiltrés* in the northwest… they cut visits completely and reduced the food. We only ate on Wednesdays and Sundays and we couldn't get supplements from our families. There were 600 to 1,000 prisoners in Mulindi at that time. They included military, and civilians arrested because they were accused of being traitors or infiltrés.
>
> The *infiltrés* arrested on the frontline were also put there. They were refused food almost completely. They went to the toilet in a ditch inside which they emptied every two to three weeks. It was impossible for us (military prisoners) to talk to the *infiltrés*. They were in a separate room and never went out. There were about 150 of them. They included civilians rounded up along the way. We were outside and we saw them being brought in. We knew some of them. We could see they had been tortured. Some couldn't walk and were carried in on stretchers.
>
> There was a feeling of despair and discouragement. We could hear information on the radio. They blamed us [the ex-FAR] for collaborating with the *infiltrés*. We ended up feeling guilty whenever the *infiltrés* attacked. The guards and the DMI, who sometimes came to interrogate prisoners, accused us of collaboration. We were very worried and we used to talk about it among ourselves. Some of the prisoners were from Ruhengeri and Gisenyi [where the attacks were taking place]. Later, they found out their families had been killed in the military operations."

1998 was also the year of the second war in eastern Congo, and the Rwandan government launched a programme of forced recruitment to boost its ranks across the border. Prisoners were among those rounded up for the front in Congo. Many of the prisoners chosen for this role were ex-FAR, including some from Mulindi. According to one prisoner, the military authorities chose those who they knew were not opposed to the government and who were from lower ranks. Mulindi prison was close to Kanombe airport, so the prisoners were taken straight there, and on to Congo. Some died on the frontline. Others returned and were later demobilised. During this period, civilian prisoners were also recruited from some of the central prisons and were sent to Congo, either to fight or to work in the mines. An RPA soldier who had fought in Congo between 1998 and 2001 remembered regularly seeing a group of 150 to 200 Rwandan prisoners digging for gold.

Other military detention centres

Camp Kami, a military camp used as a prison in Kigali Rural province, had some of the worst conditions. One prisoner told us: "I will never forget Kami prison. It keeps coming back to me. Even if I'm released, I will never forget it."

An ex-FAR who was arrested in 1995 after being integrated into the RPA spent two years in Camp Kami. For him, the conditions there were "indescribable". There were two rooms: one for RPA detainees, who numbered about 60, and one for ex-FAR and those accused of being *infiltrés*, who numbered about 75. Even though he had joined the RPA, he was put with the ex-FAR and the *infiltrés*. They were held in an underground room about five metres long and five metres wide, which was formerly used to store weapons. The room was so dark that the prisoners suffered serious eyesight problems. Once a day, they were given a plate of food to be shared between four people. There was no drinking water. They were never allowed out, except to empty the bucket they used for the toilet; then, the detainees seized the opportunity to collect rainwater, whenever they could. When there was no rain, they resorted to licking the grass outside.

Many detainees in Camp Kami died from untreated illnesses and injuries from beatings. Others were taken out and shot dead. One prisoner told us how they used to see the smoke rising from the burning bodies; he recalled one occasion on which 12 or 13 prisoners accused of infiltrations were killed in one day. The Red Cross tried to intervene in Camp Kami, but the soldiers guarding the camp told the detainees themselves that they had denied access to the Red Cross.

Towards the end of his two years there, the ex-FAR prisoner we spoke to was moved to the RPA cell. Conditions there were better; the RPA prisoners were reasonably well-treated. Eventually, after some senior military officials visited the camp and saw the life-threatening conditions in which the ex-FAR were held, the ex-FAR were allowed to receive some of the same food as RPA prisoners, as well as medicines supplied by the military authorities.

Rilima prison, in southern Rwanda, housed civilian and military prisoners, in separate sections. The majority of the prisoners were civilians – several thousand of them; there were only a few hundred military. The civilians in Rilima were held in much worse conditions than the military and many civilians died as a result of acute overcrowding. There were also cases of ill-treatment of both military and civilian prisoners. An ex-FAR prisoner told us of several prisoners who had become impotent after having heavy stones tied to their testicles during interrogations.

Ill-treatment of prisoners was systematic in other military camps and in some of the smaller military detention centres. In Camp Ngoma, a military camp in Butare, the guards used to take the prisoners out one by one to a special room set aside for this purpose and beat them with electric cables for 30 to 60 minutes at a time, calling them "*interahamwe*" and "*génocidaire*" and trying to force them to confess.

One of the most disturbing testimonies of torture in military custody came from a civilian who was detained for 28 days in a DMI brigade in Kibungo, in 1995. When he was taken there, he thought he was going to die:

> "They took me and another detainee who was arrested with me to the brigade at Kibungo, but they didn't tell us where we were going. Some soldiers said they would kill us. I knew that others who had been taken away before us had been killed. I was very frightened. When we reached a barrier, I heard a conversation among the soldiers. They were asking each other whether they should kill us. One of them said no, because the accusations against me were not true.

At the military brigade, they put both of us in a container. At the time, I didn't know it was the DMI. Four other detainees were already in there. They were all civilians too. They included a former *bourgmestre* [mayor], a businessman and a butcher. The container was four metres by two and a half metres. After about a week, my wife found out I was there, but she couldn't visit or bring food. They gave us a saucer of food. It was not even full and not enough for four people. There were lots of stones and salt in the food. We didn't get any water for about two weeks. I weighed only 35 kg (before, I used to weigh 62 kg). If there was a kind guard, we could go outside, but some were nasty. The toilets were 50 metres away. We had to go there on our knees. There were stones and broken glass on the ground... In the early morning, we were beaten at least 20 times. They opened the door and came in. They made us lie down on our front and beat us.

They questioned me. I told them what I knew. I said I had participated in actions [during the genocide] but that I hadn't killed. They rejected this and wanted me to say I had killed.

After 17 days, the soldiers took me outside and asked me whether my name was C. I said no. Then they took out the prisoner they called C. and shot him dead. They shot him at point-blank range... I saw it myself. C. had been a policeman before the war. He was about 35. He was accused of genocide. After that, they put us in another room for four days, without food or water.

They took me to a torture room for questioning. They tied a rope on a wooden beam. They tied my feet, legs and arms behind my back. One of them took a stick and beat my head. A second hit me on the ears and a third one lifted me up. The soldiers stayed with me from 3am to 4pm. I was just hanging there, turning in the air. They brought a metal bar which weighed more than 50 kilos and placed it against my back, between my shoulder blades. At about 4pm, a soldier untied the rope and I fell to the ground. Another soldier came with a stick and beat me on the backside at least 80 times. At about 3am, I was sent back to the cell. All five of us went through the same torture. I still have the scars and injuries on my shoulders and chest."

Eventually he was transferred to Kibungo Central Prison, where he was treated for his injuries, then to Nsinda prison later the same year. He used to work as a carpenter, but because of the chest pains he still suffered as a result of the torture, he was no longer able to do this work, even in the prison. I asked him about the other five civilians who had been detained with him in the brigade. One had been released, another had died as a result of the torture at the DMI, after his transfer to Kibungo Central Prison; a third was in Nsinda prison with him, and was still suffering ill-health as a result of the torture, nine years on.

CHAPTER X

"You could count yourself as dead":

memories of the *cachots* and brigades

However bad the conditions were in the central prisons, the treatment of prisoners in the *cachots* and brigades was even worse, especially between 1994 and 1999. The *cachots* are local detention centres where civilian prisoners were held when they were first arrested. Prisoners could be detained there for weeks, months, or even years, before being transferred to one of the central prisons. Some of the prisoners we met had spent longer in the *cachots* than in the central prisons. Some *cachots* were located in towns, others in remote rural areas. Local district authorities were officially responsible for running the *cachots*, but those in charge of guarding the prisoners were military or police. Some prisoners were held in local brigades – detention centres run by the gendarmerie – rather than *cachots*; the conditions were very similar.

The *cachots* were like micro-prisons, holding several hundred prisoners in one or several very basic buildings. Some of these buildings were never designed to be used as prisons, but local authorities resorted to detaining people there when all existing detention centres became full. As in the central prisons, there were no individual cells, and many of the *cachots* did not even have separate sections. The prisoners were all stuffed into empty rooms, where they slept on the concrete floor or on bricks. Sometimes the rooms had no windows, or the windows were covered, so the only light which came in was from under the closed door. The overcrowding was as bad as, if not worse than, in the prisons. In some *cachots*, as many as 500 people could be held in one room. Prisoners were piled on top of each other and had to take it in turns to sit or lie down, or sat squashed between each other's legs.

The state provided no facilities whatsoever in the *cachots*. Until the ICRC and other international organisations were able to intervene from around 1998, prisoners were left to fend for themselves. They were not given any food or water; there were often no washing facilities, so they would spend weeks or even months without washing; they could not take any exercise; they were not allowed to talk to visitors; and they were tortured and ill-treated by the military or police guards. Hundreds, probably thousands, of prisoners died during this period. One prisoner told us: "Then [in the early days], if you were arrested, you could count yourself as dead."

When we started talking to prisoners in the central prisons, we were not intending to interview them about the conditions in the *cachots* where they had been held beforehand. However, many of them wanted to talk about this period because it still haunted them. Several described it as the hardest period of their lives. As our interviews progressed, it became apparent that the experience of detention in the *cachots* had affected them deeply and had shaped their attitudes towards their imprisonment in the years that followed.

We did not visit the *cachots* as part of the research for this book, but I had visited several, in different provinces, in earlier years. The visual effect of the *cachots* was less immediately shocking than that of the central prisons, simply because there were fewer prisoners in each location, but the physical condition of many of the prisoners was much worse; many were visibly suffering from hunger, poor health and ill-treatment. There was also a darkness and sense of abandonment in the *cachots* which was absent from the prisons. Especially in the *cachots* in remote areas, there was a sense that anything could happen there, and nobody would know or care.

Torture and killings

Some of prisoners' most haunting memories were of torture and killings in the *cachots* between 1994 and 1998-1999. Many people died during this period. Prisoners were taken out of the *cachots*, usually at night, and shot dead. The other prisoners could hear the screams, and sometimes gunshots, and they never saw those people again. Others died of starvation, disease and absence of medical care. One prisoner estimated that in the *cachot* where he was held, there were about ten deaths a day, mainly as a result of untreated diarrhoea, hunger and thirst: "When people got diarrhoea, we used to put them in an area they called 'the morgue'; it was the toilet. I watched one person I knew die there. It was horrible."

Almost all the prisoners we spoke to who had been detained in *cachots* and brigades recalled the deaths of fellow detainees and could list by name many of those who had died. A prisoner who had spent one month in a brigade met 11 other prisoners from his own area there; by the time he left the brigade, nine of them had been killed. They were shot dead by soldiers; the other prisoners were made to load their corpses onto a lorry for them to be taken to the morgue. An elderly man remembered 14 young prisoners from his *cachot* who died as a result of beatings: "I carried their bodies... They didn't die straightaway. They used to bang people's heads against the walls until blood came out of their ears."

Patterns of torture were replicated across *cachots* and brigades in different parts of the country. The military and police guarding the *cachots* could do as they pleased; no one held them to account. Usually, prisoners were severely beaten immediately after their arrest and during interrogations intended to extract confessions of guilt. One man told us how soldiers tied bricks to his testicles when he was sitting down and told him to stand up; they did this in order to make him confess.

In many *cachots*, there was a regular routine of beatings and humiliation, several times a day. Prisoners called it "the morning tea", because it was often administered first thing in the morning. Prisoners were also systematically beaten and humiliated when they were taken out to go to the toilets. Twice a day, the guards would take the prisoners out, one group at a time, to the open-air toilets located at some distance from the *cachot*, and beat them all the way there and all the way back. The prisoners were allowed at most one or two minutes at the toilets, then all of them had to go back at the same time. The soldiers or police threw stones at them while they used the toilets, especially if they hadn't finished in time. One prisoner recalled: "We only had a few seconds. We were like baboons. It was all in the open, in the forest. It was a hole covered with logs. Some people fell through the logs as it was wobbly, into the pit." In one *cachot*, the prisoners first had to dig the hole themselves: "We put wood over it, like a bridge," one of them told us. "It wasn't covered or sheltered; it was in the open air. Around 40 of us would go to the toilet at one time, half of us facing one way, and half the other. When the ditch was full, we covered it and dug another one."

In some detention centres, there was a slightly different routine. A prisoner who had been held in a brigade told us: "We had to defecate into plastic bags which we threw into a bucket (in the cell), but there was urine all over the floor and we mopped it up with old fabric and wrang it out into the bucket. The bucket was emptied in the morning and in the evening, carried by two people handcuffed to each other, one walking backwards. Once they got to the toilets, they couldn't even use the toilets as they couldn't take their trousers down because of the handcuffs."

Prisoners who were suspected of reporting incidents of ill-treatment could be punished for doing so. One man told us how he and another prisoner had been beaten after they were seen talking to an ICRC representative who visited their *cachot*. "The Red Cross woman used to visit to help the prisoners. Sometimes they didn't allow her in, so when we saw her, we all used to clap. We liked her a lot. One detainee in the *cachot* had bad sores on his legs and really stank. When she saw this, she was very concerned. She went to the IPJ [*inspecteur de police judiciaire*, local police investigator] and made a complaint. After she had gone, the IPJ called me to punish me for talking to her. He made me lie down next to the sick man. He beat us both for several minutes with a club studded with four very big nails. We both screamed."

Prisoners were also subjected to relentless psychological torture and humiliation. A former prisoner recalled: "They used to say to us: 'You're killers, you're less than shit. You'll stay here forever.' Once a sub-lieutenant said: 'Why are there so many people here? Why hasn't the military in charge got rid of all these people?' "

Visits

In the *cachots* and brigades, visits were literally a matter of life and death for the prisoners: the government did not feed them, so they were entirely dependent on their families for their survival. Knowing this, the families struggled to visit every day, or almost every day. They spent all their money and time – sometimes several hours a day – going backwards and forwards to feed the prisoners. Failure to do so would have meant letting the prisoners starve to death. According to a representative of a non-governmental organisation, the situation was so serious that it affected the entire rural economy, as the prisoners' families didn't have any time left to grow their own crops.

Prisoners who received no visits at all had to rely on other prisoners to share their food with them; many spent several days in a row without eating. A man who was detained in a brigade estimated that at least 30% of the prisoners held with him never received any food from outside. In 1997, during a period of widespread shortage of food and general hunger in parts of Rwanda, prisoners in some *cachots* were reduced to picking up scraps which had fallen on the ground during the visits or rummaging through the wheelbarrows of rubbish. An elderly prisoner remembered the shortage of water: "Whenever we saw a few drops of water on the ground, it was a big thing." Two prisoners who became friends worked out an arrangement with their families, who were neighbours: they asked each of them to come to the *cachot* on different days, three times a week, so that both families would not have to come every day. The prisoners then shared what they brought, as far as they could. One of them asked his mother to bring extra food for some of his co-detainees, but she was unable to.

In the first few years, visitors were not allowed to talk to the prisoners. If they were lucky, the prisoners could peep out from the door of the *cachot* to see their visitors, or the visitors could peer through the window to see the prisoners. One prisoner said that in the early days, he just used to look at his children through the window, and they used to blink to indicate they had seen him. Sometimes, the prisoners were allowed to come out and see their visitors from a distance, but not to talk to them. A prisoner who had been detained in a military brigade said some of the guards there deliberately made the prisoners put their heads down so that they couldn't see the visitors at all.

Visitors were made to drop the food at a specific point and leave straightaway. One prisoner was designated to come out to collect the food and take it back to his colleagues. The process was completely depersonalised. In some *cachots*, prisoners had to recognise the food destined for them by the container in which it was brought. A prisoner explained: "We identified the visitor from the objects, for example by the plates or bowls, but if a bowl had been bought later so that we didn't recognise it, or if we didn't recognise what was brought for us, we didn't get it. Visitors didn't specify the prisoner they were visiting. They were afraid of being beaten. We had to identify what was for us from the utensils."

Women were harassed when they came to visit their husbands or brothers in the *cachots*. A woman whose husband spent seven years in a *cachot* was harassed by several military guards, including one who wanted her to become his wife. "Once they held me for one hour... They beat me three times and said: 'Why do you keep coming back to see that *interahamwe*?' Once a military guard from the *cachot* came to my house and asked me to be his wife. He said: 'Why are you running after that killer?' I said I would not abandon my husband. He came twice, then he stopped. When I visited the *cachot*, I saw him again. He threatened me. He was transferred later."

There were reports of women being raped by soldiers guarding the *cachots*. A prisoner who was detained in a *cachot* for six and a half years told us: "Wives of other prisoners were often beaten, chased away or raped. We used to hear the screams. There was nothing we could do because those who were doing it were the ones who were in charge – the soldiers. My wife wasn't raped but she was beaten a lot. It felt like suicide for her to visit me. For the first two years, it was like this."

There was also the prisoner's humiliation at being beaten in front of the family, and the family's pain at having to witness this. A former prisoner still remembered the day when his son had visited him and brought him tea in a container. The container fell on the ground. As his father bent down to pick it up, a soldier beat him hard on his back, in front of his son. Once, a man detained in a brigade was beaten in front of his mother when she came to bring him food. He watched her crying while the soldiers bashed his foot. That was the last time he saw her. She told his wife she would never go back to that place where they beat her son. She died one year later.

Eventually, thanks to the intervention of international organisations, the abuse of visitors decreased and detainees were able to talk to their families for a few minutes. Visiting time was bought. One prisoner recalled that the price set by the police guards for five minutes of visiting time was a bottle of beer, but the exact price varied according to the price of Primus, one of the most popular makes of beer in Rwanda. The wife of another prisoner had measured the improvements over the seven years her husband had spent in a *cachot*: "Things have changed over time. In the first phase, I saw him through the window. For the whole of the first year, I only saw his face in the window of the *cachot*, from a distance. It was just a look. We couldn't even wave or talk. He could see I had come, that was all. In the second phase, I saw his whole body. In the third phase, we had a brief visit and we talked. We could give 500 francs to the guards to get three minutes to chat outside. The detainees came out to get the food themselves and we talked."

Prisoners' testimonies

The testimonies below, from those who survived the *cachots* and the brigades, act as a kind of testament to those who died there.[1]

47-year-old man from Kibuye:

> "I spent two and a half years in the *cachot*... I was seriously beaten by the assistant *bourgmestre*, the police and the military There were more than 300 of us, all accused of genocide... all in one room. We used to try to get pieces of paper to use as fans, just to be able to breathe. There were windows but they were always closed. When we tried to open them, people from outside threw stones at us, so we preferred to keep them closed. We couldn't stand up. We were sitting all day. We tried lying down but we couldn't sleep. As soon as we lay down, the police poured water in through the door or the windows, deliberately, to stop us from sleeping. We had to clean up the water. There was no question really of sleeping or lying down.
>
> There was water to wash but we weren't allowed to use it. To go to the toilet, it was painful... They waited for us at the door of the

---

[1]   Most of these testimonies refer to the period 1994 to 1999, before international organisations intervened to improve the conditions in the *cachots*.

cachot and each one was beaten as he passed. It was the same on the way back. We all had to go at the same time. Those who couldn't wait had pots or old wrappings. They urinated in them and emptied them the next morning. Sometimes people were beaten as they held the pots, so the contents fell out and they made us pick it up with our bare hands.

I was transferred to [the central] prison in September 1998. We were beaten along the way. One person died from the beatings. 124 detainees were taken in one truck. We couldn't breathe. Our stomachs were squashed against the chests of others. We were piled in. The truck had difficulty driving as it was overloaded, and almost broke down. We had to hold onto the collar of the person in front so as not to fall. One person died of suffocation in the truck."

43-year-old man from Gitarama:

"I was arrested in January 1996… I was taken to the *cachot*. I stayed there until March 2003. There were 700 or 715 prisoners at the beginning. At the end, there were about 500… In 1997, a detainee was killed when he went to the toilet outside. Soldiers took him to one side and killed him. I witnessed it. Then the prisoners who had witnessed it were threatened.

We were always afraid. Every morning, we were beaten. They used to called it "tea". On my first day, the prisoners asked me: "Have you had your tea?" I didn't know what this meant so I said: "No, my family hasn't come yet." They explained what it meant. The military and survivors [of the genocide] outside used to beat us. The toilets were outside, about 200 metres from the *cachot*. We used to have to run there. They called it *kimbia*, which means 'run' in Swahili. The survivors lined up and hit us with sticks…

This huge fear meant that people kept quiet and said nothing. We didn't dare speak about the ill-treatment…

Each of us had two bricks. That was our bed... it was forbidden
to have a blanket. We had to sleep on the concrete. We could see
people's bones and their wounds."

46-year-old woman from Kigali:

"Outside there were dead people who had been buried.
Sometimes the rain would wash away to show a leg sticking
out. This was what we saw on the way to the toilet. I also saw a
man half-dead across our path, naked, unconscious but
unrecognisable. He had been tortured and thrown there. We had
to walk over him. He didn't move. He was in agony. He was
there throughout the time I was there."

62-year-old man from Butare:

"We were so many, I can't remember the number. There were
epidemics and lots of deaths... When you wake up, you find that
the person next to you is dead. It is terrible to wake up next to a
corpse. I suffered from that illness, I think it was typhoid, and
almost died. Sometimes the police took us to the dispensary but
they couldn't take all of us as too many were sick. They just took
the most serious cases. There were dead bodies everywhere in the
cachot. About 45 people died...

An official questioned me and told me I was accused of genocide.
He asked me if I had killed. When I said no, he beat me. He took
me into a room and locked it. He closed the curtains and beat me
so seriously I thought I would die. He aimed for the sensitive
parts, kicking me in the testicles. When I came out, I couldn't
walk as he had stamped on my legs... I spent one week lying
down. I couldn't sit or stand. Other prisoners poured a bit of
water over me. I had abscesses all over... My whole body was
swollen. The swellings continued until I was transferred to
prison... I still suffer from the after-effects. My body burns where
I was beaten."

46-year-old man from Cyangugu:

> "After one week, an officer came with the *bourgmestre* and said my
> file didn't contain enough evidence and I should be released...
> They were going to release me, but a commander intervened. He
> intimidated me and made me admit I'd killed people. He took out
> his gun and said: 'I kill five people every day, so I can easily kill
> you too.' I admitted I had killed other people in order to save my
> life...

> One day, a prisoner escaped. They beat us morning, midday and
> evening as a punishment. One of the guards particularly beat us.
> One person died as a result. We were kept in 11 rooms... To
> punish us, they moved us all into just five rooms. I had a whole
> month with no sleep. We could only lie back on the chest of the
> person behind to sleep. 28 people died in that month. I had a
> book where I noted the deaths and the causes. People died of
> weakness, sickness from lack of food or lack of sleep, suffocation
> and beatings. I saw two people beaten to death."

Improvements in conditions of detention

The conditions in the *cachots* were slower to improve than those in the
central prisons. The transfer of prisoners from the *cachots* to the central
prisons was supposed to be a continuous and regular process, but as the
prisons filled up to several times their capacity, transfers stopped, and the
overcrowding in the *cachots* increased further. In 1998, approximately 40,000
out of Rwanda's total prison population of around 130,000 were held in
cachots. Over the following years, transfers gradually resumed as prisoners
started being released from the central prisons. The living conditions in the
cachots also began improving after the ICRC and other international
organisations intervened. As in the central prisons, prisoners talked of two
phases in the *cachots*: a first phase in the early years, when many people died,
and a second "easier" phase after the ICRC intervened. Ill-treatment by the
military and police decreased, and detainees were finally able to receive
visits, talk to their families, and even work outside. The non-governmental

organisation Dignité en Détention set up a work project which ran for four years in six different *cachots*. The project was designed to be beneficial not only to prisoners, but also to their families and to survivors of the genocide. One of the aims was to bring the prisoners and the genocide survivors closer together; part of the profits from the prisoners' work were donated to survivors in the local area.

In some *cachots*, the regime eventually became so relaxed that questions could legitimately be asked about whether it really constituted detention. Some prisoners managed to go outside without even pretending to join a work team and could pay the guards to allow them to go and see their family. Some even set up their own business from the *cachot*. We were told about one group of detainees who were running a taxi business. Prisoners held in rural areas were spotted in the capital, Kigali. As prisoners in the *cachots* do not wear uniforms, they would not have been easily identifiable as prisoners. These prisoners apparently used to travel regularly to Kigali to work, stay out all day, then go back to the *cachot* to sleep at night.

By the end of 2004, almost all the *cachots* had been closed after prisoners had gradually been transferred to the central prisons. Only a handful of *cachots* remained open, in Gitarama and Butare provinces.

CHAPTER XI

Three minutes:

prison visits

In the dusty courtyard in Kigali Central Prison, in November 2004, a prisoner draws two lines in sawdust on the ground. The metal gate of the prison rests slightly open, and there is a group of prisoners clustered behind it, peering out. Three or four guards lounge nonchalantly outside the gate. A few metres away, a large crowd of visitors is waiting patiently in an amorphous group which stretches up the hill towards the main barrier. They are mostly women, some children, not very many men. The women are dressed in a jumble of bright colours: green, yellow, purple, red. They carry baskets full of provisions or stand next to large bags which they have put down on the ground. The children stand by quietly.

The first group of prisoners, around 50 of them, emerges from the gate and sits down on the nearest row of long benches which have been placed on one side of the sawdust line. A guard whistles, and the first group of visitors lunges forward to take their seats on the second row of benches opposite the prisoners. It takes a few seconds for the visitors to spot the prisoner they have come to visit, but the procedure is not as chaotic as might be expected. The families have perfected it with years of practice. The prisoners on one side and the visitors on the other are packed together so tightly on the benches that they barely have room to move. There is a frantic exchange of provisions and full and empty containers, and a frantic exchange of words. Two or three guards patrol these exchanges half-heartedly, on either side of the two benches. Suddenly, one of the guards blows his whistle again and the visitors have to leave. They grab their empty baskets, throw out a few last words, step over the bench and make their way back up the slope to where the next group is waiting. Those who dare to linger for more than a few seconds are chased away by guards wielding thin sticks. The prisoners inspect their new provisions, then amble back in through the gate.

From the first whistle to the second whistle, the visit has lasted less than two minutes. Then the next group of prisoners comes out, the second group of visitors rushes forward, and the whole routine is repeated. Some of these families had travelled for miles, for hours, for those two minutes, to be able to hand over a bowl of food, a few bananas, to say a few words of greetings, and to leave again. Until the next time.

Many prisoners had already spoken to me about the conditions of visits before I witnessed these visits with my own eyes. They had told me the visits lasted a maximum of three minutes. I had thought they were exaggerating. They were not. I timed the visit in Kigali Central Prison. If anything, the prisoners were overestimating.

Once, in Kigali Central Prison, I interviewed a female prisoner on a visit day. We were sitting just outside the guards' office, in view of the general visits on the benches. I noticed she was keeping an eye on the yard while she was talking to me. I asked her whether she was expecting a visit. She said maybe, she wasn't sure. A little later, another prisoner came to tell her that her visitor was waiting for her, and she excused herself. She returned within about three minutes. She had spoken to her visitor, everything was fine, she said, and we resumed the interview. I was shocked that the visit could really have taken place in such a short time, and that she wasn't showing any sign of emotion, but I didn't say anything. For her, it was normal. It didn't even occur to her to comment.

A special day is designated for children to visit. The children's visits take place in the same conditions, on the same benches in the same position. The only difference is that there are fewer visitors, so the guards may be slightly more generous with the time, perhaps granting four or five minutes instead of three. The children are mostly unaccompanied; in some cases, the adults may be waiting outside. Some of them are dressed in their best clothes, as if they're going to church or to a wedding. Little boys in three-piece suits, little girls in stiffly ironed dresses with bows and lace. Some bring bags of food, but are less heavily laden than the women. When the first whistle blows, they take their places on the bench and sit quietly opposite their fathers, their uncles (we watched the men's visit). Observing from a distance, most of the conversations appear to be one-sided, and less animated than during the general visits: it is the prisoners who speak, and the children listen. On one end of the bench, an older prisoner is talking to a teenage girl, almost certainly his daughter, gesticulating with his finger, dispensing some advice or instruction on how she should lead her life. It seems that fathers are still figures of authority, or think they are, even when they are dressed in pink uniforms. At the other end of the bench, I spot a prisoner we had interviewed a few days earlier, sitting with his arms around his children, chatting with them calmly and affectionately. When the second whistle is blown, most of the children leave immediately, but a few are allowed to linger. We walk towards the father who is still talking to his children. He greets us warmly with a beaming smile and introduces us to his children one by one. The oldest is 13, the second one is nine; the two youngest ones are eating wafers. Perhaps he treated them to these wafers himself. I talk to the children but they are too shy to engage in a conversation with me, despite their father's best encouragements. We all smile, everyone is relaxed, it is as if we are visiting this family in their living-room. We stand there in the sun for another minute or so, making idle conversation, until the guards round up the last stragglers and the children leave. We say goodbye. Just three days earlier, we had spent two or three hours talking to this man about his hopeless situation. He is accused of genocide and was just starting his eighth year in prison. He has been sentenced to death.

We witnessed visits in other prisons too. The basic conditions and the absurdly short time were the same in all of them, with some slight variations, depending on the goodwill of the prison director and the mood of the guards.

In Cyangugu Central Prison, the atmosphere was different. Visits were highly organised and strictly monitored. When we arrived at the prison one morning, we found a very long queue of visitors snaking up the steep path of red earth which leads up to the barrier – again, mostly women, carrying heavily laden, brightly coloured baskets. At the barrier, at the front of the queue, in addition to the usual guards snoozing at their posts, there was a reception team of two or three prisoners sitting on chairs with paper and pens on their laps, conscientiously recording the names of the prisoners to be visited. Here, even more than in Kigali, many of the women would have travelled for miles to reach the prison from remote, rural areas, and would have spent hard-earned money on the journey. Those who had no money would have walked for hours, carrying their heavy provisions. They stood there waiting for their turn, their faces expressionless, dulled by exhaustion and the relentless monotony of this routine.

We greeted the guards and the prisoners sitting on the chairs and walked past the queue, past the barrier, and up the hill to the prison building. At the top, outside the forbidding brick fortress of the prison, a large group of prisoners was already in the throes of a visit. It is the same ritual as in Kigali, but in Cyangugu, there are no benches. Neither the prisoners nor their visitors are allowed to sit down. A tight row of prisoners faces a tight row of pre-dominantly female visitors, all standing up, all squashed together. A thin rope delineates the visiting area. Here, the guards patrol more vigilantly, randomly searching the contents of a woman's basket or a prisoner's pockets, waving their sticks and hitting people without hesitation. The guards don't physically hurt the visitors when they hit them; in fact most of the time, they lift their sticks as if to hit them but hit their baskets or bags instead. It is a game, a mindless show of authority.

The conditions of visits are among the most distressing aspects of life in the Rwandan prisons. They are distressing because of the completely unnecessary strictness and humiliation, the frustration, the sadness, the physical, mental and economic exhaustion of the families, and the denial of the basic comfort which visits should bring.

Visits from foreigners are the exception to this rule. Whenever we were working in the prisons, especially on visit days, I was painfully conscious of the huge disparity between the conditions in which family visits took place, and the conditions in which we, as complete strangers, were allowed to talk to prisoners. Armed with our letter of authorisation from the Ministry of Interior, we were granted almost unlimited access and unlimited time, without having to pay a single franc to any of the prison staff. We could stroll into the prison on any day of the week, except Sundays. We would be allocated a special office in which to work; the prisoners we wanted to speak to would be called out individually, and we would sit down, one to one, and talk privately for two or three hours, or as long as we wanted, with virtually no interruptions. The most serious inconveniences we encountered were the deafening sound of heavy rain on the corrugated iron roof, a loose piece of roofing flapping noisily in the wind, splashes of rain on our notebooks, or the coming and going of guards who were fetching documents from the office we were using. Even they would usually apologise for the interruption. In Gitarama Central Prison, where we were allocated the office used by the prisoners' *gacaca* committee, we occasionally had to pause while a nosy prisoner pretended to search for something in the room in the hope of listening to our conversations. The rest of the time, we were left alone.

On our last visit to Gitarama prison, my colleague was talking to a prisoner we had met several times before when his wife happened to turn up for her regular visit. We had met her previously too, and we were beginning to know and understand the story of their family. My colleague invited her into the little office so that she could chat to her husband. They embraced formally and sat down next to each other on the wooden chairs. My colleague offered to leave them together but both eagerly insisted that she stay. Her presence was their passport: it allowed them to meet in these exceptional conditions. They talked for about 50 minutes, constantly and quietly, maintaining a certain physical distance. This was probably the longest and calmest visit they had experienced in the nine years he had spent in prison. Both of them expressed their warm appreciation for this opportunity, pointing out that it would have cost them a lot of money to pay for a meeting like this in normal circumstances. Towards the end of the time, they became anxious that the guards might intervene, so although no one interrupted their meeting, they voluntarily stopped and the wife left.

I recall an earlier visit to Kigali Central Prison, in 1999, when I went to see a friend in prison who was very sick. I had timed my visit badly, as it coincided with a day of family visits, and I didn't have a special authorisation. Hundreds of people were gathered in the yard. I was told that it would be impossible for me to see my friend because there were too many people. I pleaded with a friendly guard, and after a few minutes of negotiation, he agreed. Then I was told that my friend was too sick to see me. I insisted, slightly desperately, as I only had a few days left in the country. The guard went back to see what he could do. Eventually a group of prisoners brought my friend out on a stretcher as he was too weak to walk. They put the stretcher down in the middle of the crowd of waiting visitors. I sat down on the dusty ground next to him and we talked for about half an hour, with the sound of other visitors' conversations buzzing around us. Even though he was weak and demoralised, it was an uplifting moment. When he became tired, we said goodbye and he was taken back in on the stretcher. I was deeply grateful for this visit, but overwhelmed by guilt as I knew that none of his relatives would ever have been able to secure this amount of time with him.

Conditions of visits in the central prisons

There are two or three days allocated for prison visits: one or two days during the week, and Saturdays for employees of the state. Families who live near the prison and who have sufficient means can visit once a week. We met some prisoners who received weekly visits, and many more who received a visit only every few weeks, every few months, or even just once or twice a year. They were at pains to point out that the frequency or regularity of visits was not an indicator of the extent of commitment of their family, but rather of the family's ability to support them financially and the distance from their home to the prison. In a typical example, one prisoner told us that his wife and 18-year-old son visited him in alternate months. The journey from their home to the prison took six hours, and the visit lasted two minutes. Some families live so far away that they have to spend one or two nights along the way before reaching the prison.

In most prisons, the standard length for a visit is still three minutes. In practice, it may be a little more, or even a little less. In the words of a former prisoner: "If the guard is in a good mood, you get two minutes. If he is in a bad mood or has had a row with his wife, you get a few seconds." "We line up in two rows, behind ropes, like the Berlin wall", said a prisoner in Cyangugu. "We throw words at each other. We get a few crumbs of minutes, never more than one or two. Then the guards whistle and everyone is chased away and shoved around." For most prisoners, these two or three humiliating minutes may be the only opportunity they ever have to step outside and get a breath of fresh air.

The names of the prisoners to be visited are jotted down on a list, which a prisoner then calls out on a loudspeaker, inside the prison. The prisoners line up in the yard inside until their name is called out. It is a long process as there can be hundreds of names on the list. They call out the names block by block, then 50 to 100 are taken out at a time. The *capita général* of Gitarama prison described the timetable there: "Families arrive from 6.30am and come into the yard from 7.30. From 8.30 we call prisoners from the lists given by the families and ask them to come out. From 8.30 to 2.30, prisoners come out. They talk for two or three minutes then go back inside, then the next group comes out." Before going out to meet their visitors, the prisoners have to put on their pink uniforms; no prisoner is allowed out into the yard without a uniform. Those who don't own a uniform have to borrow one.

The cruelly short time-limit on prison visits has completely altered the nature of communication between prisoners and their families. In societies where visits in reasonable conditions are considered a basic right of prisoners, one of the main purposes of a visit is to talk to the prisoner, provide reassurance, encouragement and comfort, as well as news. In Rwanda, there is no time for this, unless it can all be squeezed into one or two sentences. The visits are functional, not social, and serve two basic purposes: to provide food or other items to the prisoner, and to give the prisoner news of the family. In practical terms, it is a one-way relationship: the family gives – food or information – and the prisoner receives. The prisoner has nothing to give, except a shopping list for the next visit, advice on family matters or an often futile request for the family to follow up the case-file with the prosecutor's office. One prisoner summed up the situation: "You can't call the visits real visits. It's just time to pass over a bag... It is a pretence of a visit."

An offering of food, clothes or other basic necessities is a self-imposed imperative for all visits. A visitor who has nothing to bring might as well not come. The prisoners expect every visitor to bring something, even when they know that those outside are struggling to make ends meet. The prisoners' families feel this pressure and may not visit for months on end if they cannot afford to bring anything. The very functional nature of these visits is also apparent in the frequent practice of wives or husbands sending someone else, usually a child or a neighbour, to take provisions to the prison instead of going there themselves. The priority is sustenance and the duty is to provide material support, however meagre it may be. The rest takes second place.

Visiting day, Kigali Central Prison, 1999   © Fiona Lloyd-Davies/Panos Pictures

The rules on what visitors are and are not allowed to bring to prisoners have changed over time. In most prisons, visitors are allowed to bring cooked food or food which can be eaten raw, such as fruit, but not food which has to be cooked before being eaten. However, some prisons are more flexible and visitors can bring in almost any type of food, which prisoners then arrange to cook themselves with their own semi-clandestine cooking facilities, separate from the official kitchens. Visitors also bring other items: sugar, tea, clothes, soap and other toiletries, books and newspapers. In some prisons, such as Gitarama, visitors are not allowed to bring in items which are sold in the prison shop if they have bought them elsewhere; goods bought from the shop are marked with a label to enable guards to identify them. In practice, this rule is regularly flouted. Visitors also bring medicines to prisoners who are sick. The provision of medicines is important, as only a limited range is available in the prison hospital.

The quantity as well as the quality of provisions varies enormously, depending on what the families can afford. During the visits that we witnessed, we couldn't see everything that families had brought, because the food was neatly wrapped up in bags or containers. However, we noticed one lucky prisoner in Cyangugu receiving a large shopping bag full of huge, bright green, luscious avocados. He piled the avocados into a large plastic bucket, right up to the brim; as he kept adding more, others tumbled out because there were too many to fit in the bucket. He would probably start selling them to his fellow inmates as soon as he got back inside.

Money

Money is forbidden in the prisons. Yet the prisons run on a cash economy, and most of this cash comes from the families. In the words of one prisoner: "Nothing is very prohibited so if we're caught, it's not too serious."

It is easy to smuggle money into the prison. Those who are supposed to stop the inflow of money are the first to benefit from it, and the percentage for the guard who allows it in can immediately be deducted and handed over. Sometimes this traffic is negotiated directly between the prisoner – or the visitor – and the guard, and a handling fee is agreed in advance. In other cases, a guard may intercept the money on a random search and help himself to some or all of it. Visitors conceal money in a variety of ways, sometimes so skilfully that the intended beneficiary doesn't even find it. A woman who had been detained in two different prisons had seen this happen several times: "Visitors used to hide things or slip money into the food. A prisoner could receive a pineapple and sell it to another prisoner, for example for 100 francs, without realising there was a 1,000- franc note inside. The buyer could get a surprise. The person who received it from her family didn't even know. The visitors didn't have time to tell her, or the guard was there so they couldn't say anything."

Families who have sufficient means may slip money to their prisoners for general use inside the prison, but most times, prisoners ask their families for a specific sum of money for a specific purpose: for example 5,000 francs to buy a better space to sleep, or a few hundred francs for a uniform or a pair of sandals. The family then scrapes the money together as best they can before the next visit. In practice, this money would not always be spent on the specified purpose, or only a proportion of it would be; the remainder would go to the *capita* for his commission. Likewise with food, clothes and other items which the families carefully choose for their relatives: very often, these items are not consumed or used by the prisoners themselves, but are sold on to other prisoners for cash.

Money is particularly useful for buying time – extended visits. It is usually the visitors rather than the prisoners who pay the guards for this privilege. Through arrangement, they can then talk quietly, privately, away from the crowds, for a few extra minutes, or even half an hour or an hour. In the yard in Kigali Central Prison, we noticed a prisoner sitting on a small bench with one or two visitors in a sheltered alcove, away from the mêlée on the long benches in the glaring sun. They sat there talking and talking, as if they were sitting on their own front doorstep. Meanwhile, several successive groups of prisoners and visitors came and went under their three-minute curfew, just a few metres in front of them.

The prison directors are fully aware of this practice but do nothing to curb it. It is a matter to be negotiated directly with the guards. The fee varies, depending on the duration of the visit, the disposition of the guard and the number of guards who have to be paid. Sometimes several guards get involved in the transactions: a visitor can pay one guard and start talking to the prisoner, then the guard leaves, and another one comes and demands to be paid too. These longer visits are extremely valuable to prisoners and their families, even if they can't afford them on a regular basis.

Exceptional visits

In addition to the general visits, families can arrange a special visit through the *social* if there are specific problems which require a longer discussion, for example deaths in the family, financial problems, or difficulties with the children. These special visits are intended to be exceptional and cover a limited range of situations. Either the *social* or a guard is usually present during the visit. One prisoner had arranged several such visits for his family. He said being able to participate in these meetings and in family decisions make him feel like he was still part of the family. However, these special visits always take place on a weekday, so families who work during the week are usually unable to take advantage of them.

Prisoners in positions of responsibility – the *capitas*, those responsible for security, and others – are automatically granted longer visits, usually at least 15 minutes, and sometimes longer. These longer visits are free: they are one of the perks of the job. One of the *capitas* admitted that it was somewhat unfair: "It is like a favour. Favours are not equal. The representatives of prisoners have longer and better visits. They put out benches for us. The director authorised me to get visits without paying, even when it is not a visiting day." Prisoners who work in the carpentry, sewing or other work-shops in the prison compound also find it easier to receive longer visits as the workshops are situated outside the main prison building and are less closely monitored by the guards.

The other category of prisoners who benefit from exceptionally long visits are those who work outside the prison. Prisoners on the work teams are in a uniquely privileged position to be able to fix an appointment to meet their relatives or friends in a designated place at a designated time, sometimes far away from the prison. These are better described as social meetings and are as different from the prison visits as can be imagined. Prisoners or their families pay the guard accompanying the work team and can spend several hours, even a whole day, chatting near the site where they are supposed to be working. A former prisoner said that the guards who supervised the work teams were not really guards at all, but *accompagnateurs* – just there to accompany them. There are different tariffs, according to the length of the visit. The guard calculates the "service"; each time, the prisoners and the families have to start the negotiations from scratch. A prisoner told us that in Byumba Central Prison, the price of a meeting with the family depended on the status of the prisoner: a peasant paid 100 francs, while a better-off person paid 500 francs. His wife had had to pay 1,000 francs, but he said it was worth it.

A man whose father had been in prison for more than nine years said that when his father joined the work teams, it transformed the nature of their contacts: "In 1998 my father could work outside. He made bricks, built houses, and cultivated. He used to give us appointments to meet him, in writing, and told us where he would be. We had to go to the guard and give him 1,000 francs for each rendezvous. He found us a house or a quiet place near where they worked. We were completely free there. We could talk for a long time, even a whole day. We could do it every day if we wanted to. It was profitable for the guards. A group of five to ten relatives used to visit him like this." A similar situation prevailed in some of the *cachots* in the later years. A former prisoner who was held in a *cachot* used to see his wife regularly when he worked outside fetching water and firewood; his youngest child was conceived during this period of his detention. Another prisoner specifically arranged to go out to work when he knew the team was likely to be working close to his house. He was able to see his house from the place where they collected straw for the tomatoes, and was very pleased to see with his own eyes that his wife had had electricity installed.

Working outside the prison was also an opportunity to meet other acquaintances, by chance. Prisoners never knew whom they might meet. A former prisoner had not received any visits from his family until 2000, when he started working outside the prison. One day he met somebody he knew outside: "He had thought I was dead and I had thought he was dead. He told my family he had seen me. They had not visited me until then, I don't know why. I like to think they didn't know I was there. Afterwards, they started visiting me, occasionally."

Aeroplanes

For most prisoners, however, the only outlet for the frustration of the three-minute visit is the written word. Letters are officially forbidden in the prisons, but many prisoners smuggle letters out to their families. These letters are called *avions* – aeroplanes – or *indege* in Kinyarwanda. When a prisoner receives a letter, a plane has landed. There is a special language, a special technique for folding the paper, and a special strategy for sending letters out of the prison. The language is one which is unique to the prisoner and their relative (usually the husband or the wife), so it is intimate and personal, yet the information or requests contained in the letter are usually very mundane. The letters are normally written on a thin sheet of paper, in elaborately small handwriting, with no space between the lines and no margins. It is then folded up tight, many times, until it can fit in the palm of a hand or be tucked into a sock or a shoe. The strategy for sending it out of the prison is simple: the prisoner pays a guard who will either allow the prisoner to give it directly to a visitor or agree to send it out himself. Some prisoners entrust their letters to fellow prisoners who have maintained extensive contacts outside. A creative young man, who was only 15 when he was arrested, sent his mother four cassette tapes which he recorded for her in the prison. In his taped messages, he talked to his mother about his life in prison and thanked her for supporting him.

The aeroplanes fly in both directions: families employ similar stratagems to write to the prisoners. There are a number of standard tricks which families use to escape the attention of the guards. One of the favourites is stuffing the tiny letter into the food they bring; letters are buried in the cooked food or inserted into fruit or vegetables. Once they had learnt to work the system, some prisoners and their families relied almost entirely on these letters to communicate with each other, instead of struggling to talk during prison visits. Sometimes aeroplanes even flew between prisoners held in different prisons. Some messages were more valuable on paper than if they had been communicated verbally, because they had a certain permanence: a prisoner who had received a letter from his wife comforting him after he was sentenced to death had kept this message and would take it out and read it whenever he had difficulty sleeping at night.

In the early days, the Red Cross distributed forms to prisoners to write to their families. This was a vital channel of communication. It enabled many prisoners and their relatives to get back in touch with each other, especially if their families were still in exile. But there were restrictions on what could be said in these letters. They could only be used for greetings and for communicating innocuous news. Their main function was to inform the family that they were still alive and in which prison they were detained. Letters which contained messages deemed too "political" were not delivered.

Solitude

A significant number of prisoners receive no visits at all. Several thousand, at least, fall into this category. They include the old and the young, and every age in between.

Some have made tireless efforts to try to trace their families, year after year, using every possible avenue to contact their relatives. Others have given up. After a number of years, exhaustion sets in, and prisoners may be afraid of finding out the real reasons why their families have not visited them.

Those who never receive visits are among the most vulnerable of all the prisoners; they are also often economically the worst-off. Their links with the outside world have been completely severed. A few of those we met – the more sociable and enterprising ones – had formed close friendships with other prisoners, but most had retreated into further isolation, drawing themselves inwards into a private solitude within the crowd.

In Kigali Central Prison, I met a 41-year-old prisoner who had not received any visits since his arrest ten years earlier. He didn't know whether members of his family were alive or dead. He had tried sending messages to them via the Red Cross but had never received a reply. Every aspect of his ten years in prison had been unrelentingly bad; he had no money, slept outdoors, and didn't take part in many activities in the prison. He didn't want to join any of the work teams as he was afraid it would make him think about the world outside. He answered my questions simply and briefly, but didn't have much to say; his life had been reduced to so little. His ten years of suffering didn't even appear to elicit any indignation, although he told me that he had still not got used to life in prison. He talked but did not expect our conversation to be of any consequence. It seemed that the silence from his family had pushed him into a corner from which he no longer even hoped to emerge.

The absence of visits also affects prisoners' material quality of life. Even though all prisoners are provided with food in the prisons, those who don't regularly receive supplements from their family face shortages and no variety. On the frequent occasions when there is a shortage of food, they simply do not eat, unless other prisoners share some of their own supplies with them, or unless they can afford to buy extra food from other prisoners. Occasionally, religious organisations visit the prisons and donate food, clothes and other items. In addition, prisoners have their own system of solidarity to help those who don't receive visits. In a number of prisons, every prisoner who receives food from a visitor puts a proportion aside into a "bank" to redistribute to the most needy. Substantial quantities are sometimes collected in this way.

There are various reasons why prisoners may receive no visits: in the most extreme cases, their relatives may all have been killed, while others may have fled the country. In other cases, they may still be alive, possibly even living in

Rwanda, but lost touch after the genocide and never resumed contact. Some simply live too far away. Others may live close by and know that their relative is in prison, but a lack of means or a combination of fear and hopelessness prevents them from visiting.

In Butare Central Prison, I met a prisoner in his forties who was married with six children and had had no news of his family since 1997. He was very poor and suffered from chronic ill-health, in large part due to beatings he had received in the brigade where he was previously detained. Several times during our conversation, he had to rest his head on the table because he was suffering from acute pains. He had no possessions, no money, and slept outside, in the prison yard. His family used to live in the neighbouring province of Gikongoro. He had made three separate requests to be transferred to Gikongoro prison, to be closer to his home area, but had never received a reply from the authorities. He seemed to have lost hope, not only in his own situation, but of ever hearing from his family again. I offered to try to contact his family as we were planning to go to Gikongoro. He said he would be delighted and gave me vague directions to the place where his wife used to live, and the address of an uncle. Some days later, we travelled to Gikongoro but discovered that the place where his family lived was very far away and the road had become impassable because of the rain. Instead, we wrote a short letter to his wife, explaining that we had met her husband in Butare prison, and entrusted it to a priest who regularly visited the area. A couple of weeks later, we returned to Butare and visited the prisoner again. We explained the difficulties in reaching his home area and told him we had sent a letter to his wife instead. He was very grateful, but seemed almost more appreciative of our second visit than of our attempt to contact his wife. It was unclear whether he expected our letter to produce any results.

Visits: the early years

In the first few years after the genocide, prison visits took place in even harsher conditions, if they were allowed at all. Families could spend months without knowing where their relatives were detained or even if they were still alive. Visitors and prisoners alike were physically ill-treated, insulted and humiliated by the guards who, at that time, were military. A prison director could suddenly suspend visits without warning and without explanation. Sometimes the guards took the food but didn't deliver it to the prisoners; at other times they threw the food away for no reason or stamped on it, in front of the visitors. They used to stir the food to check whether anything was concealed inside. In some prisons, the prisoners were forced to eat all the food which the visitors brought right there on the spot, in front of the visitors and the guards, in just one or two minutes; anything they couldn't consume within that time was left behind. The guards indulged in other forms of gratuitous humiliation, making the visitors sit on the ground or crouch down like frogs. A prisoner recalled a visit during which a guard ripped off a nun's headdress and threw it on the ground.

The ill-treatment during visits caused some families to stop visiting completely for several months. A man described the first visit he received from his son: his son, who was in his early twenties, was beaten by a guard for daring to come forward to embrace his father. He never came again.

Prisoners and their visitors used to have to stand several metres apart and shout to each other, or make signs; it was impossible to hear or to talk properly as hundreds of people were shouting at the same time. One prisoner compared it to a flock of birds, all crying out together. In some prisons, they were not even allowed to touch each other or to embrace. This situation continued in some prisons until relatively recently.

A young man who was arrested in 1995 had lost all direct contact with his family, who had fled to Congo, until 1997. Two years after his arrest, he received his first visit. "My sister came. I was very happy but the conditions were impossible... We just saw each other and looked at each other. We couldn't talk. There were three metres between us. You could only shout. Around 150 people were shouting at the same time." A former prisoner described the mad scramble when the starting signal was given: "The prisoners lined up outside. Visitors peered to see if the prisoner they had come to visit was in the line. A guard whistled. A person at the end of the line may have to run to the other end of the line if his visitor happened to be there. People ran in both directions. They bumped into each other, there was pushing and shouting, it was chaos. Sometimes food fell on the ground. On a good day, prisoners and their visitors would be two metres apart. On a bad day, it was ten metres. Visitors were told to put their food down at five metres. Prisoners picked it up and went back in." He and his wife had worked out a code for indicating where he would stand in the line so that they wouldn't have to run from one end to the other, to save a few precious seconds. One prisoner told us that before each visit, he would prepare things to say, but when the time came, he didn't manage to say anything at all.

In the chaos surrounding the mass exodus from Rwanda in the last days of the genocide, many families got scattered. The huge number of arrests in the period that followed and the absence of records made it even harder to know who was where, who was alive and who was dead. The Red Cross operated an extensive tracing system to try to unite separated families and to establish communication between those who had stayed in Rwanda and those who were still refugees. Their success rate was impressive, but in the initial period, many people spent years without any news of their families and the letters they wrote remain unanswered or were returned to them.

When families eventually traced their relatives in prison, the reunion was often tinged with sadness, as almost always, the family brought news of other relatives who had died. The sadness was compounded by the impossible conditions in which the news had to be relayed.

A former prisoner who was among the first wave to be arrested, in July 1994, told us:

> "At the start my family didn't know I was still alive, so I didn't get any visits for the first six years. My family were refugees in Congo but I didn't know that at the time. It was only in 2000 that my cousin heard I was alive and started visiting me. They looked in all the prisons without finding me. My cousin knew a guard at PCK [Kigali Central Prison]. She gave him a piece of paper with my name and he found me... She came several times. The visits lasted one minute or less. There was a distance of two and a half metres. We had to shout as everyone else was talking. She told me most of my family had died, except my mother, who was very old. There were eight of us before. My mother came back to Rwanda while I was in prison. She was too old and poor to visit me."

The significance of visits for prisoners

Contact between prisoners and their families was the topic which elicited the strongest emotional response among the prisoners we talked to. For those lucky enough to receive even infrequent visits, these occasions were a mixture of joy, sadness and worry. For prisoners who had lost all contact with their family, the absence of visits was a source of immense grief and loneliness.

The majority of prisoners remain deeply disturbed by the conditions of prison visits. The impossibility of using these visits to discuss any issues of substance, together with the absence of privacy, are difficult to bear. Even those who have observed minor improvements over the years still find them painful. A man who had been in prison for ten years said: "Yes, things have changed with time. We used to have three minutes. Now we may have five minutes, but never more."

Nevertheless, for the prisoners, these visits remain a lifeline. In addition to catering for their physical needs, they provide a reassurance that they have not been completely forgotten and link them back to the world outside. But that link can be a mixed blessing. Along with the temporary feelings of comfort and belonging, it revives anxieties about the past, the present and the future: painful memories of the genocide and the war; worries about the family struggling to cope; and apprehensions about the life which awaits them outside, if they are ever released.

A former prisoner summed up the significance of visits for prisoners:

> "Visits are important for prisoners in three respects, in the following order of importance. 1) Food is the most important for everyone, both peasants and intellectuals. If you visit without bringing food, it's not worth it and you're considered good for nothing. 2) News from outside. 3) Seeing someone from outside and being able to say: 'I've seen my wife' or 'I've seen my child'. Prisoners either love it or hate it when there are visitors. They come close or stay away. I used to love it."

Another former prisoner was in the category of people who hated it. Whenever he was called out for a visit, he used to worry and sweat. He said the visits didn't give him any pleasure.

The topics of conversation during visits were always the same: exchange of greetings, news about the family, things the prisoners needed. Husbands and wives tried hard to keep each other's hopes alive, but as the years passed, it became increasingly difficult. A former prisoner said that there was little they could say to lift each other's spirits: "I told my family to bear the situation. Whatever happened, God could work a miracle and I could be released. That's all prisoners can tell their families to cheer them up."

For many prisoners, the memory of the first visit was still very strong. One prisoner remembered his wife's first visit vividly: "I took this visit as a resurrection, because I saw my wife. She put her hand on her cheek and looked at me. She had no words to say." A prisoner who had been severely tortured in a military brigade described his first visit from his wife and children after he was transferred to the central prison. He was still in very poor physical condition: "The first time, something else happened in my heart. My wife cried. We just looked at each other and we couldn't say anything. It was sad to see my children at the prison and to think about their life. They were angry. They saw me looking thin, beaten, with injuries which were clearly visible. They cried. They understood."

Family visits sometimes had an additional purpose for the prisoner: keeping abreast of developments with their case-file. Many prisoners relied on their families to find out what progress there had been with their case-file, if any, and to try to accelerate proceedings in the courts. The families who were able to do this were usually the better-off and the better-educated. Their efforts to monitor the progress of their case-file was an important source of encouragement to the prisoners, almost regardless of the outcome. To the prisoner, the family became a symbol of eventual justice, a bridge to the bureaucratic and corrupt world which had the power to release them from prison. Prisoners who didn't have any contact with their families simply assumed that there was no progress with their case-file because they had no one outside to chase it for them.

As the years have passed, some prisoners' families have become discouraged and visit less and less frequently. A prisoner in Kigali whose wife lived in Cyangugu, at least five hours away, had seen his visits drop over a period of six years from once a month to once or twice a year. Most prisoners didn't seem to hold this against their families. They understood that supporting a relative in prison was a thankless task.

Others, however, felt badly let down by their relatives. A prisoner whose parents had died a long time ago said his brothers visited him in the first two years after his arrest, but had not returned since 1996. He suspected they wanted him to die so that they could take his possessions. He said he would find it difficult to live with them again if he was released.

According to one prisoner, some prisoners became so angry with their families for giving up that they played a sinister trick on them: "There have been several cases of prisoners who have pretended that they were dead. They get a note sent to the family telling them they have died. The family comes to get their body and finds them alive. The prisoner then scolds them for only coming to the prison when they think they're dead."

Worries about the family

Visits always bring to the fore prisoners' worries about their families and their own inability to support them. Male prisoners were especially concerned at the loss of earnings resulting from their imprisonment, which meant that their wives had to struggle even harder. A prisoner who used to be a wealthy businessman told us that once, when his wife and daughter visited him, he failed to recognise them at first because they were so thin and dressed in rags.

The main casualty of the economic situation was the children's education. Some families managed to borrow money from relatives to pay for their children's school fees, but many children dropped out of school because the family could no longer pay for their schooling. This was one of the prisoners' main preoccupations. It was partly a matter of pride: they felt humiliated at being unable to provide a good education for their children, especially those who were well-educated themselves. One prisoner we spoke to was very upset that his 11-year-old son had dropped out of school: the boy's grandfather had advised him to stop studying and to work on his land instead, to compensate for his father's loss of earnings. He urged his boy to return to school whenever he visited him, but the boy had "disobeyed" him, and he felt unable to influence the situation from behind the prison walls.

Monitoring their children's success at school was hugely important for parents in prison. In addition to his own children who had since grown up and moved away, a 72-year-old prisoner had brought up several orphans who considered him as their father. They were now between 12 and 15 years old. They often cried when they visited him. "They say if I wasn't in prison, they would have grown up better. One just missed her entrance exam into secondary school, by one point. She said if I'd been at home, she wouldn't have failed." He felt he had failed in his responsibility towards them.

On the positive side, when their children were doing well at school, it was one of the few sources of pride for their parents in prison. Several prisoners told us how their children would bring their school reports to show them when they visited them in prison. One prisoner gave his two children some money to congratulate them on their good results; his wife had secretly given him the money beforehand, so that he could hand it to them as a reward when they visited him. We met another prisoner who used to prepare lessons from the prison for his three children who were at secondary school: "I wrote notes for them on French, English and maths. It was difficult to get the notes out to my wife, as I was watched, but I could pass them to her tucked into a book. I gave the book to a prisoner who worked outside and asked him to put it somewhere for my wife to collect. In return, I gave him a portion of porridge or 100 francs; sometimes a friend would do it for free. The children knew it was hard for me in prison, but they came to thank me for sending the notes."

Prisoners' feelings towards their children dominated their thoughts and many said that their own suffering paled in comparison to that of their children. Their descriptions of their children's visits to the prison were very emotional. Even the most hardened prisoners melted when they started talking about their children. One prisoner, whose children were aged 11 and nine, spoke in a very articulate and detailed way about every other aspect of prison life, but said he could not begin to describe how he felt when he saw his children.   Another prisoner, who came across as cold and unfeeling, suddenly took his head in his hands when I asked him about his children's visits to the *cachot* where he was detained for four years, and said he did not want to talk about it. He didn't explain whether a particular incident had occurred, or whether it was the general conditions of visits which still made him feel angry, several years on. He had not seen his children for five years.

For some prisoners, the experience of seeing their children in prison was simply too humiliating. A 60-year-old father of five, the youngest of whom was 16, had spent six and a half years in prison. He had been tried and sentenced to death. "I don't like my children to see my shame so I prefer them not to come. Anyway, when they come, we can't really talk… They leave in a different state of mind. They're confused. I don't even have time to ask them how they feel."

Similar emotions came to the surface when prisoners talked about their parents and their inability to care for them in their old age.   Prisoners' relationships with their parents often dwindled when their parents were too old to visit them. A 44-year-old woman who had been in prison for seven years said her mother, who was about 70, had visited her only once. Her father was too old and sick to visit. She said he didn't count her among his children any more. He had already lost four other children during the war.

A prisoner who was 20 when he was arrested had seen his mother only once during his ten years in prison. On the day she visited him, she was ill, and she cried when she saw him. He said he didn't want her to come again as the visit had caused her too much suffering. He even stopped sending her aeroplanes as they made her cry every time. The last time he had seen her before her visit was six years earlier, when the whole family had been in Congo; they had fled there in 1994. His mother had tried to warn him against returning to Rwanda. He told us: "I had spent eight months in Congo with my family. I came back because I was nostalgic. I didn't feel at ease in Congo. I used to go to the border every day to look at the hills in Rwanda. I came back on 16 February 1995. I was arrested the same day. I didn't expect to be arrested at all. Only my mother, who is a Tutsi, had warned me. She had said: 'Wait, my son, we don't know what will happen', but I was impatient, so I came back alone."

Another prisoner had received just one visit from his father over a five-year period: "I saw him, but I couldn't talk to him. He was crying. I gave a guard 500 francs just so that I could shake his hand. The guard let me shake his hand, then said 'that's enough' and the visit ended. My father never came again."

Mourning from prison

Finding out about the deaths of close relatives was one of the hardest experiences for prisoners. Often they received this news weeks or months after the event, or found out accidentally.

One of the most shocking examples was the way one prisoner found out about the death of his 14-year-old son. The conditions in which prison visits took place had made normal communication impossible. "Once, my wife brought me food. I shouted to her: 'Next time, send my son.' She said: 'Your son is dead.' But I didn't hear her, so I said: 'Tell him to bring me a pair of trousers.' Then some other prisoners who had heard what my wife had said told me that my son had died. It was a dialogue of the deaf."

Often news of a relative's death was communicated by other prisoners. The wife of a 42-year-old man died one year after his arrest in 1995. A prisoner who heard the announcement on the radio told him; he never found out how she had died. Since her death, he had gradually lost contact with the remaining members of his family, including his three children, who had returned to their home area, more than five hours away. He had not seen them for ten years.

In 2004, a prisoner who had been detained for ten years and had received regular visits from his wife began wondering why she had not visited for about a month. Then some prisoners who were working outside told him they had met a woman from his home area who had told them his wife had just died and that she was going to be buried the next day. The next morning, he heard the confirmation of her death on the radio. His sister visited him on her way to the funeral. She said she would call again on her way back, but never did. He was not able to find out the cause of his wife's death and, like all prisoners, was not allowed to attend the funeral.

A man who was released in 2000 recalled the death of his mother while he was in prison: "The first time my mother came to see me in prison, she cried and didn't say anything. The second time, she said: 'My son, are you sure you will get out of here?' I said yes. I am her favourite son. The third time she came was on 30 August 1998. Before she even started talking, I could see she was desperate. She said: 'My son, I don't think you'll get out of here.' That night, she died. The next day, a child came to tell me. I said: 'It's not possible. She was with me yesterday.' She was about 60. She was very strong. She used to come all the way to Kigali from Byumba."

The question of friendships

Few prisoners received visits from people other than their close family members. Visits from friends and colleagues, if they took place at all, tailed off rapidly after the early days of their imprisonment. We asked prisoners why they thought their friends no longer visited. Some said that especially in the first few years, people were afraid to visit prisoners accused of genocide in case they were perceived as sympathising with them and their alleged crimes. Apparently some people feared being arrested themselves if they were seen visiting these prisoners. Prisoners offered this explanation as a kind of excuse for their friends, but it was obvious that they only half-believed it.

Prisoners felt let down by their friends. A prisoner who had had many friends before his arrest said he had never seen them at the prison: "It makes you wonder whether people are your friends or not. When I'm released, I won't talk to anyone." Friends who had done well for themselves since the genocide – who had started a family, got a good job and started saving money – were the least likely to visit, especially if they had developed close links with the government or the military. A prisoner told us: "Prison creates a distance between us and our friends. We're accused of being killers, so people don't want to associate with us. I feel abandoned by my friends."

There is of course a special stigma attached to the accusation of genocide, but even common criminals accused of offences unconnected to the genocide found themselves abandoned by their friends. A man who spent almost two years in prison accused of a common crime said only one of his former colleagues ever visited him: "There was a general indifference. Not everyone has the courage to go to those places. There are myths: that the prison is inaccessible, etc. I don't blame them. In the first few days, I felt abandoned. I expected colleagues to visit and to give me lots of support. It was the opposite."

What was particularly disturbing for prisoners was the realisation that some people they used to consider friends had begun to question their innocence. A man who had spent more than seven years in prison explained that the simple fact of being in prison was enough to start creating suspicions among his friends, even though everyone in Rwanda knows that many innocent people have been imprisoned: "There is total mistrust. People are beginning to wonder how come I am spending so long in prison. They end up thinking that maybe I'm guilty. This hurts me, of course. But I try to understand... I think it's just human nature."

Sometimes it was just time that wore down the friends and acquaintances outside. According to the prisoners, they lost patience with a situation which seemed to have no end. A man who had been detained for nine years said simply: "My friends waited and gave up." Sometimes there were chance meetings. Visitors may come to the prison to see a relative and happen to recognise other friends among the prisoners. They may then return and chat to them, or bring them something small on the next visit, but this didn't happen very often and rarely developed into a sustained routine.

From my own observations, I concluded that the failure to visit was not necessarily a sign of indifference. There are so many people in prison in the country that it is no longer exceptional or even noteworthy to have a friend in prison. Imprisonment in Rwanda does not have the same value that it may have elsewhere. Many people I spoke to expressed genuine concern about the imprisonment of their friends or colleagues. Yet this concern didn't translate into a desire to visit them. These people had simply succumbed to the hopelessness of the situation.

CHAPTER XII

"The time of crying is over":

the effect of imprisonment on the family

Prolonged imprisonment has taken a huge toll on the families of prisoners, financially, socially and psychologically. Tens of thousands of families have been affected. Husbands, wives, brothers, daughters and sons of prisoners spoke to us candidly about their hardships and how the imprisonment affected their daily lives. In some cases, we managed to speak to the families of prisoners we had interviewed, so we were able to start piecing together the fragments of their parallel, broken lives. In other cases, we met the families without meeting the prisoner and were just presented with the bleak picture of a life outside taken over by the needs of life inside. In many more cases, we met the prisoners without meeting their families, so we only saw the suffering of the families through the eyes of the prisoners.

The economic burden

Families of prisoners are being suffocated by their economic problems. Rwanda is a poor country where many people struggle to survive. A family with one or more relatives in prison finds its financial commitments doubled, or tripled, for an indefinite period. Many of these families had just returned from exile when their relatives were arrested, so had little or no possessions, no employment, and in some cases no home.

Prison visits are the symbol of the family's economic burden, and the provisions which families carry to the prisons are a symbol of their commitment. There is a certain type of large, sturdy bag made of sheeting, with handles, which many visitors use to carry food and other items to the prisons; these bags are often made by prisoners. I was told that whenever you see a woman carrying one of these bags, you can assume she has a husband in prison. Rwandans call these bags "*nzamurambaho*": it means "I remain attached to him" or "I won't abandon him". The wife of a former prisoner complained of the physical effects of the routine: she had difficulty bending her arm because of the weight of the bags she carried to the prison every week.

Families make huge sacrifices to support their relatives in prison. The wife of one prisoner we met divided everything she and her children had at home by two. Sometimes she even forgot about the children because she was so worried about what to take to her husband in prison, or she would send the children off to their grandparents so that she wouldn't need to worry about them for a while. She used to beg people for food and go to bed without eating. A woman whose husband and brother were both in prison was in a state of perpetual anxiety about how to support them: "I have to cater for both of them. My main problem is finding all the things I have to take them. I worry how I will find something for next Tuesday. It is in two days' time but I don't have anything. It haunts me. It's an obligation and I worry when the day approaches." In the most extreme cases, a family may be so poor that the woman is forced to prostitute herself to support her husband in prison.

There is also the cost of travel to the prison, which can be significant, especially in the rural areas. Most of the central prisons are located in the provincial capitals or main towns. Families living in remote villages have to travel miles to reach the prison. They become drained by the cost and physical exhaustion of travelling backwards and forwards, all for a matter of two or three minutes. Many families make this journey on foot (very few people in Rwanda can afford a car). Some may take the bus, but the buses travel only along the main roads, so families may still have to trek for hours across steep hills. One prisoner said it used to take his wife three days to visit him: she would travel on the first day, visit him on the second day, and travel back on the third day. A young prisoner told us that his 70-year-old mother's journey from her home to the prison, which she undertook partly by road and partly by boat along the lake, took her five hours: she would set out at 6am and reach the prison at 11am.

For several years after the genocide, many prisoners were held in prisons miles away from their home, in the area where they happened to have been arrested. Later, in preparation for *gacaca* (see Chapter XVII), they were gradually grouped together and moved to the area in which their alleged crime had been committed. In many cases, this coincided with their home area, so their transfer was a huge relief both for the families and the prisoners. A prisoner who was originally from Cyangugu but spent three years in prison in Butare was finally transferred back to Cyangugu Central Prison in 1997, along with a group of about 250 others. He remembered them all dancing and singing with joy in the lorries which transported them there.

The strain on relationships

Prison visits are a constant, painful manifestation of the social break-up of families. The conditions of visits make it impossible for families to relate to each other through the normal rites of conversation. Even where family relationships remain strong, there is little pleasure to be derived from a three-minute encounter, surrounded by hundreds of other prisoners and visitors and by guards waving their sticks. For many families, the first few visits following the prisoner's arrest were difficult and emotionally charged. One man said he would never forget the first time he visited his wife in prison: "The visits were torture… We were three metres apart. I could just touch her furtively before the soldiers saw. The visit lasted one or two minutes. It was painful to see her. She was wearing pink and her head was shaved. She used to have beautiful hair."

Some families were so overwhelmed by the situation that they were at a loss as to what to say in the few minutes granted to them, or would forget what they had intended to say. "I was just happy to see him/her alive" or "at least I could see him/her" – meaning literally to set eyes on each other – were common responses, especially during the early years when there was no certainty of surviving from one day to the next. Indeed for some families, the primary purpose of the visits, during this period, was simply to check whether the prisoners were still alive.

Ten years on, these conditions have just become part of the normal routine and any expectations of meaningful communication between prisoners and their families have long been abandoned. They just greet each other, the whistle blows, and they leave. Whether a visit has gone well or not, for the family, is often measured by the basic well-being of the prisoner: if the prisoner is in good health, the family is happy. If he is sick, the family is sad. The visit has been reduced to that simple equation. A woman whose husband had been in prison for more than seven years told us: "Before, I used to cry all the time. Now, the time of crying is over."

The conditions of visits, and the experience of imprisonment itself, are an endurance test for relationships. Some relationships survive this most extreme of ordeals, but others crumble. In every country, marriages fall apart as a result of prolonged imprisonment and the resulting loneliness, frustration and impatience. Rwandan prisoners and their families both alluded to this problem, but only a few admitted that it had affected them personally. As there are more men than women in prison, the usual reference, in this context, was to women who had given up on their husbands in prison, but the reverse also occurred, with men abandoning their wives in prison in favour of other women.

For many male prisoners, in particular, their wife's loyalty was a matter of pride. For example, a prisoner whose wife had only visited him three or four times since 2001 was confident that whenever she managed to get some money together, she would come back to see him. He was keen to explain: "She loves me very much. She didn't get another husband."

Some women were willing to befriend other men without abandoning their husband in prison, in order to receive some material support which they could then channel to the husband in prison. A prisoner who had been detained for ten years told us that his wife had slept with another man who had lent her money so that she could visit him in prison; she had had a child with him. She had told her husband herself, apparently because she didn't want him to hear rumours. He seemed quite philosophical about it, perhaps because he had had no choice in the matter. His wife had since died.

A woman who had been in prison for nine years said her husband only visited her once a year, on New Year's Day. He had been in prison too but was released after three years. It was not clear why he did not visit more frequently. He didn't have far to travel to the prison. He told his wife that he didn't want to see her suffer, but there may have been other reasons. After so many years of separation, prisoners can lose the sense of what motivates their partner or their family, and a relationship can be disintegrating without them realising it. The woman told me: "He sends the children to see me and he sends me all I need… We could write letters but my husband says he can't write to me. I don't know why… I suffer from the absence of my husband but I've got used to it. My husband is a nice man, but I don't know if he's changed after five years."

In an extraordinary interview with a very sick prisoner, I discovered that some relationships not only survive this prolonged separation but can be enhanced by it. This was a disturbing and intense conversation with a highly educated man who had spent more than ten years in prison and stood very little chance of being released, as he was in Category 1, although he hadn't yet been tried. A colleague who had known him before the genocide told me that he used to be an imposing and physically strong man. When we met him, he was so weak from his third attack of tuberculosis that he could barely walk and had to be propped up by two other prisoners. He was tall, gaunt and painfully thin. He was 58 but looked about 20 years older. I thought he might be too weak to talk to us, but his eyes were burning and it was obvious that he had a lot to say. Sickness was eating away at this man's body, but his spirit was fighting to survive, and inside he was as hard as steel. He sat down slowly on the wooden chair and launched into an impassioned monologue, about the injustices of the system, the corruption of the government, the horrors of life in prison. It was an extremely bitter, negative and highly politicised discourse, delivered in a beautiful language full of graphic images mixed with brutal sarcasm. It was almost as if he took pleasure in the suffering around him. In the middle of this invective, he started talking about his wife, who was a Tutsi. She visited him twice a week. "I tell my wife that the fact that we're separated increases my love for her, that growing old separately increases our love. I wrote this to her on our 30th wedding anniversary." His sudden expression of affection was totally disarming.

There are many other, less extreme but equally moving, cases of a husband or wife's unconditional commitment to supporting their partner in prison and to finding ever more thoughtful ways of expressing that support. A man whose wife was in prison for four years was so distraught when she was first arrested that he went to see the Minister of Justice, who was a friend, and asked to be put in prison instead of her. (The minister told him not to be so naïve, or he might stay in there too.) He felt revolted at not being able to do anything about his wife's situation and indignant that she was in prison while he was free. He visited her regularly and often throughout her imprisonment and never hesitated to spend his earnings on buying her "things which would reduce her suffering and show I was supporting her. I used to buy her expensive things, like cheese, meat, chicken, cosmetics. I used to ask other women for advice because I didn't know what to buy. I bought things which would last at least a week because I couldn't go there every day. I bought fruits as I had heard people in prison could catch beriberi from lack of vitamins." She had asked him for religious books, which he bought her; he also bought her other books which he thought might encourage and inspire her, such as books written by survivors of concentration camps. He spent a lot of time and money befriending the guards and bribing them so that they would allow him to talk to her for longer and to give her money. His wife reciprocated these gestures of affection as best she could. She wrote him lots of letters, and on their wedding anniversary, she sent him cards made by the prisoners. She even sent him some of the dry biscuits which the Red Cross used to distribute to prisoners, just to be able to share something with him.

The gulf between prisoners and their families

One of the most striking aspects of our interviews with the families of prisoners was the difference between their perspective and that of the prisoner. Sometimes they were poles apart. Even in the case of families who appeared to be close, their experiences were different, and, crucially, not shared. Each lived in their own private world of suffering.

The family will never fully understand the daily life of the prisoner because the general public is not allowed inside the prison. Visits always take place in the outside courtyard. Only those who have been in prison themselves or whose profession has taken them into the prisons in the past, for example journalists, priests or members of the judiciary, will have any idea of the world inside. The life of a prisoner in Rwanda cannot be truly understood without understanding the conditions in which they live, because they are so extreme. The fact that this experience is not shared creates a permanent gulf between the prisoners and their families. Some prisoners have attempted to describe these conditions to their families during their brief visits, but most choose to keep their suffering to themselves. A woman whose husband had been in prison for almost eight years said he rarely talked about the conditions so as not to upset her: "Prisoners have their secrets. They don't always talk. I don't know much about the life inside." One prisoner said that whenever his family visited him, he always asked them for their news so as not to have to talk about his own living conditions, especially with the children: "Anyway, they don't ask and we don't have time." In some cases, the silence persisted even after the prisoner was released, reinforcing the sense of alienation. Prisoners and former prisoners told us – complete strangers – things which they had never told their closest family.

The families, for their part, complained that prisoners failed to understand their situation. Some families chose not to tell the prisoner about the hardships they were experiencing in order to spare them the worry – much as the prisoners didn't talk about their own living conditions. A former prisoner whose wife had supported him steadfastly through several years of imprisonment was shocked by the poverty he found after his release. "When I got home, I saw how they were living and I cried. I asked my wife: 'How could you find money to bring me food when you were living like this?' My wife and three children were living in one small room. She suffered a lot."

But the wives of several prisoners who had been detained for many years spoke bitterly about their husbands' lack of understanding of their situation. Some accused their husbands of having become selfish and of forgetting the harsh realities of life outside. One woman continued to visit her husband every week – he had been in prison for eight years – but was critical of the expectations which male prisoners placed upon their wives. She was a strong, well-educated woman with few illusions about the world around her, yet she cried when she thought about her husband. Her account encapsulated many of the contradictory emotions and conflicting priorities for prisoners' families:

> "I feel good when I am with my children. When I'm with them, I
> don't think about it. I think about my husband mostly on Fridays,
> as I have to think about what to take him on the Saturday…

I talk with other women whose husbands are in prison, especially about our financial problems. There are two colleagues. We meet by chance. Their husbands are in different prisons. We compare our experiences sometimes but these are not real friendships. Friends have abandoned us. We are alone.

The children are a big relief. They talk and play, but education is difficult. The children lack the authority of their father. They listen to me but something is missing.

In rural areas, some children miss school to go and visit their fathers in prison. They get up very early and it takes all day. They may walk four or five hours, for example for 20 kilometres. Even if their mother is alive, she works and sends the children to take the food to their father. In other cases, the mother has died. Or the mother may be in prison. Sometimes both parents are in prison… People talk about these things on visit days.

Sometimes people give better food to their relatives in prison than they eat themselves at home, especially in the rural areas. I know a 13-year-old girl who told her mother that she wanted to live in prison because her father there was getting chips and she didn't get any. Families deprive themselves to give good food to their relatives in prison. I took the decision to cook the same food for my husband and for us so that the children don't feel he is getting better treatment.

Some fathers ask for things for themselves without thinking about their children… For example they say: 'Before, you used to bring me good food, where is it now?' or 'Did another man give you money for that?' They just think about themselves. It is not because they don't know. They know everything: the cost of living and prices outside, they can follow our movements, they know who we talk to. They have become selfish and jealous. Some tell each other they are not going to go back to their wife because she has been talking to other men. If a wife doesn't visit for one week, they assume she's with another man. Some say:

'When I'm released, I don't want to go back to that wife, I want
another wife.' "

Another woman complained that her husband expected her to do all sorts of
things that required money, apparently forgetting that she didn't have any. As
we were planning to visit him in prison after seeing her, she said to us:
"When you see him, tell my husband I have problems too. It's not only him.
He thinks he's the only one." However, she was aware that her husband was
suffering from depression and was becoming gradually disengaged from the
real world. She said he had changed since he had been in prison. "He used
to be psychologically more active. He seems traumatised. When we talk, he's
not always OK. Sometimes he tells me I just have to take responsibility, that
he can't do anything and that I have to deal with it. Sometimes he doesn't ask
much about the children, but he asks to see them. He doesn't react. He is
elsewhere."

The selfish attitude of some male prisoners was illustrated by a number of
comments made by prisoners themselves on the subject of marriage:
marriage was an investment, and little consideration was given to how their
wife may feel. A prisoner in his thirties told us that he regretted not being
married, because if at least he had a wife, she would be there to support him
in prison. Another prisoner was even more blunt: "When I'm released, the
first thing I want to do is get married. I may take the first girl I meet when
I'm past the prison gate and ask her to marry me. That way, if I have other
problems, the whole burden won't be on my mother. My wife will share the
burden. I never thought I'd end up in prison. If I'd thought of it, I would
have got married before." A prisoner who was detained for five years on an
accusation of genocide, released, then re-arrested five years later for alleged
theft, said the first thing he had done after his release was get married: "My
family found me a wife. My father said I should concentrate on my family
and get married so that if I was arrested again, at least I wouldn't be without a
wife or children." Indeed, when he was re-arrested, his wife did visit him. It
was only then that he realised the pain and suffering it caused her. Now, he
was constantly worrying about his family and felt desperate when his young
children came to visit him.

Another male prisoner made a revealing request at the end of our interview. A former local official, he had spent eight years in prison and had confessed to participating in the genocide. He was a serious, intelligent man who didn't give much away in his facial expressions. He spoke quietly, with his head tilted downwards, but his eyes peered at me over his glasses in the dark room. At first he gave the impression that he was not very interested in talking to me, but I discovered, after about an hour, that his manner was deceptive. He was precise and clear and, unlike some prisoners, understood immediately the type of information I was looking for. Most of what he told me was hard and painful, but he told it in a matter-of-fact, unemotional way. After the interview, we sat and chatted for a few minutes. Like so many other prisoners, he relaxed once the questioning was over and I had closed my notebook. We talked about his family. He was keen that I should meet his wife and daughters and told me how to get in touch with them. Then he asked me if I would come back and tell him what they had said. I laughed and reminded him that all our interviews were confidential, even with members of the same family. He laughed too and suggested a compromise: "All right, find out what they think about me. Have they had enough? Then you can come back and tell me if what they say is good, but not if it is bad." The tone in which he made this request indicated that he had no idea what his family was really thinking. Unfortunately, I didn't have time to meet his family and I didn't go back to see him. He probably thought it was because they had said bad things about him.

Deaths in prison

One of our visits to Kigali Central Prison happened to coincide with the recent death of a prisoner from tuberculosis. There was some commotion around the gate as the prisoner's sister had come to collect the body. A group of prisoners from the prison Red Cross association seemed to be in charge of the process: they lifted the body carefully and put it into a truck which was waiting in the prison yard, along with a large hand-made wooden cross – presumably manufactured by the prisoners themselves. The truck drove off slowly.

When a prisoner dies, the prison is supposed to inform the family and allow them to collect the body for burial. In the early years after the genocide, thousands of prisoners died without their families' knowledge. Later, procedures were introduced, but many families were still not directly informed of the deaths of prisoners, or found out accidentally. Some were told by other prisoners that their relative had died when they happened to come to the prison for a regular visit, sometimes weeks or months after the prisoner had died and had already been buried. It was especially difficult for prison authorities to contact families in rural areas outside visit days, so the question of whether a family had the opportunity to bury the prisoner themselves might depend on the day of the week on which the prisoner happened to die. If a prisoner died on a Monday, they would be buried by the prisoners without waiting for the family, as visits took place only on Fridays and Saturdays. A man who had spent more than seven years in prison said he would never forget those who died in prison without their family to take care of them: "They are buried like dogs."

The system has improved in the last few years. Prison directors communicate the information on the day of the prisoner's death through the local authorities of the family's area. If the family has not come to collect the body after two days, the prisoners are asked to bury the body themselves, in a special section of the public cemetery, because the prisons do not have the facilities for keeping the bodies for any longer. The prison directors reassured us that this system worked, and that families usually responded within two days. But prisoners told us that there were still cases where the families didn't turn up, either because the message hadn't reached them, or because the prisoner had no family left in the country. One prisoner told us that some families received the message but didn't collect the body because they felt the government should take responsibility for the burial: "Instead of giving us back a healthy person, they give us a corpse. Let them deal with it."

In Kigali, we met a young man who often used to visit his father in prison. His father, who was in his sixties, was detained for five years. He died in prison in 2001. His son used to take great pleasure in visiting him; he and his brothers and his sisters used to fight over whose turn it was to visit him. The fact that his father died in prison had had a deep effect on him, especially as his mother died less than a year later:

"My father wrote a letter for his children. It was his last letter before dying. He told us what to do after his death. He named me as the head of the family. His prisoner friends signed it as witnesses. He died the day after he wrote the letter. A prisoner friend asked his own family to inform us that my father was dead. We went to the prison to see if it was true. I took my mother... The prisoners brought out his body on a stretcher. One of his friends went to get the letter and gave it to us. They gave us the body and we took him home.

My father's death completely changed the situation at home. Whenever we got together, my mother used to say: 'I always remember your father who died in prison.' She was always talking about his death. She just stayed at home all the time. Sometimes she used to look at photos. I used to tell her it was not good to look at the photos all the time, but she insisted. My sister even wanted to hide the photos as it was not doing any good for my mother. About eight or ten months later, my mother died. She was very discouraged after my father's death. She was tired...

Some of my father's friends are still in prison. I go to visit them. The first time I went back after his death, I felt bad. Even just passing by the prison, it touches me deep inside."

Even while a prisoner is still alive, the family may start behaving, in some respects, as if he has already died. It is a form of acceptance of long-term absence and adjustment in order to survive. The wife of a prisoner told us: "Sometimes I think my husband will be released, but sometimes I think he'll die in prison and they may call me to fetch his body. I start behaving like a widow, but I'm not really a widow. Widows get assistance but I don't. Yet I don't have a husband. So what am I?"

The wider social circle

Families of prisoners accused of genocide are among the most stigmatised groups in Rwandan society. They have had to endure the insults and taunts of neighbours and colleagues and have even been ostracised by members of their own families, on the assumption that the relative in prison must be guilty. Wives of prisoners, in particular, were affected by the stigma in the first few years after the genocide. They were perceived, and some ended up perceiving themselves, as "wives of *interahamwe*". Those who had jobs often tried to conceal the fact of their partner's imprisonment from their colleagues. Colleagues who already knew rarely made explicit reference to it, but the knowledge created an atmosphere of distrust, sometimes leading to discrimination. A woman whose husband was in prison for several years had difficulty finding a good job while he was in prison. She used to work as a manager in a bank but after her husband's arrest, tensions developed with her Tutsi colleagues, and her bosses asked her to work as a receptionist or a cleaner. Her husband told us: "Anyone who has a relative in prison is considered an enemy... A woman with a husband in prison is considered an *interahamwe* herself. The irony was that my own brother was killed by *interahamwe*. Then I was called an *interahamwe* myself, and so was my wife."

The situation of mixed couples is the most delicate of all. A significant number of Hutu prisoners accused of genocide have Tutsi wives. These women have to maintain a careful balance in their daily lives and may find themselves rejected by both sides. A smaller number of Hutu women prisoners have Tutsi husbands. Their situation is equally difficult.

In some cases, friends and neighbours gradually cut off social relations with a prisoner's family. In other cases, they actively encouraged the family to abandon the prisoner. The wife of one prisoner had heard some dispiriting words from some of her friends. They used to tell her: "It's useless. Your husband's going to die in there. You're wasting your time." In fact, her husband was tried, acquitted and released. A man whose wife was released after spending several years in prison was also shocked by the advice of some of his friends, who used to tell him: "She may die in prison. Why don't you get another wife? And if she's released, she can be the second one."

The suffering of prisoners' families is mostly invisible and silent. Several wives of prisoners told us they felt they didn't have the right to speak, and that even if they dared to speak, they wouldn't be heard. There is no support network for these families. Some occasionally talk with other families of prisoners whom they have got to know during prison visits, and derive some comfort from those contacts, but their conversations are limited and rarely develop into strong friendships. Some prefer not to spend extended time with other prisoners' families because such conversations will inevitably dwell on the most painful aspects of their lives. The only other support they receive is from members of their own family or occasionally from church-based groups. The wife of a prisoner said she deliberately avoided talking to people other than those closest to her: "It makes me nervous. I keep a low profile. People don't even know where I live. I avoid people and I don't like to have visits. I only feel at ease in my family and in my religious community. In the religious community, we say everything, Tutsi or Hutu, but it doesn't go outside the group. I joined this group after my husband was arrested."

A man whose wife was in prison for several years tried to set up a support group for families of prisoners, but it never got off the ground as all the people he approached were too afraid to take part. Nevertheless, he developed an informal solidarity with other men whose wives were in prison: "Each Saturday, after the visits, we used to go for a drink together. I helped one of them with his children's school fees. I met these men at the prison, three or four times, in the same circumstances. We used to visit each other at home. We encouraged each other. If we stayed faithful to our wives, it was a victory against those who had taken our wives away from us. I am still friendly with some of them. Prison has enabled us to make new friends. This is the only positive thing about it."

For some of the women we met, talking to us about their suffering seemed to be an important form of release, as there were few other people they could talk to openly. A woman whose husband and brother were both in prison told us at the end of our conversation: "I feel relieved after this meeting. I had been hoping someone would come to whom I could talk like this. My dream has come true."

CHAPTER XIII

"Your father is a killer":

the next generation

A parent's long-term imprisonment, especially without justice and in such harsh conditions, will have a long-lasting effect on their children. Many of the families we spoke to described a dramatic change in their children's behaviour, ranging from difficulties concentrating at school to serious psychological disturbances. Young as well as older children were traumatised not only by the fact that their parent was in prison, but by the gravity of the accusation of genocide. The fact that, in the majority of cases, their parents had not yet been tried created confusion in their minds and raised many difficult and unanswered questions: could their father or mother really be a killer? How would they ever know what they had really done? Friends and neighbours would tell them: "your father / your mother has killed." Could it be true? As children grew up and started acquiring a better understanding of events, they became angry towards the individuals – often anonymous – or the government who, in their eyes, had taken their parents away from them, and their interpretation of the situation became increasingly politicised.

Visiting parents in prison

The conditions in which children had to visit their parents accentuated their distress. A former prisoner remembered his six-year-old daughter being beaten when she visited him: "One day my wife came with our daughter. The guards beat the girl. It was the first and last time she came to visit me at the prison. I saw them hit her. I just left the food there and walked away. My wife told me that from that day on, the girl was traumatised and didn't want to talk."

Even in subsequent years, when conditions had relaxed slightly, prisoners said their children were often tearful and not very talkative during the visits. They stood in front of their father or mother without knowing what to say, then after a few minutes of one-sided conversation, they left. An elderly prisoner said his children seemed happy to see him, "but I watch them and sometimes it doesn't feel right. Something is hidden. The youngest is 14. He is sad, and very young. It is a long road, a four-hour walk, so when he arrives, he is very tired. Sometimes he cries... We sit on benches 1.5 metres apart. We just greet each other, they give me the bags and go."

Yet the children were always keen to visit, even if they did not communicate through words, and were reluctant to leave at the end of the visit. The youngest son of one prisoner had learnt to count the days of the week. Whenever Friday came around, he told his mother it was time to see his father, but his mother couldn't always take him as it took them four hours to walk to the prison. He visited his father twice. On the second visit, he said to his father: "Come on, let's go home". His father replied: "You go home, I'll join you later." The boy was crying as he left.

A prisoner who had spent almost nine years in prison said that when his children visited him, they looked at him but didn't talk. The boy was 11, the girl was eight. "My wife tells me they get impatient before the visits and keep looking at their watches, but when they come, they don't talk, even though they want to see me. I find it very hard. My wife tells me they're OK at home. She may be hiding the problems." His daughter was born just after his arrest and had never known him before he went to prison. He would send her photos of himself and tried to have these photos taken outside so that it wouldn't be obvious that he was in a prison.

A man who had spent ten years in prison, and whose wife had died two years after his arrest, sometimes received visits from his daughter. She was about six or seven when he was first arrested. She used to visit him with her mother, then after her mother died, she visited him alone. "We had nothing to say to each other. We didn't really have any conversation. I could see she was alive, that was all... After my wife died, I saw my little girl was all alone. My friends here tried to comfort me."

Some children wrote to their parents in prison. These letters gave them the freedom to express feelings which they may not have known how to articulate face to face. The wife of a prisoner said her husband was always pleased to receive letters from his children; it lifted his spirits, momentarily.

His youngest son, who was eight years old and was conceived in the period between his father's two stints in prison, once asked why his father had not confessed, after hearing on the radio that those who confessed would be released. He wrote to his father: "I want you to be released soon and when you are released, make sure you come straight home and don't go anywhere else." The eight-year-old daughter of another prisoner became jealous when she felt her father wasn't paying her enough attention. The prisoner told us: "Once I sent two cards to my wife. My daughter said to her mother: 'Why does he only write to you?' So I stopped sending cards to my wife for a while, and sent two cards to my daughter instead. When she visits me, her mother gives me money and I buy her a Fanta and cards and sculptures made by the prisoners."

Explaining prison

Mothers and fathers have struggled to explain to their children why their other parent was in prison. However, most of the families we spoke to were convinced, or had convinced themselves, of the innocence of the relative who was in prison, so they didn't have to broach the question of how to tell a child that their mother or father had killed. There was one exception, the wife of a former local government official who had confessed to playing a role in the genocide. Her two children often asked her why their father was in prison: "I tell them to wait for justice. I explain to them what happened: that a whole population was massacred, that their father was an authority and that he has to answer for what happened as he should have protected the population. I only talk about it when they ask me questions."

The wife of another prisoner had tried to explain the situation to her 11-year old daughter in a more roundabout way. "She keeps asking me when her father will be back, and why all these people are wearing strange uniforms. I tell her they've committed sins and are in prison. She asks what sins. I tell her some are thieves and some have committed genocide. She tries to understand if her father has also killed."

Many parents whose children were very young at the time of their arrest tried to conceal the fact that their father or mother was in prison and pretended that they were studying or working. The parent in prison as well as the one who was at home both tried to perpetuate the myth for as long as possible. For a while, the children believed it, but when they grew old enough to understand, or if other people blurted out the truth before their parents were ready to tell them, some became distressed.

The wife of a prisoner started taking her two children to visit their father from the second year of his imprisonment. Initially, she didn't tell them the truth as she felt they were too young. The eldest was only about six:

> "The boy cried the first time he saw his father. He used to say to the soldiers: 'Go away! You took my dad away!' Later, he asked me lots of questions: 'Who put him in prison? Why is he in prison? What has he done?' I lied and said he had become a pastor and had gone there to preach. He said: 'When you next go, ask Dad to preach as quickly as possible so that he can come back quickly.' Gradually, neighbours started mentioning that his father was in prison, so two years ago, I decided to tell him. I said to him: 'I'm sorry, I lied to you, this is the situation.' The boy took it badly. He wanted us to move away from the area. He doesn't trust people anymore. If a neighbour gives him a sweet, he'll take it but won't eat it without asking me. He really looks like his father. Everyone comments on this. It affects him to hear this."

For a former prisoner accused of a common crime, his children's understanding of the situation manifested itself in different ways:

> "I didn't like the children's visits... The oldest two were about six and four. They didn't understand the situation. My wife never told them I was in prison. She said I was studying. The children used to ask her: 'Why is he studying with armed men next to him? We don't have that at school.' After my release, they saw prisons on the TV. They asked me: 'Were you with those people? We were told you were at school.' But the older one understood and didn't say anything. Once while I was still in prison, my oldest son went up to some prisoners in uniform outside and asked them: 'Is Dad here?' They asked him what my name was,

then they told him I was not working with them. The prisoners told me later. I realised that my son had understood, but he never asked me anything afterwards...

When I was released, my daughter was three. The first night I came home, she asked my wife: 'Is this man going to go away?' Now, whenever the children see people in a similar uniform to the prisoners, they want to say something, but they don't dare. If I travel for a few days, they're worried. They keep asking my wife where I am, if she has heard from me... My wife wants me to tell them in advance when I'm going away, because when she tells them I'm at work, they think she may be lying again."

For a former prisoner who was detained for six and a half years, the lies he and his wife used to tell their child turned into a family joke after his release. Their eldest boy was only two when he was arrested, and nine when he was released. "My wife used to tell him I was studying. Later, he asked why I wasn't coming home when it was the holiday period. When he learned to read, he saw the sign '1930 prison' outside the prison and asked his mother why she had lied to him... Now, whenever we pass the prison, he jokes and says to me: 'There is your university.' "

Some prisoners felt rejected by their children. A former prisoner accused of genocide, whose wife was killed in 1994, was extremely hurt when he found out that some members of his wife's family, who were looking after his children while he was in prison, had persuaded them that their father was a killer and deserved to be in prison. They eventually kicked the children out of the house and they had to stay with another family. One of his sons had become seriously traumatised by the experience. After his release, the father described his most positive memory of the seven years he had spent in detention: "My biggest joy was when my daughter, who was 12 at the time, came to pray with me once in prison. She said: 'I thank you God for keeping my dad alive.' It showed me I was still a father for someone and I had some value. Otherwise, I was condemned. I thought my children saw me as a killer. I felt very encouraged when I went back in."

Children of *interahamwe*

Children of prisoners have experienced difficulties at school, including problems of concentration and a loss of interest in studying. Children who had been top of the class commonly dropped to the bottom following their parent's arrest, though some subsequently climbed back up again. Children whose parents were accused of genocide had to contend with a shift in their relations with their schoolfriends and teachers. To explain their parent's absence, some pretended that their father or mother was working in a different part of the country, or abroad, or simply said they had no father.

Children who told the truth about their parents could end up regretting it. "Your father is an *interahamwe*" was an insult that flowed freely in the classrooms and the school playground. Teachers were not always more sensitive than the children. The wife of a prisoner told us that her 13-year-old son had "made the mistake of telling his teacher, who was a survivor of the genocide, that his father was in prison. Since then, whenever there is trouble at school, the teacher often blames him."

One prisoner we talked to – a thoughtful and highly educated man – had a more philosophical attitude towards this problem. He acknowledged that his two children were stigmatised by the insults of their friends and neighbours, but saw it as a kind of rite of passage. "My children have classmates who say: 'your father is a killer, your father is an *interahamwe.*' They have to bear it. I don't have time to talk to them about it. Even if I did, I don't want my children to talk about this and I don't want to see this feeling in them, so I focus on other issues with them, like their studies. Sometimes I don't really regret what's happening to my children. It's a discovery, they learn from it."

For some children, though, the experience has been so distressing that they have become unable to carry on living their lives as before. We met one prisoner who had been arrested, sentenced to death, acquitted on appeal and released, then re-arrested. His children had reacted badly to his imprisonment, especially after his re-arrest. One of his sons, who was in his early twenties, suffered a breakdown and had to give up his job. He told one of his sisters that his mental state was directly linked to his father's imprisonment, that he felt guilty because his father had done so much for him and he could do nothing for him in return. His family asked him not to visit his father in prison any more, to spare him any further distress. Two of the daughters had been subjected to taunts and intimidation at school. After their father was sentenced to death, a military commander visited the school where one of his daughters was studying. He made her stand up and humiliated her in front of everyone, accusing her father of killings during the genocide. The same evening, a student taunted her, asking her how she could eat that night when they were about to kill her father, and whether she was going to drink her father's blood. The daughter complained to the school director, who was unsympathetic and simply told her that her father had been a local authority in the area, implying that he must therefore be guilty or at least expect to be found guilty. After this incident, the daughter, who used to be top of the class, dropped to 19th place, then to 22nd. Later, she picked up again and her family moved her to another school.

For children whose mother and father were both in prison, it was even more difficult. A woman whose husband was also in prison told us that her daughter had not told her boyfriend that both her parents were in prison until he asked her to marry him; when she told him, he left her. The mother was close to her children but felt she didn't know everything they were going through: "There are things I'm waiting to ask them when I'm released. I don't want to ask them too many questions now. I just ask them general questions about their studies and how they are."

Separation

Many parents in prison have spent years without seeing their children. A mother who was arrested in February 1995 had not seen her children for five years until they visited her in 2000. She said it was a great joy to see them, but she cried all night after they left. Children who were very young when their parents were arrested sometimes had difficulties recognising them in the alien environment of the prison, where everyone was wearing the same uniform.

A prisoner who had spent nine years in detention, most of them in military prisons, had not seen his ten-year-old son since 1998, when his wife left him.

The separation coincided with a period when visits were suspended in Mulindi military prison, where he was detained at the time. "After visits were cut in Mulindi, my wife went her separate way. The child is with her and she won't let him come. He's never visited me. She never had the courage to tell me. I haven't seen him since 1998. I ask friends for his photo. I write to him and he writes back. He writes: 'Don't worry, I'll get you out' and other things. His mother refused to let him visit me. She's a bad mother."

In some cases, all contact between parents and children has been severed. A woman in her thirties, whose mother and father were also in prison, had not seen her eight-year-old son since her arrest. The boy didn't even know his mother was in prison, as his grandparents, with whom he was staying, had told him she was in hospital. The grandparents didn't want to bring the boy to the prison and didn't visit themselves either, so she had no information at all about how her son was growing up. A woman in her forties, whose husband had died during the genocide, had not seen any of her three children, aged ten, 13 and 18, since her arrest in 1998. An elderly relative who occasionally visited her in prison told her that her second child had died of sickness in 2003, and that the oldest child had stopped going to school since her mother's arrest. The children knew their mother was in prison but had never been able to visit her.

Another woman had not only lost touch with all of her six children, the youngest of whom was born in prison, but her husband had died in prison. She was eight and a half months pregnant when she was arrested in 1995 and her baby stayed with her in prison for the first three years. Her husband was in the same prison as her, but she had never been allowed to see him there. When the baby was born, she asked to see him so that they could decide on a name for the child. That was when other prisoners told her that her husband had died. She wasn't told the cause of his death, nor how long ago he had died. When the child was three years old, he went to stay with his aunt. She had had no news of him since, nor of the aunt who was supposed to look after him. She didn't know what had happened to the other children either. She had had no visits at all since her arrest in 1995. I asked her whether she had contacted the Red Cross to see if they could try to trace her children. She hadn't. She seemed to have given up, a long time ago. At this point in the conversation, she broke down in tears and said she didn't want to talk about her children any more. But she insisted on continuing the interview, so we talked about other things: her activities in the prison, her friendships with the other women, and her hope in God.

The future

In the longer term, the prison situation in Rwanda is likely to create serious difficulties among the next generation. Children who have seen their parents imprisoned for years without trial will find it difficult to erase these memories. They are growing up harbouring feelings of injustice, incomprehension and victimisation. Many prisoners, former prisoners and their families had noticed significant changes in their children's attitudes and social relations as a direct consequence of their imprisonment and of the resulting social discrimination. One former prisoner remarked that his daughter, who was only about six years old when he was in prison, had started "to take an interest in Tutsi and Hutu". Many others said their children had become suspicious of all those around them, even their closest friends. A prisoner who received a visit from his 19-year-old son four years after his arrest discovered that even the most basic parental advice could no longer be taken at face value. When he told his son that it was important for him to continue his studies, his son replied: "Dad, haven't you thought that it's because you studied that you ended up in prison?"[1] Prisoners, their families and other Rwandans we spoke to expressed their fears for the future if the government did not move quickly to remedy the situation and to prevent these children's feelings of injustice from turning to thoughts of revenge. One prisoner told us: "They have created a system of vindictiveness in people's hearts."

---

[1] The boy's remark is a reference to the belief held by many "intellectual" prisoners that it was because of their level of education that they were arrested. In the mass arrests which followed the genocide, "intellectuals" were especially targeted by the new government. Some had participated actively in the genocide and were among the leading figures who ordered people to kill, but others were singled out merely because they were "intellectuals". "Intellectuals" in prison are still seen as a body of opposition to the government and are regularly accused of trying to indoctrinate and influence other prisoners.

CHAPTER XIV

"It's more human inside than outside":

relations between prisoners

There is a surprising social cohesion in the prisons, transcending pre-conceived boundaries. Each prison is a potentially explosive environment, where tens of thousands of Hutu prisoners accused of genocide have to live side by side, in the closest proximity, with a small number of Tutsi prisoners. But Hutu and Tutsi, *génocidaires* and common criminals, all are in the same boat. "There are no divisions," one prisoner told us. "We are all prisoners. Once you come in here, it's finished. We live together."

As in any society, there are friendships and enmities, jealousy, power struggles, and occasional fights. But most of the time, tensions are kept under control. Incidents of serious violence are fairly infrequent. Most of the prisoners we spoke to – from different categories and different backgrounds – confirmed, with a certain sense of pride, that overall, relations were good, and that open expressions of hostility were rare.

For the sake of their own survival, prisoners have a tacit agreement to preserve order and calm. The resulting atmosphere is superficially harmonious, but it is a harmony based on self-interest and pragmatism, rather than serenity. The calm has an edge, or multiple edges, but the edges blur and dissolve among the mass of prisoners, and it is sometimes difficult to pinpoint precisely where the tensions lie. Mostly, they remain unspoken.

Violence and the absence of violence

Overall, the prison culture in Rwanda is not a culture of violence. Yet all the ingredients are there: an extraordinarily high number of prisoners, the strain imposed by intolerable living conditions, and the extreme violence of the crimes of which most of these prisoners stand accused.

A former prisoner was amazed when he first arrived in Kigali Central Prison: "Before, I had a mental image of the prison being a brutal place, but I didn't see any violence or abuse… I asked the prisoners: 'How come there is no violence?' They said: 'What do you expect?' " Many prisoners experienced a similar sense of surprise and relief when they first arrived. A young prisoner accused of genocide remembered his first day: "I was so frightened, as I thought the prison was full of *interahamwe*. I was afraid of the other prisoners. In fact, it was the opposite. I was well received."

There were exceptions, of course, especially in the early days, when conditions were so extreme that prisoners sometimes ended up fighting over food or water, and incidents of physical aggression were more common. In Gikondo and Kimironko prisons, in particular, groups of prisoners repeatedly clashed in 1997 and 1998. These fights were mostly about control of the leadership of the prison. In 1997, Gikondo prison – which closed in October 2003 – was run by a clique of prisoners described as "bandits" or hardened criminals.[1] These leaders ruled through intimidation and violence, operating with the tacit assent of the prison director. One prisoner told us about an incident in which a member of the prisoners' security team beat another prisoner to death: "The brutality there was terrible. We all knew about it but could do nothing. The director was informed but nothing was done." Eventually, there was a clash between these "bandits" and a group of "intellectuals". One of these "intellectuals", a former politician, explained: "When they saw us intellectuals, they felt threatened. They accused us of organising strikes or revolts. They reported this to the director who put seven of us in the punishment cell for 20 days. The seven included engineers, politicians and former authorities. The *capita général* accused us of plotting and planning a revolt. The director told us: 'You are not in Mugunga or Benaco here'.[2] Other prisoners were beaten. All seven of us were in the cell together. It was like a mud room, three metres by two metres. We couldn't

---

[1]   Prisoners sometimes use the term "bandits" to refer to common criminals, as opposed to those accused of genocide.

[2]   Mugunga, in the Democratic Republic of Congo, and Benaco, in Tanzania, were two of the largest refugee camps from 1994 to 1996. Members of the former Rwandan government, military and *interahamwe* militia were among the hundreds of thousands of refugees who fled Rwanda at the end of the genocide and settled in these camps. From there, some reorganised their structures and carried out military training in exile.

use forks or spoons and they refused us plates. We were like animals when we came out. We had no water to wash and didn't go out at all for 20 days."

A younger prisoner also managed to get on the wrong side of the leaders when he first arrived in Gikondo: "The *responsables* were illiterate and un-reasonable. Most were people from the countryside. They were not used to leading different types of people. They were just in it for their own interest and tried to extort from other prisoners... Every time they saw a group of people talking who were not their friends, they suspected we were against them... It was a form of intimidation. I was beaten once, but others were beaten even more seriously."

In Kimironko prison, a similar power-struggle in around 1998 turned to violence. A prisoner who observed what happened described it as an internal coup d'état: "It was at night. We saw a new security group trying to take over from the *responsables* of the blocks. There was a big fight inside... Soldiers intervened. The director of prisons [from the Ministry of Interior] came and sorted out the problem. Those responsible for the trouble were transferred to Kigali Central Prison and are still here."

Since 1998, such incidents have become rare, and physical fights between prisoners have decreased. Tensions remain, but they are not expressed physically, or even verbally. For example one prisoner talked about the tensions between rich and poor prisoners: "There is jealousy between people: there are the rich in their châteaux, and at the other end, there are people sleeping in the open air in the rain. You can't see the jealousy, as these two groups don't really meet, but they don't like each other."

There are occasional indications, however, that violence is not as far from some prisoners' minds as it may seem. In Butare Central Prison, the prison director showed us a large sack of weapons he had confiscated. It was full of knives, machetes, metal bars and other lethal weapons which prisoners had manufactured themselves or had managed to smuggle into the prison. Whether they were intending to use these weapons against each other or against an unidentified enemy outside remained a mystery. The *capita général* told us: "Every week, we search and find weapons, usually metal bars which they have sharpened. They get the metal from the welders and those who do metalwork. Prisoners make all sort of things, knives, keys... [he showed us his own bunch of keys which had been made by prisoners]. Or some of those who work outside may come back with a piece of broken machete or scrap metal which they pick up from building sites or elsewhere. Prisoners don't reject or throw out any piece of metal. The guards don't seem to search them."

When violence does erupt, it is usually brought under control by the prisoners themselves. The prisoners' security team is always on the lookout for signs of trouble and tries to nip them in the bud. Disputes may be sparked by trivial arguments over food, money, theft, or personal animosities and settling of scores. A former prisoner told us how he was almost attacked by a group of prisoners in 2003 because during a *gacaca* session, he had denounced a local government official for participating in the genocide; the prisoners who tried to attack him were loyal to the government official. Members of the security team intervened and prevented the conflict from developing into a full-blown fight.

There are occasions when the security team is not able to intervene in time. A former prisoner in Butare remembered three or four incidents when prisoners had ended up killing each other: "One hurled a stone at another prisoner. Another was killed with a knife. Another was beaten with sticks." The director of Butare prison told us about an incident when a prisoner was killed in 2003: "One day, a prisoner was smoking hemp. Another prisoner tried to steal it from him. The first prisoner killed him with a knife, stabbing him seven times. We put him in the punishment cell, then transferred him to another prison. He had already been sentenced to death."

Troublemakers are sent to the punishment cells for a few hours, days or weeks, depending on the severity of their offence. Prisoners talk of a strict regime of discipline which they claim acts as a deterrent, but in practice, this attitude reflects their active compliance with their own system of internal governance more than a fear of punishment. Confinement to a punishment cell is not really confinement at all, and the punishment is more symbolic than practical. The cells, which are located within the prison blocks, are small, narrow and barren. Prisoners are supposed to be isolated there, but up to four can share a cell, sitting and sleeping on the concrete ground. Each cell has a door with a padlock, but in some prisons, the doors are left unlocked during the day, and the prisoners can chat with their friends. Their food rations are either brought to them in the cell, or, in some prisons, the prisoners are allowed to go out and fetch them themselves. They can attend meetings in the prison and are even allowed visits. In practice, the only difference between this and their normal routine is that they are locked up at night. It could even be argued that the conditions in the punishment cells are slightly better than in the rest of the prison blocks, as the prisoners are temporarily sheltered from the crush and the congestion.

We did not hear of any fatal attacks among the women prisoners, but there were sometimes fierce squabbles. One of the *capitas* told us: "There are some bad characters here, who are difficult. Some fight. We don't put up with this… We talk to them. We try to change their ideas. If there is still no progress, we send her to the director, but this is very rare. I have had to do it when two women had a fight. They lost control and slapped each other very hard and pulled each other's shirts. Other women saw it and the security team put them in the punishment cell. If they say sorry, they're released [from the punishment cell]. If they don't, they have to stay in for another day… They write an apology to the director, and we help those who can't write. They also apologise at the next general meeting, to everybody."

Transferring prisoners from one prison to another is also used as a form of punishment. Transfers are decided by the prison director, not by the prisoners themselves. Transfers may succeed in temporarily reducing tensions between groups of prisoners, but can be very unsettling on an individual level, as prisoners will usually find themselves further away from their home area, and it becomes more difficult for their families to visit them. A former prisoner said: "If they want to destabilise you, they transfer you. Some people have lost count of the number of times they have been transferred."

Kigali Central Prison, 1995   © Hervé Deguine

Ethnic relations

Ten years after the genocide, ethnic divisions in Rwanda run deeper than ever, and human relations have become conditioned by fear and suspicion. Yet in the prisons, there is a kind of calm which cannot be found elsewhere. One prisoner said that from this point of view, the prison was a paradise compared to the world outside: "It's more human inside than outside."

The political and ethnic balance in the prison is the opposite of the political balance outside: it is the balance which prevailed under the previous regime. In the prisons, the Hutu, without question, are still in power, and the Tutsi are an unprotected minority. Yet somehow, the ethnic and political polarisation seems to melt away within the prison walls. To a large extent, the common experience of imprisonment seems to have ironed out these differences. Or so most prisoners claimed. "There are no ethnic tensions in the prison," said one prisoner, "I talk with prisoners openly about politics, about anything. We tell each other what we think."

This is one of the many profound contradictions embodied by the world of Rwanda's prisons. The complete breakdown of ethnic co-existence and the manipulation of ethnic hatred which culminated in the genocide in Rwanda is the reason why the vast majority of these men and women are in prison in the first place. Yet with apparently little effort, Hutu and Tutsi prisoners are able to live together without friction and with little overt violence – even though many Hutu prisoners still perceive Tutsi prisoners as allies of the RPF who imprisoned them, and the Tutsi prisoners may perceive the bulk of Hutu prisoners as their killers. Ironically, the government's official post-genocide policy that there are no more Hutu and Tutsi, just Rwandans, has been far more successful in the prisons than outside, but not as a result of propaganda or indoctrination. One prisoner told us that the question of ethnicity among prisoners was not an issue: "The only ethnic problem is with the politicians."

In any case, the question of an individual's ethnic identity is often not clear-cut. There are many mixed marriages in Rwanda. Many Hutu accused of genocide have a mother or a father who is Tutsi; others have a Tutsi husband or wife, and lost many relatives and friends during the genocide. In Kigali Central Prison, I met a Hutu woman who was married to a Tutsi man. Both were arrested in 1995, on accusations of genocide. Her husband was released three years later, but she remained in prison. The way she told her story illustrated the absurdity of rigid ethnic labels: "My husband was almost killed twice during the genocide. He is considered Tutsi. I don't know if he's really Tutsi or what it means. He's just my husband."

Prisoners' assertions that there were no serious ethnic tensions in the prisons seemed genuine. However, there were moments when it was apparent that the general fear which reigned outside, and the effects of the government's intimidation of the population, had filtered through even into the prisons. Some prisoners, just like Rwandans outside, were fearful of talking straight. When we asked a prisoner in Gitarama Central Prison to estimate the proportion of Tutsi prisoners there, he said: "We try not to go into that. We would be accused of divisionism."[3] In fact, the words "Tutsi" and "Hutu" are rarely used by the prisoners. They are replaced with expressions like *"l'autre ethnie"* (the other ethnic group). Yet, in a contradiction typical of Rwanda, these prisoners who did not even dare refer to ethnic groups by their name were very vocal in their criticism of government policy, especially on the question of ethnicity. The same prisoner in Gitarama described the policies of the government as a "vicious circle of vengeance... The government says we should get rid of vengeance and ethnic differences, yet it is creating them."

When we scratched beneath the surface, we found that ethnic relations in the prisons were not always as harmonious as they seemed. The worst periods of tension were usually the first few days following a prisoner's arrival. Tutsi prisoners, in particular, were terrified at the thought of entering what they saw as a den of Hutu *génocidaires*. Some were taunted and insulted when they first arrived. They were greeted with comments like "The country belongs to you, so come in here too" or "You put us in here. You condemned

---

[3]   The term "divisionism", along with "genocidal ideology", has been used by the Rwandan government in the years following the genocide as part of a strategy to silence dissent. These accusations have typically been levelled against Hutu whom the government perceives as critics or opponents but against whom it does not have evidence of involvement in criminal activity. In 2002, a law was passed making "divisionism" a criminal offence, punishable with a prison sentence of up to five years. Examples of how this law has been used to target civil society in Rwanda can be found in *Front Line Rwanda: disappearances, arrests, threats, intimidation and co-option of human rights defenders 2001-2004*, published in 2005 by Front Line (an organisation which works to protect human rights defenders).

us. Come and lead the life you gave us." Members of the RPF who found
themselves in prison were given a particularly rough time.[4] In Byumba Central
Prison, prisoners who came from near the Ugandan border, or who spoke
Ugandan languages, were accused by Hutu prisoners of being accomplices of
the RPF.[5]

A Tutsi prisoner accused of fraud, who had lost many close relatives during
the genocide, described his first few days in Byumba prison in 2003:

> "There are very few Tutsi in the prisons... I couldn't react or
> show I felt threatened. I tried to let it wash over me... On my
> first day, I was very afraid. The prisoners surrounded me and I
> was in the middle. They called me Tutsi and *inyenzi* [cockroach].
> I went to see the *sociale* as I was very disturbed and I couldn't
> sleep. She calmed me down and listened to me but only for a few
> minutes and didn't ask me to come back. Some prisoners from
> my home area intervened to tell the other prisoners I hadn't done
> anything wrong. At least I hadn't got anyone arrested. After that,
> I gradually got used to it. If the other prisoners heard something
> on the radio [about the government], they would come and say
> to me: 'See what your brothers are doing.' During the [2003]
> elections, it was difficult. I said I supported Twagiramungu [the
> Hutu opposition candidate] but they didn't understand. I had to
> be careful and keep quiet."

Usually, the more serious aggression many Tutsi prisoners had anticipated
failed to materialise. A prisoner who had lived in four different prisons
told us: "There were misunderstandings between prisoners, for example
between Hutu and Tutsi about the genocide. The Tutsi would say: 'You killed
my family' and the Hutu would say: 'I protected your family and now I'm in

---

4   The relations between military prisoners and civilian prisoners, and between
different categories of military prisoners, are described in Chapter IX.

5   The northern part of Byumba province borders Uganda. The RPF was based in
Uganda when it was still a guerrilla movement, and from 1990 onwards, it launched
incursions from Uganda into Rwanda. The RPF had already occupied parts of
Byumba and other areas of northern and eastern Rwanda by the time the genocide
started in April 1994. The RPF's subsequent invasion of Kigali and other parts of the
country was carried out from northern Rwanda, with the support of Uganda.

prison". But it was only ever words. When a new Tutsi prisoner arrived, he always thought he would be killed. But he soon found there were no problems."

Some Tutsi prisoners were accepted into the fold without much comment or reaction. Like everyone else, they were thrown in at the deep end, but they managed to adapt, and a few, usually those with a higher status, even climbed up the rungs of the prison hierarchy. A Hutu prisoner remembered a Tutsi *bourgmestre* detained in Gisovu prison: "He was afraid and thought that as a Tutsi authority, he would not be able to live with us. But after a year, he realised we were not so nasty. When he was released, he brought some corn and milk for the prisoners to thank us, as he hadn't expected us to be so nice to him."

A few Hutu prisoners who were initially perceived as collaborators or supporters of the current government received a hostile reception. The insults with which they were greeted often took the form of jokes, but the particular brand of humour which has developed in the prisons is sharp and unforgiving, and those on the receiving end have to develop a thick skin to withstand it.

A Hutu former prisoner in Kigali Central Prison had had to put up with caustic comments from other prisoners when he first arrived. "You are being rewarded by the regime you were so loyal to," they told him, even though he had not worked for the government. He believed the other prisoners may have been jealous of him because, unlike many Hutu, he had at least been able to find employment after the genocide. He recalled:

> "As soon as I had had my first shower, they made me impart information, endlessly, about what was going on outside, 'in that country', as the older prisoners used to say. 'What's going on out there? What were you, as a Hutu, still doing out there? The country of the Hutu is in here, not outside'... A crowd was already gathering around me to listen to what I had to say. Ten minutes later, they were disappointed by my answers, which did not meet their expectations. 'He's lying as he still thinks he's working for

the government. He'll tell us more in two months' time, once he realises he's been forgotten here, unless he's been sent to spy on us'.

Several people used to make these types of comments, and not just to me. They would say [to newly arrived Hutu prisoners]: 'Why have you waited so long? Our place is here, not outside.' Or: 'Come in, this is your final destination.' It was not a joke. There are some extremists in there. At night, you could hear people saying: 'We've had enough of the Tutsi. They're going to kill us all'.

Sometimes a group of Hutu prisoners would see a Tutsi common criminal. A few of the common criminals stayed in prison a long time. They included some former military from Uganda. The *génocidaires* would say to them: 'Your regime has forgotten you. Tell them that you're likely to die in here with us.' "

The provocative remarks seemed to be a test to judge the resilience of the new arrivals rather than a serious attempt at starting a fight. Nevertheless, there was a permanent distance between the two ethnic groups which came to the fore at times of political tension outside. The same former prisoner explained:

"You could feel the dislike, even though it wasn't expressed. But as most prison staff were Tutsi, the Hutu were afraid of harming the Tutsi prisoners. When there were the attacks in the northwest [by Hutu insurgents in 1997 and 1998], prisoners used to make comments. Some were very pleased and used to say things like: 'Our army's coming, the Tutsi will be overthrown.' Some of them said these things in front of Tutsi prisoners, but there was no reaction, as the Tutsi were in a minority."

Some individuals were singled out for harsher treatment as a result of their perceived collaboration with the current regime. A former provincial government official was very badly received when he first arrived in prison because of comments he had made in his official capacity after the genocide. Prisoners accused him of collaborating with the current government because he had once accompanied a ministerial delegation to the prison to explain the new genocide law and had described the events which took place during the genocide as very serious. On his first day in prison, he was shoved into a corner at the back of a dark room from where he could not even see the door and where there was no space to lie down. The *capita général* specifically asked the *brigadier général* responsible for security to put him there, as a kind of punishment. On the first evening, he was beaten by other prisoners, who threw dirty water, and potato and banana peel at him.   Some prisoners, including another former local government official and a priest, intervened to protect him. Eventually he was advised to pay for a better place. After asking his wife to bring him 5,000 francs, he was moved to a château where there was enough space to sleep and which had partitions made of sacks dividing it from the neighbouring châteaux.

Génocidaires and common criminals

The distinction between *génocidaires* and common criminals can be more important than the distinction between Hutu and Tutsi, and a prisoner's social status in the prison is more likely to be determined by his alleged crime than by his ethnicity. The *génocidaires* far outnumber the common criminals and dominate the prison hierarchy, so it is they who set the mood and lay down the rules.[6]

The *génocidaires* and the common criminals all live together. Some prisoners denied that there was any distinction between the two groups, just as they denied that there was any distinction between Hutu and Tutsi. "We can't tell who's who," said one prisoner. "We share everything." This may be true in some cases, but overall, the language prisoners used when talking about their fellow inmates indicated a clear awareness of difference and, in some prisons, a marked social distinction. An elderly prisoner said: "The *génocidaires* and common criminals live together as we are in the same misfortune, but we have different concerns and a different language."

---

6   According to estimates from non-governmental organisations, prisoners accused of genocide accounted for approximately 90% of prisoners at the end of 2004, or just over 75,000 out of 85,500 prisoners.

The common criminals have little in common with the bulk of the *génocidaires*, either in terms of the crimes they allegedly committed or in their attitude towards their imprisonment. Many of the *génocidaires* have spent close to ten years in prison and have resigned themselves to spending many more there. As many of the common criminals are accused of lesser crimes, they are perceived by the *génocidaires* as more likely to be released within a short time. They are in transit, and therefore cannot be taken seriously as long-term prisoners. "You'll be counting the windows," the *génocidaires* would say to the common criminals when they first arrived in the prison – an expression meaning that they would not spend long there (they would walk past the prison, count the windows and leave). A prisoner accused of genocide said bitterly: "We, the *génocidaires*, we are condemned, we are people who have to die. The common criminals will get out more quickly." The *génocidaires* also suspected some of the common criminals of being spies. Several prisoners we spoke to claimed that the RPF used to place "false" prisoners in the prisons to watch them and report back to the government on their activities. We asked them how they could tell who the spies were. "We can just tell," they said, "and they just stay for a short time, then mysteriously they're released." Those they suspected of being spies were always common criminals, never *génocidaires*.

Common criminals, for their part, complained of being treated as second-class citizens by the *génocidaires*. Apart from their dominance in terms of sheer numbers, many of the *génocidaires* are better educated than the common criminals and tend to look down on them, partly out of intellectual snobbery and partly, as indicated above, out of jealousy, because they believe they will not stay long in prison. Putting them down or depriving them of certain privileges may be a way of expressing that jealousy. A prisoner in Butare told us that the *génocidaires* there called the common criminals *abana* (children), originally because the *génocidaires* sometimes abused the common criminals, especially the children. In other prisons, the *génocidaires* called the common criminals thieves or murderers. The common criminals' feeling of discrimination was aggravated by the policy of the prison management not to allow them to work outside, in case they escaped. A young prisoner accused of a common crime complained that the *génocidaires* deprived the common criminals of certain rights, in particular the opportunity to study. He was halfway through his university course when he was arrested, and wanted to continue studying, but claimed that the books in the prison library were reserved for genocide prisoners. Once, when he had requested a copy of a magazine, the prisoner responsible for the library had told him they were not for him because common criminals were likely to steal the books. He also complained that on visit days, common criminals were the last to come out to meet their visitors, so their families had to wait for hours until the much larger number of *génocidaires* had finished speaking to their visitors.

A former prisoner accused of a common crime said it had taken at least a year for the prisoners accused of genocide to start trusting him. Eventually, he managed to make friends with prisoners in both categories: "I never saw them as *génocidaires* as such. I never presumed anyone was guilty, as there is no proper justice... Among the common criminals, we discussed our own cases. With the *génocidaires*, it was difficult as they had different types of cases, but we talked about other things. We would support each other. My closest friends included both *génocidaires* and common criminals."

A former prisoner accused of fraud complained about how the *génocidaires* treated the common criminals, but he had ended up feeling more sorry for them than resentful: "The *génocidaires* used to taunt the common criminals, saying we were just there to walk about and would soon be set free. They weren't sympathetic if a common criminal complained about his own situation. They saw their own position as more serious. But many of the *génocidaires* I saw were traumatised. Some had difficulty speaking and stayed silent... I felt I was lucky to be a common criminal."

We met several prisoners who had had two stints in prison, first as a *génocidaire* then as a common criminal, or vice versa. These prisoners offered a unique insight into the dynamics of each group and the relationship between the two, having experienced it from both sides. Their views were not always consistent. A prisoner who had spent five years in prison on an accusation of genocide was released in 1999 and re-arrested in June 2004, accused of theft. He returned to the same prison, but did not feel that his change in status had altered his relationship with other prisoners: "The accusation is not our business. It's a private matter. I have been in both categories but there is no difference. There are no tensions. Prisoners are the first to get on well together. It is peaceful here." However, a prisoner in another prison had had a very different experience. He had spent four years in prison on a genocide accusation, then was released and re-arrested four years later, accused of murder. When he returned to the same prison as a common criminal, he found that prisoners' attitudes towards him had altered, and there was not the same solidarity he had experienced as a *génocidaire*. This shift in mood had unsettled him and destroyed his confidence:

> "In prison the second time, I noticed lots of changes... The *génocidaires* treat the common criminals as thieves, except me as they knew me... Most of my friends inside are accused of genocide. They are friends from before, but I don't feel at ease with them now. When I was free, they saw that I was doing OK and I was reintegrated in society. They're suspicious of me. I haven't really made new friendships the second time."

A prisoner in Butare had first been in prison before the genocide, from 1992 to 1994, accused of theft. He was released at the height of the genocide in 1994 and fled to Congo, where he stayed until 1997. Then, two and a half weeks after his return to Rwanda, he was re-arrested, this time on an accusation of genocide. Although he was now technically a *génocidaire*, he had made friends with prisoners in both groups: "When I'm ill, a common criminal helps me. Mostly the *génocidaires* and the common criminals get on well, but the *génocidaires* are nicer. The common criminals are more arrogant and confident that they won't stay long, so they don't follow the rules. There is more solidarity among the *génocidaires* as they will all go through the same system."

Relations among the *génocidaires* are more complicated. There are those who have killed and those who haven't. Many in the latter category were very afraid when they first arrived in the prison. Over the following weeks and months, they listened in horror as some of their fellow inmates described the crimes they had committed. A former prisoner remembered the first time he overheard a conversation between prisoners about what they had done during the genocide: "They were proud of what they had done. I was very upset. I thought: 'why am I here?' I couldn't sleep at all that night". But however strong their discomfort at living side by side with these people, they eventually learned to co-exist. When the confessions programme was introduced, however, the superficial harmony was destroyed. New divisions were created: divisions among the guilty, among the innocent, and between the guilty and the innocent (see Chapter XIX).

A former prisoner talked about the occasional conflicts between the guilty and the innocent. "The criminals [the guilty ones] used to say things like: 'I've killed 100 people. I'm just waiting to die.' We used to call them '*les dangereux*' [the dangerous ones]. The intellectuals – those who felt themselves to be innocent – used to try to make them realise they were still human." A prisoner who had been sentenced to life imprisonment for genocide lived in a special part of a block reserved for prisoners sentenced to life or to death. He said some of the other prisoners there talked openly about how they had directed killings during the genocide. They mocked those who were innocent and told them: "You didn't do anything, but you've been sentenced just like us. We're the ones who really killed, but there's no difference between us now."

Friendships in prison

Prisoners talked about the friendships they had developed in prison in a multitude of ways, but in the end, these friendships tended to fall into one of two categories: functional friendships based on mutual self-interest, or deeper, longer-lasting friendships. Occasionally, the two overlapped, or friendships which started off as functional would turn into stronger, social bonds.

Prisoners were brutally honest in the way they described the "functional" friendships. These were dealings based on selfish materialism, only worth pursuing if the other person could give them something: money, favours, ways of making their lives more bearable.[7] They might reciprocate in kind, if they were able to, but the friendship did not consist of much more than that.

---

[7]   A similar attitude characterised prisoners' attitudes towards family visits: if their relatives were not able to bring them food or money, these visits were considered almost useless (see Chapter XI).

Friendship for the sake of company or moral support did not hold much value for these prisoners. One prisoner told us: "There are people I chat with, but they are not really friends. They can't do anything for me." As soon as they were released, these friendships would cease to be useful, and prisoners did not expect to sustain them beyond their period in prison.

Some prisoners apparently went out of their way not to make friends. One prisoner, despite his outwardly sociable manner, had developed a suspicious attitude towards friendships in prison: "I've avoided making friends in prison, so that I can feel freer," he told us. "It exposes you if people are too close. If you have something of great value, you could make enemies if you share it."

The concept of solidarity seemed to have different meanings for different prisoners. One former prisoner told us that in prison, solidarity simply meant money. Others gave it a more generous interpretation. One prisoner told us: "There is solidarity between prisoners. People get on well, especially those in my block. We lend each other things… Some come in with nothing, no plates, no forks. We lend them ours or we undo our beds to give them a piece of cardboard to lie on." Prisoners tried to reciprocate gestures of assistance when they could, the most common of which was sharing food. This was particularly true in the early days, when many prisoners would have died had other prisoners not come to their rescue. There were extraordinary acts of solidarity by prisoners, many of whom were almost as destitute as those they were helping. Some of the most solid friendships had their origins in these acts of generosity in desperate circumstances, especially when a prisoner first arrived in the prison. By sharing his food or offering to share his space, a prisoner could unknowingly have sown the seeds of a lifelong friendship.

Some of these friendships predated their arrival in prison – many prisoners found old friends and relatives in prison – but strangers also formed strong bonds and looked after each other "like brothers" or "like sisters". Members of the same religious community often became close friends. Indeed, solidarity based on religion seemed to come the most naturally. At first, prisoners also gravitated towards others from their own area of origin, whether they had known them before or not, and this common background could sometimes form a starting point for a friendship.

In some prisons, little cliques would develop, occasionally leading to competition or jealousy. This was especially the case when large groups of prisoners were transferred together from one prison to another. For example in Nsinda prison, a rivalry had developed between prisoners who were transferred from Kibungo, in the east of the country, and those who were transferred from Byumba, in the north. A prisoner who was in the Kibungo group complained of tensions arising from the domination of the prison hierarchy by "the northerners". Some of the women in Kigali Central Prison also complained of tensions arising from regional divisions; some claimed that positions of responsibility were dominated by women from the northwest of Rwanda. When Kibuye Central Prison closed in early 2003, many of the prisoners there were transferred to Gitarama Central Prison, but those from Kibuye retained a distinct identity and continued to stick together.

Some prisoners spoke movingly about the close personal friendships they had developed, which went well beyond material solidarity. They chose their words carefully: these prisoners were "friends", while others were commonly referred to as "colleagues". One prisoner, who spoke good English, had written a special song in English for some of his friends. He recited some of the words for us: "Friends of mine, don't forget me, I am yours, yours, and you are mine." For another prisoner, the test of real solidarity was what happened after a prisoner's release: "Whether I consider them as friends or not depends on whether the friendship will continue outside. More than 500 prisoners have been released, but they haven't visited us, so I doubt the friendships will continue. They promised to visit. Some said they would follow up my case for me, but they haven't come back."

For prisoners who have little or no contact with their family, their friendships with other prisoners may be all they have. A prisoner who was 20 when he was arrested and 30 by the time we met him said that, for him, his friends in prison were like his family: "Most of my friends are young, like me. Others are older. They are like parents and give me food, especially when I'm sick. There are some minors (the youngest are 14 or 15) whom I consider as my little brothers." A former prisoner who had spent almost nine years in prison said: "Prison friendships are like friendships from school, military camps, or convents. We are inter-dependent. A prisoner friend can be more valuable than a brother. These friendships last a long time."

A disabled prisoner described how he had to rely on others to survive the harsh prison environment from day to day:

> "Living here as an invalid means I always have to be accompanied, for example to wash or to eat. I can't do anything on my own. It's difficult even to take a bucket to fetch water. I can't easily access the hygiene facilities. It's very competitive, so people need to be strong and quick to get water and other things. Several people help me, especially a close friend who helps me a lot. I knew him before, but our friendship only really started in prison. When he's ill, I have to find someone else to help me. When he's ill, I'm ill too. He doesn't live next to me. When I sleep, I can't get up to reach him so I have to ask the person next to me. People help me, because tomorrow, they may need help themselves. There is solidarity. Relations are better in here than outside."

Naturally some prisoners are more or less sociable than others. One prisoner told us he enjoyed chatting with anyone who was willing to talk. But some of those we met had only one or two people they considered as real friends. In Kigali Central Prison, we talked to a prisoner in his forties who had been among the first to be arrested after the genocide. He had spent more than ten years in prison. He told us he had only had one friend in prison, a younger man who was arrested at the same time as him but was released in 2002. He told us his friend had visited him once since his release. He wanted him to come again and asked us to pass this message on to his friend, whom we had met earlier. He reflected on the nature of prison friendships: "You talk to people because of the circumstances, but once we're released, it will stop." He was a lonely man, and his loneliness extended beyond the prison walls. His wife and one of his children had died during his period in prison. He told us that if he was released, he would probably go and stay with another former prisoner, as he would have nowhere else to go.

CHAPTER XV

"We are always in a state of maybe":

attitudes to imprisonment

"Life in prison is just one small stone in a big mosaic, one spark in a great fire."

Prison as home

There are those who have made prison their home, and there are those who never will, who are unable to, and whose suffering never decreases, however many months and years go by.

It is fairly easy to identify the prisoners who have made prison their home. They behave, move and talk in a particular way, with a kind of relaxed authority born out of the length of time they have spent there – eight, nine, ten years – and the acceptance, explicit or implicit, that they are unlikely to get out soon. Their discourse is calm, peppered with a hard sense of humour. They have transcended their suffering and have made the prison environment their own. If asked, they will protest that it is impossible to get used to life in prison. Yet, consciously or otherwise, that is what they have succeeded in doing. It is a form of defiance against those who have imprisoned them and a way of taking control of their small world.

These are, for the most part, prisoners accused of genocide, who have witnessed and in some cases perpetrated some of the worst horrors imaginable. Some then fled into exile and would have seen many more die there, of disease in the refugee camps, or shot dead by the new Rwandan army when it invaded eastern Congo. They may have become separated from their families and lost all trace of them to this day.

In comparison to this accumulation of horror, prison life may not seem quite so grim. These prisoners have become hardened and alienated, brutalised by their actions or their experiences, then brutalised all over again by the prison environment. But within the relative safety of the prison walls, they can detach themselves from the rest of humanity and can find a kind of freedom in that detachment.

According to the prisoners themselves, those most likely to consider the prison as their home or to feel "comfortable" there were those who knew they stood little or no chance of being released. These included prisoners who had already been sentenced to death or to life imprisonment, those who were closely associated with the former government and others who were known to have participated in the genocide. One of the prisoners we met had come to terms with the fact that he was unlikely to ever be released, by virtue of the fairly senior position he had held in the ruling party under the former government: [1] "Some people can pay for a solution to their problem, but I can't. Politically, I'm finished. I'm convinced I'll never be tried. If they saw me as a political card, I would have been tried by now. I watch the politicians. I understand them. I'm just here and this is the life I'm living… Prison is my life and my home. It's no problem for me, but it hurts me to see people suffering here."

There were also those who had no family or home to go to should they ever be released, and certain types of common criminals, including repeat offenders. A prisoner observed: "Those who have killed feel like prison is their home and wouldn't survive outside. 'Delinquents' [common criminals] are the same. At least they get food here. They wouldn't be able to find work outside. They have no one outside. They think: 'My home is here.' Some don't even think about their release. They just accept it."

In extreme cases, some prisoners apparently did not even want to be released. A former prisoner remembered the reaction of one prisoner who was due to be released: "They told him to get ready to be released. He refused and went to hide. So that was that. He had killed a lot of people. He knew he didn't deserve to be released." A man who had spent ten years in prison described the attitude of some of his colleagues by quoting a Rwandan saying: *ihene yamenyereye kuzirikwa n'iyo uyizituye yanga kugenda igira ngo urayikinisha* (a goat which is used to being tied up often hesitates to leave even when it is set free). He explained: "I mean there are some people who would not want to be released because they wouldn't know where to go or what to do and where to start. So life continues, whatever the circumstances. I've noticed

---

[1]　The *Mouvement républicain national pour la démocratie et le développement* (MRND) was the ruling party under President Habyarimana.

some prisoners consider the prison blocks as their villages and give out the number of their bed as if it was their address."

But not all prisoners have managed to adapt to life in prison. Some sit on their 40-centimetre planks or in corners of the courtyard in silence and isolation. Others wander around aimlessly, with blank expressions, lost in memory, in despair or simply in the emptiness of their existence. If they had any hope in the early days, it has evaporated with the ever-receding prospect of justice. For them, the future, if it exists at all, is just a dream. A former prisoner who was released after eight and a half years told us simply: "You don't envisage anything when you're in prison." An elderly and sick prisoner said at the end of our conversation: "It is as if we are in a hole. I'll go back to my place and wait."

Hope and despair

Prisoners' attitudes towards their imprisonment filtered through in a variety of ways during our conversations, and, like almost every other aspect of their situation, were characterised by multiple contradictions. The same prisoners who shrugged off their situation as "normal" – "*c'est comme ça*" (that's how it is) – and who had evidently succeeded in adapting to life in prison suddenly became indignant when asked if the prison had become their home. Those who said they preferred not to think about their future because they had no hope of being released were also those who described themselves as optimistic and confident that justice would be done. They found themselves torn between the weight of despair and the need to keep the flame of hope alive for their own sanity. They wavered between the two, often unsure as to which corresponded to the reality. A prisoner who had been detained for eight years said: "We are always in a state of maybe."

The extent to which prisoners are able to cope with their imprisonment does not always correspond to the objective gravity of their situation. Some of those who have suffered the most are among the most resilient and optimistic, perhaps because their earlier experiences have given them a sense of perspective. "You have to be happy with what you have and not try for what you can't have," said one prisoner after almost eight years in prison without trial. It is a question of temperament, and, the prisoners would say, a question of prayer. It is also a question of money. The most desperate prisoners are often the poorest. Those who can buy themselves a few luxuries and whose families can afford to visit them regularly at least have some small comforts to distract them.

Many prisoners we spoke to felt bitter towards the RPF and the government which had imprisoned them, but still considered themselves lucky to be alive. They had expected to be killed in the aftermath of the genocide. Among them was an older, well-educated prisoner who had spent ten years in prison accused of genocide, in addition to seven years in prison before the genocide for an alleged financial crime. Seventeen years of imprisonment had not yet worn him down. He told us calmly: "The people who came in [the RPF] could have just killed me. It's normal that the RPF should hurt us like this. They conquered us. Usually, the people who are conquered are exterminated. But thanks to God, we're alive. I tell the other prisoners this, that we are lucky to be alive, even though some of our families have been killed. I can't feel cross. But the government has exaggerated: not all Hutu are killers. Keeping people in prison for so long without trial is killing them slowly. It's a form of vengeance."

Prisoners experienced sharp mood swings. Often these were directly related to developments in the justice system: whenever the government announced programmes of releases or the start of *gacaca* trials (see Chapter XVII), prisoners' hopes rocketed, then when they failed to materialise, they sank back into resignation and despair. The government's numerous announcements and promises – many of them unfulfilled – have put prisoners through the same seesaw of emotion time and time again. Even though prisoners soon realised that they should not pin their hopes on these announcements, they could not help doing so. "They [the government] always made promises," one woman explained. "We believed them. Every time, we thought: this time, it's for real."

A woman who had spent time in three different prisons described the psychological vulnerability of prisoners:

"There was a feeling of permanent fear and uncertainty. One moment, a prisoner can feel very optimistic and expect to be released. The next moment, you can expect a life or death sentence. We suffered from serious mental instability. One day, a prisoner can be very cheerful and the next day, very depressed. It is easy to frighten prisoners, like children.

Some prisoners stay alone when they are depressed. They don't want to eat or do anything. Sometimes I used to find myself thinking: 'Let me die and let this be over with' or 'I may stay here for the rest of my life.' The lack of faith in justice accentuates these feelings. When we used to see someone looking depressed, isolated or violent, we used to say 'uburoko bwamuriye' ['prison is consuming him today']. It meant they were driven to desperation and felt they had nothing to lose.

It was difficult to make plans because the authorities used to say we would be released tomorrow, but five years later, we were still in.

Some people always kept their morale and made plans, all the time. We didn't know how they did it. There was one man who used to say: 'Let's do everything we can to unsettle the prison rather than let the prison unsettle us.' It became his motto. 'Tubuserereze' [the Kinyarwanda word expressing this concept] became his nickname. He had guitars made in Gitarama for young prisoners who wanted to learn to play. He was eventually released."

Some prisoners who had not yet been tried managed to maintain an extraordinary, totally unrealistic optimism. Despite years in prison in a legal limbo and no indication as to when they might expect to be tried, let alone released, prisoners would announce confidently: "I know I will be released next month", "I will be on the next list of those due for release", or "I won't spend more than another year in here" – even when all the evidence pointed to the contrary. One prisoner explained that his optimism was based on his innocence, even though he knew very well that innocence didn't have much to do with decisions about releases. But without this belief, he would have fallen apart. He later admitted that he sometimes lost patience, and he knew he was more likely to be released through chance than through any process of justice: "Here in the prison, people come and go. It is like a rotation or a transit centre. I hope I can just be part of that rotation and that I might leave."

The prisoners who never lost hope were often those who kept themselves busy inside – obsessively coordinating, teaching, learning, praying – so busy that they almost ended up forgetting that they were in prison. They made sure they had no time to think, or to remember where they were and why they were there. A former prisoner recalled the words of a friend he found in prison, who apologised for not greeting him earlier on his first day: "I know you've been here since this morning, but I had a lot to do. Even here, we are often busy, or we have to pretend to be busy so that the years can become days."

A 30-year-old prisoner maintained a remarkably fresh outlook, even though he had been in prison for more than nine years without trial and was not one of the more materially privileged prisoners. He kept himself busy teaching and studying, every day. Unlike some prisoners, whose optimism came across as slightly contrived, his seemed genuine and natural. I asked him how he coped with being in prison for such a long time. "I don't think about it," he said with a constant smile. "It's as if I came here yesterday... the time has passed quickly."

His attitude was exceptional, even among the more optimistic prisoners. For most, the slow passage of time was one of the most painful aspects of prison life. Each had their own measure of time in prison, which they expressed in different ways:

> "One day seemed as long as two."
> "Here, one day is like lots of days."
> "One year in here is like two years outside."
> "Time goes slowly. A week is like a year."
> "The day is long and the night doesn't finish quickly."
> "I don't count the days, because there are too many. I cross off each year. It's easier."

The younger prisoners, especially, were acutely aware of the years slipping away. In the time they had spent in prison, they could have got married, had several children, finished their studies, found a job and earned some money. The prospects of doing any or all of these things after their release remained uncertain. Prisoners who were arrested in their twenties or thirties and who had spent close to ten years in prison often felt that their lives had been ruined.

Prisoners who have been tried and sentenced to life imprisonment, or sentenced to death, have a different attitude to their imprisonment. They have shifted into a different gear. They continue pursuing all their legal options for appeal, tirelessly, but their pretence of hope is unconvincing. A prisoner sentenced to life imprisonment, who spoke eloquently and passionately about his life in prison and his views on justice, had only a few words to say about the future: "We continue to live from day to day. I don't know what will happen tomorrow. I tell myself I have to succeed with my appeal… Prison has not become my home, but we have no choice, no alternative. We're just waiting."

Another prisoner, who had been sentenced to life imprisonment after three successive periods in prison for a crime he claimed he did not commit, spoke about his situation with moving humility: "Sometimes I spend four days in a row without eating, and I think about the person who has killed who was released, and I'm still here, even though I haven't killed. The situation requires me to keep calm, otherwise I would go mad. It is a lesson in self-control. To keep my morale, I think: well, I'm here, I can't do anything. And I think of all the people who were killed, who were innocent too."

Prisoners' expectations have evolved over time. Almost all those we spoke to said that when they were first arrested, they never thought they would stay in for more than a few days. Some hadn't even taken their arrest very seriously. "I thought it was a mistake", "I was innocent, so I knew I would be released" were their initial reactions – reactions of incredulity, even among those whose arrest cannot have taken them entirely by surprise. One prisoner told us: "When I first arrived in prison, naively, I thought I would get out soon. I used to tell people I would be out in a month. Now it's seven years. Prisoners joke and say to me: 'You're still here!' " A former prisoner remembered his fellow inmates' best efforts to disabuse him when he first arrived: "Some senior prisoners who have been there a long time stay together, talking and joking. They were all around us… Some of the older ones were comfortably set up. They told us we may be there for a long time and we shouldn't be getting ideas we would be released soon." At first, their warnings didn't ring true. Then the days turned into weeks, the weeks into months, the months into years. Gradually, each prisoner realised that the matter of their guilt or innocence was irrelevant, and that once they found themselves in prison, it was almost impossible to get out.

Only a few said they were not surprised to be arrested. These were prisoners who had held positions of authority under the former government, former politicians, people who were too well-known to be able to escape arrest, and others who decided to hand themselves in to the authorities, typically soon after returning from exile. They may have done this for reasons of conscience or, more likely, of pragmatism: better to be arrested than to be killed.

The incredulity which most prisoners experienced in the initial stage of their imprisonment was a reaction not only to the fact of their arrest but also to the conditions in which they were expected to live. At first, they could not imagine surviving. One prisoner compared it to arriving in a foreign country. But within a surprisingly short time, they managed to adapt. "It was just a change in life", said a former prisoner. "I had to make the mental adjustment as I walked through the gate. There was nothing I could do. The next day, we had to line up to take a shower, half naked. Everyone goes through the same routine, even people in high positions. You don't see yourself as special. You just get involved in it."

The process of adjustment was captured by another former prisoner's written account of the time he spent in Kigali Central Prison:

> "I was wondering [on my first day] whether I would be able to sleep at all in that nauseating place, where people stared at you with disdain, trampled on you, laughed in your face, shouted in your ears as if to celebrate your arrival in their midst, danced, sang and played above you – whether I would be able to sleep in

that chaos. I didn't realise I was already sleeping, in that public market, and that that was sleep, there in that new world...

That is how I discovered that life stops only when the heart cannot go on. I discovered some people's happiness through the misery of others... From that day onwards, I learned that you can sleep and eat in the toilets... that you can spend a week without eating and still survive... that life and mourning become one and the same thing. That above all, I had to resist, like everyone else – 8,000 people at that time... I learned how to live a life of order through disorder and to live apparent disorder in the name of order."

Being in prison led some prisoners to reflect on their own situation in new ways. A prisoner accused of a common crime said: "You have to change in prison. You don't think in the same way as when you're free. Now I avoid getting angry. Some people go mad because they think too much. I've seen this happen." Another prisoner, accused of genocide, said: "Prison helps us withstand the hard things in life. It trains us to be patient. Sometimes we waste our lives away. But after being here, we have a sense of the value of life... I have rethought my ideas and philosophy. Being here has taught me how to live with people, accept how they are, be patient and not get cross with other people's ideas. We should share the easy and the difficult aspects of other people's lives."

Reflecting on their imprisonment could even become a form of intellectual activity. One prisoner told us that he had organised a debate in the *cachot* where he had been detained on whether life as a refugee was better or worse than life in prison. He had won the debate, arguing that prison was worse.

One man who had spent ten years in prison had a philosophical attitude towards his imprisonment: "Personally, I've never felt depressed. I don't know why. Perhaps it's a matter of faith, perhaps it's in my character. Since I arrived here, I have really begun to discover who I am. I started to look at myself. It's as if I lived all my life in a dream until then, and now I'm waking up. It's strange... I will stay here until further notice. That time will come. History repeats itself. Life in prison is just one small stone in a big mosaic, one spark in a great fire."

Others started off feeling sorry for themselves but soon realised that many prisoners were in an even more desperate situation than they were. Their conversations with their fellow inmates put their own situation in perspective. A woman who had spent three years in prison said that when she talked to women who had been detained for ten years, she felt as if she was not in prison at all. A former prisoner, accused of fraud, was marked by his early conversations with the prisoners who happened to be living near him in his block: "I chatted to the guy sleeping next to me. I asked him what he was in for. He said genocide. I asked him if he had killed. He said yes. The guy on my other side was a tailor accused of an attempted murder, after the genocide. He was a common criminal, sentenced to life... He had been in for five years... One of the people who would have been next on the list to be executed, after the group of around 20,[2] was sleeping across from me... You just start talking to people. They confide in you. My case seemed like a joke in comparison to some of theirs. Some were on death row. Others had just missed a bullet."

Some prisoners have revised their perceptions and opinions of imprisonment as a whole. A number of them admitted that before their arrest, they had tended to assume that all prisoners were criminals, even though they knew that the justice system was imperfect. Then they found themselves in prison and realised that if they had ended up there, anyone could end up there. A prisoner accused of genocide told us: "When I came into prison, I realised other innocent people like me were accused of genocide. Before, I assumed all prisoners were guilty." For a former prisoner accused of a common crime, prison – before his arrest - was something that only ever happened to others: "Outside, you never think about being in there."

Prisoners who went to work outside, in their pink uniforms, were often insulted by passers-by, including children, who called out: "Look at those *interahamwe!*" and "There go the killers!" For those who believed in their own innocence, these comments were deeply hurtful, especially if they

---

[2]   A reference to the first executions of prisoners accused of genocide in 1998, described in Chapter XVIII.

reminded them of their own attitudes before their arrest. A former prisoner told us: "Before, when I used to pass prisoners outside, I used to think of them as *génocidaires* and terrible people. Then I got inside and I was wearing the same uniform. Once I was in a truck going to court. I heard a woman say: 'Who did these people kill?' Then you hear people say it about you. You realise it is wrong to assume that everyone in pink is a killer."

Others had ceased to worry about the social stigma, as they realised that imprisonment has become so ordinary in Rwanda that it could no longer be used as an indication of guilt. "Prison has become normal," an older prisoner observed. "The old, the young, the sick, the vulnerable – anyone is thrown into prison. Prison is an instrument of coercion." Another prisoner told us: "What's happening in this country is that all Rwandans are living with the fear of being imprisoned one day. It's as if everyone is waiting for his turn to come. Prison has become mundane."

Looking back

We asked prisoners what was their single most vivid or lasting memory of the time they had spent in prison. Some were able to pinpoint a specific moment or incident, often from the period when they were detained in a *cachot* a memory of being tortured, or of watching other detainees die. For many, hunger was the dominant memory, and nights spent sleeping outside. For others, it was events outside the walls of the prison, particularly deaths of close relatives whose funerals they had been unable to attend. Many prisoners were vague about dates, but a former soldier, who had been held in five different prisons, remembered the precise date of each transfer; he used these dates as reference points to remember other events. One prisoner said he could not single out a particular memory or incident: "The whole period I have spent in prison is in my mind. I can't forget a single day of it."

Some prisoners mentioned positive memories: a longer family visit when they could talk to their children, the day they were transferred from the *cachot* to the central prison and allowed themselves to hope that they might not die. Some of the positive memories were also the most painful. One prisoner said without hesitation that his lasting memory was of the day he was acquitted – "it was a victory for justice" – but that day was like a dream, because two months after his acquittal, he was re-arrested. Five years later, he was still in prison, without having gone through any other form of judicial procedure.

Other prisoners interpreted the question differently. Their lasting memory, they said, was simply the injustice of their imprisonment; that was the most terrible thing. Most of them were talking about their own situation when they said this, in reference to their claims of innocence. But a few, usually older, more educated prisoners, found the plight of other prisoners even more distressing than their own: they could cope with their own imprisonment, whether innocent or guilty, but the memory of so many other innocent people locked up in those conditions would never leave them.

Looking forward: dreams of freedom

Prisoners' attitudes towards their own imprisonment came through most clearly when they talked about the prospect of their release. Towards the end of each interview, we asked them how they envisaged the day of their release and what they would wish to do if they found themselves free. Some were taken aback by this question, which seemed to require a leap of the imagination in a new direction. As a result, their answers were spontaneous and often poignant. Many laughed or smiled at the very idea of being released – a warm laughter full of sadness, as if they were laughing at a child's impossible dreams. Then, for a brief moment, they allowed themselves to fantasise: if they were released, they would return to their families, they would look after their elderly parents, ensure their children got a good education, work their fields, set up a small business or resume their studies. They didn't have ambitious plans; they just wanted to lead a quiet life. An otherwise sullen prisoner chuckled when he thought about his release: "It would be like a resurrection. First of all, I would look after my family. Secondly, I would remember my friends who remained in prison and try to help them."

A man who had been in prison for more than ten years told us: "When I think about the day of my release, it will be a big celebration. It will be one of those great days in life, like a birth or a marriage. But I try not to dwell on it too much. If I get disappointed, it will be too heavy to bear. We just take it slowly." A prisoner who had spent nine years in prison had a similar vision: "There are unforgettable days in your life, for example my wedding day. I think the day of my release will be the same or even better… My parents are both alive; they are 84 and 82. For six years, I haven't seen them because they're not strong enough to visit. Their last visit was in 1998. I didn't have grey hair then. They would notice lots of changes in me. But going home would be a big celebration."

For some prisoners, the terrible experiences they had undergone before their arrest were still present in their mind when they thought about their release. A prisoner who had been arrested in 1997 on his way back from Congo said his release would be like a double freedom: he would have survived life as a refugee and life in prison. A 58-year-old prisoner, who was among the more optimistic, told us: "I often think and dream about my release: how my wife, even though she is old, will kiss me and my children will embrace me. These thoughts comfort me and I integrate them into my life." Another prisoner, who had been sentenced to ten years, said he thought so much about his release that he was worried he might never get there.

Some prisoners had made specific plans. A prisoner who had worked as a technician before he was arrested told us: "I've planned for the day of my release. I've prepared everything. I'm planning to work for myself, not for someone else. I will do agriculture and rear animals." He had also started preparing his social reintegration and had taken steps to repair relations with the people who had accused him of genocide: "I've written to the people who accused me to say I've forgiven them. They went to see my wife and apologised to her. They now have good relations with her. Some have come to visit me in prison. Reintegration won't be difficult, apart from the poverty." Others had more spiritual ambitions. One prisoner told us: "Sometimes men amongst themselves are animals. I want to work within the Church to bring people together and build a bridge between the good men and the bad men."

For a former schoolteacher in his late fifties who had spent nine years in prison, the moment of his release would be highly symbolic. He could visualise it precisely: "When I leave here, I'll put on my blue suit and my red tie and I'll go proudly."

For some, however, the prospect of release was so distant that it belonged firmly in the realm of fantasy. A man who had spent more than eight years in prison said: "I can't imagine the day of my release. It would just be wonderful. I don't know if my feet would touch the earth or if I would fly like the angels." A 68-year-old woman said she could not imagine what she would do if she were released: "I would just go home and hold out my hands and thank God." Some did not even allow themselves the luxury of dreaming: "I don't think much about my release," one prisoner told us. "I would be deceiving myself and creating false hopes." And others, who were much further down the road of despair, didn't even want to talk about it. They expected to die before then. Even some of the younger prisoners had resigned themselves. A man in his mid-forties who had spent ten years in prison told us: "If God decides I will die in prison, I will die in prison". Another prisoner, who had also spent ten years in prison, said: "Sometimes I lose hope. A prisoner died last week. He had been here for nine years. We all believed he was innocent. There was nothing in his case-file… At night, I think a lot. I imagine things. I can't sleep. I see my house closed up with no one living there. If I die in here, how will my child survive?"

Others were worried about the impact of public perceptions on their economic prospects. They knew that after spending years in prison, especially if they were accused of genocide, finding work outside would be difficult. A woman who had spent ten years in prison said she would not expect to find a good job but might be able to work on her parents' land. "But people take land which belongs to prisoners and sell it. When we're in prison, we're considered like the dead."

One of the most cheerful prisoners we met was a physically disabled man in his early thirties, who was completely dependent on other prisoners to help him from day to day. He was very poor and rarely received visits from his family, yet he was determined not to let prison life grind him down.

> "I've gone through mental and physical suffering… I try to manage and not to think too much about my disability. I try not to isolate

myself... I chat a lot with prisoners to forget the conditions of life. Chatting and joking cheers me up. When you chat, you forget your own situation and it is a relief. I realise it is not just me who is suffering. Unhappiness strengthens solidarity. We talk about the conditions here. We avoid comparing with the world outside. Some feel nostalgic and want to go out on the hills, even for a few minutes, then come back. Others say they have no idea what their hill is like any more, if they haven't been out for ten years, and they have no desire to return."

When I asked him whether he thought about his release, he laughed: "If I think or dream about my release, I won't be released. I have to avoid having these dreams. It's like when you dream of a girl, you don't get her."

In Cyangugu Central Prison, we met one of the rare prisoners whose release was an objective reality, and a reality within reach. A common criminal accused of theft, he was just completing his ten-year sentence and was due to be released in 27 days' time. "I'm going to be released on 30 December 2004. The days are going by too slowly. I wish it was tomorrow. I would like to talk to you on 30 December. My family has promised me a big celebration, a double New Year."

Escaping

One of the mysteries of the Rwandan prisons is that, despite the accumulation of suffering, there are very few suicides. We asked some of the prisoners if they knew of any cases of suicide. None of them did, not even those who had spent ten years in prison. It just doesn't happen, they said. Even prisoners with severe depression and other serious mental illnesses didn't commit suicide. They didn't really know why. Some thought that religion, which occupies such a central place in the prisons, may have played a part. One prisoner offered a more pragmatic explanation: "It doesn't happen because of the overcrowding. You can't do anything without people seeing or knowing." Others speculated that the extreme experiences prisoners had undergone before even reaching the prison, compounded by the life-threatening conditions they had to endure when they were first arrested, meant that many of them were still grateful just to be alive. In this context, the idea of suicide seemed strangely inappropriate.

We only met one prisoner who referred to thoughts of suicide, but in a hypothetical way, and not in relation to the present. He had been arrested soon after returning from exile in Tanzania and said that if he had known he was likely to be imprisoned, he would never have returned to Rwanda. "Instead, I would have committed suicide, either by throwing myself into the Akagera river, or by jumping from the car which brought me back from Tanzania." But now that he found himself in prison, he was trapped. For some reason, suicide was no longer a possibility, even though he had still not got used to the idea of being in prison, seven years on. He had been a successful businessman before the genocide, and his fall in status was what hurt him the most: "I don't have anything anymore. I used to be very rich. Now I'm poor... I'll never forget how I fell from high up. I used to be an important person. Now I'm nothing."

The second big mystery of the prisons is the low number of escapes. From an outsider's point of view, one of the most striking features of prisons in Rwanda is the absence of security and the ease with which prisoners could escape. The only padlock is on the front gate of the prison. With the exception of this gate, and the punishment cells inside, there are no locks and no keys. The walls are not very high, there is no barbed wire, and there is usually no second wall or fence outside. Where there is, the entrance stands permanently open, or is marked by a symbolic boundary, such as a flimsy piece of rope. There are no alarm systems; the few look-out towers that exist are unmanned; and often, there isn't a guard in sight. Prisoners could just climb over the walls and run out in the wide open fields which surround the prisons. At any given time, during daylight hours, there are scores of prisoners outside the main building, milling about in the courtyard. They could stroll out into the street without even needing to scale a wall. As prisoners are often seen working outside, the sight of people in pink uniforms would not cause a stir. There are no security measures or controls, other than a cursory, random search of prisoners when they come back into the building after working outside; even then, the guards' main motive for searching them is the hope of finding a few hundred francs in their pockets. The number of guards is tiny compared to the number of prisoners:

approximately one guard for every 800 prisoners. Yet escapes, or even attempted escapes, are relatively rare. The prisoners are in prison, and that is where they remain.

Some of the prisoners we spoke to mentioned individual cases of escapes in passing, but these were few and far between. There may be one escape every few months, and sometimes none for a whole year. Prisoners may be deterred by the knowledge that if they are caught trying to escape, they may be shot dead by the prison guards. Such incidents have occurred in the past. All the guards carry firearms, and their first reflex on seeing an escaping prisoner would probably be to fire. A guard at Butare Central Prison told us that night shifts could be difficult: "We have to patrol and look out for escapes. If we see someone trying to escape, we shoot, but we try not to kill them." He didn't know of anyone who had been killed in the one and a half years he had been working there. In previous years, however, shootings of prisoners were more common.

But the fear of being shot is not the principal reason why more prisoners do not escape. Most prisoners do not even attempt it because they would have nowhere to go. Rwanda is a tiny and tightly controlled country. If a prisoner were to return to his home area, everyone there would recognise him and he could easily be re-arrested. The authorities would also have no trouble tracking down an escaped prisoner in another part of the country if they felt it worth their while to do so. And for anyone with a certain level of prominence or notoriety, there is no place to hide in Rwanda.

The only other option would be to leave the country. But as prisoners look around across the borders, their possibilities are limited. Neighbouring countries are either in a state of conflict and insecurity (the Democratic Republic of Congo to the west, Burundi to the south) or have political and military links with Rwanda (Uganda to the north, and the eastern part of Congo to the west), so they would feel just as unsafe there. Tanzania, to the east, would be the only direction in which some safety and anonymity might be found, but for reasons which were not explained, few prisoners seem tempted to go there. The handful of prisoners we were told about who had succeeded in escaping had gone much further afield, in some cases as far as

Europe. Only those with substantial reserves of money and networks of contacts outside could afford to entertain such dreams.

Most escapes take place when prisoners go to work outside the prison. The deputy director of Gitarama Central Prison told us that there was usually just one guard for every 20 prisoners working outside. According to a guard at Butare prison, sometimes there were only one or two guards accompanying a team of up to 200 workers. In such circumstances, escaping is as easy as just walking away. We asked one of the guards why more prisoners didn't try to escape from the work teams. In his view, it was because the conditions were comparatively good for those who could join the work teams: "They can live as if they're not prisoners. They can meet people and talk with their family." In his eyes, escaping was almost unnecessary, as these prisoners could do almost anything they wanted anyway.

Attempting to escape, or failing to prevent colleagues from escaping, is considered one of the most serious acts of indiscipline for prisoners, and one of the most serious professional failures for guards. Whenever an escape did occur from the work teams, all the other prisoners on the team, as well as the guards who were supposed to watch over them, were made to pay the price. After a prisoner ran away from one of the work teams in late 2003, the *capita* of his block was put in the punishment cell for one week and was prohibited from working again for several months. The *capita général* in Cyangugu Central Prison said the last escape he knew about was in October 2003: "A guard was taking about 50 people to work quite far away. One of them escaped when the guard wasn't looking. When that happens, the anger of the authorities lands on everyone involved: the members of the work team, the guard. Privileges are cut."

The majority of prisoners who escape are those accused of common crimes. As a result, in most prisons, common criminals are not allowed to join the work teams, so they have had to resort to other means of getting out of prison. Some have succeeded not by escaping, but by sheer ingenuity. Prisoners told us that common criminals excelled at forging release documents, official letters, government stamps and seals, and banknotes – all within the prison. We were told about a common criminal in Kigali Central Prison, a former customs agent, who was released after forging his own release document. He left Kigali for Ruhengeri, but his luck ran out there, and he was re-arrested, not because his forgery was discovered, but on an accusation of genocide.

The more generalised lack of interest in escaping is an attitude peculiar to prisoners accused of genocide. The *capita* in Cyangugu prison described the difference in attitude between those accused of genocide and those accused of common crimes: "The *génocidaires* have been here much longer and have only a remote hope of leaving. They are more patient with prison life. They've learnt how to live without losing hope. The common criminals are more ambitious. They think they'll be out of prison in two or three months. They get discouraged if they're here for longer." A prisoner accused of genocide had a more mundane explanation as to why common criminals were more likely to escape: "Most common criminals come in for things like corruption or stealing money, so they want to get out in order to get their hands on that money."

The prisoners accused of genocide are caught up in a different dynamic and a different way of thinking. Even the above explanations offered by prisoners themselves do not fully explain their apparent resignation to remaining in prison when it would be comparatively easy to escape. It is certainly not due to a lack of imagination or resourcefulness, as prisoners have found ways around almost every other restriction in their day-to-day lives. A minority of prisoners may be deliberately biding their time, watching events unfold outside, quietly and patiently, calculating, weighing up their options. It may suit some of them to remain confined within those walls, until or unless the political situation starts unravelling. But for most, their unwillingess even to consider ways of extricating themselves from this situation is part of a more complicated psychological phenomenon. It illustrates their painful and complex relationship with the outside world and a profound fear of re-engaging with that world and with their past.

CHAPTER XVI

Talking

Prisoners in Rwanda have seen many foreign visitors traipse through the prisons in the aftermath of the genocide. Journalists, representatives of humanitarian and human rights organisations, students and academics have passed through, year after year, picking their way through the crowds and the filth. Some have visited the prisons in order to provide material assistance to improve their conditions; others have interviewed prisoners as part of attempts to document the genocide. But we gathered that this was the first time that prisoners had been asked simply to tell their own stories and describe their day-to-day existence in its most mundane details.

We tried to speak to prisoners who had not already talked to many outside visitors, so that they would not have preconceptions about what they would be asked or deliver rehearsed speeches. For many, this was therefore the first time they were speaking to a foreign visitor. We did not put pressure on any of them to speak to us; it was an entirely free choice, which almost all of them welcomed. They were delighted that someone was taking such a close interest in their situation and surprised that we wanted to hear their thoughts and opinions. One prisoner listened carefully to my introduction about the purpose of my research, then expressed his gratitude in a little introduction of his own, delivered in a slightly formal but intense manner: "We don't have the opportunity to express ourselves," he confided. "We are used to receiving orders. No one asks us what we think of our imprisonment." Towards the end of our interview, he again stressed the importance of prisoners being able to talk about their experience: "It's a reality which is difficult to express, and which people don't think about. Everyone is focused on the survivors [of the genocide]. They don't worry about what the prisoners think."

Even prisoners who were initially suspicious of our motives let their guard down after a short time. They talked and talked, sometimes for several hours. After we had reached the end of our questions, they wanted to carry on talking. Their sense of relief was palpable. One prisoner described the chance to talk to us as "absolutely extraordinary". Another told us our visit would help him sleep that night. Even the most cynical prisoners expressed their appreciation for the opportunity to unburden themselves. One man who had shown little emotion or enthusiasm for talking thanked me warmly at the end of the interview: "We like to have visitors. When we talk, we forget our problems and our conditions, even when we are talking about them." Many prisoners told us that this was the first time they had told their story in such detail to anybody, even to members of their own family, even to other prisoners. "Prisoners don't talk much about the conditions here," one prisoner told us. "We talk mostly about superficial things. We hide the rest. We need to talk. We miss that."

An old man recounted to us the whole story of his arrest and his imprisonment, then, when we started winding up, he wanted to tell us about his past, his parents, his grandparents, his cows. "I don't want to leave you," he said. He smiled and his eyes were shining. I didn't want to leave him either, but other prisoners were waiting to talk to us. We stood up and shook hands. He didn't want to let my hand go.

The younger men, especially, just wanted to sit and chat. They were full of curiosity and asked lots of questions – questions about my research, about the book I was planning to write: what would the title be? how could they get hold of a copy? They wanted to know which country we came from, about the situation in England. Several prisoners, as well as prison staff, asked us how prisons in England compared to prisons in Rwanda. They were surprised to learn that prisoners lived in individual cells, and were not sure whether this was a desirable way to live. During one of these informal chats, one prisoner told us he would rather be detained in Rwanda than in the prison of the UN-run International Criminal Tribunal for Rwanda in Arusha, Tanzania, where a very small number of detainees are held in individual cells, in excellent conditions – simply because he would hate to be locked up in a cell on his own.

Prolonging the conversation was also a way of prolonging the luxury of being outdoors and delaying the moment when they would have to return to their dark blocks. For many of these prisoners, these few hours were the longest period of time they had spent outside their prison block since their arrest.

Normally, this privilege could only be obtained for a price. "Today is a cause of celebration for me, because I'm getting fresh air for free," said one prisoner. Another told us at the end of our conversation: "Inside, I feel desperate, but now that I'm with you, I feel a bit relaxed." It was difficult watching the prisoners walk back into the prison building after each interview. Some lingered in the courtyard after leaving us and just stood around soaking in the fresh air for a few moments longer.

The prisoners we interviewed expressed themselves in many ways. The amount they were willing to tell, and the manner in which they told it, varied enormously, depending on each individual's personality, their emotional and psychological awareness, their level of trust, their expectations of the conversation, the accumulation of their experiences and their general outlook on life. The language they used and their ability to express themselves in an articulate way did not always correspond to their level of education. Some highly educated men and women spoke at length but failed to convey vividly the reality of their experiences. Others, who had never been to school, spoke directly, precisely and passionately.

All the prisoners were unfailingly courteous in the way they told us their story, however distressing their experiences, and they took the trouble to explain every detail. In many cases, their lives had been an accumulation of tragedy and violence. Some prisoners expressed bitterness, frustration, sorrow. Mostly these emotions rose to the surface when they relived specific events through our conversations. Yet they told their stories calmly, with an acceptance which indicated that anything was possible, and that anything could be overcome, almost.

Many aspects of these prisoners' stories were similar, but each prisoner and each conversation was unique. The personality unravelled with the story. Even those who were not very voluble were highly expressive, in their facial features, in their movements, in their silence, in their presence. Some spoke with such passion that it was difficult, as a listener, not to be swept away. Others had an inspiring stoicism about them. And others had an air of humility and resignation which was almost unbearable to see. Each prisoner's world was an individual world of intense sadness, separation, death and perceived injustice, illuminated by flashes of defiance and humour.

Every evening, I relived the stories I had heard and the faces I had watched tell those stories. I had to remind myself that most of those individuals whose lives I had been drawn into were accused of genocide and that those faces which now lived with me could be the faces of killers. I knew that a significant number of prisoners were innocent, but even according to the most generous calculations – various prisoners who hazarded a guess estimated that about half the prison population might be innocent – at least half were guilty. Statistically, it was therefore extremely unlikely that all those I had spoken to were innocent.

The matter of what these individuals had done during the genocide was not the object of my research and I did not broach it during my conversations with prisoners. Some volunteered the information, mostly in order to protest their innocence. Many seemed to be in a state of denial about the genocide. Only a tiny minority admitted having killed. For the rest, the question remained unasked and unanswered. Nevertheless, it was impossible not to wonder what these people had done and what they had seen. Prisoners themselves claim to know exactly who did what during the genocide. One prisoner told me: "People can't hide in prison. They are exposed. Everyone knows who has killed and who hasn't. We know and we never get it wrong." But as an outsider, I was not in a position to jump to conclusions in the absence of explicit comments or hints.

On a few occasions, I discussed this question with my Rwandan colleague as we were leaving the prison and sharing our thoughts about the day. He had a clearer sense than I did of where people stood – or where he thought they stood – in relation to the genocide, but even he found it baffling. He was able to isolate just a handful of cases where he had had the impression that the prisoner we had talked to may have participated in some way in the genocide – Rwandans use the expressive phrase *"tremper dans le génocide"* (literally, "to dip into the genocide") – but this feeling could not be substantiated by any evidence or specific remarks made by the prisoner. Anyway, there were so many ways of "dipping into the genocide" that it was not even clear exactly what that meant.

One was a man we interviewed together in Cyangugu Central Prison. As soon as my colleague mentioned him, I knew what he was referring to, but I couldn't have put my finger on it or explain why I shared his feeling. I asked my colleague what made him think that this man may have been guilty. He replied: *"Il avait froid dans les yeux"* (there was a coldness in his eyes).

He was the only prisoner out of all those we interviewed who seemed not to want to cooperate with us. In this sense, he was an exception, but a significant one. Most of our interviews with prisoners had taken place in a relatively relaxed atmosphere, with many of the characteristics of normal, social conversation. Typically, their comments about their imprisonment were based on an insistence on their part that they were innocent. This man's attitude was completely different. Suddenly, we were faced with the stark reality: the fact that some of these prisoners were indeed brutal murderers. Yet even with this prisoner, the reality was never articulated in words. Instead, it took the form of a silent, uncomfortable truth weighing down on our conversation.

He was a peasant in his late forties who was arrested in 1995, accused of genocide. He had spent four years in two different *cachots* and was badly tortured there. In 1999, he was transferred to Cyangugu prison and had remained there ever since, even though he had confessed on his first day in the prison. He had not seen any of his ten children since 1999.

Although it was obvious from his manner that he did not want to talk to us, he had agreed to meet us. He had sat down and listened to our questions, reluctantly, and with very little eye contact. When he did look straight at us, his eyes were impenetrable and his face was like stone. We sat on small wooden chairs, huddled together in a false intimacy in a corner of a huge, empty room. Each question I asked was met with a few seconds' silence, a silence that was dismissive, hard and hostile. Nevertheless, he answered our questions, and gave detailed information on certain aspects of his imprisonment, in particular the period he had spent in the *cachots*. To the questions he didn't like, his answers were full of disdain, almost aggressive. He had entirely lost hope in his situation, but unlike others, he didn't even pretend to believe things might change one day. He was very bitter about the justice system: *"Gacaca?* It's just a slogan. The whites may believe it, but I don't. People chant 'gacaca' but what *gacaca*? I don't know about the future… This is just our life. The situation here is so sad that all other sadnesses pale in comparison." But sadness was the wrong word. There was no sadness in his voice, just dull, blunt pain.

He told us that his wife could afford to visit him only once a year, so I asked him if they tried to send messages to each other. He replied: "Even if my wife could write, what could she say? She has nothing." Had he made any friends in prison? "What for? If we exchanged problems, we would just be adding to our problems. Even now, talking to you reminds me of my problems." At this point, I told him we didn't have to continue the conversation if he was finding it too painful. He sat in silence for a few seconds. I asked him again whether he preferred to stop the interview. He said no, we could continue. So we asked him how he spent his time in prison. He told us he had lost his appetite for everything. Nevertheless, he had joined a choir, which he had never done before his arrest, and had learnt to read music. As we edged towards the end of the interview, I didn't dare ask him how he imagined the day of his release. Instead, I just asked him what was his lasting memory of his time in prison. "Ask me when I get out," he replied, "I'll think about it then."

CHAPTER XVII

"Innocence can be subjective":

justice

"We are waiting.
We don't know what for, and we don't know how long for."

The question of how to bring to justice the hundreds of thousands of people who participated in the genocide has been Rwanda's most intractable challenge since 1994. A senior official in the Rwandan Ministry of Justice presented the dilemma to us very clearly: "The question is: how much and how hard to punish?" That question will probably never be satisfactorily answered. Even if it has been partly addressed by a series of formal mechanisms and provisional releases, it leaves open the bigger question of what constitutes punishment. The fact that tens of thousands of people have effectively already been punished by spending more than ten years in prison without their guilt having been established by any court is rarely discussed.

By the end of 2004, ten years after the genocide, the vast majority of the 85,500 prisoners had not been before a court at all. When we visited Gitarama Central Prison in November 2004, only 252 out of 8,827 prisoners had been tried and sentenced. In Butare Central Prison, the figure was 506 out of 10,781. In Kigali Central Prison, it was slightly higher: 870 out of 6,093. Most of the remaining prisoners had been denied their basic right to a fair hearing for up to ten years. For prisoners accused of lesser offences, the period they had spent in prison may well have exceeded the sentence they would have received had they been tried. By mid-2006, more than three-quarters of the prison population were still awaiting trial.

As soon as the RPF took power in Rwanda in July 1994, mass arrests of people suspected of participating in the genocide started taking place across the country. Tens of thousands of men, women and children – the majority of them Hutu – were rounded up in towns and villages, in their homes, in their workplaces, on the street. Given the huge scale of popular participation in the genocide, the fact that such large numbers of people were arrested was not surprising. However, many of these arrests were carried out arbitrarily and indiscriminately. Some of those arrested had undoubtedly participated in the genocide, but others were arrested on the basis of unsubstantiated denunciations. A simple accusation of genocide by one person against another was enough to warrant arrest without any form of investigation. Some of these denunciations were made in good faith by people who had witnessed killings during the genocide, but others were motivated by the desire to settle personal scores. For many ordinary Rwandans, as well as for the government, this was an opportunity to get rid of real or perceived enemies and rivals.

Post-genocide Rwanda had none of the structures or mechanisms needed to process such a large number of cases or to perform the delicate task of gathering evidence and sifting the guilty from the innocent. Nor did it have the personnel or the expertise to manage such a fast-growing prison population. The whole justice system had been destroyed during the genocide, as had the police force, the prison service and the entire machinery of administration. But this did not stop the new government in its tracks. Before long, thousands of suspected *génocidaires* were locked up in prisons and detention centres around the country. There was a further sharp increase in the number of arrests from the end of 1996 after the mass return of hundreds of thousands of predominantly Hutu refugees who had fled to Congo, Tanzania or Burundi in the last days of the genocide.

As the months went by, the case-files piled up in the prosecutors' offices. A new law governing the prosecution of genocide crimes was adopted in 1996 and the first genocide trials began in December 1996. But arrests continued, and it was a race against time which the newly reconstituted courts were bound to lose. The prison population grew inexorably, and by 1998, it had reached around 130,000.[1]

Many Rwanda observers have tried to divine the government's motivation for continuing to arrest such large numbers of people when it was clear that it would never have the capacity to process their cases, and in the full knowledge that many of those arrested were innocent. Furthermore, the conditions in the prisons were so extreme that it was obvious many prisoners

---

[1] This is an approximate total which human rights and non-governmental organisations working in the prisons used as an unofficial estimate at the time. Official figures were slightly lower. No one knows exactly how many prisoners were held during this period. Official statistics were unreliable and did not include the hundreds or possibly thousands held in unofficial or secret detention centres.

were likely to die before their cases got anywhere near a court. The generous interpretation was that the government was overwhelmed by events and lacked the capacity to cope with the consequences of the genocide. Some commentators argued that, after all that had happened during the genocide, it was normal that such large numbers of people should be arrested, and inevitable that a few innocent ones would accidentally be caught in the net. The alternative was to allow thousands of killers to walk free, possibly to commit further atrocities. Some claimed that imprisoning large numbers of suspects would also help prevent revenge killings and vigilante violence. The Rwandan government became exasperated with human rights organisations for criticising the slow progress of justice. It dismissed these criticisms as unrealistic and implied that in some way, they minimised what had happened during the genocide.

At the other end of the spectrum, there were those who believed that the new government was pursuing a policy of vengeance, imprisoning as many Hutu as possible, regardless of their guilt or innocence, in order to establish a secure power base for the new Tutsi elite and to silence potential opponents; and that the likely deaths of thousands of Hutu prisoners suited their political agenda. Some believed that prisoners were deliberately left there to die. Many prisoners shared, and still share, these views.

The scale of popular participation in the genocide meant that the government could get away with arresting huge numbers of people without anyone – other than the prisoners themselves, and a few human rights groups – worrying about the legal basis for these arrests.[2] Gambling on the guilt of the international community after it had failed to intervene to stop the genocide, the government calculated that the prison situation was unlikely to adversely

---

[2] The number of people who participated in the genocide may never be known. The question is complicated by the need to distinguish between different levels of participation, the motivation behind the crimes committed, and the fact that many people were forced to kill. Studies by academics and others have produced figures ranging from tens of thousands to several million. In what appears to be one of the more rigorous calculations, academic and former journalist Scott Straus estimates that between 175,000 and 210,000 people participated in the genocide (see Scott Straus, *The Order of Genocide: race, power and war in Rwanda*, Cornell University Press, 2006).

affect its relationship with foreign donors, no matter how many prisoners died. After all, these were genocidal killers who attracted little sympathy.

The government's calculations were right. The crisis in the prisons – which would have provoked outrage had it occurred in almost any other country – elicited barely any response from foreign governments. Nor was there much concern for the fact that the genocide had become a licence to arrest anybody without even asking any questions, and, in many cases, without evidence of participation in any crimes. All this was passed off as an inevitable consequence of the genocide. In these exceptional circumstances, perfection could not be expected, said the government, and most international actors embraced this message wholeheartedly.

The genocide trials

Since December 1996, around 10,000 people have been tried on genocide charges by the Rwandan courts – a figure which would seem impressive in almost any other country, but in the Rwandan context, accounts for only a small minority of those detained in connection with the genocide.[3]

Various local and international organisations, as well as journalists, followed the progress of the genocide trials in Rwanda in the initial period, but most of the attention tailed off after a short period. Interest peaked again, briefly, with the execution of 22 people found guilty of genocide in 1998, but since then, there has been little media coverage of the trials. Some of the most valuable and sustained monitoring was carried out by the Rwandan human rights organisation LIPRODHOR, which set up a special team to observe and report on the conduct of trials across the country. LIPRODHOR carried out this work conscientiously for several years, publishing regular reports on the

---

3   This figure excludes those tried under the *gacaca* system from 2005, as described elsewhere in this chapter.

progress of justice in Rwanda, until the government's crackdown on human rights groups resulted in the organisation's near-dissolution in 2004.[4]

The 1996 genocide law classified genocide suspects into four categories, later reduced to three in a law passed in 2004. Under the 2004 law, Category 1 includes those responsible for organising and planning the genocide; individuals in positions of leadership at the time of the genocide (including officials at various levels of government, in the security forces, the militia, and religious denominations); those who carried out killings with particular zeal or "excessive wickedness"; and those who committed torture, rape, sexual violence or mutilation. The penalties for defendants in Category 1 are the death sentence[5] or life imprisonment, which can be reduced to 25 or 30 years if the defendant confesses. Category 2 is for people accused of killings or "serious attacks", and their accomplices. Sentences for Category 2 defendants can range from three to 30 years, depending on a number of factors, including whether they confess to their crimes. Category 3 is for those accused of looting and crimes against property, punishable by reparation but not imprisonment.

Justice in the aftermath of the genocide was never going to be easy. There were the immediate problems of lack of resources, logistical difficulties and a shortage of trained judges. There was also a general lack of a sense of urgency. Court hearings were repeatedly adjourned, for a variety of reasons, and sometimes apparently for no reason at all. It could take years for a trial to be concluded, not necessarily because the case was complicated but because of the inefficiency of the system.

In addition, the political environment in which trials were launched from late 1996 did not encourage an approach based on fairness. The genocide had torn Rwandan society in two, and each side viewed the other with deep distrust. The government did little to instil faith in the independence of the justice system in this initial period. There were numerous instances of

---

[4]   The Rwandan government has effectively destroyed most independent human rights activity in the country. For details, see *Frontline Rwanda: disappearances, arrests, threats, intimidation and co-option of human rights defenders 2001-2004*, published in 2005 by Front Line.

[5]   Rwanda abolished the death penalty in July 2007 (see Chapter XVIII).

political interference in the judiciary, intimidation of witnesses and pressure on judges to obtain the desired result: convictions. The quality of trials varied enormously. Some judges tried to resist interference, but others succumbed, willingly or otherwise.

Many defendants were tried without a lawyer and given heavy sentences, including the death penalty and life imprisonment. For those without much education or familiarity with the law, the process was overwhelming. Only the lucky ones benefited from the assistance of Avocats sans frontières (Lawyers Without Borders), a Belgian non-governmental organisation which set up a project in Rwanda to provide legal assistance in the genocide trials. Even then, many trials dragged on for so long that the lawyers – most of whom were foreign and only stayed in Rwanda for short periods – were unable to see them through to the end. Appeal courts were often willing to confirm the verdicts of trials which had been deeply flawed and in which defendants had had no legal representation. Rwanda had only a very small number of trained lawyers of its own, the majority of whom were too afraid to take on the defence of genocide cases for fear of being associated with the *génocidaires*. Even prisoners who did manage to secure the services of a lawyer complained that they (the prisoners) ended up doing most of the work themselves.[6]

The presence of lawyers, prosecutors and judges among the prison population came in handy here: they often guided other prisoners through the contents of their case-file and helped them prepare their arguments before their trial. Prisoners were usually given just a few days to read their case-file before their trial. The case-files were often voluminous, and in many cases, this was the first time the prisoners had seen the specific accusations against them. They would often use these few days to copy their file out by hand, in its entirety, so as to keep their own copy and have more time to study it. A former prisoner whose trial began in July 1998, and eventually resulted in his acquittal in 2000, recalled:

---

[6]   These problems were not limited to genocide cases. Common criminals also complained of difficulties in finding a lawyer, and, once they had hired one, of their inefficiency and failure to attend court hearings.

"My case-file was about 50 pages. There were lots of accusations. After four days, I just put it to one side. I thought I could never defend myself. I was accused by people I didn't know of killing people I didn't know. They were very serious accusations. I was shocked. For four days, I couldn't get over it. A prisoner who was a lawyer told me not to worry. He said I had to study my case-file. He helped me and advised me on the law...

I copied out my case-file word for word. Two other prisoners helped me copy it out. I remember Misago's file [the Bishop of Gikongoro] was more than 200 pages. As he was becoming discouraged, the *capita* found some people to copy it out for him. Prisoners who couldn't read used to get other prisoners to copy out their case-file for them."

After a trial which consisted of 19 hearings, five of which were adjourned, the date of this prisoner's judgement was eventually set. However, on the appointed day, the judges didn't turn up, so it was postponed by a further week.

"That week was like a year for me. I couldn't eat. A prisoner who was a doctor said I had to do something, otherwise I would die. He told me I was disturbing other prisoners at night. I wasn't even aware of it. He gave me some sleeping tablets. The day before the judgement, I couldn't control myself. Someone gave me some whisky. It calmed me down. It came from a rich prisoner, who was a millionaire. I didn't even know whisky existed in the prison...

The trial started at 3pm. The judges hadn't come. I started sweating as I was afraid. I felt very fragile. The judges came at 4.30pm. After about 45 minutes, they announced I was acquitted... After the first page of the judgement was read out, I knew I would be acquitted. I could tell from the atmosphere. One of my wife's friends wanted to start celebrating before the end of the hearing. After the judgement, people banged drums and pans in the prison. It was a big celebration."

We spoke to a number of other former prisoners who had been acquitted. Both prosecution and defence witnesses testified in these trials, though some were intimidated and came under pressure from the prosecution to withdraw or alter their testimonies. But at least in these cases, judges weighed up the evidence carefully and were willing to order the release of those against whom there was insufficient evidence.

However, even when judges acted objectively, the final outcome could not be guaranteed. In a number of cases, as described below, court judgements were overruled by politicians or prosecutors, and verdicts blatantly ignored.

"Buying innocence"

Many prisoners have bought their freedom – or tried to buy it – for various and large sums of money. Several prisoners we spoke to complained that they remained in prison only because they could not afford to pay for their release. A prisoner who had been detained for seven years told us: "I asked about paying for my release through an intermediary. It would have cost 400,000 francs [around US$715]. I can't find that money. Lots of people have done this. Some are now free, but some have paid and are still in prison. A friend's wife paid 100,000 francs but he was not released."

Corruption is rife in the judiciary, and many, though not all, officials can be bribed. The money is usually paid to the prosecutor's office, sometimes directly to the prosecutor, sometimes to the *substituts* (assistant prosecutors). It is usually the prisoner's relatives who have to find the money. They pay the bribes in several instalments, without knowing when, or even if, these payments will secure the prisoner's release. It can take months, it can take years, or it can never happen. Indeed, many prisoners' families and friends have been let down by officials who promised to release the prisoner for a fee. For the prisoner's husband or wife, chasing up the case-file is an extremely time-consuming, expensive and disheartening business. It involves writing and personally delivering dozens of letters, making repeated visits to the prosecutor's office, bribing a whole range of officials and intermediaries, and vast reserves of patience and determination. Some families persisted for a few years, then gave up when they realised that even money could not guarantee a release or an early trial, or that the price kept rising beyond their means. Even personal relationships with prosecutors did not always bear fruit. Prisoners and their families carefully documented the progress of their file and meticulously kept copies of all the relevant documents, but their efforts were often futile.

Some judges have also accepted bribes to order a prisoner's release. In some cases, the judges were approached by the prisoner's family and agreed to "help" them. In other cases, the judges themselves asked for the money from the family. Sometimes they shared the money with officials from the prosecutor's office. A prisoner told us how he was tried and sentenced to death for genocide, while his four co-accused were released: "They had each paid 200,000 francs [around US$357] to the *parquet* [prosecutor's office] to be released. The *parquet* was to share it with the tribunal. I couldn't get this money so I was sentenced… The charges against the four who were released were more serious than the charges against me."

The same "system" applies to prisoners accused of common crimes. A young prisoner accused of a common crime had missed out on an opportunity to buy his release because he was not yet wise to the ways of the courts. "The trial lasted five minutes or less. I said very little as I knew the complainant had cleared me. The only accuser was the *substitut*… I realised later that the judges and the *substitut* were waiting for me to pay them, but they didn't tell me, or else I would have got the money for them. The *substitut* was making signs at me, but I didn't understand what he meant. The trial never concluded. There was no judgement."

The "big fish"

Meanwhile, in what seems like a parallel universe, the leaders of the genocide are being tried by the International Criminal Tribunal for Rwanda (ICTR) in Arusha, Tanzania. The ICTR – the second such international tribunal, after the International Criminal Tribunal for the former Yugoslavia – was set up by the United Nations in November 1994 to prosecute those who played a leading role in the genocide. Its targets were meant to be the "big fish": senior members of the former Rwandan government and military, and other individuals who were instrumental in organising and inciting the killings. Many of these individuals had remained in exile since 1994.

By April 2007, the ICTR had handed down 27 judgements involving 33 accused. Eleven trials involving a further 27 people were still pending. The work of the tribunal will soon be drawing to a close: it is supposed to have completed all its trials by the end of 2008 and all appeals by the end of 2010.[7]

Despite its slow progress, the ICTR has at least succeeded in apprehending, trying and sentencing some of the key individuals behind the genocide. The ICTR only ever intended to prosecute a small number of people, but these were individuals bearing the greatest responsibility for the deaths of more than 500,000 people and without whom the genocide would probably never have happened.

The ICTR, like the Rwandan courts, has been criticised for corruption and excessive bureaucracy, but in every other respect, it operates in a world of its own. The contrast between the treatment of the big fish in Arusha and the small fry in Rwanda could not be greater. The dignitaries of the genocide have become dignitaries in the justice system too. As a UN institution, the ICTR is obliged to respect international standards in terms of prison conditions and due process. The somewhat absurd result is that the individuals who bear the heaviest responsibility for the genocide enjoy the best conditions of detention – including individual cells and availability of a range of facilities – and have teams of lawyers to ensure that none of their rights is violated, while tens of thousands of untried suspects in Rwanda lie waiting in prison in life-threatening conditions, with no legal assistance and no idea if or when they might ever be tried. In addition, the ICTR cannot impose the death penalty, whereas the courts in Rwanda handed down thousands of death sentences before the death penalty was abolished in July 2007 (see Chapter XVIII).

However, few of the prisoners we spoke to in Rwanda expressed feelings of jealousy about the treatment of the genocide detainees in Arusha. They followed the news of the ICTR trials closely on their radios, but the reality was many worlds away. Only one said that he would prefer to be tried in

---

[7]   Further information about the work of the ICTR can be found at www.ictr.org

Arusha than in Rwanda, because the judges were from different countries, and therefore neutral in his eyes. Most of the others seemed resigned to their fate.

Gacaca

Genocide trials in Rwanda ground on painfully, year after year, until it became apparent that the conventional legal mechanisms were never going to be able to process so many cases. Calculations were made that it could take several decades to try all the people in prison, let alone others who had not yet even been arrested. An alternative had to be found.

The model eventually produced by the Rwandan government was *gacaca*: a form of local justice loosely based on a traditional system of community participation. Historically, *gacaca* – meaning "lawn" in Kinyarwanda – had been used in Rwanda to resolve relatively minor local disputes, such as disagreements over land or inheritance. Now, it was to be adapted to try the most serious criminal offences, across the whole country.

Under *gacaca*, residents of each area gather and speak out about what happened during the genocide in that particular locality. Individuals accused of participation in the genocide appear before the assembled crowd and everyone is expected to state publicly what they know about that individual's actions during the genocide, before a panel of judges selected from the local population. The idea was that by drawing on eye-witness testimonies of local people, it would be easier to reach the truth. *Gacaca* offered the additional advantage of involving the population directly – both as judges and witnesses – in the process of justice for crimes which had affected the entire country.[8]

Gacaca jurisdictions are to try all genocide cases, with the exception of those classed as Category 1 who are to be tried by the normal courts. The *gacaca* jurisdictions are responsible first for categorising the defendants into one of

---

[8]   The workings of *gacaca* were first set out in Organic Law no.40/2000, adopted in January 2001. Revisions were contained in a law passed in 2004, Organic Law no. 16/2004. Further amendments were contained in a third law passed in March 2007, Organic Law no.10/2007. Most of the information in this book predates the 2007 law.

the three categories defined in the law, then for holding the hearings where evidence would be heard, and ultimately for the judgement and sentencing of those in categories 2 and 3.

The Rwandan government, with foreign government support, has invested a huge amount of resources in *gacaca*. To a large extent, it has staked its reputation on its success. Presented as a radical but creative solution to the justice crisis, *gacaca* has become one of the main planks of the government's strategy in post-genocide Rwanda. *Gacaca* jurisdictions have been set up all over the country. The recruitment and training of thousands of *gacaca* judges (none of whom had prior legal training), the campaigns to inform the population about how the system would operate and to encourage broad popular participation (without which the whole system would fall apart) and the logistical arrangements have been a massive undertaking. The *gacaca* system itself is complicated and multi-layered, with different stages taking places at different levels, from the lowest administrative level of the *cellule* through to the *secteurs*.

The preparatory phases of *gacaca* have taken several years. There have been numerous false starts, unrealistic deadlines and long delays. First, there was a "pre-*gacaca*" phase, during which detainees were presented to the local population in their area with a view to releasing them provisionally if there were no credible accusations against them. Then a pilot project was launched in 2002, covering around 10% of the country.[9] *Gacaca* trials across the country started in earnest only in March 2005, three months after we carried out the research for this book; the first judgements were handed down in mid-2006.

The pros and cons of *gacaca* have been debated endlessly inside and outside Rwanda, by government officials and advisers, lawyers, academics, human

---

9   For details of these two phases, see Penal Reform International, *Integrated report on gacaca research and monitoring. Pilot phase, January 2002-December 2004*, December 2005.

rights organisations and others.[10]   Ordinary Rwandans have debated them too, though mostly in hushed tones or behind closed doors.

Aside from the numerous technical and legal difficulties posed by *gacaca*, and the disregard of certain basic rights (for example the accused are not allowed legal representation under *gacaca*), there were more complex, political questions hanging over the whole scheme. For *gacaca* to be true to its aims, it needed the cooperation of the Rwandan population, at all levels, across the whole country. It was also dependent on a public commitment to telling the truth, and the ability to do so without fear. Yet from the outset, it was apparent that *gacaca* would be plagued by many of the same problems as the rest of the justice system and could not be divorced from the political realities of Rwanda. *Gacaca* was unfolding in an atmosphere of deep political and ethnic division, fear, suspicion, intimidation and corruption; within such a climate, it would be extremely difficult to forge a clear path to truth and justice. *Gacaca* could easily turn into a tool of vengeance and be misused to settle scores, accuse enemies and exonerate friends, while setting aside its primary aim: finding the truth about who did what during the genocide.

In the early stages of *gacaca*, a number of people were arrested for "not telling the truth" to the *gacaca* jurisdictions. One man who was called to testify before a *gacaca* court in October 2003 explained: "I told them what I saw. For them, it wasn't enough. The president of the *gacaca* said I should go to prison so that I would think and give them more information." He, and several others arrested in the same circumstances, spent ten months in prison. He was never questioned and was eventually released in August 2004. There have been other cases where people who stood up and defended individuals on trial in *gacaca* were themselves threatened with arrest. Accusations that they too participated in the genocide came out of the blue, simply because they had dared testify in favour of the accused. Such cases have discouraged people from speaking out freely in *gacaca*.

Even if *gacaca* were to succeed in making headway through the backlog of cases awaiting trial, there is no guarantee that it would solve the problem of

---

[10]   Penal Reform International, Amnesty International and Avocats sans frontières, among others, have published detailed reports on *gacaca*, available at www.penalreform.org, www.amnesty.org and www.asf.be.

Rwanda's prisons.   On the contrary, it has already led to many new accusations and arrests. Official data from the *gacaca* courts indicated that by the end of 2006, 818,564 people had been accused of genocide since the *gacaca* system started functioning. The scale of the problem remains overwhelming.

When we met government officials in late 2004, they made it clear that they were not envisaging further mass arrests or a dramatic increase in the prison population.[11] The solution could be found in an interesting new element in the government's strategy: the introduction of a system of community service, referred to by its French acronym TIG (*travail d'intérêt général*). The concept of TIG was introduced in the law on *gacaca* and formalised in a presidential decree in 2005.[12]   TIG would not replace prison sentences entirely, but defendants in Category 2 – who make up a significant proportion of the prison population – would spend the second half of their sentence out of prison, doing community work.   Widespread use of this scheme could significantly cut down the long-term prison population. The programme also aims to promote "reconciliation" between prisoners and the local population and assist the reintegration of prisoners into society.

By the end of 2004, the TIG programme and the commission set up by the government to implement it were still desperately under-resourced and faced numerous logistical difficulties. It was clear that the implementation of TIG, like every other aspect of the justice system, was going to take a long time. The scheme was eventually launched towards the end of 2005. Originally, it was intended that prisoners work on projects in their local area of origin. In the initial phase, however, this did not happen. Instead, prisoners were grouped into centralised camps and performed community work from there.

---

[11]   These assurances have since been overtaken by events. From the second half of 2006, the number of arrests shot up again as a result of new denunciations through *gacaca*, leading to a sharp increase in the prison population (see Chapter XX).

[12]   Presidential Order no.10/01 of 7 March 2005 determining the modalities of implementation of community service as an alternative penalty to imprisonment.

The work included stone-cutting and building houses.[13]   By March 2007, around 18,370 people tried by *gacaca* jurisdictions had been sentenced to a period of community work. Around 2,500 of them – now known as "tigistes" – had started this phase of their sentence.

The prisoners' *gacaca*: "the real truth is in the prisons"

Long before the *gacaca* courts started functioning, prisoners had already set up their own *gacaca* inside the prisons. With their usual efficiency, they organised themselves into groups, according to their areas of origin. Each group sat around and discussed what had happened in the genocide in their particular area. Prisoners were asked to speak out about what they had done, what they had not done, what others had done and not done.

By the time we visited the prisons in late 2004, the prisoners' *gacaca* system had already been going for several years and was extremely well-organised. *Gacaca* sessions took place once or twice a week and had become part of the institutionalised routine of prison life. In each prison, a special committee of prisoners was responsible for running the sessions and carefully recording the proceedings in writing. These committees also held meetings with prisoners to raise awareness of *gacaca* and advertise the confessions system (see Chapter XIX).

The prisoners' *gacaca* sessions were usually held in one of the large rooms in the prison blocks or in the inside yard and were presided over by a panel of prisoners. We witnessed one such session in Butare Central Prison: a large room was filled with hundreds of prisoners sitting on rows of benches, facing a desk behind which sat the prisoners' judges, secretaries and other "officials" – all of them prisoners. It was just like a courtroom. Prisoners acted out their roles naturally and convincingly. More than ever, in these *gacaca* sessions, you could forget you were in a prison at all.

---

[13]   For a description of the initial phase of TIG, including the reactions of prisoners and the local population and a description of life in the camps, see Penal Reform International, *Monitoring and research report on Gacaca. Community Service (TIG): areas of reflection*, March 2007.

As with the system of confessions, some of the information provided by prisoners during their *gacaca* sessions may be of questionable quality: prisoners make deals with each other about what to say and not to say, in order to further their own interests. Nevertheless, most prisoners seem to take the whole enterprise very seriously. One prisoner explained: "If someone lies, someone else will point it out and say it is not true. The information from the prison *gacaca* is very reliable. The Tutsi prisoners – the common criminals – also help us. For example, they may say: 'I survived the genocide but I escaped thanks to X or Y' and they confirm whether X or Y killed their relatives. They participate sincerely in the prison *gacaca* without any problems."

More generally, prisoners state confidently that they know exactly who did what during the genocide. Whether from the *gacaca* sessions or from their own private conversations over their years of incarceration, they claim to know the truth about each other. A former prisoner told us: "A prisoner could deliver justice better than the Ministry of Justice, as we know who is innocent and who is guilty."

As with every other aspect of the prisoners' lives, the prisoners' *gacaca* mirrors events in the world outside. The difference is that the prisoners' version of *gacaca* is much better organised than the real thing. While the real *gacaca* around the towns and villages of Rwanda has been moving at a snail's pace, the prisoners' *gacaca* is speeding ahead. The prisoners' committees have been beavering away for several years, producing reams of testimonies on what happened during the genocide. Unlike the government and the population outside, the prisoners have little else to do, so they can devote as much time and energy to this process as they wish, or as much as the government asks them to.

The prisoners' *gacaca* is not purely a prisoner-inspired initiative. The government has been behind the prisoners from the beginning. In 2004, the then Attorney General, who was Minister of Justice when the government started pushing through the idea of *gacaca*, claimed that it was his idea to set up a parallel *gacaca* system in the prisons. Prisoners have willingly cooperated, in the hope that by doing so, they might speed up the process of justice. Ultimately, the initiative may be of greater benefit to the government than to the prisoners. The system is intimately bound up with the programme of confessions, through which the government has been urging prisoners to confess to their crimes in exchange for a reduced sentence or early release. The prisoners' *gacaca* sessions are one of the main vehicles for producing confessions and denunciations and are thus extremely useful for the government. The Executive Secretary of the National *Gacaca* Service, a body set up by the government to oversee the entire *gacaca* system, described the prisoners' own *gacaca* as "an institution of mobilisation". She told us: "The *gacaca* committee in prison is doing the sensitisation and is helping us."

The relationship between the prisoners' *gacaca* and the real *gacaca* outside is ambiguous. In theory, the prisoners' *gacaca* has no real status and no judicial institution is bound by its findings. But the results of the prisoners' *gacaca* sessions are carefully collated and forwarded to the *gacaca* jurisdictions and judicial authorities outside, to complement their own investigations. Exactly how much weight they carry is not known, but the government's continuing encouragement of the initiative would indicate that the prisoners' findings are, at the very least, taken into account.

Knowing this, the prisoners responsible for the internal *gacaca* sessions go about their business with a sense of great self-importance. The mass of ordinary prisoners – with some exceptions – also go along with the system, as no opportunity to claim their innocence can be wasted. Even those who have a scornful attitude towards the process usually attend the sessions which are pertinent to their area. The initiative has built up such a momentum that prisoners end up believing in it as a real judicial process and place great faith in their colleagues' judgements. This was apparent in the language they used when describing the sessions.   Some prisoners told us they had been "acquitted"; when we probed more deeply, it turned out they had not been acquitted by any court – and had not even appeared before a court – but had been "declared innocent" by the prisoners' own *gacaca*, in other words by other prisoners. The prisoners' *gacaca* is a world of make-believe, but the illusion it provides – that justice is progressing – is crucial to keeping prisoners' hopes alive.

The paralysis of the justice system

Gacaca was meant to unblock the paralysis of the justice system, but until it got fully under way in early 2005, it had the opposite effect. While everyone was anxiously waiting for *gacaca* to be launched, month after month, year after year, virtually all other judicial procedures ground to a halt. The paralysis became almost complete in 2004 after the government introduced a wide-ranging reform of the courts and judicial personnel. As a result of this reform, even the normal courts which had been trying criminal cases ceased to function; but *gacaca* was not yet up and running, so there was no functioning system under which prisoners could be tried.

That was the situation which prevailed when we carried out the research for this book. The prisoners we spoke to were in a state of confusion and uncertainty. Many of them didn't even know which jurisdiction would try them, let alone when. Cases which had started snaking their way through the court system before *gacaca* started had got stuck, and it was not clear when the system would be unblocked. Prisoners who had been tried and had appealed against the verdict had been waiting for years for an appeal hearing. Others were pinning their hopes on *gacaca* without really knowing whether it would be *gacaca* or the normal courts which would try them. A prisoner who had been detained without trial for eight years said that, even with *gacaca*, he didn't expect to be released for many years yet. In deference to the common practice of corruption in the justice system, he added with frustration: "Now you can't even pay to speed up a normal trial, because the courts are not functioning at the moment. All the taps are shut."

Numerous cases had either got stuck between the two systems, or had been shunted from one to the other and back again. A prisoner in Butare was one of four people accused of genocide whose trial began in 2001. In 2002, they were summoned to the court to hear the verdict, only to be told that the whole trial was cancelled as the case was to be referred to *gacaca*. The four defendants appealed against this decision and demanded that the court finish trying the case. They took their appeal to the Supreme Court, but by then, the Supreme Court had stopped functioning because of the reforms. They had heard nothing since then, despite writing several letters to the authorities.

The government has presented the ever-changing face of the justice system as a positive development. In 2004, the Secretary General at the Ministry of Justice described the government's policy on justice over the last ten years as "very flexible. We try not to be too rigid. The road map can change, or we can wait for debate, or introduce new things." There is little regard for the impact of these repeated changes in laws and procedures on those awaiting trial. Nor does there seem to be much concern about the continued illegal detention of so many people. The Secretary General admitted: "When you're innocent, even one hour is a very long time. However, innocence can be subjective... We regret this type of situation, but it's a practical question: we can't just release people without investigation." The fact that so many were arrested without investigation in the first place did not seem to cause undue worry.

Acquitted and still in prison

During our visits to the prisons, we came across a number of prisoners who had been formally acquitted by the courts but never released. The motive behind their continued detention may well have been political – these were not mistakes or administrative errors – but the exact reasons were not always clear, even to the prisoners themselves. In Butare prison, we were told there were two groups of prisoners in this situation, whose trials dated back to 2000: one group of three and another group of about eight. These cases were well-publicised in Rwanda at the time. The prisoners and their families wrote numerous letters to the highest government authorities, including the Minister of Justice and the Attorney General, and human rights organisations took up their cases, all in vain.

We talked to one of these prisoners, a softly spoken man in his forties. He told us his story fully and precisely. He was sharp and alert, remembering every detail of his case, but his voice, though gentle, was lifeless. Sitting on the edge of his chair, he barely moved as he spoke. The only expression was in his eyes, which betrayed a pleading look through the sunlight reflecting off his glasses. We saw him briefly a second time when we returned to Butare a few weeks later. This time, he greeted us with a glimmer of a smile, but when we sat down to talk again, the weight of his misery returned.

He was first arrested in April 1995 on an accusation of genocide, spent three months in Kigali Central Prison, then was released after a *commission de triage* (a preliminary mechanism to sift through cases before trials got under way) found no evidence against him. For two years, he led a quiet life. Then in June 1997, he was re-arrested when he went to collect his new identity card in his home area of Butare.[14] He was held in a *cachot* for two years and eight months. Then his case was added to the file of 40 other suspects accused of genocide, and he was transferred to Butare prison.

The trial started in 2000 and lasted three months. He and seven other defendants were found not guilty. The rest received sentences ranging from six months to life imprisonment, and four death sentences. He returned to prison to prepare for his release:

> "They sent the documents for the release for five of us, but... three of us remained in prison... After three months, they sent another arrest warrant saying there were new accusations against us. We were not told the content of the new accusations. After we wrote to the authorities about our problem, the prosecutor at the appeal court wrote to the prosecutor in Butare telling him to clarify the new accusations and release us. He said the investigations could continue while the three of us were released... The prosecutor of Butare replied that he couldn't release us and would send him the new accusations. They quickly made up a case-file and sent it to the court.
>
> We went to court again on 19 June 2001. The court said we should be released unconditionally as the second case-file contained the same accusations as the first and we had already been found not guilty. Our release documents were given to a staff member of the *parquet*... On 26 June, when we came out to be released, we were met by a policeman. Even before we came out, we had been told the police were waiting. We tried to refuse to go out. The prison

---

[14] After the genocide, the new Rwandan government introduced new passports and identity documents. All Rwandans had to apply for a new identity card from their area of origin. In 1996 and 1997, many people were arrested while collecting their new identity cards from their local government office.

director asked the police what they had come for. They showed him new arrest warrants... They took us to the brigade in town, where we spent 20 days, then we were brought back to the central prison. I have been here ever since.

It is still the same case-file. We don't have a lawyer any more as they got tired of the trial being adjourned 30 times. We asked the police about our re-arrest. They said they had just been given orders to arrest us... After two days, the prosecutor came to the brigade. He told us directly he wasn't happy with the decision of the court and we should stay in prison...

Then there was the reform of the judicial system, so we are just waiting, all three of us.

Nothing is clear, nothing is precise. Everything is changing. If *gacaca* were done as it is supposed to be, it could have been OK, but the years are passing and nothing has happened. I could have hope if I could see something positive happening but I don't see anything positive."

We also met his wife, who had done everything she could to protest at his illegal detention after the verdict – all in vain:

"When my husband was supposed to be released but wasn't, I was screaming and crying and banging my head against the wall... I have written to everyone about his case, but there is no reply. Now I'm folding my arms and waiting... I've shouted every-where, but no one wants to listen. There is no justice in Rwanda. It will drive me mad. It's all lies. The documents are there. What justice? There is none. It's a huge burden. I don't know when we'll be able to put it down."

We raised this case with Rwandan government officials, as it struck us as one of the most flagrant examples of injustice. The Secretary General at the Ministry of Justice admitted that there had been "gross abuses in the early days" but said he would be surprised if such cases were still pending. He told us that following legal reforms, suspects should be released even while the prosecution appealed against their acquittal. When we raised the case with the then Attorney General, we got a very different response. The Attorney General, who is originally from Butare and is known to take a closer interest in cases from his province, was Minister of Justice at the time of these men's trial; other sources had told us that he was fully aware of these cases. However, he did not indicate any knowledge of them, nor did he show any concern for the way the verdict of the court had been ignored. Instead, he told us it was quite possible that new accusations could come up against someone who had been acquitted, implying that the men's continued detention after their acquittal might be justified.

An equally distressing case was that of a provincial government official in Cyangugu who had been arrested in March 1995 on an accusation of genocide, tried in February 1997 and sentenced to death. He was acquitted on appeal and released in July 1999, but he was unable to enjoy his freedom: for the following two months, he was effectively under house arrest, guarded and followed everywhere by soldiers. The authorities claimed the soldiers had been sent to protect him, as some people had protested against his release. Finally, in September 1999, he was re-arrested. He remained in prison five years later. There had been no second trial or any other court hearing. He had been told that this time, he was accused of crimes which had taken place in 1992, as opposed to participation in the 1994 genocide which had formed the basis for the charges the first time around. In July 2004, he spoke to the *substitut* during one of his visits to the prison. According to the prisoner, the *substitut* admitted there was no serious evidence against him but claimed that his first trial had not been conducted properly and he would have to be tried again. The prisoner asked him whether he was being charged with the first or second set of charges. The *substitut* told him he should expect either.

Also in Cyangugu Central Prison, I tracked down a prisoner I had met in a different context five years earlier, whose case had stuck in my mind because of the particularly perverse course it had taken. His story was, in a sense, the reverse of the case described above: he was first acquitted, then sentenced to death on appeal.

He and his younger brother had been detained on three successive occasions since 1994 on accusations of genocide. Additional accusations against the elder brother, relating to alleged membership of an opposition group in exile, were suddenly brought in halfway through the process, but were dropped equally suddenly, without explanation. The first time, the brothers were detained for just under a year and were provisionally released for lack of evidence. They were re-arrested a few months later. In 1998, they were tried, formally acquitted, and released again. However, the prosecution appealed against their acquittal and one year later, in 1999, they learned that the court of appeal had found them guilty and sentenced them *in absentia*, without giving them a chance to defend themselves. The older brother was sentenced to death and the younger brother to life imprisonment. They were re-arrested.

Five years later, I met the two brothers in the same prison and talked to them separately, for a long time. They were very different in temperament and manner of expression. The older brother, a teacher in his mid-fifties, was the one I had met before. He seemed to have grown harder and more brittle with time, but he spoke eloquently and retained a sharp sense of humour. The younger brother was a farmer, about ten years younger, a warm and straightforward man. As the more educated and wealthier of the two, the older brother tried to look after his younger brother in prison. The second time they were arrested, the younger brother didn't have to worry about finding a place to sleep in the prison because his older brother, who had been arrested just before him, had bought two 40-centimetre places: he was keeping one for him, as he knew he would be arrested too. The two brothers often talked together in the prison, but they had given up talking about their case-file: "Now we talk about other things, like brothers do."

In their conversations with me, however, they talked extensively about their case and their desperation with the justice system. The younger brother told me:

> "The worst thing is that they didn't even call us to the appeal hearing to explain the reasons. We had the right to know and to defend ourselves. I was like someone who had gone mad. It was as if the world was falling apart. Who could I address myself to?

How would I get out? I felt very destabilised. Now, I'm gradually better. The destabilisation lasted about a year. Five years have gone by now."

The older brother had become very bitter.

"This government operates a system of vengeance. It does not look at responsibility in the genocide. The truth for them is not the truth for us. There will be no compensation even if I'm released. I may spend the rest of my life here… I don't see any way out.

Sometimes I re-read my case-file. It's like a novel. I dare to read it now because I'm not afraid any more. It is like a travelling companion. It has become normal.

When you have strength of character, you always hope to get out. I'm still optimistic I'll be released. It won't make me go mad."

In October 1999, he had appealed to the Supreme Court. At the time of our conversation, five years on, he was still waiting for the outcome of his appeal. In June 2005, I learned that the Supreme Court had confirmed his death sentence.[15]

Prisoners' views on justice

The absence of justice preoccupies prisoners almost more than any other issue. A prisoner spoke for many when he pleaded with us: "Justice is the most important thing. Please give out this message. Tell the government to judge people as quickly as possible. We have done bad things but we accept the punishment and want reconciliation." Not all prisoners accepted having done "bad things", but whether innocent or guilty, all were equally affected by the absence of justice. Many did not expect to receive a fair trial.

---

[15] His death sentence would have been commuted after Rwanda abolished the death penalty in July 2007 (see Chapter XVIII).

Nevertheless, they longed to be tried, simply in order to put an end to the uncertainty.

Listening to these prisoners' experiences of the justice system, one after the other, was overwhelming. It was an endless catalogue of bureaucratic blockages, indifference, corruption, and, sometimes, revenge. Of those we spoke to, many told us that there had been no progress with their case-file since the day of their arrest. Many had not been through any form of judicial procedure other than a cursory interrogation soon after their arrest, usually intended to extract an admission of guilt (often under torture) or fabricate an accusation rather than ascertain facts. Some prisoners didn't even know the specific accusations against them.

When we asked these prisoners about their expectations of the justice system, their standard answer was: "I'm just waiting." Some were no longer waiting for justice as such, but waiting "to see whether justice will happen", as if they were outsiders observing from the sidelines. Some seemed to have lost track of what they were waiting for.

We met some prisoners who didn't even know whether they were accused of genocide or of some other crime. One was a prisoner who had been detained since 1997. He and a number of other people were arrested by soldiers who raided a market in search of people who didn't have identity documents. He had his identity card, but the soldiers took it away. He was then detained in a brigade for four years, where he was repeatedly beaten. He was detained along with more than 200 people, some of them accused of genocide, others of common crimes. He didn't know which category he belonged to as he was never questioned. In 2002, he was transferred to Butare prison, where he remained at the end of 2004. He told us:

> "I consider that my case-file doesn't exist. I could be accused of a common crime because there are no specific genocide accusations against me. I don't know the charge. All I know is that I haven't done anything wrong... If there was the will to do justice, they would release me... I feel the day of my release will never come. I'm waiting for something, but that something will never come."

Frustrated by the endless delays, many prisoners had given up believing in any prospect of justice at all. They felt they had been forgotten. Their loss of faith was based on a series of very real experiences: the arbitrary nature of many arrests, the impossibility of redress for miscarriages of justice, the absence of due process, and the authorities' apparent lack of concern about all these problems. A man who was released after nine years said that it had never even occurred to him that he would be tried while he was in prison. He avoided even using the terms "trial" or "case-file", as he considered them irrelevant.

The main problem for prisoners who claimed to have been wrongfully arrested was that it seemed impossible to undo the wrong which had been done. Prisoners and their families sent off numerous, handwritten letters to the authorities, pleading their innocence, explaining the circumstances of their case in minute detail and begging for a hearing. In all but a tiny handful of cases, their letters remained unanswered. Sometimes prisoners would approach the prosecutor or the *substitut* when they visited the prison, and these officials might promise to look into their cases, but usually, nothing more was heard. The frequent turnover of staff in the prosecutors' offices was an added complication. Sometimes, a sympathetic official was willing to investigate a case, but was then dismissed or moved to another location. The prisoner then had to start all over again with a new set of officials, because these small promises were only ever based on personal favours.

Once in prison, it made no difference whether someone's arrest had been based on substantial evidence of participation in a crime, whether it had been maliciously orchestrated, whether it was arbitrary, or whether it was simply a mistake. Even when people outside came forward to testify to a prisoner's innocence or to retract earlier accusations, nothing happened. As one prisoner told us: "You can be accused by one person and confirmed innocent by 30 people but still not be released... It is quick and easy to put someone in prison, but it's almost impossible to get out."

The case of a prisoner accused of a common crime illustrated this predicament. He was a driver, now in his early thirties, who used to live and work in a neighbouring country and who sometimes drove passengers across the border into Rwanda. One day, in 1995, he gave a lift to some Rwandan soldiers. The next day, he was arrested. He was questioned about the where-abouts of the soldiers, who had been accused of stealing some money. When he said he didn't know where the soldiers were, he was detained and accused of complicity. Nine years later, he was still in prison. There had been no hearing, no trial, no form of judicial procedure whatsoever. He didn't have any relatives or friends in Rwanda, so there was no one to follow up his case for him. He tried to keep himself busy in the prison, but there were times when he despaired. "I don't know if or how I'll be released," he told us, and added, in a typical understatement: "Time is passing by."

Some people have ended up in prison not through deliberately wrongful accusations, but through sheer error. Once in prison, they have got caught up in the paralysis of the system, like everyone else. A prisoner told us: "A man I know is accused of killing a woman who used to be his girlfriend, but she's still alive. He's told the authorities, but nothing has happened. He has been in prison since 1995, without a trial. He is not thinking about anything any more. He is waiting for God to decide."

Prisoners' views on *gacaca*

Initially, the introduction of *gacaca* raised hopes among prisoners. Here was a new system, a different system, one which, in theory at least, would offer them a chance to stand before the population and be judged by those who were really in the know: not professional judges or prosecutors, but ordinary people, from their own area. Prisoners who claimed to be innocent said they desperately wanted to appear before a *gacaca* court as they were convinced they would be acquitted. Even those who were sceptical about the quality of justice to be delivered by these improvised jurisdictions held out some hope. Despite its imperfections, *gacaca* had to be better than nothing.

Of the prisoners we spoke to, a surprising number said they trusted *gacaca*. Whether they really did or whether they just forced themselves to for the sake of keeping their hope alive was not entirely clear. Some were in favour of the principle, but feared it might not be applied properly. A woman who had spent nine and a half years in prison without trial said: "*Gacaca* will be positive if people tell the truth... But more generally I don't feel confident, as there is still a lot of hatred... I doubt people's truthfulness."

As the years went by, some prisoners stopped believing in *gacaca* simply because it had been postponed so many times. One prisoner told us: "*Gacaca* is an utopia… *gacaca* is a cloud." Another complained: "*Gacaca*, *gacaca*, *gacaca* is all we hear, since 1998. Nothing ever happens." Each time a new date was announced on the radio, prisoners would prepare themselves psychologically and start looking forward to the possibility that they might be tried. Each time, the date was postponed, and a new date was set. It went in cycles, about three months at a time. Prisoners claimed they no longer took these announcements seriously, yet every time, despite themselves, they started counting the days again.

Some prisoners dismissed *gacaca* as a mere slogan, a ploy on the part of the government to impress the international community. They didn't believe it would provide any guarantee of objectivity. "*Gacaca* won't resolve the problem. It will increase it," one prisoner told us. "The judges are not trained in law… I am not confident I will be able to defend myself fairly." Another described *gacaca* as an opportunity for retaliation by the population and said he would prefer to be tried by a normal court because there were more safeguards: "You have the law, evidence, rights, a lawyer, and you can challenge the decision. I have witnesses… all this is not possible with *gacaca*."

One of the more cynical prisoners was equally negative about the two systems: "I don't believe in the justice system, neither the courts nor *gacaca*. They drag things out so that they don't happen. Those who die will die. They make excuses. They say, 'we'll start in January', 'we'll start in March', and so on. They get money from donors. *Gacaca* is just intended to blind the outside world. Every year, it is delayed… It's just lies. Lying has become a political art."

Blame and frustration

Many prisoners accused of genocide were arrested on the basis of denunciations by people they knew, but most of their anger was directed towards the government rather than towards the individuals who had denounced them. The matter of relationships between former friends and neighbours in the aftermath of the genocide is complicated, but ultimately is one which prisoners feel able to deal with on an individual level, each in their own way. However, prisoners were much less forgiving towards the state. Many attributed the endless delays in the justice system to ill-will, rather than lack of means, and described their continued detention without trial as a calculated policy of vengeance on the part of the government. "Politics and justice have merged," one prisoner told us. "They [the government] pretend to show their good side but deep down, it's vengeance," said another. "It would be better for them if we weren't here. The justice system is sick. The principle is that they don't want us to get out of prison."

Many prisoners believe that the justice system, like almost every other institution in Rwanda, has become politicised along ethnic lines and they expect the ethnic composition of the courts to affect the outcome of trials. One prisoner complained that it would be difficult to obtain justice because most judges were Tutsi. Another asked: "Is it justice or settling of scores? A judge can say: 'You're innocent, but I don't care as my family was killed [in the genocide].' That is not justice for me." Another described it as "the justice of the victors over the vanquished. How can a judge try someone when the person he sees is the one who killed his family? Justice should come from outside. Even Arusha [the location of the International Criminal Tribunal for Rwanda] is not far enough away."

Some prisoners blamed Ibuka, the organisation representing survivors of the genocide, for ensuring that certain individuals remained in prison for political rather than criminal reasons, and for blocking the release of people against whom there was no evidence.[16] A prisoner whose name was on a list of people to be released but who ended up back in prison said: "Whenever the government wants to release people, Ibuka intervenes to stop it. I have no hope because the genocide survivors always have their word to say. The government keeps changing the law and moving the goalposts. The law is fashioned around lies."

---

[16] Ibuka, one of the most prominent groups representing survivors of the genocide, is a highly politicised and influential organisation, active at national and local levels. Its members have denounced numerous individuals for participation in the genocide. Government authorities have been willing to arrest people solely on the basis of Ibuka's recommendations, without carrying out independent investigations. Ibuka has opposed some of the large-scale releases of prisoners accused of genocide.

Justice for RPF and RPA crimes

Aside from the question of their own long wait for justice, prisoners were very bitter about the blanket silence surrounding the tens of thousands of killings by the RPF. They were angered and frustrated not only by the government's refusal to admit that the RPF, and later the RPA, had carried out massacres, but by the political impossibility of even talking about these crimes, let alone demanding justice for them. By the end of 2004, only a small handful of RPA soldiers had been prosecuted by military courts, and some of those had been released. Despite the government's repeated assurances that it was taking such cases seriously, it has been extremely difficult to obtain precise or comprehensive information on these cases.[17]

Gacaca, for its part, was set up explicitly to try only genocide cases, not crimes committed by the RPF. RPF crimes would continue to be dealt with by the normal civilian or military courts, if they were dealt with at all. For many Rwandans, this set *gacaca* off to a bad start. How could they trust a system which was so unashamedly one-sided and which excluded crimes committed by those who were now in power? A prisoner told us: "Justice is not objective or neutral... They are only judging one set of crimes." In one prison, prisoners had included names of people killed by the RPF in the list of victims and perpetrators which they had drawn up during their own *gacaca* sessions. They had done this out of a sense of duty to report the truth, but they did not expect any response or action.

Many miles away, in Arusha, the ICTR has not prosecuted any RPF officials either, even though crimes committed by the RPF are covered by its mandate.[18] Intense political pressure and obstruction by the Rwandan government has ensured that this has simply not happened. To date, no RPF official has been indicted by the ICTR. Prisoners therefore believe the ICTR

---

[17] For details of some of these cases, see Fédération Internationale des Droits de l'Homme (FIDH), *Victims in the balance: challenges ahead for the International Criminal Tribunal for Rwanda*, November 2002, page 16 and Annex XI ("Statistics of human rights abuses by RPA soldiers"), pages 64-70.

[18] The ICTR was set up to prosecute individuals responsible for genocide and other serious violations of international humanitarian law committed between 1 January and 31 December 1994.

is as one-sided as the Rwandan courts. A prisoner told us: "Prisoners follow the ICTR trials on the radio, but justice there is unilateral too. Before, they used to talk about 'genocide and massacres'. Now, it's just genocide. People don't talk about the deaths of Hutu any more."

Many of the prisoners we spoke to expressed their fears for the longer-term future of the country as a result of this suppression of a whole set of events and crimes. "The RPF massacres were never acknowledged," one prisoner complained. "If there is to be reconciliation, everything should be out in the open and they should look at both sides. We should seek mutual forgiveness, especially for our children in the future. Otherwise, the gulf will never be closed and there won't be total forgiveness."

CHAPTER XVIII

"The heaviest sentence":

prisoners sentenced to death

When the genocide trials started in Rwanda at the end of 1996, there was a strong desire for retribution. The first wave of trials resulted in numerous death sentences. According to the genocide law, only defendants in Category 1 (such as those who played a leading role in the genocide) were liable to be sentenced to death. However, in the early phase, the process of categorisation was rushed and deeply flawed, and many individuals who probably should not have been classed as Category 1 found themselves sentenced to death, often after summary trials and without a defence lawyer. Over the years that followed, judges continued handing down death sentences, but proportionally fewer than in the initial period. By 2004, hundreds of people had been sentenced to death.

Rwanda abolished the death penalty in July 2007, but at the time of our interviews with prisoners in late 2004, the death penalty was still in force.

The 1998 executions

On 24 April 1998, 22 people were executed after being sentenced to death for genocide. These executions all took place on the same day, in public, in five different locations. These were the first and the last executions of people tried in Rwanda for genocide.

Those executed included at least one prisoner who was widely believed to have played a leading role in the genocide: Froduald Karamira, a prominent member of the extremist "Power" faction of the MDR party (*Mouvement démocratique républicain*). But not all 22 were notorious for their actions during the genocide, and several of those executed may have been innocent. Among them was Silas Munyagishali, an assistant prosecutor in Kigali who was arrested on an accusation of genocide after protesting at corruption and political interference in the justice system. Many of his fellow prisoners, as well as journalists, human rights activists and others, were convinced he had been made a scapegoat, and that his arrest and his execution were politically motivated.[1] I had met Silas Munyagishali in Kigali Central Prison in 1996. I still remember his face clearly. Returning to the prison six years after his execution brought back memories of our conversation and of his case which I had found deeply disturbing. I also remembered meeting his wife about a year after his execution. She had been completely distraught and seemed to have lost all points of reference. Friends told me, several years later, that she had never recovered from his execution.

The 1998 executions sent shockwaves through the prisons. Several prisoners who had been told that their names were next on the list believed they escaped execution on that day by a whisker. Even prisoners who had not yet been tried were thrown into a state of panic. They were convinced that further death sentences would be carried out. A former prisoner told us they started thinking they would all be killed soon and that some used to say it didn't matter whether they carried on eating or not.

Prisoners had lived side by side with those who were executed for several years and had got to know them well. Seeing these prisoners taken out of the prison, then hearing on the radio that they had been executed was an altogether different experience from watching prisoners die as a result of harsh prison conditions, or even torture. This was a coldly calculated programme, officially sanctioned by the highest levels of government and carried out as part of a political strategy. The prisoners' sense of dread was heightened by the knowledge that the trials which had resulted in these executions had been grossly unfair, and by their belief that some of those executed were innocent.

In their reactions, prisoners differentiated between the individuals who were widely known to have taken part in the genocide, such as Froduald Karamira, and those who they believed to be innocent, such as Silas Munyagishali. An older prisoner reflected: "Silas died unjustly. He got swept up in a current where he did not belong. But Karamira was a politician. It was different."

---

[1]   For details of the arrest and trial of Silas Munyagishali, see Amnesty International statement, *Rwanda: fear of imminent executions*, April 1998.

The prisoners we spoke to who had been in prison at that time all had vivid memories of the day of the executions, especially those who were held in prisons from where people were taken to be executed. We spoke to a young prisoner who used to live in the same block as Karamira in Kigali Central Prison and who had also known another of those executed, a young man who had been in his volleyball team:

> "On the morning of the executions, we saw them being taken away on a truck. I saw them through the gate. It was hard for us. People were afraid. Two other prisoners who were sentenced to death were also called, but it turned out their case-files were not complete, so they stayed here; they were not executed. The fear continued. It took some time to pass. We thought it could happen to the rest of us at any time."

A former prisoner in Kigali had a vivid memory of Karamira: "Karamira... was a high personality. I don't know what he did in the genocide, but in prison he used to keep our spirits up. He used to joke, he used to say he would win his trial, he played sports and trained others, he learned German. But no one visited him because people were scared."

Three of those executed were from Butare. A former teacher, who had been in prison since 1994, remembered the period leading up to their executions.

> "Two of them had been my students. I had taught them in high school. I didn't use to talk about their sentence with them but we talked about their case-file and the accusations... We expected them to be executed. The president had indicated that. The feeling on that day was horrible. Nobody spoke about it, but you could read the sadness on everyone's faces, especially those of us who knew that some of them were innocent. It was as if we were mourning their deaths before the executions even took place. Other people said I could have been among those executed. I missed it by an inch. But I never felt this risk, as no one had accused me, and in my heart, I was clean."

A former female prisoner in Gitarama Central Prison remembered the only woman who was executed.

> "She was uneducated. She never thought she would be executed. She thought her appeal would be accepted. She was very naive. She didn't believe in her execution until they came to fetch her in a truck. In the prison, we had beds on three floors. The women on the top floor saw the people tied up on a truck, ready for the execution. It was shocking. When they read out the list on the radio, we heard that she really had been executed."

A prisoner in Gitarama told me that about two years after the executions, officials brought a list of prisoners to be released from the prison. The name of the woman who had been executed was on this list.

A former prisoner in Kigali Central Prison was moved to write a detailed description of the impact of the executions as part of a longer account of his imprisonment:

> "One of those executed was Froduald Karamira, one of the brains behind the 1994 genocide... On the rare occasions when I caught sight of him in prison, he seemed to be in good spirits, like all politicians. He used to pray and always wore his rosary around his neck. After the three o'clock prayers, he used to play karate 'to fight off old age', as he liked to say. Some said that after his death, he left behind plans to build a railway network in Rwanda, which he was planning to launch after his release – except he never said who he thought would release him. Whenever he was asked that question, he would just say that everything is possible in politics, as in football.
>
> In April 1998, the authorities announced their final decision: that the first group of people found guilty of genocide would be executed on a specific date, in all four corners of the country... The list was circulated and one day, in the prison where I was living, they came to fetch eight of the prisoners who had been sentenced to death, including Mr Karamira. I remember another

one called Bazumutima who said, as he was climbing down from his bed for the last time: 'Die like brave men.' I asked where he was going. I didn't know that he too had been sentenced to death and was about to die.

All the prisoners were in a state of heightened emotion. Everyone was afraid and there were lots of rumours about the list of people to be executed. Even those who hadn't exhausted their appeals were afraid, even those who hadn't yet appeared before a court. Their fears were well-founded as some of those who were called out came back ten minutes later, after their cases were checked, after they had already got into the truck... For example there was one prisoner who narrowly escaped because his case was still in appeal. Another old woman came back a week later. Even though her case-file was in order, she was made to wait, I don't know what for... for death, and she's still waiting because there haven't been any more executions since then.

Above all, I remember the face of a young man who used to sleep outside in the central courtyard... I can still picture the astonishment on the face of this young man, who believed it was a mistake. He kept saying: 'My case is still in appeal, let me drink some tea.' Some of the other prisoners commented with indifference: 'What's the point in drinking tea? You'll be dying anyway!'

We learned a week later that the convoy went round the prisons picking up those who were to be executed. On the penultimate day, they gathered them in an isolated room we called Rukomera within the compound of Kigali Central Prison... We also heard, but couldn't confirm, that Silas Munyagishali... had protested that it was a mistake, until the very end, that his time had not come, and that he had even struggled when they tied him up...

I have been haunted by that terrible scene ever since, and I'm sure I'm not the only one...

But what surprised me on the day of the executions was that people did not mourn. Not because mourning was prohibited or because people believed that those who were guilty should be held accountable for their actions, but because each person in prison is mourning his own death from day to day and has become indifferent to the fate of others. We used to say: 'Each person to his pain, and each person's turn will come.' One prisoner whispered in my ear that he didn't see why they should shed tears for Karamira: 'At least he really participated [in the genocide].' And we sat down to eat our few grams of beans and corn as usual. They say that everything is normal when nothing is normal.

During the week that followed, we had to put up with rumours and comments, some of them exaggerated, on the way the executions were carried out. We didn't need to search far for this information... We talked with the guards and within a short time, the information, whether accurate or not, circulated among the 8,000 prisoners, in 8,000 different versions."

With hindsight, it became clear that the 1998 executions were show executions. The government did not carry out any further executions, and eventually, in July 2007, it abolished the death penalty. Many prisoners believed that the shift in the government's strategy was largely due to international pressure.

In the absence of further executions, prisoners' fears began to recede. "Now, people are calm," a prisoner told us at the end of 2004. "We don't believe there will be more executions. Sentences are being reduced. We have seen criminals confess and be released." A former prisoner believed the executions were one of the factors which persuaded prisoners to confess: "After the executions, the confessions started. Before, no one admitted having killed... The executions frightened people into confessing. They thought: 'If I don't confess, they will put me on the tree' ('bazamushyira kugiti'). This meant they were finished, they would be killed, like Karamira and the others who were tied to a tree before being shot."

Life under sentence of death

When we visited the prisons at the end of 2004, there were still hundreds of prisoners under sentence of death. Some were convicted of genocide, others of common crimes.[2] In some prisons, a separate block was designated for prisoners sentenced to death or to life imprisonment, but the separation was not adhered to rigidly, and prisoners drifted in and out of the blocks, mixing freely. In other prisons, they were not separated at all and lived side by side with the other prisoners.[3] Prisoners sentenced to death were not allowed to work or to participate in activities outside the prison building. In some prisons, they were not allowed to hold positions of responsibility in the prison administration.

Many of the prisoners sentenced to death appealed against their convictions as soon as they were sentenced. In a number of cases, the appeal courts confirmed their death sentences. In others, prisoners were still waiting for a hearing several years after lodging their appeal. Many of these appeals got stuck in the system when the courts effectively stopped functioning during the period of judicial reforms in 2003-2004.

The prisoners we spoke to who had been sentenced to death were still angry about the severity of their sentence, and most of them vehemently protested their innocence. But they no longer believed in their death sentence as a real sentence, even though it would be another three years before the death penalty was formally abolished. One prisoner said: "Even though I've been sentenced to death, I haven't realised it." Another, despite feeling very angry about the justice system, said: "I don't believe in my death sentence. I laugh about it." While they expected to spend many more years in prison, they did

---

[2] According to a report by the organisation Ensemble contre la peine de mort (ECPM, Together Against the Death Penalty), there were 814 prisoners under sentence of death in July 2006. Of these, 590 had been sentenced to death for genocide and 224 for common crimes. The ECPM report, *La peine capitale au Rwanda: enquête dans les couloirs de la mort de la prison de Mpanga* (The death penalty in Rwanda: investigation on death row in Mpanga prison), also provides detailed information on other aspects of the death penalty in Rwanda.

[3] More recently, the government has begun transferring all prisoners sentenced to death who have exhausted their possibilities for appeal to the new prison of Mpanga.

not expect to be executed; it was as if somewhere along the way, their death sentence had imperceptibly changed into a life sentence.

Some prisoners told us they had never believed in their own death sentence, even before it became clear that further executions were unlikely. Convinced of their own innocence, and spurred on by their religious faith, they had succeeded in maintaining an irrational optimism and a detachment from reality.

Some had been deeply shocked when they were first sentenced to death, but had got used to living with their sentence as they realised that the prospect of being executed was becoming increasingly remote. One prisoner, who described his trial in Byumba as a pretence of justice – "you wouldn't know whether to laugh or cry" – said that he had expected to be acquitted and released. Instead, he was sentenced to death. "I felt as if I was struck by lightning. When I heard the judgement, I couldn't speak. I just signed the paper. I couldn't eat or drink. Friends in the prison came to comfort me and made me tea. I was in this state for about a week. But after two weeks, I was laughing about it with the others. There were about 80 of us in Byumba sentenced to death, so it was comforting to know I wasn't the only one."

By the time we visited the prisons in late 2004, most of those sentenced to death shared this fairly relaxed attitude about their fate. Nevertheless, there was a noticeable difference in tone in our interviews with prisoners who had been sentenced to death and a certain heaviness to these conversations. They spoke about their hope, but this hope seemed artificial and did not ring entirely true. To some extent, the same was true of prisoners who had been classed or knew they would be classed in Category 1 but had not yet been tried. They had resigned themselves to spending the rest of their lives in prison.

In Kigali Central Prison, I interviewed a man I had first met in 1998 and again in 1999; at that time, he hadn't been tried. He recognised me and greeted me warmly. As we sat down to start the interview, he told me: "You know, since we last met, lots of things have happened. I have to update you on my situation. I've been sentenced to death." As I listened to his story, I noticed he had changed since our meeting several years ago. I had remembered him as an optimistic, friendly and outwardly caring man. He was still charming, and spoke with a big smile even when describing his harshest experiences, but there was a harder edge to him now. His death sentence and his long years in prison had chipped away at his generosity. But if he had succumbed to depression, he still hid it fairly well. "I won't be executed," he announced confidently and categorically, "I don't feel discouraged at all."

He had been tried along with four co-accused. He described the agony of waiting for numerous adjournments, which extended over a period of three years:

> "In July 1999, I received notification that my trial would start in August 1999. But judges kept resigning and there were delays. It was postponed until 17 February 2000. The trial started on that date... On 8 December 2000, the judges said we should bring our conclusions on 18 December. On 18 December, no judge turned up. It was postponed. We waited. It was postponed again and again until 9 October 2001. Then on 9 October 2001, it was postponed *sine die*. They gave various reasons, for example a judge was sick, a witness had challenged a judge, etc. I was going crazy... Finally, the judges fixed the date of 24 June 2002... They said they would give the judgement on 11 July. They only came on 26 July. They took us to the court. There they said that all my accomplices were acquitted, but that I had been responsible for everything so I was sentenced to death. My family was there. They all screamed. I thought I was going to faint. I tried to stay calm. I was brought back to prison and wrote my appeal...
>
> It never occurred to me that I could be sentenced to death. Until then, I had thought that all the other people sentenced to death were probably guilty. After my trial, I realised that some of those sentenced to death before me might also have been innocent."

I asked him how he coped with life in prison. As a well-educated man, with a family who supported him, he seemed to have both the material means and the moral strength to make his situation bearable: "I try to stay calm and hopeful. I read. There are lots of classes. I'm learning German for three hours a week. Prisoners come and ask me for advice or I help them write letters... I have no choice but to live here, and I manage, but it doesn't stop me from thinking about my family. I try not to be overcome by unhappiness, sadness and injustice. I pretend to make myself at home. It helps me not to get too depressed. It is very hard for a prisoner to spend years in prison without feeling guilty."

Another prisoner who had been sentenced to death had been less successful in overcoming his despair. His feelings alternated between hope and resignation, but the resignation seemed to be winning. A businessman and local representative of the former ruling party, the MRND, he was arrested in 1998, three years after returning from Congo. His trial began in 2000, and in 2001, he received what he called "the heaviest sentence". The lawyer he had hired didn't turn up at the trial, so he had to defend himself. He believed – rightly or wrongly – that if the lawyer had done his job properly, he would not have been sentenced to death. The court convicted him of participation in the genocide on the basis of the position he had occupied in the ruling party. He pleaded not guilty and appealed against his conviction, but in 2003, the appeal court confirmed his death sentence. He then appealed to the Supreme Court and was still waiting for a hearing when we met him.

> "I didn't expect to be sentenced to death. I was expecting to be acquitted. Even now, I can't believe it. I will continue until the end. I can't rest until this is finished... I am waiting to see what their justice comes up with... Most of all, I am waiting for the justice of God to overcome their justice.
>
> I would be afraid if I felt guilty, but while I feel innocent, I am not afraid. If it happens, it happens. If it doesn't, it doesn't. What is death? There is the death of the body. When death comes, it comes."

I asked him about other prisoners sentenced to death and how they felt about their situation. He replied: "I know some of them here but we don't really discuss this. What can we say? I prefer to talk to God than to other prisoners."

We also met common criminals who had been sentenced to death. A man charged with a murder apparently unconnected to the genocide was tried in 1997, two years after his arrest. His co-accused, a former neighbour, stated during the trial that she had been tortured into confessing and into denouncing him as her accomplice. Nevertheless, they were both sentenced to death. They had no defence witnesses and no lawyer. They both appealed immediately, but four years later, their appeal had still not been heard. They had been given numerous dates, but each time the hearing was postponed. The last assignment they had been given was for 29 September 1999, but five years later, nothing had happened. The prisoner had written to the authorities about his case 12 times, but had received no response since 1999.

As with so many other issues, whether a death sentence stuck or not could come down to a question of money. A woman accused of murder was tried in 2000. She had written to the authorities asking for a lawyer, but had not received any reply, so had had to defend herself. The following day, she was sentenced to death. The judges had asked her for 50,000 francs (about US $90) in exchange for an acquittal but she had been unable to pay. She appealed against her sentence. "They called me to appear before the court without warning. I asked for a few days to read my case-file. They allowed me only two days to read a file of 178 pages. I didn't even have a lawyer... At the appeal, they asked me for 100,000 francs." One year after the appeal hearing, the appeal court confirmed her death sentence. She appealed to the Court of Cassation, but was told that it didn't exist any more, because of the judicial reforms. She had been waiting since then.

The abolition of the death penalty

On 25 July 2007, Rwanda abolished the death penalty. A new law was passed, commuting all death sentences to life imprisonment or "life imprisonment with special provisions". Crimes punishable by "life imprisonment with special provisions" include genocide. Those affected by these special provisions are not entitled to "any kind of mercy, conditional release or rehabilitation" unless they have served at least 20 years in prison, and are to be held in isolation.[4]

Until now, the International Criminal Tribunal for Rwanda (ICTR) in Arusha has not been able to hand over suspects to Rwanda as they may face the death penalty there. The abolition of the death penalty in 2007 will mean that suspects indicted by the ICTR could now be tried in Rwanda. It also paves the way for the extradition of suspects to Rwanda from other countries which had previously ruled out extradition on the basis of their opposition to the death penalty.

---

[4] The law does not explain what is meant by "isolation". It does not specify whether these prisoners are to be detained in a separate location or section from other prisoners or whether they are to be held in solitary confinement (the latter would be practically impossible, given the state of Rwanda's prisons). The most likely scenario is that this category of prisoners would be moved to a different prison.

CHAPTER XIX

Where the guilty are kings:

confessions

"I wonder: is it a crime not to have killed?
Or is having killed the best way of getting out of prison?"

As part of its strategy to reduce the burden on the justice system, the government set up a programme to encourage prisoners to confess to the crimes they committed during the genocide.   If their confessions are accepted, they can be released or benefit from a reduced sentence. In some respects, the system is similar to arrangements which exist in other countries where those who plead guilty may receive a lighter sentence. But in Rwanda, the confessions programme has a twist in its tail. Prisoners who confess have to describe not only what they did during the genocide, but what others did too.   If they do not denounce others, their confessions are not admissible. The government's barely concealed ulterior motive is to demonstrate that as many people as possible participated in the genocide. In this way, the bulk of the Hutu population is "proved guilty", not through any process of trial but by self-incrimination.

A range of means have been deployed to encourage prisoners to confess, including subtle and not so subtle forms of coercion and bribery. These methods may help the government reach its target, if the target is a large number of confessions, but there will be huge casualties too: justice, truth, and the fate of thousands of innocent people in prison.   The confessions programme has turned the principle of justice on its head: it has resulted in a situation where people guilty of the most terrible crimes walk free, while those who are innocent remain in prison.   One prisoner summed up the situation as follows: "A person who is innocent and does not want to lie accepts to stay here."

Some prisoners fabricate confessions just in order to qualify for release. They take responsibility for crimes they have never committed, implicate others in crimes they may not have committed either, invent incidents which never took place, confess to killing people who are still alive or who don't exist. Deals are struck: guilt and innocence can be bought, and truth doesn't even enter into the bargain. Some prisoners are driven to confess only by the fear that others will denounce them in their confessions, so they try to anticipate this by getting there first; or they confess as soon as they learn they have been denounced by someone else, so as not to be caught out later. It is like a game where each person has to guess his opponent's strategy. Others confess to crimes their relatives or friends may have committed, to protect the real perpetrators, who are still free. The truth becomes more and more elusive, until the confession loses its very meaning.

Propaganda, pressure and enticements

Initially, prisoners were suspicious of the government's motives for encouraging confessions. The few who did confess in the early days of the programme, which was launched in earnest around 1998, were viewed with mistrust by their fellow prisoners. "As soon as someone confessed," a prisoner told us, "he stood out from the crowd and those who hadn't confessed didn't want to speak to him." Two camps were created: those who confessed were called cowards by those who hadn't confessed, and those who hadn't confessed were called recalcitrants by those who had confessed.

A prisoner who was a lawyer linked some prisoners' initial reluctance to confess with events which were taking place outside. In 1998, the insurgents known as *infiltrés*, who included people who had participated in the genocide, stepped up their attacks in the northwest of the country, and prisoners who had sympathies with these groups believed that they were about to be "liberated". This prisoner told us: "In May 1998, I explained the law to the prisoners and told them about the possibility of confessing. People thought I was crazy or that I was a government spy. They asked how they could possibly confess. When the real *génocidaires* among them heard about the *infiltrés* attacking, they were happy and said: 'Good, they're coming to release us.' So there was no question of confessing at that time... There was a direct link between the armed conflict and prisoners' reticence to confess. People really believed the government would be overthrown and they would be released... But the attackers were losing the war."

In the months and years that followed, the thinking started to change. Small groups of prisoners who had confessed were released in dribs and drabs, and prisoners realised that confessing might represent their only chance of getting out of prison. The number of prisoners willing to confess gradually increased, and was further boosted by the first large-scale releases in early 2003. According to the Attorney General, about 50,000 prisoners had confessed by the end of 2004, more than half the total prison population.

The start of the confessions programme marked a turning point for prisoners and altered the psychology inside. Hopes were raised: for the first time, people who had spent years in prison without trial were offered a real prospect of release. But there were continuing frustrations too, as not all those who had confessed were released, and there seemed to be no clear rationale as to why some were left behind.

The government's campaign to encourage confessions was still in full swing when we visited the country at the end of 2004. Officials from the government and from the judiciary continued touring the prisons, extolling the virtues of confessing. Prison directors also encouraged prisoners to confess. Prisoners were bombarded with the message from all sides, and the deadline for confessions was extended several times. There was no presumption of innocence here: the assumption underlying the government's campaign was that most, if not all, of these prisoners were guilty and had something to confess. Their vulnerability and desperation were exploited to the full.

A former prisoner said that these meetings with government or prison officials often produced results: "The pressure worked. Lots of people confessed after those meetings. Some confessed to things they hadn't done to be released. We all knew each other and we knew who was lying... The list of people who had confessed was publicised in meetings."

The government took its campaign to the *cachots* as well as the prisons. A prisoner who had spent eight years in a *cachot* described the intense pressure on prisoners when the authorities visited: "A team from the prosecutor's office came to the *cachot* about once a month, from early 1999 to 2000. They asked what we had seen in the genocide. They tried to force us to admit things. We had to think hard about what we hadn't done or seen. They said: 'If you don't admit, you'll stay in forever, until you confess.' They forced us through questions: 'Were you in the country during the genocide? Were you sick? If not, what did you see? The government ordered you to kill, so why didn't you kill?' I was questioned like this at least five times."

The government has denied putting pressure on prisoners to confess. The Secretary General of the Ministry of Justice claimed that the only arguments used by the government to persuade people to confess were legal and moral arguments. He explained that in addition to the benefit of reduced sentences, confessions gave prisoners a chance to tell their story. "Some truly regret what they did and feel they were misled by their leaders. Confessing gives them an opportunity to say that. It is a moral encouragement. We are reviving the culture of the honest personality... Some believe they've lost their personality forever. Confessing is part of the process of returning their personality to them."

The Attorney General presented the government's confessions campaign as part of the search for the truth about the genocide. He said it was easier to reach people inside the prisons than outside. "The information from the prisons helps us a lot. It's not a trial, but preliminary information. Some give half-confessions. They say what they think has been seen... but even half the information is useful, as it can lead on to something else. It's like a chain."

However, according to prisoners themselves, the content of many confessions is unreliable, and the truth is disappearing fast. Had the confessions programme been run rigorously and conscientiously, it could have been an important step towards establishing which prisoners were guilty and which prisoners were innocent. Instead, the manner in which it has been driven, and particularly the extensive corruption which has influenced the quantity as well as the quality of confessions, has further muddied the waters and rendered the distinction between guilt and innocence almost irrelevant.

The sensitisation committees

The most keen advocates of the confessions system are some of the prisoners themselves. These prisoners are effectively working for the government. Under heavy encouragement and inducements from the authorities, prisoners have set up their own committees to persuade their fellow prisoners to confess. Referred to as the sensitisation committees (*comités de sensibilisation*), they double up as the prisoners' *gacaca* committees, as they also organise the *gacaca* procedure in the prison. Their duty is to propagate and manage the confessions system inside. They organise regular meetings with the prisoners to remind them, over and over again, of the advantages of confessing, and to explain the *gacaca* system. On visit days, they talk to prisoners' families in the hope that they too might persuade prisoners to confess. Some committee members, such as those in Gitarama, also tour prisons in other provinces to spread the word, sometimes for several weeks at a time. The Executive Secretary of the National *Gacaca* Service – the government-appointed body in charge of overseeing the *gacaca* system – told us that she was planning to give these prisoners computers and disks to record the confessions electronically: "They are doing the work for us."

When we visited Butare Central Prison in December 2004, one of the sensitisation meetings was going on in the background while we interviewed a prisoner. He was a 70-year-old man who had not confessed. He pointed to the meeting as an example of the constant pressure: "They go on and on about it and it's like brainwashing. I can't confess if I didn't do anything. But listen to that: that's the pressure we're under. The *gacaca* committee come to see us here in the yard all the time."

We met members of these committees in most of the prisons we visited, especially in Gitarama Central Prison, where one of the leading members of the committee – an over-enthusiastic man with bright eyes and a keen grin – lent us his office for our interviews. He and his colleagues had been given their own special office in the prison compound, outside the main building, where they spent their days collecting and filing confessions. On the wall of the office, they had chalked up the statistics of the number of confessions so far. The list was updated every day. When we visited on 3 November 2004, there was a grand total of 4,186 confessions – about half the population of the prison.[1]

---

[1]   The proportion of prisoners who have confessed was not as high in all the prisons. In Butare prison, for example, around 3,000 out of 10,000 had confessed at the end of 2004.

Some members of these committees clearly expected to be rewarded in proportion to their success rate. A member of the committee in Butare prison told us that he and his colleagues had written to the prosecutor asking for all the members of their committee to be released, because they had worked so hard and had "found almost 4,000 people to confess. Encouraging people to confess is heavy work." They had even offered to continue with their sensitisation work outside once they were released. They had not received a reply to their request.

The members of the committees not only make it their business to encourage and collect confessions, but facilitate the process by advising prisoners on what to include in their confessions and how to write them. Some prisoners confess to them directly, as if it were a religious confession. A member of one of these committees compared his work to that of a priest who helps a penitent: "He comes to talk, you listen to what he did and you advise him. I like this work, but listening to people who have killed many times is really difficult. For example, someone told me he took a two-month-old baby by the feet and smashed it against the wall. It was horrible taking that confession."

Another committee member explained that they gather prisoners who have been denounced by others during the internal *gacaca* sessions and "advise them seriously"; some decide to confess there and then and the committee writes down their confession straightaway. In other instances, prisoners approach the committee themselves. The members of the prisoners' *gacaca* committee are supposed to respect the confidentiality of each confession, but clearly don't, as we discovered when we asked a member of one of these committees to show us a sample of confessions. He did so readily, without even bothering to conceal the names at the top of the sheet.

We asked members of these committees about the likelihood of prisoners fabricating stories just to be released. They told us no, all confessions are sincere, there are no lies, or not many. They said that one of their duties was to warn prisoners not to make false confessions, because if they lied, they would be found out once they were released and could be re-arrested. They also denied that prisoners were under pressure to confess and claimed all confessions were purely voluntary.

Most of the committee members we met seemed comfortable with their role, but one felt ill at ease and had been threatened by prisoners who refused to confess. He said they accused him of deceiving them and telling them they would be released when this was not true. He told us some prisoners had written tracts threatening to kill him and other members of the *gacaca* committee because they were working for the government. They had reported the matter to the prison director, who had put those who signed the tracts in the punishment cell for a few days, but according to the prisoner we spoke to, the people who were really behind the plot were not the ones who had signed the tracts, and no action had been taken against them.

The fact that not all prisoners who have confessed have been released has made the work of these committees more difficult. Sometimes, their attempts to persuade prisoners to confess have been met with dismissive reactions. One committee representative admitted they were starting to lose hope. "We have lost the rhythm of the confessions because people are not being freed. But if they free some more people, the rate of confessions will go up again." A man who had spent three years waiting for a response to his confession said that prisoners used to feel motivated to confess, but since things were moving so slowly, many had lost interest. Some of those who hadn't been released wondered out loud: "I've killed lots of people, so why haven't I been released?"

In addition to the committees inside the prisons, the government has co-opted released prisoners to add their voices to the campaign. A prisoner who was released after confessing said that he and other former prisoners went to visit their former colleagues in prison: "We try to convince people to confess and tell them we are not having problems outside. Once we went on the request of the prosecutor. He came with us and took us to our colleagues in the prison. He said to them: 'See, they're OK outside, we weren't lying, you can talk to them.'"

The bureaucracy of confessions

Confessions follow a specific procedure. The confession is made in writing and special forms are distributed to the prisoners. Those who cannot write ask another prisoner or a member of the committee to write their confession for them, then they sign it.   In addition to the basic requirements – confessing to their own crimes and denouncing others – prisoners have to make an apology, according to a set formula. They have to ask forgiveness for what they did from the survivors of the genocide, from the Rwandan people and from God. The substance of most confessions is only about two or three pages long. There is a page for the prisoners to describe the crimes they committed, a page for them to describe the people who were with them and the crimes they committed, and a page to ask for forgiveness.

Prisoners have the option of sending their confession directly to the prosecutor's office, but in practice, this rarely happens. The normal procedure is to channel the confessions through a representative of the prisoners' *gacaca* committee.   The committee then passes the confessions on to the prison director, who signs off on them (without taking responsibility for the content) and sends them to the prosecutor's office.

After that, the prisoner just sits and waits to find out whether the confession has been accepted. This may take months, or even years. During this time the prisoner is unlikely to receive any feedback from the authorities on the admissibility of his confession. Even the members of the *gacaca* committee deplored the slowness of the procedure and the failure of the prosecutor's office to respond to the confessions submitted.

Rewards for the "guilty"

In case the lure of an early release is not enough, an informal system of other benefits and privileges has been introduced into the prisons to favour those who confess. When we were first told about this, we assumed it was an initiative of the prison directors, or even of the prisoners themselves, but we soon discovered that it was a national policy which came from the top levels of the government. Prison directors told us that the suggestion to "motivate" prisoners in this way had come from the authorities in the prosecutor's office. The Attorney General himself told us that it had been his idea and that he wanted those who confessed and denounced others to enjoy certain advantages.   It was a kind of early payment, a reward for helping the government.   It was also a bait to those who had not yet confessed. The Secretary General at the Ministry of Justice, however, denied that this was government policy. He said it had been debated within the government but no directives had been given, and it was the prison management who had decided to use these means to encourage confessions.

The privileges accorded to prisoners who have confessed are small but significant. In the words of one prisoner, those who confessed were treated like kings. Another said with contempt that privileges were given to those who confessed "like you give a piece of sugar to a dog". Those who confessed were given positions of responsibility in the prison; they were the ones picked to join the teams which worked outside; they were the first to be called out on visit days and were granted more time with their families; in prisons where visits usually take place standing up, they were allowed to sit down; they were given priority when new uniforms or blankets were distributed; they were served their food first, and in some prisons, when the system was first instituted, they were given different food, though this practice had apparently stopped by 2004. Taken together, these privileges could transform the life of a prisoner.

One of many prisoners who had confessed in order to enjoy some of these privileges told us: "What I wrote is true, but I only confessed to make life in prison easier and to have peace, and so that I can go out to work and not be stuck in here being shoved around." He did not believe that his own confession would resolve anything in terms of justice or the search for the truth.

Those who hadn't confessed became second-class citizens. Not only did they have to watch their colleagues enjoy an improved quality of life, but they were barred from taking part in certain activities, in particular from joining the teams that worked outside. This discrimination in the composition of the work teams hit prisoners where it hurt most. One of them, who hadn't confessed, told us that being able to go outside, or simply being active, was one of the most precious things for a prisoner, and taking this away could make someone confess. Several prisoners told us how they had been pulled off the teams because they had not confessed. For example, a prisoner in Gitarama who used to work in the team which chopped firewood outside was taken off the team in January 2004. He and ten others were told by the head of the prisoners' *gacaca* committee to "go back inside" because they had not confessed. He said it was the same in all the work teams in Gitarama prison. Once, this policy drove a prisoner to violence. A prisoner told us: "The *gacaca* committee go outside to watch over the work teams and take out anyone who hasn't confessed. Once a member of the committee took a prisoner off the work team because he hadn't confessed. The prisoner got cross and threw a stone at the *gacaca* committee member and injured him on the head."

A prisoner who had been detained for ten years decided to confess to a minor crime (stealing a cow) simply in order to keep his job on the hygiene team. He said he did not invent the crime, but he had not intended to confess until he realised that his position on the work team depended on it. Another prisoner was able to join the team which went out to fetch water, after he had confessed. When there was running water in the prison, everyone had equal access to water, but when there was a shortage of water, he and others who went to fetch the water were given priority.

Divide and rule

The two-tier system created by these privileges changed the dynamics between prisoners in a fundamental way. New divisions were created. It was not only a question of jealousy about small advantages. There were deeper and more serious grievances and anxieties. As every confession has to include a denunciation of others in order to be valid, prisoners began eyeing each other with suspicion and fear. If a prisoner who had already confessed was denounced in someone else's confession, it did not pose a problem. But if a prisoner who had not confessed found himself implicated in another prisoner's confession, the consequences were more serious.

As tensions rose between those who had confessed and those who hadn't, the psychological segregation became formalised in a physical segregation: some prison directors decided to separate the two groups, and those who had confessed were moved to a separate block. The separation was partly intended to thwart the efforts of prisoners who were allegedly intimidating others and preventing them from confessing; a Ministry of Justice official described these intimidators as "hardliners who are still convinced about killing people and feel they have no life any more".

In Butare prison, the two blocks reserved for those who have confessed are called "Arusha", named after the town in Tanzania where the International Criminal Tribunal for Rwanda is trying the leaders of the genocide. The remaining section of the prison – for those who have not confessed – is called "7,000" (approximately 7,000 people live there). Prisoners who are planning to confess but have not yet done so are allowed to move into "Arusha" before they have written their confession, to maximise the chances of "success" once they are surrounded by colleagues who are converted to the cause. But the segregation is not watertight. Prisoners who have no intention of confessing are allowed to drift in and out of "Arusha", and viceversa: by the end of 2004, more than 3,000 prisoners in Butare had confessed and there was no room for them all in "Arusha", so some lived in the other blocks.

In Cyangugu Central Prison, prisoners who had confessed were put in a separate block from the second half of 2004. The block that they moved to, in the old part of the prison, is called "Tingi-Tingi", as many of the prisoners who were originally detained there had come back from Tingi-Tingi and other locations in Congo where they had been refugees. Since mid-2004, Cyangugu prison has two *capitas*: one who has confessed and is responsible for the block of those who have confessed, and one who hasn't confessed and is responsible for the rest of the prisoners. But as in Butare prison, some prisoners who haven't confessed live in "Tingi-Tingi", and others who have confessed live in the other part of the prison. The *capita général* of those who hadn't confessed was not worried about this: "So long as security is OK, they can stay. If they're afraid, they can ask to be moved. About 50 people who have confessed have stayed here. They don't have any problems."

The decision to confess

Overall, we did not detect a clear pattern in the profiles of prisoners who decided to confess. Even prisoners sometimes found it difficult to predict who would confess and who would not. A former prisoner who had been detained for eight years said that prisoners used to talk to each other about what happened in the genocide, sometimes very frankly. Some had no qualms about telling their friends that they had killed, but these were not necessarily the ones who confessed formally. Others who never talked about what they did during the genocide ended up confessing.

There is a general belief, especially among government officials and prison staff, that less-educated prisoners or those from rural backgrounds are more likely to confess, whereas "intellectuals" will resist. The deputy director of Cyangugu prison said that in Rilima prison, where he was previously based, more than 3,000 out of around 7,000 or 8,000 prisoners had confessed very quickly when the programme was first launched. In Cyangugu, however, only around 1,000 out of 5,600 prisoners had confessed by the end of 2004: "In Rilima, the prisoners are mostly peasants. They took the lead for the confessions... Here in Cyangugu, it has worked less well. There are different ideas. There are more intellectuals and they are not convinced by confessions." This belief seems to be based on the assumption that it is easier to manipulate those who have a low level of education, and that prisoners who are illiterate, ill-informed about the law and who have little contact with the world outside are more likely to succumb to pressure. However, among the prisoners we spoke to, there were both peasants and "intellectuals" among those who had confessed, as well as among those who were determined never to confess.

A representative of the elderly prisoners in Kigali Central Prison believed that overall, old prisoners were less likely to confess than young ones: "The young prisoners have their whole life ahead of them. They are ready to confess to killing more easily, even if they are innocent. They have a different conception of life. The old ones reflect harder and are more careful. They don't want to accuse themselves if they are innocent. They don't want to say things rashly. They are not so concerned about their own well-being. They feel insulted. They think in the present."

We talked to many prisoners who had confessed but were still waiting to be released. We asked them whether the decision to confess had been a difficult one, and what had motivated them. Some had agonised over the decision for a long time. In most cases, it was the desperation at the thought of remaining in prison for an indefinite period which spurred them into action. A few talked about the sense of relief they experienced after confessing, but for the majority, confessing was simply a means to an end, the only exit route to freedom that was within their reach. Watching the release of the first wave of prisoners who had confessed was a turning point, and even some of those who had vowed never to confess changed their minds. The constant pressure from the authorities and from some of their own peers also wore them down. One prisoner who confessed after listening to the speeches of the authorities said that the decision had been 70% his own.

The confidentiality of confessions is not taken seriously by anyone, least of all the prisoners. A prisoner told us: "Nothing is secret here, even if it should be." Everyone knows who has confessed and who hasn't, who has said what, and who has implicated whom. In some cases, this is because prisoners speak openly about what they did and saw during the genocide. But prisoners also talk among themselves, one to one, or in small groups behind the scenes. Knowing what others have said or are planning to say is a critical factor in deciding whether to confess. Confessing is often a collective decision, as explained by a prisoner who had confessed as part of a group: "We confessed together... There were about ten in the group. We discussed it among ourselves first, to remember what happened and who killed whom. Then we said what we had done."

The religious factor

Many prisoners told us that their faith had been a strong motivation in persuading them to tell the truth. In some ways, these confessions had more in common with religious confessions than with confessions to a crime before the law. A prisoner who had carefully weighed up the consequences before confessing told us: "After you confess, you feel right with God. God has forgiven us even if the victims haven't." It was not always clear whether this religious motivation was sincere, or whether the prisoners just thought it would add some dignity to what was otherwise a purely pragmatic decision.

Church-based organisations, especially the more evangelical ones, regularly visit the prisons and encourage prisoners to confess to their sins in order to clear their conscience and make peace with God. In their work too, there is a fine line between the religious preaching and the political agenda. The government has been working closely with some of these organisations, having realised that they could be valuable allies and that prisoners are more likely to listen to a priest than to a prosecutor. They have mobilised and trained priests and pastors in justice-related issues and asked them explicitly to encourage prisoners to confess. A former prisoner said he used to find some of the preaching "a bit political, especially in the new Protestant or Pentecostal churches. The government used them to incite confessions. They became like government emissaries for the programme of confessions."

A pastor from an evangelical organisation which preached in the prisons talked to us about the difference between religious confessions and confessions to a crime, but even in his explanation, there was a blurring between the two. He was open about the relationship between the churches and the government:

> "Confessions are done spontaneously, in front of the congregation, after the preaching of the gospel. The prisoners pray and sing, then we leave time for people to confess publicly. Some confess to specific events and ask us to find the survivors from their area to reconcile them... Religious confession is a different procedure from a formal or judicial confession. Some people confess formally simply in order to be released. Our focus is to transform the heart.

> When people have confessed to us, they are no longer afraid of confessing to the authorities or in front of *gacaca*. Many say they don't mind whether they are in prison or not as they are free in their heart. This is helpful for the government. Every year we give a report to the government. The government is talking with church leaders and asking them how they can help with the process. Church leaders are helpful to the government, so the government asks us to do things."

Another pastor, however, said some prisoners were fully aware of the difference between a religious confession and a judicial one. He said prisoners who were likely to be classed in Category 1, in particular, would often be willing to repent in the religious sense, but not in the judicial sense.

The impact of confessions on prisoners' families

Prisoners' decision to confess also affected their families, but of those we spoke to, only a few had discussed it with their families beforehand. Most had just presented them with the *fait accompli*. Their families had no choice but to agree, although in some cases, it was apparent that they did not fully support the decision. Some prisoners had not even told their families they had confessed, so as not to raise their hopes in case they were not released. A 62-year-old man explained that the confessions programme had not only affected relations between prisoners but also relations between their families:

> "Our families have become mistrustful towards us and towards each other. At the start, the families of those who had confessed did not get on with the families of those who had been denounced in the confessions. Since the releases of 2003, families have become more understanding and trust is returning. Now, the families of those who haven't confessed are encouraging their prisoners to confess in order to be released. Their wives say to them: 'Do you want to stay here forever? Why not confess like your neighbour?'
>
> I didn't discuss my decision to confess with my wife. I took on my responsibility. At the start, she wasn't happy that I was accusing myself instead of letting the justice system accuse me. Once she and my daughter visited and were cross with me. They asked me why I had done that. But later, they understood and said: 'Whatever you do, don't lie and don't cause problems for us outside by denouncing other people.' Families felt motivated and pleased when they saw the prisoners who had confessed coming out first for visits, being given more time for visits and sitting down and having proper conversations."

When only a proportion of those who had confessed were released, many families, just like the prisoners, were left frustrated and confused. Some families felt they had been deceived and began regretting the prisoners' decision to confess.

A 68-year-old woman, who confessed in March 2004, was one of the few to admit that she regretted confessing: "The *gacaca* committee told me that if I confessed, I would be released. I've never killed anyone. I confessed to stealing some pots and I denounced the people who killed my neighbour. Prison was weighing down on me. This was the only way to get out. My children were very cross with me because I had confessed. They were upset that I'd lied. Now it's too late to take it back." When we asked her whether she had been pressured to confess, she was visibly close to tears and said she couldn't reply to the question. Then she calmed down and explained: "To say those things is to throw yourself to the lions. Some prisoners push other prisoners to confess. Genocide is a kind of business. It's terrible. It makes you lose your mind."

Killing without killing

We did not question prisoners about the contents of their confessions, as we had explained to them that it was not our role to judge whether they were innocent or guilty. However, some of them were keen to talk about it. With just a few exceptions, all those we spoke to claimed they had not killed during the genocide. Yet they had confessed. What had they then confessed to? They told us they had confessed to participating "indirectly", for example by being part of a group of people who had killed. They did not accept personal responsibility for the killing which the group had carried out, but for the failure to intervene to prevent it. Some said they had had a weapon in their possession but denied using it. Others confessed to looting, but not to killing. Various other stories were told, some more plausible than others. Almost all these stories indicated that the author of the confession had been at the scene of killings but stopped short of implicating him directly in acts of violence. A prisoner told us: "I confessed to indirect participation. I didn't kill but I was in a group looking for families. If we had found them, we would have killed them. There were other sins too, such as breaking into houses, and telling about people who were hiding Tutsi."

It was not clear whether this was really all these prisoners had written in their confessions, in an attempt to qualify for release without labelling themselves as killers, or whether they had confessed to more but didn't want to tell us. One prisoner was unusually honest about the strategy behind his and many other confessions and said that if and when he was tried, he would disown his confession. He had come under so much pressure from other prisoners to confess that, in the end, he had had to confess "just in order to have a bit of freedom. You can give information in your confession about someone's death but say you didn't participate. That's how people confessed. I've confessed, but if I go before a court or before *gacaca*, I will deny that I have confessed. I will tell them the whole story of what happened in the prison which pushed me to confess."

The way prisoners spoke about their confessions illustrated the state of mind of many prisoners accused of genocide, who have convinced themselves, and tried to convince others, that they have not killed, even while admitting that they have. Their descriptions of their confessions were riddled with contradictions. Many told us that their conscience had compelled them to confess and that they believed individuals should take responsibility for their own actions, while at the same time insisting that they were innocent and had done nothing wrong. They recited their apology like a kind of mantra – "I have asked for forgiveness from the victims of the genocide, from the Rwandan government, from the Rwandan people and from God" – but it sounded flat, like a lesson learnt by heart.

These confessions leave a lot of questions unanswered: if none of these people killed with their own hands, then who did? Will those they have denounced also claim in their own confessions that they participated only indirectly? How many of these confessions were made in good faith?

"False confessions"

A lot hinges on a prisoner's confession: ultimately, their freedom may depend on it. Prisoners who have been detained for ten years without trial will be desperate, and for some, the idea that at last, there may be light at the end of the tunnel is too hard to resist. A 60-year-old woman who had been in prison for eight years said simply: "I lied so that I could be freed. God will judge."

In theory, the authorities in the prosecutor's office are supposed to cross-check the contents of each confession with the information in the prisoner's case-file and other evidence of the crimes in question. If the confession is found to be inaccurate or incomplete, it should not be accepted. In practice, this verification does not happen systematically. The process would take too long, and it seems that for the government, obtaining tens of thousands of confessions and denunciations is in itself a more interesting target than the truth.

Confessions are big business in the prison, and a source of easy revenue for prisoners. The programme has opened up a whole new world of deals, counter-deals and blatant extortion. Prisoners discuss and reach agreements with each other on what their confessions should contain before even starting to write them. A prisoner can pay another prisoner to denounce someone he doesn't like; he can pay not to be cited in someone's confession, or pay someone to declare in his confession that he is innocent; he can pay another prisoner to say or not say anything he wants, to let himself or others off the hook, or to implicate others. Some prisoners offer to claim responsibility for a particular crime in exchange for a favour from the person who really committed it. The practice of paying another prisoner to declare your innocence is called "getting coltan" – a reference to the mineral found in eastern Congo which the Rwandan army plundered when it invaded the country in 1998, and which enabled senior Rwandan military and government officials to get rich very quickly.

A prisoner who had already been tried and sentenced to life imprisonment told us how another prisoner had accused him of having a weapon during the genocide in his confession. He asked him why he had said this. The other prisoner replied: "I did it to get out of my situation. If you want, you can also invent something about me, if that would be useful."

A prisoner who had not confessed described the extortion and the victimisation of those who refused to pay:

> "Those who've confessed demand money from the rest in exchange for not denouncing them in their confessions. Each time they need money, they come and intimidate the others.

They also threaten to denounce people who refuse to share the food that visitors bring them.

Someone can confess to a crime to cover another person and get paid for this. Everyone knows about this, the prosecutor and the prison director too. If you're innocent, they threaten to denounce you unless you pay. Fear makes people pay. But I've refused categorically to give any money. So I was denounced in prison. One group said I had killed, another group said I was innocent. Those who had confessed demanded money from me several times. I got someone to intercept a message between two people who had confessed about my case. The message said that if I didn't pay, they would denounce me. I cited this message directly to the prosecutor in a letter and submitted it to him when he visited the prison. The prosecutor told the prison director to call a meeting in the prison about my case, for all the people from my area. People there either accused me or defended me. Those who defended me won the case."

Another prisoner also wrote to the prosecutor's office about a prisoner who had offered him 400 francs in exchange for not citing him in his confession. He was still waiting for a reply one year later.

Government authorities themselves have sometimes tried to interfere directly in the content of prisoners' confessions. One prisoner told us that several of his fellow inmates had been approached by a *substitut* who had asked them to denounce the prisoner in exchange for their release. Another prisoner knew of a case where an official from the prosecutor's office told a prisoner who had confessed that he should add certain specific details to his confession before it could be accepted.

In Cyangugu prison, one prisoner had become notorious for inventing crimes. A prisoner there told us: "He is being paid to say people are guilty or innocent. He is paid by people inside or outside. He accused a lot of people and got others released. He was first arrested in Congo for another crime and was transferred from a prison in Congo to here. Then he confessed to his participation in the genocide as if he had participated everywhere, even though he hadn't participated at all. He did it just to get money. Later, he was exposed... It is a business. If you give someone sugar, he won't accuse you... It was becoming impossible to find the truth."

The confessions system has resulted in some absurd scenarios. A prisoner told us that people went around saying they were looking for a crime to confess to. Prisoners were heard fighting over who was responsible for a particular death during the genocide, saying: "No, you didn't kill that person, I did!" Others vied with each other over who had killed the largest number of people. Sometimes the temptation was so strong that one or two common-law prisoners, who were not even accused of genocide, claimed they had participated in the genocide just to be able to get onto the confessions list and qualify for release.

A prisoner, who said he had never been tempted to confess, was distressed to see that so many prisoners lied without stopping to consider that lying was also a crime, especially if it involved false denunciations. He thought some prisoners realised the consequences of false confessions, but felt they had nothing to lose: "It's like a suicide."

"Real confessions"

There are, of course, sincere confessions too. After years of reflection in prison, some prisoners feel ready to confess, in some cases out of genuine remorse. Those who were forced to kill under threat of being killed themselves are more likely to be willing to confess, as are some who were widely known to have participated in the genocide or ordered others to kill. Some had voluntarily confessed to the authorities soon after their arrest, long before the formal programme of confessions was instituted. A few had even handed themselves over to the authorities. These early confessions should have been noted in their case-file, but in many cases, they were not. These prisoners have therefore had to confess again under the new system.

In Butare, we met one prisoner who, unlike most, was prepared to tell us frankly that he had participated in the genocide. He had confessed to killing three people. In 1996, he returned from Burundi, where he had been a refugee, expecting to be arrested straightaway. After two days, he had not been arrested so he handed himself over to the local authorities: "I told them I had killed people and that I should be in prison. I had decided to do this before leaving Burundi." He confessed formally in September 1998. At that time, the government had not yet announced that those who confessed would be released. He had decided to do so because he felt he had done something bad in his heart. It had been a difficult decision, but afterwards, he felt relieved and "free". He had since been given a position of responsibility in the prison, but was still waiting for his release.

In Gitarama, we met another prisoner who told us he had killed. He said that during the genocide, he hid a man in his house to try to protect him; a crowd of people forced him to kill the man he was protecting. He explained this in his confession in 1998. Some of the people who had forced him to kill were also in prison. They knew he had denounced them in his confession, and initially, relations between them were tense, but they later decided to confess too, and the tensions died down. His account sounded more sincere than many others. He said that even though he had not killed voluntarily, when he looked back on his life, the thing which troubled him the most was the crime he had committed. Few other prisoners expressed a sense of guilt in such an explicit way. However, even in this case, it was the prospect of a reduced sentence, rather than the burden on his conscience, which was his main motivation for confessing.

Other prisoners may confess to crimes they really committed, but without feeling any regret. We met one such prisoner for whom confessing was a purely functional affair. He didn't even pretend to show remorse for what he had done; it was just opportunism. But his strategy had not worked, and several years on, he had still not been released. He had turned bitter and hostile, and regretted having confessed at all. "They promised us we would be released. It was just lies… I wrote my confession, on 17 February 1999… I'm still waiting. I confessed to stealing cows and participating in an attack in which several people were killed. I confessed so that I would be tried and find out how many years I would get… If I could go back in time, I wouldn't have confessed. If I could get the document back, I would withdraw it. But even if I could withdraw it, you can't erase it in people's minds… I only believe in providence or God. Men lie."

Prisoners who were well-known political figures or local authorities under the former government have little to lose by confessing, though not all of them have done so. We met several former local government officials among the prisoners. One of them, who had confessed, explained to us what the decision had meant to him. He was also one of several prisoners who agreed to testify for the prosecution in one of the genocide trials at the International Criminal Tribunal for Rwanda (ICTR) in Arusha.

"I confessed in March 2004... As a former local government official, I am automatically in Category 1. I decided to face God... I led people and I should have protected them, but I didn't. I didn't have the courage to stop events. I failed through weakness and fear. As I didn't resign from my position either, the accusations against me are even heavier...

I now encourage people to confess. I tell them that certain things happen, and you can't erase history. You have to admit your sins. Even if you don't confess, God will punish you. You must ask for forgiveness. Religion plays an important role. When priests came to the prison, I always went to confess. If you repent to God, you must also repent to the state...

Before, I was seen as someone who didn't want to tell the truth. They didn't expect me to testify. I thought a lot before confessing. I told my wife in advance. She said it was the right thing to do. I then added further testimonies separately. It was my decision to add more information. Sometimes you forget things, then you remember later.

I also added my testimony in Arusha and testified at the ICTR. People [prisoners] here reacted. They felt betrayed. They said to me: 'You have betrayed our people, our ethnic group, you're working for the RPF and the government.' But for me, it's just the truth."

Since he had testified in Arusha, some prisoners had continued taunting him and several who had been his friends no longer talked to him.[2]

"The innocent"

Among those who have not confessed, the system has created deep feelings of resentment and injustice. A 68-year-old prisoner who had spent more than ten years in prison said: "If you refuse to confess, you have no rights... I've seen nothing good in prison in more than ten years, but I won't prostitute myself to plead guilty. It would be good to be free, but not at that price."

Those who are innocent and who are not prepared to lie or incriminate themselves feel they are condemned to remaining in prison. One prisoner who had not confessed told us: "I might spend the rest of my life in prison as I haven't even witnessed any killings, and I can't invent things I haven't seen."

We asked some of these prisoners whether they had ever been tempted to confess, simply in order to stand a chance of being released. This question provoked indignation and even outrage, with some swearing that they would never confess to a crime they had not committed, not to their dying day. It was a matter of principle which, for them, was more valuable than their freedom. Some of the elderly prisoners were the most categorical on this point. A 73-year-old man who had been in prison for eight years told us: "I would never confess to something I haven't done, even if they cut my head off." Similarly, a 79-year-old woman who had been in prison for nine years said that she would rather die in prison than accept responsibility for a crime she hadn't committed, especially if it also meant lying about someone else.

---

[2]   The circumstances surrounding prisoners' testimonies in Arusha were the subject of much gossip and jealousy. Prisoners said they were coaxed into testifying for the prosecution at the ICTR, much in the same way that they were coaxed into confessing to their crimes. Some admitted that government authorities had offered them money and promised them an early release if they agreed to testify in Arusha. Some agreed to testify even though they knew nothing about the case or the defendant. A prisoner told us: "The ICTR has difficulties finding prosecution witnesses. Even those prisoners who do testify are not the real witnesses. They just arrange to go... They lie to get advantages."

A common response on the part of prisoners who hadn't confessed was simply that they had nothing to say. "How can I confess to nothing?" they asked. An elderly prisoner told us: "I'm still wondering: who have I killed? I thought about lying to confess, but I don't have enough to say." Another prisoner laughed when I asked him whether he had ever been tempted to confess: "No, it's not possible. You can only confess to what you've done. I can't invent things. If I start confessing to something I haven't done, I would be encouraging those people who always accuse others of crimes... I don't succumb to pressure. No one could persuade me to confess."

The prisoners we spoke to who had not confessed seemed to fall into two categories. There were those who were innocent and who, on principle, would not confess to crimes they had not committed and believed that lying was a sin. And there were those who may have been innocent or guilty but who strongly disagreed with the way the government was putting pressure on prisoners to confess and refused to cooperate with such a system. For one prisoner, resisting the pressure for as long as possible was a matter of pride. Despite having spent ten years in prison, he had never been tempted to confess: "I'm not at that stage yet." A prisoner in his seventies not only refused to lie to qualify for release but had turned down an offer from his daughter to pay the prosecutor's office to release him, because he believed passionately in his innocence.

An older prisoner was among those who strongly objected to the programme of confessions and to the pressure exerted on prisoners. A peasant and father of eight children, he had spent six years in prison and had never been tried. The absence of justice and the manipulation of prisoners by the state made him angry, even though he said he tried to remain calm "like a man. Men have to be able to stand it." He delivered a spontaneous and passionate speech about the politicisation of the justice system.

> "I was never tempted to confess. I'm sufficiently mature. My age wouldn't allow it... For this regime, everyone who stayed in Rwanda during the genocide is suspected. When you say you haven't killed, they say you're not helping the Rwandan state. They ask us to accept we were manipulated by the former government. When we refuse to say that, it becomes a crime. If I

managed to resist that manipulation, why do I have to lie and say
I killed, just to please this government?…

What bothers me the most is being in prison for nothing. Crimes
were committed, but they arrested people indiscriminately. If they
had only tried to arrest the criminals, we could have helped the
justice system identify them.   Now the guilty make fun of the
innocent. We're all lumped together. The guilty have a greater
chance of release, that's why I think they're laughing at us. I often
talk to them. I agree with the guilty who confess. It's a brave thing
to do. I can repeat endlessly that I haven't killed but in the end,
I'll probably be punished more harshly than those who killed."

An even older prisoner, a man in his mid-seventies, talked about the relations
between the guilty and the innocent in prison. He too had become angry
about the way justice had been turned upside down:

"Now they're ready to release people who've confessed to killing.
They are well treated. We who don't confess are called liars. This
is incomprehensible to me. I tell other prisoners: 'You've killed
people and dragged us into this, and we're the ones suffering the
consequences.' Those who killed in the genocide are pleased to
see the innocent in prison and tell us: 'You didn't do anything but
you're rotting in here with us.' They ask me why I don't confess. I
tell them I have nothing to confess. They tell me I'll rot in here
anyway. There are killers who are proud of killing. It gives them
value. I'm not the only innocent one in prison. There are many.
A criminal says 'I've killed' and they say: 'Go, you're free.' I don't
understand this."

These views are shared by many Rwandans, both inside and outside the
prisons. An elderly prisoner was distressed by some of the things he heard
from his fellow prisoners – some of whom were later released: "Sometimes
when I hear what people say in their confessions, I cry. I can't believe those
things happened, for example someone who describes killing babies. We
know what some of them did." A former prisoner was also shocked by the
release of certain people who he personally knew had participated in the

genocide: "I know at least two people from my area who were terrible during the genocide and who have been released. But others stay in prison for years even though they haven't done anything. It's astounding. We can't understand it. There is a lack of concrete evidence so they [the government] prefer people to accuse themselves."

We came across many prisoners who told us that others had confessed to the crimes of which they themselves had been wrongly accused. They had written to the prosecutor's office to explain the situation but had never received a reply. A prisoner who had spent nine years in prison wrote to the authorities in January 2004 stating that he was innocent and enclosing a copy of the confession of the man who had claimed responsibility for the crime of which he was accused. He was still in prison at the end of 2004 and had not received a reply to his letter. The prisoner who had confessed, however, was released in 2003.

Some prisoners, including many "intellectuals", objected to the confessions programme on more political grounds. They denounced it as government propaganda, a trap to ensnare the weaker prisoners. Because these "intellectuals" were able to articulate their views clearly, and were not afraid to do so, the authorities labelled them as troublemakers. They accused them of mounting a counter-campaign and preventing people from confessing. Several, particularly those who had held positions of responsibility under the former regime, were transferred to other prisons, apparently because they were seen as obstructive and their views detrimental to the government's campaign.

A prisoner described the predicament of "intellectuals" who refused to confess:

> "Some of those who've confessed are the instruments of politics…
> They want everyone to be implicated. They push you to implicate
> others. They've done this to me too. They wrote in a newspaper
> that I was stopping others from confessing. There are little groups
> of prisoners who push others to confess… The political authorities
> want to use the peasants to push those who haven't yet confessed.
> They accuse the intellectuals of preventing confessions. This is the

card they play. It's like walking on eggshells. We have to go slowly, because we will be the first to be nailed."

Another of the more politicised prisoners told us:

> "There is brainwashing… The [prison] director is over-zealous. He wants to score points. They called me once and asked me to convince others to confess. I said: 'I don't accept responsibility so how can I convince others?' I didn't accept it… People are traumatised and will cling onto any hope. It's like an act, a role-play. The prisoners are asked to play the roles of judges, prosecutors etc. They defend themselves in here as if they are before a tribunal, but they're all prisoners."

Double standards

For prisoners whose family members were killed by the RPF, contemplating a confession was even harder. Prisoners found it difficult to accept the contrast between, on the one hand, the official silence surrounding killings committed by the RPF, and, on the other, the government's very public campaign to persuade people to confess to their participation in the genocide.

A 68-year-old man whose son, daughter-in-law, five nephews and two nieces were killed by the RPF in 1994 was harsh in his criticism of the confessions programme, but said that if the government, or the RPF, recognised what they had done, then he might be prepared to do so too.

A prisoner who had lost several members of his family to the RPF massacres in Rwanda and in Congo said this had not stopped him from confessing, but for others in a similar situation, it represented a big stumbling-block:

> "Some of us wonder why we should confess when the RPF don't admit their crimes. My father was killed in Rwanda by the RPF after July 1994, and my mother, sister and others were killed in Congo. I've confessed because I wanted to in my heart, but others may say: 'Why should you confess when they've killed your

family?' This problem will come up in *gacaca*… I will go to *gacaca* and confess to what I did, but I won't be able to say anything about the killings of my father, my mother and others. I resign myself to that, even though I don't agree with it, but others find it difficult. Inside, we talk about it but only with our friends, not openly. They can ask me in *gacaca* about the destruction of Tutsi houses but I can't talk about the destruction of my own houses."

CHAPTER XX

Freedom:

a mirage

The programme of releases

As the years passed, the political and particularly the financial cost of keeping such a large proportion of the country's population in prison became too high for the Rwandan government.   From 1998, even the most hardline members of the government realised that this was no longer a viable strategy. On a practical level alone, the International Committee of the Red Cross, which had borne the brunt of the cost of feeding and caring for the prisoners, was threatening to withdraw its assistance and the government was facing the prospect of having to take full responsibility for the welfare of the entire prison population.

Confronted with this unmanageable situation, the only option for the government was to start releasing prisoners.   A succession of different mechanisms were set up to sift through the cases and recommend the release of those against whom there was no evidence. As early as 1995 – before the genocide trials had even begun – there were the *commissions de triage*, then the *groupes mobiles*,[1] and other short-lived, improvised procedures, but each one became bogged down in corruption, political interference and incompetence. Many of the prisoners released through these mechanisms in the two or three years after the genocide were promptly re-arrested. The genocide trials which began at the end of 1996 resulted in some acquittals, but these were too few to make a significant dent in the prison population. Releases were still far outnumbered by continuing arrests.

---

[1]   The *commissions de triage* were screening committees set up to identify prisoners against whom there was insufficient evidence to justify their continued detention. They were replaced by the *groupes mobiles*, whose functions included cursory investigations and creating case-files for prisoners who did not have one.   These mechanisms are described in the Amnesty International report, *Gacaca: a question of justice*, 17 December 2002, Chapter V (2).

Fearful of public reactions, particularly those of the survivors of the genocide, the government had to tread carefully. A general or even partial amnesty had been ruled out, so a more gradual approach had to be found. In 1998, the government announced that it would start releasing the old and the very sick, as well as those known as the *sans-dossier* – those without a case-file or whose case-file was empty. Between 3,000 and 4,000 prisoners from these categories were released. This first step was controversial, as some sectors of society remain opposed to any releases at all, and the political environment into which the prisoners were released was extremely polarised. In any event, the number of releases at this stage was still too low to have any appreciable impact on the congestion in the prisons.

In 2001 and 2002, around 3,000 more prisoners were released, mostly those against whom there was no evidence. But it was not until January 2003 that the government decided to act more boldly. In a New Year's Day communiqué on 1 January 2003, President Kagame announced a wider-ranging programme of releases. The categories to be released included, once again, those who had nothing in their case-file, the old and the very sick, as well as those accused of common crimes who had already spent more time in prison than the sentence provided for them under the law, those who were under 18 at the time of their alleged crime, and those who had confessed to their participation in the genocide. These were provisional releases; the prisoners were liable to be re-arrested at any time should fresh information come to light about their participation in the genocide or other crimes.

The first big wave of releases – about 24,000 – took place between January and April 2003. In early 2004, a further 4,500 were released, mostly prisoners accused of common crimes, whose time already spent in prison exceeded the length of their sentence had they been tried and found guilty. When we visited the prisons at the end of 2004, there was talk of further large-scale releases, but dates and details had not yet been announced. All eyes were on *gacaca*.

Eventually, in the summer of 2005, a few months after *gacaca* had started, a further 22,000 prisoners were released – not as a result of *gacaca*, but as a continuation of the programme of provisional releases which had begun in January 2003. By early 2006, the prison population had gone down to around 70,000, and there were tentative hopes of a more lasting solution to the prison crisis.[2] But as *gacaca* gained speed, the number of arrests began creeping up again. The prison population rose alarmingly, despite the release of a further 6,700 prisoners in the first quarter of 2007 and despite the government's assurances that *gacaca* would not result in further large-scale imprisonment. Among these new arrests were prisoners who had been provisionally released on the basis of their confessions, but who were sent back to serve their full sentence after their confessions were judged to be incomplete or inaccurate.

Returning inside

Since 1995, a significant number of prisoners who have been released have been re-arrested, some several times. Some enjoyed just a few days of freedom, others may have been lulled into a false sense of security by spending several weeks, months or even years outside. Some did not get a chance to taste freedom at all, as they were re-arrested before they could even walk through the prison gate.

Many of these prisoners, particularly those accused of genocide, were re-arrested on the same charges, even though they may have been released the first time because there was no evidence against them. Some were even re-arrested after being formally acquitted by a court. Others were told that their release had been a mistake, or that witnesses had suddenly come forward with fresh evidence against them. Some were initially re-arrested on different charges, which mysteriously reverted to the old charges over the following months. Others were re-arrested on completely separate accusations: a number of those we spoke to had first been in prison on a genocide accusation, then were re-arrested for a common crime.

---

[2]   In September 2006, Rwanda adopted a new law on the organisation of the National Prisons Service. Carefully worded and with liberal references to Rwanda's human rights obligations, the law outlines the responsibilities of the new National Prisons Service, as well as procedures of detention and conditions of imprisonment. The law highlights the responsibility of the state prison service to protect prisoners' fundamental rights.

For all these prisoners, the second period in prison was harder to bear than the first, and the third period even harder to bear than the second. For those who found themselves back in prison in direct contravention of a judge's decision, the situation was the hardest of all, as it proved that the justice system could not be relied upon, and that even when it delivered a favourable verdict for the prisoner, there were other, more powerful interests which could overrule it.

Walking back into the same prison was a terrible moment for re-arrested prisoners. Any temporary comfort brought about by the familiarity of the faces and the surroundings did not last long. A number of prisoners we spoke to said they were given back their old space, in their old block. This may have been intended as a gesture of welcome on the part of the other prisoners, but inadvertently, it rubbed salt in the wound. Returning not only to the same prison but to exactly the same space was like returning to a place from which there was no way out. It had the inevitability of a recurring nightmare.

Re-arrests are common enough not to cause much surprise among prisoners when they see an old colleague walking back in through the prison gate. The returnees were greeted with a mixture of sympathy, resigned shrugs and sharp jokes. Some of the more hardened prisoners who had been in prison for a long time couldn't resist expressing satisfaction when they saw old colleagues, whose release they may have secretly resented, returning to the fold. For the returning prisoners, the shock and humiliation at finding themselves back in this environment were not helped by the mocking comments of some of those they had left behind. In some cases, it took them months to readjust to life inside.

Most prisoners who were provisionally released were so afraid of being re-arrested or killed that they were barely able to enjoy their freedom. A prisoner who was first arrested in May 1995 on an accusation of genocide was provisionally released one month later. He was free for three and a half years, but during this period, he had found it impossible to relax as the fear of re-arrest was always hanging over him. He said that even when he was at home, he was on his guard every day, and whenever someone knocked on the door, he thought they were coming to arrest him again. He had not been accepted by people around him. He told us that socially, he had felt more comfortable in prison than out.

In December 1998, he was re-arrested on the same accusation and taken straight back to the same prison:

> "You feel belittled, humiliated… The beginning was not easy. I found some of the same people in prison again. Some were jealous because I had got out and they had stayed in. They made comments like 'at least you could get out'. They asked me for lots of news from outside. I found it difficult to be reintegrated… but gradually they accepted me."

Eventually, he was tried, and in 2002 was sentenced to life imprisonment.

Quite often, the period between a prisoner's release and his re-arrest is much shorter. A prisoner who was first arrested in 1995 on an accusation of genocide and detained for six years was provisionally released in 2001 after the prosecuting officials said there was not enough evidence to keep him in prison. He spent 17 days at home, then was re-arrested and ended up back in the same prison, where he remained at the end of 2004. He had never been questioned since his re-arrest.

A man who was first arrested in 1994, on an accusation of genocide, was one of the few who did not expect to be re-arrested when he was provisionally released in 1999:

> "I just went straight home and settled there. My family found me a wife… My father bought me a house and gave me fields. I didn't have any problems with my neighbours… I continued thinking about my time in prison for about one month, then life went on. I never expected to return to prison."

Five years later, he was re-arrested, this time on an accusation of theft. He claimed the owner of the shop where he worked accused him and a colleague of stealing money so as not to pay them, and got them both arrested. The routine that followed was alarmingly familiar:

"We were taken to the police station for four days, then to the brigade for one month, then back to PCK [Kigali Central Prison]. It was the same brigade as last time. I knew what was going to happen. I knew I would be brought back to prison again and I wasn't sure I would be released this time. At the police station, they beat us and tortured us to make us confess. I was beaten, but I didn't confess. My co-accused didn't confess either...

When I came back to PCK the second time, I was warmly welcomed. The prisoners asked me for news of my family and the situation outside. They gave me blankets, plates and other things. There hadn't been much change in the conditions. There is still a lack of blankets and plates and a lack of space. The second time was hard, but at least it was familiar to me."

Re-arrests were also very hard for prisoners' families. A prisoner who was released after being tried and acquitted, then re-arrested after two months, often thought about his elderly mother. After his release, he had gone back to his home area. His mother, who was 82 and blind, had travelled all night to his sister's house where he was staying. It had been an emotional reunion and everyone had celebrated. His mother had said to him: "Now that I've seen you again, I can die in peace." After his re-arrest, she said she would die of sorrow. He didn't expect to ever see her again.

A minority of people who had been in prison before the genocide were released in the chaos of the war in 1994 only to find themselves back in prison a few months or years later. One of those we met was a man in Butare Central Prison, who was first imprisoned from 1992 to 1994 after being sentenced to five years for stealing a shirt. At the time, there were about 3,000 prisoners in the prison. Then there was the genocide. When he returned to the same prison in 1997, the population had risen to more than 6,000 and would eventually reach more than 10,000. He was one of about five prisoners in Butare prison who had already been in prison before the genocide. They were nicknamed "les dangereux" (the dangerous ones).

When the genocide had started, he was still in prison. He was released when the killings were at their peak, in June 1994:

"They evacuated the prisoners on 16 June 1994. The prison authorities opened the prison and said the RPF troops were approaching and were just a few kilometres away. They let us go according to our sentence. Those who had not been tried or who had served half their sentence could go, as there was not enough food for everyone. Those sentenced to death or life stayed.

I had heard the genocide was going on outside. There was a place in the prison where we could stand and see what was happening on the hills. We could see people chasing each other and killing, but we didn't know exactly who or why. We saw houses burning and people fleeing and sleeping outside. We were afraid. We felt surrounded and exposed as we couldn't run away.

I had served half my sentence so I was released... Then on 1 July 1994, everyone fled. I went to Congo, until June 1997.

I came back to Rwanda because it was not safe in Congo... Three of my brothers were killed. One was killed by the RPF on the day they took over our area, in July 1994. Another went to Congo but decided to come back and was killed as soon as he came back. The third one died in a refugee camp in Congo. He was shot dead during the mass repatriation.

Nineteen days after I came back, I was arrested. The prosecutor asked me where I was during the genocide. I told him I was in prison. He asked why. I explained about the stolen shirt. He said: 'You have to go back to prison to finish those five years.' The prosecutor said I had to start the five years again. I have now done eight.

How will I be released? It is beyond me. I don't see why I should even be tried as I haven't done anything wrong... How can I catch up on lost time?"

Stopped at the gate

Some prisoners whose release was ordered by a court did not even manage to set foot in the outside world before being re-arrested. These were usually the more political cases – prominent individuals such as former politicians, government officials, members of the military, or people suspected of opposing the government.

A former military prisoner charged with fraud was tried and sentenced to three years' imprisonment. He served his full sentence in Mulindi military prison, from 2001 to 2004, then was immediately re-arrested on a different accusation. He believed his arrest on both occasions was linked to his outspoken criticism of the government and the army.

> "The day I was released, policemen were waiting for me at the gate with a pick-up truck and an arrest warrant. They took me to the brigade. After two hours, a *substitut* came and said he would write up a case-file. They accused me of divisionism on an ethnic basis. As examples, they said I had insulted a Tutsi; that while I was in Mulindi prison, I had a football team in which I didn't accept Tutsi, which was not true; and that whenever I saw the president on TV, I laughed and denigrated him. The same people who had got me arrested the first time engineered it again. The same day, I was brought to PCK. I have been here for six months."

In another case, a judge ordered the release of two men accused of fraud about one week after their arrest in 2002, on the basis that they had been wrongfully arrested and that there was insufficient evidence against them. But just as they were about to leave the prison, they were re-arrested. One of them told us:

> "We were given our belongings back. We packed our bags and walked up to the barrier at the outside gate. Suddenly, a plain-clothes policeman said: 'No, you're under arrest.' We explained we had been acquitted. They hadn't even changed the accusations against us. On the arrest warrant, it said: 'Any necessary force will be used to ensure their arrest.' "

They were taken back to the police headquarters, then to the brigade, then back to Kigali Central Prison. There, they received a warm, though slightly smug, welcome from their former friends, some of whom had reminded them of the case of four other prisoners who were due to be released three times on the orders of a court but who had remained in prison.

> "The prisoners said to us: 'We told you! We had kept your place for you.' I realised it would be a long battle, a different battle. When the judge had ordered our release, I had felt vindicated. It was like a bad joke. This time, it felt more serious… I knew it would be a long time the second time."

But there was a third time too. Seven or eight months later, they appeared before a judge again. The judge ordered their provisional release, but the prosecutor intervened with a new arrest warrant and they were sent back to prison again. After appealing to the Supreme Court, they were eventually released about a year later. The prisoner remembered that on the day of their release, the courtyard was full of prisoners wishing them well. He said he was so touched he almost felt like going back inside.

The *ingando*: "touching freedom"

From 2003 onwards, prisoners who were due to be released had to pass through one of the solidarity camps known as *ingando* before being let loose on the outside world.

The *ingando* were set up by the government as a transition phase for prisoners, to prepare them for life as free men and women.[3] Ostensibly, the purpose of these camps was to ease the process of reintegration, re-educate the prisoners and equip them with information about changes which had taken place in the country in the years they had spent in prison. But critics, including some prisoners who went through the *ingando*, called them indoctrination camps.

---

[3] Similar camps had already been set up for students, returning refugees and demobilised soldiers.

Prisoners due for release had to spend three months in an *ingando*, in an indeterminate state between incarceration and freedom. During their stay there, they followed an intensive programme of classes organised by the government's National Unity and Reconciliation Commission (NURC). They also took part in community work projects. After three months, they were allowed home to start rebuilding their lives.

At least that was the theory. Through our conversations with prisoners, we discovered that in 2003, at least 800 prisoners who had attended the *ingando* in preparation for their release were sent straight back to prison at the end of the three months; most of them remained in prison more than 18 months later. None of those we spoke to knew precisely why they had been sent back to prison. Some said there were supposed to be fresh accusations against them but had no idea what these accusations consisted of.

It is difficult to imagine a more cruel deception for a prisoner who has spent eight or nine years in prison without trial, in desperate conditions, than to be sent back to prison just as he is expecting to be released. The authorities had made them go through all the motions to prepare for their release only to imprison them once again. It was a form of psychological torture. Some of the prisoners we spoke to, as well as their families, were still reeling from the shock. For the first time, they had allowed themselves to start hoping and to make plans for the future, and they had come crashing down.

"A percentage of freedom"

The *ingando* was a halfway house between prison and the world outside. Almost all the prisoners we spoke to described it in these terms. They told us: "we were free but we were not free", "we were free but not completely" or "we had a percentage of freedom... we were half-free". The impression of freedom came in part from the contrast with the environment of the prisons from which they had just emerged and in part from the prospect of real freedom which was finally within their grasp. In reality, they were still prisoners and they were closely watched.

We did not carry out an exhaustive study of life in the *ingando*,[4] but we asked some of the prisoners and former prisoners we met to describe their activities there.

In 2003-2004, there were 18 camps across the country. The number of prisoners in each camp ranged from about 700 to close to 2,000. The daily routine was intensive and the discipline was strict. The general atmosphere was reminiscent of a military training camp. The prisoners slept in tents and took part in physical exercises every morning. A prisoner who attended a camp in Gitarama said that when he first arrived, there was a phase which he compared to an initiation rite, "with people being pushed in the mud, beaten about, etc" but the authorities running the camp told his group that they could skip this first phase "because we had suffered enough". Prisoners took part in community work projects, for example chopping wood and building homes and schools, many of which were designed to benefit survivors of the genocide.

The NURC was responsible for the overall management of the camps, as well as the organisation of all the activities. Security in the camp was the responsibility of the police or the paramilitary Local Defence Forces; there were no prison guards. A number of prisoners were appointed as leaders within the camp; they were the equivalent of the *capitas* in the prison. To go outside the camp, for example to work or to fetch water, prisoners needed a special authorisation. There were other rules too. Alcohol was forbidden and there were restrictions on what prisoners were allowed to buy outside. If anyone was caught infringing these rules, they could be disciplined and they might be beaten. Returning to prison was the ultimate sanction. For example, a prisoner in a camp in Butare who was caught with some beer which his wife had given him when he had gone to work outside was sent back to prison for this offence.

Families could visit the prisoners on Saturdays or Sundays. The visits were much longer than in the prisons, typically between 30 minutes and one hour,

---

4   For more detailed information on the *ingando*, see Penal Reform International (PRI), *From camp to hill, the reintegration of released prisoners* (Report VI, May 2004). PRI carried out research in a number of camps. The report includes testimony from prisoners and an interesting analysis of the history courses taught in the *ingando*.

and took place in a more relaxed environment. One prisoner said that he could chat to his family for as long he wanted to. Another mentioned that they could even ask for permission to visit their family at home if there was a serious family problem.

The main activity for prisoners, in all the camps, was attending classes. There were classes or lectures all day, every day except Sunday, with just a one-hour break each day. Attendance was compulsory. A variety of topics were covered, including the history of Rwanda, the genocide, the new administrative structures in the country, the economy, governance, justice (with a particular focus on *gacaca*), reconciliation, social relations (including relations with survivors of the genocide), domestic relations (for example how to readjust to living with their husband or wife after many years apart) and HIV-Aids. The teachers came from a range of backgrounds: some were from the government, or government-appointed bodies such as the NURC, others from the university, from the Church or from civil society. Specialists were brought in as necessary, for example on the topic of HIV-Aids awareness. All the lessons heavily emphasised the notion of Rwandan national identity. In conformity with the government's official line, which strongly discourages reference to the existence of distinct ethnic groups, prisoners were urged to think of themselves as Rwandans, not as Hutu or Tutsi.

Prisoners' reactions to the lessons varied. Some followed them with interest, if only because they brought them up to date on the many changes which had taken place in the country since their arrest. One prisoner said that in this respect, the lessons had been useful to prepare them for the new life outside: "Here, in prison, it's another world. After ten years, we have been overtaken." Others – possibly the majority – were so impatient to get out that they did not bother listening to the classes, especially as many already knew most of what was being taught. One prisoner summed up the general attitude: "For me, these courses were not necessary. What they taught us was not that important. What was in our heads was the thought of freedom and the thought of going home."

Prisoners attending a class at an *ingando* in Myaga, near Butare, 2003
© Per-Anders Pettersson/Getty Images

The more perceptive – and the more politicised – dismissed the lessons as propaganda and brainwashing. With more than a touch of contempt, they described being taught "how to behave in society" and "how to be careful and nice towards families of survivors". But they listened, or pretended to listen, obediently, as doing otherwise would almost certainly have cost them their freedom. In theory, prisoners were encouraged to debate the issues raised in the classes. In practice, few did, because they feared that anyone perceived as questioning the government's doctrine would be viewed as suspicious and could be sent back to prison; it was not worth taking the risk. This resulted in a situation where most of the prisoners agreed, or pretended to agree, with what was being taught. One prisoner said: "History has changed. They taught us the new version. We accepted it without accepting it. We listened and stayed silent. If you question it, they accuse you of the ideology of the former government. Some tried asking questions but you could see they were not welcome." The idea that there could be any real debate in the classes was not taken seriously by any of the prisoners. The only real discussion that took place was among the prisoners at night, or when they went out to work.

One prisoner felt that the way in which the classes were taught was insincere. He was critical of the political control exercised in the *ingando*:

"When we did something wrong, for example if we went outside the limits of the camp, the police beat us. This cancelled out everything we had learnt. How can someone teach you to love your country while they beat you? The whole situation didn't make sense. You come out of prison and you're put in a training, which is like military training... I didn't see the point of it. We discussed things, but within certain limits, as defined by the state. For example, they told us there were no different ethnic groups, no Hutu, no Tutsi, only clans. Some people in the audience knew the history of Rwanda better than the teachers. If you don't agree with these 'statements of fact', you're not allowed to say so, even in the discussions. Some tried to disagree and were accused of being divisionists and having a genocidal ideology.[5]

We felt we were about to be sent to a completely different country."

Other prisoners shared this view and found the lessons alienating: "They taught us things to learn by heart," one prisoner told us, "things about the politics of their country. It's not my country. Maybe it will be my country when I'm free. But I have no rights in this country, therefore it is not mine."

There was a distinction in the *ingando* between prisoners who were there because they had confessed and those in other categories. The unofficial hierarchy had been transposed from the prisons, and those who had confessed continued to enjoy certain privileges. One prisoner said that even though everyone lived together in the *ingando*, there were two groups: "We were separate psychologically, and there was unspoken tension between the two groups. The people who had positions of responsibility in the camps were all prisoners who had confessed. They were chosen by the camp authorities [representatives of the NURC]. Those who hadn't confessed were given less good places to sleep in the tents." During the classes, those who had confessed were encouraged to do most of the talking. Those who had confessed were also the first group to be released from the *ingando*, in some cases about a week before the others.

---

5   For an explanation of these terms, see Chapter XIV (footnote 3) and Chapter XXI.

Psychological torture

We spoke to a number of prisoners, in different locations, who had been sent back to prison after passing through the *ingando*. Over the years, many of them had developed a certain scepticism in relation to the government's numerous unfulfilled promises, but this time, the intention to release them had been explicit. Most of them said that once they reached the *ingando*, their doubts evaporated, and it did not occur to them that they would not be released. Then, suddenly, they found themselves back in prison, as if the three months in the *ingando* had been a cruel dream.

In some cases, the sense of deception was aggravated by the way the authorities misled or even lied to prisoners up to the last minute. One prisoner said that on the day he was expecting to be released, he and about 200 other prisoners in the *ingando* were told that their papers were not quite ready. First they were told to wait for the *parquet* to complete their release documents. The next day, they were told to be patient and that their situation might be clarified within two weeks. They waited, then they were simply sent back to prison.

A prisoner who had spent seven years in a *cachot* was initially sceptical when he was told that his name was on the list for provisional release, but any reservations he may have had were soon overtaken by the anticipation of freedom. "Sometimes these hopes are illusions," he told us, "but that time, it was more real." He was taken from the *cachot* to the *ingando* in March 2003 and spent three months there:

> "We all expected to be released after three months but there were interventions from outside. The first to leave the *ingando* were those who were sent back to prison... 106 people were sent back to prison. I still haven't been informed why I was sent back to prison. I don't know of any new accusations against me. We asked the prosecutor when he visited the prison and he said we had been accused again. Recently the Minister of Justice came and said we should be given proper information about the new accusations, but we have not been told anything.

On our last day in the *ingando*, our families came to see us. It was supposed to be the last visit before our release. Then the police chief came with the prosecutor, other authorities and representatives of Ibuka [the genocide survivors' organisation]. They called a list of names. They started insulting and threatening us, calling us killers. They kicked us. They put us in trucks. We had to leave our things behind. It was very hard. We were taken straight to the central prison, on 3 May 2003. I have been here since then. All the 106 are still here, including some who had confessed, but apparently their confessions were incomplete.

Since then, there are rumours that those of us who came back from the *ingando* are going to be released, but nothing happens...

My son visited me in the *ingando*. When I first went there, he was ticking the days off the calendar. Then I didn't come home. When he heard I hadn't been released, he was traumatised. He cried every time he saw me... He comes to visit me in prison and is a bit better now. I write letters to him to encourage him and I ask my wife to buy him balls to play with."

His wife told us how she found out that her husband was not coming back:

"When my husband was in the *ingando*... there were Ibuka meetings taking place day and night. One of their members told me that they were planning to prevent his release...

Two days before the end of the *ingando*, I went to the camp to visit my husband and took him food for two days. I didn't know he wasn't going to be released. Then a whole group of them were sent back to prison. I saw them getting on the truck. My husband saw me there. I followed the truck to the prison, on a bicycle, so that at least I could give him the food. Then I went back to the *ingando* to collect his belongings.

That day, when I went home, it was very difficult. The children saw I had brought his things back and still thought he was coming home. We had prepared special food. We ate, then I told them everything. My son went mad; he threw up all his food. He got bad results in his school tests, less than 50%, whereas before, he was third in the class... The girl stood it better. She had never known what it was like to have her father at home."

Her husband's physical and mental health worsened after he was sent back to prison. He also started having trouble remembering names, even those of his own family.

Some prisoners were more worried about the shock to their family than about their own well-being. A prisoner who had been detained for more than nine years was among 35 people who were made to return to prison after three months in an *ingando*. The prosecutor brought the list of names to the *ingando* one evening, and the next morning, the police told the 35 to pack their bags and arranged their transfer back to the prison. He was not given any official explanation but had heard through his family that some people in their area had not been happy with the prospect of his release and had gone to the *parquet* with fresh accusations; however, he had not been questioned about any new accusations in the 18 months since he returned to prison. He said that he had felt unstable for a whole month, but for his family, the suffering had been even greater: "My family had been preparing for my release. Together with my neighbours, they had looked for work for me. When I was not released... my 71-year-old mother fell ill. I think she will die of anxiety. She used to visit me. She has come once since I returned to prison... I tried to calm her down. She was shaking and couldn't talk properly. Since then, she sends me messages."

We met one of the few women who had been sent back to prison after staying in an *ingando*. She and her husband went to the *ingando* in February 2003 in preparation for their release, after almost eight years in prison. They didn't live together in the camp, as men and women were housed in separate quarters, but they were able to meet during the lessons and at meal times. In March, her husband was sent back to prison. Even then, she didn't think that the same fate awaited her. One day, the prosecutor came to see her and said he would release her if she gave him 300,000 francs (about US$535). She refused, and in May, she was sent back to prison too. She believed the prosecutor had personally ordered her return to prison because she had refused to pay him. When she re-entered the prison, the other women there were very surprised. She said they thought she would cry, but she didn't. For her, the suffering of her children was what pained her the most. In the *ingando*, her three children had visited her together after their father was sent back to prison. "They were upset about their father, but they said to me: 'At least you'll be coming home.' Then it was terrible. They had been preparing for my return. The children suffered more than we did." She was a strong woman, but she cried when she talked to us about her children waiting for her to return home.

Some prisoners lost all hope of ever being released after being sent back to prison from the *ingando*. One prisoner told us:

> "I was torn between disappointment and courage. I thought: never mind if I'm not released, I've already done nine years in prison, I'm used to it and I'm no longer surprised...
>
> I have no hope I'll be released. It's been the same old song for nine years. They make us believe we'll be released but nothing happens. That's how they operate. Judicial reforms, *gacaca*, etc – we've had enough. We can't base our hopes on this. We get on with our lives in prison. The others get on with their careers of manipulation. It happens every year. We've never seen any serious progress in terms of justice. I don't even think about my release. I mustn't despair, but I mustn't dream either. If I think about it too much, I will get depressed. But in the *ingando*, I did believe that I would be released and that the end was in sight."

Ibuka, the organisation representing genocide survivors, played an influential role in deciding who should and should not be released from the *ingando*. The authorities did not even try to conceal this. A prisoner explained how he was thrown back into prison following protests by Ibuka, acting in league with the local authorities:

> "I asked the *substitut* why I was brought back to prison. He said there were no accusations, but the mayor of my district is also the

president of Ibuka for the province. He had made a list of the
people he knew in the *ingando* and added a comment: that he
didn't want those people to be freed. The *substitut* showed me this
list.

Since then, the authorities from the *parquet* have come here and
told us we would be freed, but the days pass... The authorities can
do whatever they like. It's nasty and racist. It's to do with ethnicity.
They use their power to threaten us.

I don't have any hope of being released because there is no justice
in our country... How can you have hope when the others – the
genocide survivors – control the prosecuting authorities?... I see
that it's finished for me. I just pray to God."

Some prisoners withstood the shock of being returned to prison better than
others. One prisoner admitted that the return to prison had been hard, but
he had managed to adjust. He said that for him, these events had to be put
into perspective in relation to the suffering he had experienced in the past.
His father had been killed by the RPF in 1994. The rest of his family had fled
to Congo, and his mother and sisters were killed there after the RPA attacked
the refugee camps in late 1996. He was injured too: his eye was irreparably
damaged after he was hit by a fragment of a grenade. After this, he decided
to return to Rwanda. Two days later, he was arrested; he was detained for
almost six years. In 2001, he confessed to participating in the genocide and
in 2003, he was put on the list of provisional releases and sent to an *ingando*:

"While I was in the *ingando*, I used to think about my release,
about being welcomed in my family, although I did think there
could be obstacles to my release because of Ibuka meetings and
propaganda.

On the last day of the *ingando*, very early, we packed our bags,
thinking we would receive our release documents. The *substitut*
came, but with lists of people who would go back to prison. I was
on that list. From the camp where I was, 165 returned to prison.
Still now, we don't have any information on why.

It was a shock. Coming back here, we had problems… Two people who had been in the *ingando* went crazy. One went completely mad because he had been returned to prison. Before, he was quite sane. Another has heart problems which he didn't have before…

I stay calm because I pray. I have trust. I had lots of problems before coming to prison, so it's not the end of the world. I don't know when I will be released. It won't be soon, but one day."

We heard about other prisoners who had fallen apart after being sent back to prison. One prisoner told us about a young man who had suffered serious psychological problems. He used to be active and sociable and used to work in the carpentry workshop, but after his return from the *ingando*, his behaviour changed: "He has had mental problems ever since. He wasn't like that before. He used to talk to people but now he doesn't talk to anyone any more. He stays alone. It is very noticeable. He thinks in the opposite way to everyone else. He is absent when you speak to him. He doesn't even see you."

In Butare Central Prison (and possibly in other prisons) the prisoners who returned from the *ingando* were not allowed to join the work teams when they returned to prison; they were viewed as more likely to try to escape if they found themselves outside. It was a source of further frustration for them that even this possibility of temporary distraction was denied to them.

The *ingando* were used as a recruiting ground for further confessions and denunciations. More than half the prisoners who were sent to the *ingando* in 2003 had been selected for release because they had already confessed to their participation in the genocide. Authorities from the *parquet* continued visiting the camps, as they had visited the prisons, to incite yet more prisoners to confess. Prisoners who had not confessed but had been sent to the *ingando* because there was no evidence against them were encouraged to confess while they were in the camp; some of them did so, to be doubly sure that they would be released. Prisoners who had already confessed were asked to add further elements to their confessions. Some of those who were returned to prison were told that their confessions were incomplete; it is not clear why the authorities did not check the content of their confessions before deciding to send them to the *ingando*. One prisoner, whose case was well-known to the government, told us that the *substitut* had asked some of his colleagues who were sent to the *ingando* to denounce him, otherwise they would not be released. They refused to denounce him and they returned to prison.

The perverse way in which the government's programme of confessions has played out was illustrated by the case of one prisoner who had not confessed but was sent to the *ingando* because there was no evidence against him. Another prisoner, who had confessed to killing the person whom the first prisoner was accused of killing, was also in the *ingando*. The prisoner who had confessed ended up being released, whereas the prisoner against whom there was no evidence was sent back to prison.

Cases such as this precipitated a rush of further confessions in the prisons. The above prisoner decided to confess two weeks after returning to prison and told us many others had done the same thing:

> "When I came back to prison, I explained what had happened to me to the team of prisoners who encourage others to confess… They told me if I didn't confess, I would never get out of prison. I believed them, so I wrote my confession. Before, I had never even thought about confessing because I thought if I was tried, I would be acquitted… In my confession, I gave the name of the person who had denounced me in the *ingando*… Now I'm waiting.
>
> The other prisoners who came from the *ingando* are very sad… Almost all of them have confessed since then. They saw no other way out of prison."

Among the prisoners sent to the *ingando* in early 2003 were a small number of people who had already been tried and sentenced, and whose cases were pending in appeal. It was not clear whether these people ended up in the *ingando* as a result of a decision by the authorities – because they had already served a proportion of their sentence – or as a result of ineptitude. A prisoner in Cyangugu Central Prison was aware of 12 such cases; there may have been others. We met one of them, who had been sentenced to 15 years for participation in the genocide. He had appealed against his sentence in 2001 and there were no further developments until he was sent to the *ingando* in February 2003. After three months, he was sent back to prison. The prosecutor later acknowledged that he had been sent to the *ingando* by mistake. The prisoner told us: "I thought I would be released after the *ingando*. I felt I was touching freedom."

The government's response

The fact that at least 800 prisoners were sent back to prison from the *ingando* was brushed under the carpet by the government in its enthusiasm to advertise the success of its reintegration and reconciliation policies. The government officials we met would almost certainly never have mentioned the issue had we not raised it with them directly. When we did raise it, they were unapologetic about sending people back to prison after building up their expectations that they would be released and claimed that only "a small number" of prisoners had been affected. The Attorney General did not acknowledge that this was problematic at all, either from a judicial point of view or even from a humane point of view. He claimed that the government had told these prisoners that if, while they were in the *ingando*, someone singled them out as having participated in the genocide, they would be sent back to prison. We asked him on what basis specific individuals had been sent back to prison. His reply was both an admission that the authorities had not done their preparatory work properly and that the *ingando* had been used to parade prisoners before the population and give people a last chance to denounce anyone they didn't want to see released: "Some people killed in a lot of places [during the genocide]. There were too many cases to investigate them all beforehand. In the *ingando*, prisoners did community work with the population. People talked and reported back. Those who were returned to prison from the *ingando* had either made incomplete confessions or had been denounced as guilty. We ask for testimonies from the population while the prisoners are in the *ingando*. If there is really no evidence against them, they are released."

None of the prisoners we spoke to had been warned that they might be sent back to prison, nor had they been informed that the population would be invited to vet their cases. As far as they were concerned, a transfer to the *ingando* was a stepping stone to freedom, not a test of innocence by the back door. It was clear from what both the prisoners and the authorities told us that organisations of survivors of the genocide, in particular Ibuka, had played a central role in deciding who should be sent back to prison. They had reviewed the lists of prisoners sent to the *ingando* and had drawn up their own lists of those who, in their eyes, should not be released. The government then acted on their recommendations. Even if new accusations had been levelled against some of these prisoners, it was highly unlikely that the authorities would have been able to investigate them within such a short time.

We discussed the programme of releases with the head of the NURC, the government-created body responsible for running the *ingando*. She told us that initial feedback from the *ingando* had been positive. A polished and outwardly sensitive woman, she delivered a well-rehearsed presentation of the government's strategy of reconciliation. Throughout the first part of our discussion, she showed compassion both for the survivors of the genocide and for the prisoners who were about to be released. But when we asked her why some prisoners had been sent back to prison from the *ingando*, suddenly her mood changed. She snapped at us: "No, it's a lie." She then composed herself and admitted that the releases in 2003 had been "rushed". There followed a convoluted explanation of why some prisoners had been returned to prison. Apparently, mistakes were made: "Some were not supposed to be released, for example those in Category 1. Those released should have been those in the lower categories. Some prisoners said themselves that they were not supposed to be there because they were in Category 1. Those released should be in Categories 2 to 4, those who've served half their sentence, the elderly, the terminally ill, those without a case-file and those accused of minor crimes. If they were not in these categories and they fluked in, they would not be released. Some had forged documents and used false names. It was only a small number that weren't released."

CHAPTER XXI

Freedom:

the reality

*"We're always afraid of going back in there... It frightens us.
We are not free."*

Of all the people we talked to in Rwanda as part of the research for this book, those who expressed the most intense feelings of fear were former prisoners. Although technically free, they were tense and nervous. Many had a hunted look and were constantly glancing over their shoulder as they spoke. They insisted on arranging clandestine meetings with us and, assuming that they were always being followed, took numerous precautions to cover their tracks. In comparison, the real prisoners seemed relaxed and able to express themselves openly. Strangely, the detachment of the prison world provided a form of security and comfort which did not exist outside.

Our conversations with released prisoners were also more emotional than the majority of conversations with those who were still detained. Once they found themselves outside, their deepest fears, their humiliation, their confusion started rising to the surface, along with the memories they had stifled for so many years. Some of these former prisoners were so traumatised that when we first met them, they could barely speak; yet it was clear that they desperately wanted to talk about their experiences.

Suddenly, after spending years in prison without knowing when their ordeal would end, these men and women had been cast out into the real world and found themselves ill-equipped to function in a place they barely recognised. While the world stood still inside the prison walls, the country had changed outside. However hard these prisoners may have tried to prepare themselves for their release, the reality still came as a shock. They were haunted, terrified, unsure as to who they were or how they would survive. Even those who were fortunate enough to have the support of family and friends felt vulnerable and alone.

It is common for people who have spent years in prison in any country to experience difficulties in readjusting to life outside. The process of readjustment can feel like an obstacle course. There are the challenges of resuming and repairing family relationships, financial difficulties, negative public perceptions, and the constant search for a new, or an old, identity.

In Rwanda, all the same difficulties exist, but there is an additional dimension: fear. This fear is different from the general anxiety brought on by the unfamiliarity of the surroundings and worries about integration. It is a deeper fear arising from the particular political and social environment which prevails in Rwanda in the aftermath of the genocide. Partly as a result of the genocide, and partly as a result of new forms of political repression by the current government, divisions have deepened, trust has been destroyed, and social relations are fragile and cautious at best. Any perceived criticism of the government in the post-genocide era is labelled as ethnic 'divisionism' or 'genocidal ideology' – new offences punishable by imprisonment, and which have gradually replaced the blanket accusation of 'genocide' as the primary tool for criminalising dissent. People do not dare to talk openly about their thoughts, opinions and emotions. Self-censorship has become a reflex, paranoia a way of life. As one prisoner told us: "All Rwandans are afraid of being arrested one day... Innocent people are no longer even sure they are innocent."

For a former prisoner accused of genocide, trying to pick his way through this politically hostile environment is like walking on eggshells. Even if he has been released because of a lack of evidence, even if he has been tried and acquitted through a formal process, he will find it almost impossible to shed the label of "*génocidaire*". As such, he is likely to be a prime target for accusations of genocidal ideology or divisionism. For those accused of common crimes, the stigma is less pronounced, but the nervousness can be just as strong.

The greatest fear for the former prisoner is the fear of re-arrest. It is a constant and well-founded fear. With the exception of those who have been tried and acquitted, the majority of releases to date have been provisional releases. Those released provisionally can be re-arrested at any time. Re-arrests are common enough for former prisoners to know that this is not an idle threat.

A former prisoner sees his own fear and distrust reflected in the eyes of those around him. In fact, his friends, neighbours or colleagues may not all harbour feelings of hostility, but the projection of his own fear may be so strong that it replaces the reality. He is convinced that all those around him doubt his innocence. His long-awaited physical freedom has led to a new form of psychological imprisonment. A released prisoner is still a prisoner and may feel less free than he did when he was in prison.

The moment of release

Many of the former prisoners we spoke to had not been given advance notice of their release. With the exception of those who were released as the result of a formal acquittal or who had served their full sentence, the moment of release came as a surprise. Out of the blue, prisoners were simply given the official document ordering their release and were told they could pack their bags and leave. Often they were not even informed of the reason for their release.

Sometimes other prisoners found out someone was due to be released before the prisoner concerned heard about it. For example, one man first found out he might be released when one of his co-detainees who occasionally worked at the *parquet* told him he had seen a piece of paper lying on a desk indicating that he would be released. Another former prisoner remembered that on the day of his release, he had left his château to have a shower, unaware that his routine was about to be disrupted. While he was having his shower, he heard a prisoner say on the internal radio: "Why are you wasting our water when you're about to be released?" He was released a few hours later.

The news of a prisoner's release was as much of a surprise to the family as it was to the prisoner. A woman who had spent two years in prison, accused of genocide, told us:

> "I was not told in advance that I would be released. I don't even
> know what led to my release. I was just given a piece of paper...
> When I got outside, I phoned my husband, but he wasn't at work.

I went home. When my small children saw me, they came up to me slowly and greeted me. My son went to call my husband, who was in a different room, and said: 'Mum is here.' My husband heard my voice but he thought it was my sister as we have a similar voice. The child insisted, so my husband came out. I was just standing there with my shaved head. He was very surprised. It was as if he thought I was a ghost."

Several prisoners described the moment of their release as a dream and said it took them some time to realise it was true. One man who had spent seven years in prison without trial told us: "It was a Friday. My wife usually came to visit on Saturdays. I saw her coming and looking at me, smiling. I understood immediately. When I came out, I thought it was a dream. While I was inside, I used to dream of my release all the time."

A man who was released after being tried and acquitted described leaving the prison:

"I saw the sky. I was opening my eyes wide and seeing the world as if it was something new. I wanted to walk out immediately, but the *capita* told me to wait and that I had to say goodbye to the director. The director was in a meeting. I burst into his meeting and I said: 'I'm free – goodbye!' I was crazy with joy. My lawyer was waiting for me outside. We went to his office. I didn't have the confidence to go home alone. I was afraid of being re-arrested, as others had been. My lawyer asked me if I knew my way around town. I said no, even though I did, because I was afraid."

When some of the released prisoners got home, they rediscovered the basic comforts which they had taken for granted before their arrest. A woman who had spent three years in prison described sleeping on a bed as a miracle. Most prisoners celebrated with their family and friends as soon as they got home – sometimes for several days, with special food and drink. But some preferred to avoid large social gatherings and public celebrations, for fear they would draw attention to themselves. They kept a low profile, sometimes for many months, in the hope that they would remain unnoticed.

The road outside Kigali Central Prison   © Carina Tertsakian

On the day of their release, some were afraid of going straight home – afraid of the reactions of their neighbours or of coming face to face with the people who had accused them in the first place. A young man who was only 15 when he was arrested, and 23 by the time he was released, chose to stay with a former prisoner during his first few days of freedom. His friend then gave him some money so that he could travel to his mother's house. But others didn't dare settle back in their home area, even several years after their release. Their families were sometimes equally fearful. A former prisoner from Gitarama went straight to his family's house when he was released. He spent the first night there, celebrating with his mother, his eldest son and other relatives. But the next day, his family sent him away, not because they didn't want to welcome him but because they were afraid. He moved to Butare, and subsequently to Kigali, but chose not to return to Gitarama.

Those who are provisionally released are given a letter specifying a number of conditions and requirements. Usually, the released prisoner is required to live within a particular location, is not allowed to travel abroad, and is asked to report to the *parquet* once a week or once a month. In the period immediately following their release, most of those we spoke to had reported regularly, as requested, but after a certain period elapsed, officials at the *parquet* indicated informally that it was no longer necessary to do so. A man who was provisionally released remembered that the first time he went to report to the *parquet*, he was shaking because he was so afraid they would put him back inside. The second time, he was "shaking a bit less as I had already been once". Then, he got used to it, and eventually he was told he didn't have to report any more.

The process of readjustment

The former prisoners we spoke to included men and women who had been released just a few weeks before we met them and others who had been released several years earlier. Some had spent two or three years in prison, others eight, nine or ten. The degree to which they had succeeded in adapting to life outside did not always correspond to the length of time they had spent in prison or the length of time they had spent out of prison. The experience of imprisonment had affected some much more deeply than others.

A woman told us about her difficulties in adapting after her release: "I was afraid of people... you feel no one trusts you or likes you. I was ashamed of being with people. At first, I preferred to talk to friends in private rooms, not in the lounge, in case other people came in... this is a small town and everyone knows about you."

A man who had spent seven years in prison told us: "Outside, you don't feel at ease. You think everyone who passes by knows you've come out of prison. It takes a long time to get over it. I was afraid of the military. Every time I saw a soldier, I thought he would send me back to prison." By the time we met him, three and half years after his release, he was no longer afraid to move around, but the memories of prison still haunted him: "Still now, I often dream of the prison. It disturbs me. I wake up and I pray. Gradually it is getting better, but it is not going away."

In some cases, the experience of imprisonment has all but destroyed individuals who had been confident and self-reliant in their previous life. Even the most simple tasks seemed insurmountable, especially in the initial period.

A man who was released after being tried and acquitted described the long and painful process of regaining even the basic confidence to go out. He spent his first six months of freedom at home, without leaving his compound:

> "On the first day, I heard people saying: 'These are *interahamwe* and killers coming out of prison', so I didn't want to go out... I used to sit in front of the house all the time. Once, a woman approached me. She said she didn't want to disturb me – this is not a typical greeting here – but she could see I was alone. She said it was not good to stay alone. She offered to buy me a beer. I accepted. It was the first time someone had approached me when I was alone. The woman was the owner of the house where we lived. Her husband was also in prison. I drank two beers. I was drunk but I was happy. She helped me to start going out and encouraged me. She is still a friend of the family.
>
> Some of the other tenants didn't even greet me. They knew I'd been in prison. People saw me as a killer. They were not happy I had been released. I was the only prisoner released in the area. There were negative attitudes from people who didn't know me, as I didn't live there before...
>
> Six months later, a colleague who had also been in prison came to see me. He wanted to take me to a bar for a drink. I said: 'No, let's have it at home'. He insisted, so we went out. Three people I knew offered me a drink. I refused because I was afraid, even though they welcomed me. My former colleague helped me out of this fear. I realised he had suffered more than me. I asked him to visit me once a week so that each time, we would go 100 metres further. Once, he said: 'Let's just go round the town.' There was no problem and we went to different places. The only place my wife said I couldn't go to was the place where I'd been arrested. For every 100 metres we walked together, I was able to walk 10 metres alone. Eventually, I managed to go out alone. After one or two months, I realised I didn't need to be afraid any more."

A 34-year-old man who had spent more than eight years in prison without trial described his gradual readjustment to life outside. He had been a member of the prison choir, and joining a local choir after his release had been a lifeline for him:

> "I didn't want to walk around as I still felt the fear... I thought everyone hated me and saw a killer in me. I didn't trust anyone. Gradually I got used to other people. My friend took me into the choir. People who knew me knew I was innocent and they comforted me. People were not hostile. Now the only problems are unemployment and poverty. I found some temporary work, but now I am not working. I had to sell my house.
>
> Now I feel calm but I pray it won't happen again. I do think about my time in prison, especially the hunger, the people dying of dysentery because of the lack of medicines. I would like to see the people I sang with in the choir in prison. Some are still in prison, others have been released. I have gone to visit some friends there. We were very happy when we met. They asked me to pray for them to be released.
>
> In the future, I would like to work or borrow money to do some business as I want to get married. I am already engaged to a woman I met since my release."

Finding work

Economic difficulties were among prisoners' main concerns following their release. The practical and psychological hurdles of finding work were overwhelming. Well-educated men and women with professional qualifications – former teachers, nurses, office workers, businessmen – experienced great difficulties in finding employment, at least in the initial period; some didn't even have the courage or energy to go out to look for work. Their difficulties were in part a reflection of the increasing economic strains in Rwanda and the high level of unemployment; in part an indication of the political and social shift which had occurred during the years they had spent in prison; [1] and in part a symptom of their own loss of confidence. When so many Rwandans are competing for scarce positions, former prisoners fall to the bottom of the pile. Some tried to conceal the fact that they had been in prison when they applied for jobs, then lived with the daily anxiety of their colleagues finding out. A woman who managed to find a job about a year after her release still felt uncomfortable at work: "There are lots of RPF people there, and I don't know what they know or don't know about me. I sometimes wonder if I should say something myself. Otherwise, it's like a secret."

In the private sector, employers were less reluctant to hire candidates who had been in prison; after all, a large proportion of the population, including many well-educated people, fall into this category. The greatest difficulties were in the state sector. Some former prisoners tried to claim back the position they had occupied before their arrest. In most cases, these jobs had since been filled by other people, or scrapped altogether. Former prisoners' requests to take up their old job often remained unanswered or were turned down without explanation.

The government specified that prisoners who had been released for lack of evidence should be reinstated, but employers did not always respect these guidelines. A former prisoner who had worked as a statistician told us: "I wanted to go back to my old job. I wrote a letter requesting reintegration but nothing happened. When I went to ask, they said there was no vacancy. Then they said mine was a difficult case. A woman there said that because I'd been in prison, the matter could not be settled. I showed them the letter I had from the Ministry of Labour saying that those who were released without a sentence should be reintegrated and paid, but they told me it didn't apply

---

[1]   After the genocide, many Tutsi who had been living in exile for decades returned to settle in Rwanda. The new political and economic climate was favourable to them; many were able to secure jobs and started to prosper. This shift occurred while tens of thousands of Hutu were locked up in prison. After their release, some of these former prisoners complained that it was extremely difficult for them to find work. They claimed that many jobs, including the posts they had occupied before their arrest, had become the preserve of Tutsi, especially in the civil service. More generally, many Hutu (not only prisoners) have complained of ethnic discrimination in recruitment practices since the end of the genocide.

to me. They advised me not to insist, otherwise I could go back to prison." Eventually, he found a job elsewhere.

Other former prisoners, especially the younger ones, decided they wanted to study rather than work, to make up for lost time. But finding the means to pay for a college course was a challenge, as was the intellectual effort required to resume studies after a gap of several years. As with the search for jobs, it was generally easier for former prisoners to enrol in private schools or colleges rather than state schools; fewer questions were asked.

Support for released prisoners

In late 2004, there was no form of therapy or counselling to assist former prisoners in readjusting to life outside, or at least none that they felt they could take advantage of. Some had heard of the existence of counselling services, but were aware that these were intended primarily for survivors of the genocide. Even if these services did not explicitly exclude other categories, the former prisoners believed they would not be welcome there and could not even contemplate placing their trust in these services. Rightly or wrongly, they expected to encounter among the counsellors the same hostility that they encountered elsewhere. Yet the need for professional counselling is immense. A woman who had been free for several years but was still suffering from the psychological scars of her imprisonment told us that if ever she were lucky enough to travel to Europe, the first thing she would do there would be to seek counselling. "We try to forget things," she told us, "but we still feel ill at ease all the time. It's like a bomb waiting to explode."

The few psychological and support services that do exist in post-genocide Rwanda are indeed geared towards survivors of the genocide.[2] There is nothing surprising in the fact that the Rwandan government should choose to channel its funds, as well as money from foreign donors, towards this sector of the population. The provision of support for former prisoners

---

[2]   Even these services have been fraught with problems. Some have come under criticism for inefficiency and corruption, and many genocide survivors, especially those in rural areas, have been unable to access them.

accused of genocide is one of the lowest priorities on the national and international agenda.

The released prisoners we spoke to did not express resentment towards the survivors of the genocide who might benefit from these services, but their own invisibility in the new Rwandan society was clearly painful for them. They had been forgotten and abandoned in freedom, just as they had been forgotten and abandoned in prison.

The only sources of support for released prisoners have been their families, their friends and, in some cases, their religious congregation. But even with their wives, husbands, brothers or sisters, former prisoners did not always feel able to express themselves freely. A former prisoner told us: "This is the first time I've talked about it at length. My wife doesn't want us to talk about it at all, so who am I going to talk to?"

Fitting back into the family was a difficult experience for many released prisoners. In some cases, marital relationships had broken down. The wife of a prisoner, who had made friends with other wives of prisoners, told us: "After being released, some have not returned to their wives as they have accused them of seeing other men while they were in prison. They have settled with other women. Even those who stay together after their release don't get on... About 80% of couples of released prisoners are very unhappy."

Even when couples had remained faithful, the long years of imprisonment had created a distance between them, which it could take several years to bridge. Each partner would notice changes in personality and habits in the other. A man whose wife had spent several years in prison described some of the more noticeable effects of her imprisonment: "It took her a long time to get used to life as a free person. Whenever there were a lot of people around, her head would start spinning. It was like a film going too fast... She had forgotten people's names. Even now, it still happens. She thinks it's because when she was in prison, she trained herself to disconnect from the outside world, so as not to have too much pain... Before, she was very confident. Now, if she has to ask for something, someone has to go with her. Her confidence is gradually coming back. But she is less optimistic than before... She is also more religious than before."

Some prisoners found it difficult to restore the relationship with their children after missing out on crucial years of their development. Their children, for their part, had got used to growing up without a father or a mother. The sudden return of their parent was usually welcome, but in some cases, it felt like an intrusion, especially when the parent tried to reassert his or her authority.

A mother of four children, aged between eight and 17, said that when she was first released, her children were afraid of seeing her: "The youngest didn't want to touch me and hid from me, for three months. It was very difficult. He was two when I was arrested. He was with me when I was detained in the brigade, but I left him when I went to the central prison. Now, he's very attached to me and doesn't want to leave me. He is afraid of losing me. The other children got used to it after about a week. They're OK, but they hate talking about prison."

A father of four who spent seven years in detention had serious problems re-establishing a relationship with one of his sons after his release. His son was about 14 when his father was arrested; his mother had been killed just one year before, in 1994. When his father was finally released, his son rejected him and started behaving aggressively towards him. Their relationship became so fraught that the son went back to live with the family who had looked after him during his father's detention. The father attributed some of the difficulties in their relationship to his son's trauma as a result first of his mother's death, then of his father's prolonged imprisonment. But he also blamed himself for not adjusting quickly enough to the new realities: "I was stuck in a time-warp of about eight years ago. For example, I would get cross if my son went out without telling me, then he would get cross with me for doing that... I haven't been around to evolve with the situation or to follow how relations between parents and children develop."

The question of friendships was also complicated. Usually, in the days and weeks following the release, friends and relatives spontaneously came to visit the released prisoner to celebrate his release. Seeing who came and didn't come to these impromptu celebrations was very telling for the released prisoner. It was an easy way of working out who their real friends were. Some found valuable support from old friends who had visited and comforted them and their families throughout their period in prison, and continued visiting them after their release. But other friends had deliberately distanced themselves or had completely disappeared off the scene.

A man who had spent eight years in prison had noticed many changes in the social interactions around him: "People are less trusting... There are new faces. After spending eight years in prison, you don't know people anymore. Those you do know may not want to spend time with you... There is a feeling of isolation and quarantine."

Even the support of close family members could not be taken for granted. A young man who had spent eight years in prison went to see his brother and sister-in-law after his release, even though his brother had never visited him while he was in prison: "I thought they would embrace me, but they didn't. They didn't talk to me or ask me what happened... I just wanted my brother to talk to me to help get over my trauma, but he didn't. I stopped considering him as my brother."

Prison friendships

Friendships with other released prisoners formed a category of their own These friendships were defined by the unique context in which they had evolved, and were characterised by a level of trust which is rare in Rwanda. Some former prisoners spoke fondly about these friendships, which continued to occupy a special place in their life. A man who had spent almost ten years in prison said he felt more comfortable with his friends who had been in prison with him than with other people: "I trust them and we can talk about our problems, but only when no one can hear us."

Others felt ambivalent about the place of these friendships in their life of new-found freedom. They were uncertain about the desirability of sustaining friendships which would always be a painful reminder of one of the most difficult periods of their lives.

One former prisoner said that sometimes, when he walked down the street, he would bump into people who had been in prison with him. "They greet me warmly. They say: 'You may not remember me. We were in prison together.' It's good to see another life saved, but you have to distinguish friendship from solidarity... I meet up with some released prisoners from time to time. They come and visit me... But I don't want to only see those people. I want to protect myself from those memories. Our conversations always go back to the prison."

Most of the released prisoners we spoke to occasionally returned to visit their friends who were still in prison. One former prisoner said the only problem on these visits was choosing who to ask for: there were so many people he wanted to see. Another told us that whenever he went to visit his friends in prison, he would hear shouts of joy when his name was announced on the list of visitors. Another former prisoner said the friends he regularly visited in prison trusted him to do things for them which other people outside could not or would not do. Some of those who were still in prison also mentioned the importance of these visits from their friends who had been released; they had already decided that they too would visit their former colleagues if and when they were released.

However, for the released prisoner, these visits could give rise to mixed emotions and revive the fear of re-arrest. A woman who had been released but whose brother, cousins and several friends were still detained in the same prison described these visits as a humbling experience, and one which made her appreciate what she had: "Now I feel I wasn't even in prison. I just think about those who are still there. When you're inside, you don't see the misery. You only see it from outside... Sometimes I dream of prison. It is frightening. I wonder whether I am still there. I dream of the women I was with and of the inside of the prison. Then it passes, but I can't forget it completely." Another woman described returning to the prison three years after her release, to visit a friend who was still detained there: "You always feel afraid of going in. You think you may just stay there. I often dream of all that, of the women in pink."

About nine months after completing the research for this book, I found out that one of the prisoners I had met in Kigali Central Prison had been released as part of a long-awaited wave of releases in mid-2005. Arrested at the age of

20, he had been detained for almost ten years without trial. I had spent many hours with him in the prison over a period of several weeks at the end of 2004; the memory of his face and his story remain among the most vivid, and several extracts from his testimony are included in this book. He was one of the most optimistic prisoners, who believed fervently in his imminent release, even in the absence of any objective signs of hope. One of his parting sentences on my last visit was that he was sure he would be released the following January. His release came eight months later.

As soon as I learned about his release, my joy became tinged with worry about how he would cope outside. Memories of my conversations with other released prisoners, who were still traumatised several years after their release, came flooding back. A few weeks later, I phoned him and we spoke for about 15 minutes. There was much to say, but little was said, maybe because he was so surprised to receive my call. I could hear him smiling down the phone. I asked him what he was doing since his release. He said nothing, yet. He wanted to resume his studies but lacked the financial means. He was one of about 1,000 prisoners released from Kigali Central Prison around the same time. I asked about some of the other prisoners I had met there, assuming some of them may have been released with him. He said most of them were still inside. Eventually, the conversation fizzled out.

Some of the prisoners I met in Butare Central Prison, including at least two elderly men whose testimonies feature in this book, were also released in August 2005. I received this news through one of the prisoners who occasionally still wrote to me. In one of his letters, he told me that around 1,600 prisoners had been released from Butare prison, but he was still inside. He wrote: "It's a shame. I'm still keeping my courage and my patience." He was eventually released in 2007.

———

This chapter is just a snapshot of the lives of around 25 released prisoners. It does not aim to cover every aspect of their new lives nor of the complex environment in which they now find themselves. It deliberately does not cover the delicate question of the relationship between released prisoners who were accused of genocide and the genocide survivors with whom they now live side by side. This question looms large over the future of released prisoners, just as it does over the future of genocide survivors. After much thought, I decided not to include this aspect in my research. It is a topic which merits a whole separate study, and it would have been impossible to do justice to it here.

There have been other studies and reports on the impact of prisoner releases on survivors of the genocide and the prospects of reconciliation in the aftermath of the genocide. Penal Reform International, among others, have interviewed both released prisoners and genocide survivors. Prisoners' expectations of how they might interact with genocide survivors after their release are also covered in some detail, and in their multiple contradictions, in Jean Hatzfeld's extraordinary book *Une saison de machettes*.

CHAPTER XXII

"I am still in that space now"

My strongest memory of all my encounters with Rwandan prisoners is of an elderly man in Gitarama Central Prison. Objectively, his story is not more tragic than any other. It is typical of thousands of prisoners across Rwanda. But his testimony moved me deeply, because of the raw misery of his situation, his vulnerability and his abandonment.

He is a peasant from Gitarama province. He is 59 but he could be 70 or 75. He is small and frail. Like all prisoners, his head is shaved but he has little shoots of grey beard. His rubber flip-flop sandals expose his bare, lined feet. He wears the regulation pink shirt and shorts which cover his knees, but the uniform is too big and falls off his shoulders. He does not own a uniform. He does not own anything. He has borrowed this uniform from another prisoner to come and talk to me.

He comes to meet me in the small office across the yard. He has no idea who I am or why I want to meet him. I explain and he listens, sitting upright on a wooden chair. He volunteers to tell his story, freely, easily, but painfully. He seems lost, animated and purposeful all at the same time.

He had stayed in Rwanda after the genocide, but his wife and three children had fled to neighbouring Congo. His eldest daughter was 19, the second 15, the youngest was still a baby. They were all killed in the refugee camps in 1996. He found out through some other refugees who had been with his family in Congo.

He was arrested in November 1994, four months after the end of the genocide. He was accused of killing two people during the genocide but pleaded innocence. He spent three months in a *cachot* in his home area, where he was badly beaten, then was moved briefly to another *cachot*. In February 1995, he was transferred to Gitarama prison, at a time when the conditions there were at their most catastrophic. He had remained in Gitarama prison ever since.

When I met him, he had been in prison for ten years. He had never received any visits. He had never been before a court. He was just there, like so many others, waiting.

He spoke for a long time, about his ill-treatment in the *cachot*, about his years in Gitarama prison, and about his loneliness.

"In the *cachot*, the conditions were terrible. I was tortured. My finger was injured by a soldier who hit me with a bayonet. He was trying to force me to confess. He wanted to cut my fingers. They tortured and beat me almost every day and night.

We were about 260 detainees in one cell. We couldn't lie down. We could only sit. We couldn't go outside. We went to the toilet inside the cell and emptied it into the ditch the next morning. Washing was officially forbidden, as was drinking water. Those who had families received food. I had no family. I survived thanks to other detainees who shared their food with me.

A soldier questioned us. He tried to make us give him names of people we had killed. That was his form of investigation. Some detainees admitted killing. Others, like me, said we hadn't killed anyone. They accused me of killing a specific person. The soldiers said they would go and see the house of that person, and that if one single tile was missing from the roof, I would be kept in prison.

One Monday morning at 5am, they put us in a truck and took us to another *cachot*, in a neighbouring area. I wasn't beaten there, but other detainees were beaten. One of them died as a result of the beatings as soon as he got to Gitarama prison.

I was transferred to Gitarama prison on 12 February 1995. It was terrible. People were dying every day, every day. You can't imagine what it was like. Many were killed by other prisoners. They were trampled on. The soldiers pushed people inside. There was a slope that led towards a cellar. People were falling in, without knowing there was a ditch. People didn't care about human lives. Every morning, the soldiers used to ask the *capita général* how many of us had died.

Often we were just on top of each other, sleeping on top of each other. In the morning, some people were wrapped up in blankets and buried, even though not all of them were dead. The soldiers used to come in, point to the bodies on the ground and say to the prisoners: 'Clear all this away.' The people in the blankets may have been sick or weak, but the soldiers just said they were dead, and they were taken away to be buried. These 'burials' were also a way of preventing people from sleeping late in the morning. You had to wake up early, to avoid being carted away.

We had to queue for the toilet from 5am; we could wait for up to six hours. There were no showers. All we could do was give our ration of biscuits to the prisoners who ran the kitchen in exchange for a cup of water to drink or to wash our teeth or face. Some of the prisoners who were there before us were killers. When we arrived, they accused us of coming to reduce their food rations.

At the beginning, I slept outside, near a prisoner who became my friend; we used to pray together. In the morning, I stayed sitting between his legs, as there was no other space. The military came and beat me. My friend said: 'Why are you beating this poor man who has no family? Let him die naturally.' He lent me his shorts, as on the first day they took all my clothes. He saved me several times even though I didn't know him before. It was a gesture from God. We are still together. We are not in the same block any more, but we are friends.

I stayed sleeping in the yard, in the open air, for one year and five months. There were 2,300 of us sleeping outside, old and young. After they built the extension, there was more space. I was among the first to be transferred to the new building because I had been there a long time. The conditions were almost the same. It was just a prison everywhere. There were four blocks, but there was a pre-selection by the *capita* and other prisoners in positions of responsibility. Some prisoners who had been allocated a place were discouraged from taking it. The poor people were pushed outside, even if they had been able to get a place inside.

It was thanks to a white man from the Red Cross that I managed to get a place inside. One day, when I was still sleeping outside, it rained heavily. We went into a room which was used as a depot. We stayed there overnight, to shelter from the rain. The next day, the military tried to chase us out. A white man from the Red Cross told the military to let us stay there. That's how I got to stay inside, thanks to that *muzungu* [foreigner]. I am still in that space now. I have a bed and a space of 40 centimetres.

Those who have a position of responsibility in the prison get meals. The rest of us don't eat properly. We get a few grains of corn and peas.

I have not had any visits at all since I've been here, so I don't receive any food from outside. Sometimes a prisoner gives me some scraps to share, for example sweet potato or cassava. Friends inside get together to buy me clothes and shoes. I have another friend who is old like me. He and the man who helped me at the beginning are my only two friends. There are others who are colleagues, rather than friends. The church people help us. I look forward to Saturdays. There are prayer sessions which lift our morale.

At one time the leader of one of the work teams [a prisoner] wanted to stop me from working outside. He was always aggressive towards me, I don't know why, maybe because I'm poor. He was trying to blame me and accuse me, but others said I was innocent. Even now, there are problems with him. The *capita* is trying to resolve it. I don't work outside. Since I've been here, this is the third time I have ever been out.

I don't want to go outside as I have no family. I stay inside, sitting or playing *igisoro*. I just sit there. At 6pm, I'm the first to go to bed. I don't do anything. Sometimes I wander into other blocks to visit people. I don't have a blanket any more. Someone stole it while I was sleeping. When I realised it had been stolen, other prisoners laughed at me.

In 2003, they held the pre-*gacaca* hearing on my hill. I was accused of killing a man and his wife. I attended, along with other prisoners. I was asked if I knew the family of the victim. I said no and that I didn't kill them. They asked the population, who said they had not seen me kill the couple. The son of the victim was there. He objected to my release. They put me on the list of people to be released, but I'm still waiting. That was in April 2003. Since then, there has been nothing.

I am not tempted to confess. If I had something to confess, I would have done so earlier on. But I have nothing to confess.

Even if I'm not released, I want to be tried, at least, otherwise I will spend ten years like this. *Gacaca* may be the solution, but I've been waiting for the results for two years now. I'm sure God is seeing me suffer and that the day of my release will come. Through prayer, everything is possible. Even though I'm old, I would prefer to die outside and be buried in dignity, instead of being thrown out like a dog.

No one is living in my house. It has probably crumbled. I have no other relatives here as my family is from Gikongoro, and they were all killed too. RPF soldiers razed the area and they killed everybody there, in 1996 or 1997.

Yes, prison has become a bit like home.

I feel relieved talking to you. It helps me forget. I am crying even though I am old. I don't know if my pain will ever go away."

Of all the male prisoners we spoke to, he was the only one who cried while we were talking.

At the end of the interview, another prisoner escorted him back, holding his arm, as if he was too weak to walk. I watched them cross the yard. He shuffled off and disappeared through the prison gate.

I went back to see him about a month later, with a new blanket to replace the one which had been stolen from him. He was not expecting a second visit. These two visits in the space of less than two months were more than he had received in ten years. Again, he had borrowed another prisoner's uniform to come out of the prison building, a different one this time, a brighter shade of pink. Like the first one, it was too big for his small frame, and it looked new and freshly ironed, at odds with his poverty. We talked for about five minutes. He said he was happy to see me. He thanked me energetically for the blanket and tucked it under his arm, still wrapped in the cellophane from the shop. He didn't have much else to say. This was a social visit, a moment of simple relaxation.

I have often thought about this man while writing this book. I have thought about him barely surviving from day to day, without receiving any visits, drip-fed by the charity of one or two other prisoners and by his religious faith. I have thought about the likelihood of him dying in prison, without ever seeing justice. I have wondered what possible justification could be found for continuing to imprison helpless and vulnerable people like him.

Postscript

Kigali Central Prison   © Ladislas Niyongira

2007

Several thousand prisoners have been released since this book was written, including some whose testimonies are included in this book. Several thousand more have been arrested, or re-arrested, as a result of *gacaca* trials.

In May 2007, the prison population in Rwanda stands at around 92,000, almost 7,000 higher than it was at the end of 2004, during the period described in this book. After dropping by around 15,000 between 2005 and 2006, the prison population increased by more than 20,000 between July 2006 and April 2007.

Among those recently arrested is a former colleague, a human rights activist with whom I worked closely over several years. In May 2007, he was accused of participation in the genocide and tried by a *gacaca* court. The trial was blatantly unfair. There were serious doubts about the impartiality and independence of the presiding judge, who had a prior dispute with the defendant. Even though the judge was challenged on this point and the defendant asked for him to be replaced – as provided for by the law in cases of conflict of interest – the judge refused to step aside and proceeded with the trial. My colleague was found guilty and sentenced to 19 years in prison. He is beginning to serve his sentence as I finish this book.

Appendices

Map of Rwanda

The names and boundaries of provinces in Rwanda have changed since this map was drawn. The references in this map were current at the time of the events described in this book.

Methodology

The primary research for this book was carried out in Rwanda from October to December 2004. Most of the information relates to the ten years that followed the genocide: July 1994 to December 2004. First-hand observations about prison conditions and other aspects of the situation in Rwanda relate to October-December 2004 unless indicated otherwise. Updates on events from 2005 to mid-2007 are based on information from sources inside and outside Rwanda, reports by non-governmental organisations and publicly available documentation.

For the field research, I worked in a team with three close friends and colleagues, one from the United Kingdom and two from Rwanda. We carried out around 200 interviews in Rwanda. The majority of the people we interviewed were prisoners. We also interviewed prison staff, former prisoners, families of prisoners, government officials and members of non-governmental organisations.

We conducted interviews in five prisons:

- Kigali Central Prison, known as PCK (*Prison centrale de Kigali*) or "1930", after the year in which it was built
- Butare Central Prison: the main prison, Karubanda, and the annex known as Rwandex
- Gitarama Central Prison
- Cyangugu Central Prison
- Nsinda prison

Through our conversations with prisoners in these five locations, as well as with prisoners who had been released from these and other prisons, we also gathered information on the following prisons (some of which have since closed):

- Gikondo and Kimironko prisons, in Kigali
- Rilima prison in Kigali Rural[1]
- Nyanza prison, in Butare province
- Kibuye Central Prison and Gisovu prison, in Kibuye province
- Byumba Central Prison (I and II) and Miyove prison, in Byumba province
- Ruhengeri Central Prison
- Kibungo Central Prison
- Mulindi and Kibungo military prisons
- Other military camps and detention centres, including Camp Kami and Camp Ngoma
- A large number of local detention centres (*cachots* and brigades) in different provinces.

We interviewed a cross-section of prisoners in each prison, including:

- Men
- Women
- Minors
- Elderly prisoners
- Prisoners accused of genocide
- Prisoners accused of common crimes
- Prisoners who had been tried and sentenced
- Prisoners who had not been tried
- Prisoners who had confessed to a crime
- Prisoners who had not confessed to a crime
- Prisoners who had been released and re-arrested
- Prisoners who had been in prison before the 1994 genocide
- Wealthy prisoners
- Poor prisoners
- "Intellectuals" (those with a high standard of formal education)
- Prisoners with no formal education
- Prisoners from a wide range of professions

---

[1]   The names of provinces in Rwanda have since changed. In this list, and throughout this book, I have used the old names, as these were the ones in use at the time of the events described and at the time we conducted our research in the prisons.

- Prisoners holding positions of responsibility in the prison
  (*capitas*, *responsables* and others)
- Sick prisoners
- Disabled prisoners
- Hutu prisoners
- Tutsi prisoners
- Military prisoners
- Foreign prisoners (non-Rwandan)

Thanks to the cooperation of prison staff, especially the prison directors and deputy directors, we were able to interview individual prisoners privately, usually in a small office in the prison. Some interviews were conducted in French, others in Kinyarwanda with translation provided by colleagues or, on occasions, by other prisoners with the agreement of the interviewee.

We spent an average of two to three hours with each of the prisoners we interviewed. We also talked to many others more casually, or in passing, in the prison courtyards.

In organising our research, we had drawn up a set of questions and topics for our interviews with prisoners. Most of our interviews were structured around this outline, but we did not always stick to the questions rigidly. The eloquence of many prisoners, and the sheer amount of information they wanted to share with us, took our conversations in many new and unpredictable directions.

Out of respect for confidentiality and the security of prisoners and their families, no names are included in this book. Likewise, the names of prisoners' specific areas of origin and other details which would enable identification of their cases have been omitted.

Glossary of terms and acronyms

bourgmestre	mayor
brigade	local detention centre run by the gendarmerie
cachot	local detention centre where prisoners were held before being transferred to the central prisons
capita	prisoner in a position of responsibility
capita général	prisoner in the top position of responsibility
Category 1	people accused of playing a leading role in the genocide or carrying out particularly serious crimes (as defined in the 1996 and 2004 genocide laws)
cellule	cell, an administrative sub-division of a *secteur*
château	prisoner's living space
chef de bloc	prisoner in charge of a block
commune	district
direction	prison management
DMI	Directorate of Military Intelligence
DRC	Democratic Republic of Congo
FAR	*Forces armées rwandaises*, the army of the former government of Rwanda
gacaca	system of local justice based on community participation, used to try genocide cases
génocidaire	person who participated or is accused of participating in the 1994 genocide
Ibuka	organisation representing genocide survivors
ibyari / icyari	improvised structures made by prisoners in which they live and sleep
ICRC	International Committee of the Red Cross
ICTR	International Criminal Tribunal for Rwanda, based in Arusha, Tanzania
igisoro	popular game in Rwanda
infiltrés	insurgents composed of members of the former Rwandan army and *interahamwe* militia, who launched cross-border attacks in Rwanda from eastern Congo from 1996 to 1999

ingando	solidarity camp where prisoners are sent before being released
interahamwe	Hutu militia who carried out many killings during the 1994 genocide
inyenzi	cockroaches (term used by extremist Hutu to designate Tutsi)
LIPRODHOR	*Ligue rwandaise pour la promotion et la défense des droits de l'homme* (Rwandan League for the Promotion and Defence of Human Rights)
MDR	*Mouvement démocratique républicain*
mine	space on the ground under the lowest row of bunk-beds in the prisons
MRND	*Mouvement républicain national pour la démocratie et le développement,* the ruling party under President Habyarimana
NURC	National Unity and Reconciliation Commission
parquet	prosecutor's office
PCK	*Prison centrale de Kigali* (Kigali Central Prison)
PRI	Penal Reform International
responsable	prisoner with a specific area of responsibility within the prison
RPA	Rwandan Patriotic Army
RPF	Rwandan Patriotic Front
secteur	sector, an administrative sub-division of a *commune*
social / sociale	prison social worker
substitut	assistant prosecutor
surveillant	guard
surveillant chef	chief guard
TIG	*travail d'intérêt général* (community service)

Further reading

Many books, reports and articles have been written about Rwanda, the majority about the genocide. The list below is not an exhaustive list, nor a complete bibliography of sources I used as references for this book. It is a small and personal selection of books, reports and websites which are either directly relevant to the issues covered in this book or which I found informative or thought-provoking. Most, though not all, of these publications are available in English and in French.

Books

Thierry Cruvellier
Le tribunal des vaincus: un Nuremberg pour le Rwanda?
Calmann-Levy, 2006

Alison Des Forges
Leave none to tell the story: genocide in Rwanda
Human Rights Watch / Fédération Internationale des Droits de l'Homme, 1999

Jean Hatzfeld
Une saison de machettes
Editions du Seuil, 2003

English translation:
A time for machetes: the Rwandan genocide - the killers speak
Serpent's Tail, 2005

Jean Hatzfeld
Dans le nu de la vie: récits des marais rwandais
Editions du Seuil, 2000

English translation:
Into the quick of life: the Rwandan genocide - the survivors speak
Serpent's Tail, 2005

Gérard Prunier
The Rwanda crisis: history of a genocide
Columbia University Press, 1995

André Sibomana
Gardons espoir pour le Rwanda: entretiens avec Laure Guilbert et Hervé Deguine
Desclée de Brouwer, 1997
(out of print in 2007 - new edition in preparation in 2008)

Hope for Rwanda: conversations with Laure Guilbert and Hervé Deguine
Translated and with a postscript by Carina Tertsakian
Pluto Press, 1999

Scott Straus
The order of genocide: race, power and war in Rwanda
Cornell University Press, 2006

Websites and reports

Amnesty International
Numerous reports and statements on the human rights situation in Rwanda.
www.amnesty.org

Avocats sans frontières
Information on the Rwandan justice system, genocide trials and *gacaca*.
www.asf.be

Ensemble contre la peine de mort
La peine capitale au Rwanda: enquête dans les couloirs de la mort de la prison de Mpanga
www.abolition.fr

Fédération Internationale des Droits de l'Homme
Reports and statements on human rights and justice in Rwanda.
www.fidh.org

Front Line
*Front Line Rwanda: Disappearances, arrests, threats, intimidation
and co-option of human rights defenders 2001-2004*
www.frontlinedefenders.org

Human Rights Watch
Numerous reports and statements on the human rights situation
in Rwanda.
www.hrw.org

LIPRODHOR
Reports and statements on the human rights situation in Rwanda,
with a particular focus on prisons, genocide trials and *gacaca*.
Some, though not all, are available at www.liprodhor.org.rw

Penal Reform International
Detailed reports on *gacaca* and related issues.
www.penalreform.org

Acknowledgements

I would like to thank the many men and women in Rwanda, in prison and outside, who were willing to put their trust in me and talk about their experiences in such great and personal detail. I have condensed many hours of conversation and hundreds of pages of notes into this book. I hope I have done justice to the essence of their testimonies and that those among them who read this book will find in it a true picture of their reality.

I would also like to thank the Rwandan authorities in the Ministry of Interior who gave me access to the prisons, as well as the prison directors, deputy directors and guards who enabled me to interview prisoners at length, privately and without interference.

There are many people in Rwanda, in the UK and elsewhere who provided invaluable help, advice, inspiration and encouragement during the research, writing and production phases of this book. It is not possible to list them all here. I have tried to single out those who have been most closely involved in this project, but many other friends, family and colleagues, who are not named here, also played a critical role.

The research in Rwanda would not have been possible without the participation, advice and practical support of Theoneste Rutagengwa and Ladislas Niyongira. They helped guide me through the complicated land-scape of Rwanda's prisons and taught me much about the intricacies of prison life, and life in Rwanda more generally.

I would like to thank Lars Waldorf and Godfrey Byaruhanga for their valuable comments on sections of the draft and Marcus Turner for proof-reading the text.

This book would not have become a reality without Darryll Patterson, who provided unlimited time, creativity and skill in the design and aesthetics of both print and electronic versions.

Most of all, I would like to thank Alison Lea for her participation in the research in Rwanda, her contributions to successive drafts of the book and the passion she put into this work. Her encouragement and unflinching support kept me going from the very beginning to the very end.

Index

Ageki 206-207

Aids / HIV-Aids 54-55, 166, 186-187, 214, 437

Amnesty International 362, 383, 426

Arusha 22, 140, 144, 343, 358-360, 378, 379, 393, 406, 417-418

Attorney General 216, 365, 368, 371, 398, 399, 403, 447

Avocats sans frontières 355, 362

Babies in prison 57, 167-169, 299

Beatings - see Torture / Ill-treatment

Belgium / Belgian 21, 23, 51, 102

Benaco 303

Biogas 52-53 (52 photograph)

Bizimungu, Pasteur 73-74

Bourgmestre / Assistant *bourgmestre* 151, 234, 244, 247, 311

Brigades 178, 191, 193, 233-235, 237-248, 264, 268, 370, 374, 431, 433-434,
     461

Bukavu 12, 13

Burundi 20, 22, 25, 26, 182, 338, 351, 415-416

Bush, George 141

Butare 51, 121 (photograph), 233, 246, 248, 369, 371, 384, 436,
     438 (photograph)

Butare Central Prison 30-33, 39, 44, 45, 47, 49-50, 52, 54, 55, 58, 62, 63, 73,
     78, 79, 84, 86, 87, 88-89, 95, 101, 103-104, 110, 111, 117,
     118 (photograph), 122, 126, 131, 132, 133-134, 137, 141, 142-143, 155,
     163, 167, 176-177, 182, 183, 184, 186, 190-191, 192, 197, 204, 208,
     225-226, 264, 278, 304-305, 314, 316, 338, 339, 350, 364, 367, 368-371,
     374, 400, 401, 406, 415, 431, 445, 464

Byumba 160, 212, 273, 310, 319, 389

Byumba Central Prison 46, 67, 97, 171, 206, 260, 310

Cachots 46, 47, 51, 116, 145, 171, 190, 191, 193, 196, 200-201, 209, 237-248,
     260-261, 271, 330, 332, 346, 369, 398, 440, 468-469

Camp Kami 227, 232-233

Camp Ngoma 227, 233

Capita / Capita général 43, 55, 59-60, 63, 64-68, 70, 72, 75, 76, 78, 82-100,
  103, 111, 120, 122, 136, 151, 164, 170, 171, 176, 181-182, 183-184, 202,
  207, 208, 211, 224, 225, 230, 256, 258, 259-260, 303, 304-305, 306, 313,
  339, 340, 356, 406, 436, 453, 470, 471-472

Category 1 prisoners 156, 219, 228, 280, 354, 360, 382, 389, 409, 417, 448

Category 2 prisoners 354, 363, 448

Category 3 prisoners 354, 448

Category 4 prisoners 448

Catholic Church, Catholics 71, 130, 142, 148, 150, 152-153, 154-155, 203

Cats 89

Children in prison - see Minors in prison

Children of prisoners 251-252, 269-271, 291-300, 441-443, 461

Clinton, Bill 141-142

Clothes 74-79
  see also Uniforms

Commissions de triage 369, 426

Common crimes / Common criminals 19, 73, 91, 119, 156, 160, 165, 174,
  176-177, 185, 193, 220, 229, 274, 295, 302, 303, 312, 313-317, 323, 330,
  331, 336, 339-340, 355, 358, 365, 374, 375-376, 388, 392, 427, 428, 451

Community work 363-364, 435, 436, 447

Confessions 95-96, 119, 141, 153, 180, 199, 200, 233, 240, 285, 294, 317, 346,
  354, 364-366, 387, 392, 395-423, 427, 428, 431, 439, 441, 444, 445-446,
  447, 472

Congo - see Democratic Republic of Congo (DRC) / Zaire

Corruption 59, 63, 74, 106, 340, 357-358, 359, 362, 367, 374, 382, 399, 426,
  459

Counselling 154, 459

Cyangugu 13 (photograph), 177, 247, 269

Cyangugu Central Prison 12-13, 30, 33, 41, 49, 52 (photograph), 53, 57, 59,
  61, 72, 76, 77-78, 85, 86, 93, 94, 95, 99, 104, 106, 110, 117, 125, 132, 135,
  136-137, 150, 160, 161, 164, 204, 205-206, 252-253, 255, 257, 278, 336,
  339, 340, 345-346, 371-373, 406, 407, 414, 446

Dance 131, 132, 135, 165

Death penalty / Death sentence 20, 86, 119, 150, 167, 193, 206, 252, 262,
  271, 297-298, 305, 323, 326, 328, 354, 355, 358, 359, 369, 371-373,
  381-393, 432

Democratic Republic of Congo (DRC) / Zaire   12, 20, 25, 136, 140, 143, 224,
        231-232, 322, 338, 413, 414
        Rwandan refugees in DRC / Zaire   25, 208, 220, 265-266, 271, 303, 316,
        334, 351, 391, 406, 422, 432, 444, 468
Dignité en Détention   116, 248
Directorate of Military Intelligence (DMI)   223, 231, 233-235
Disabled prisoners   50, 320, 335
Divisionism   309, 433, 439, 451
Dysentery   36, 54, 68, 457

Education in prison   54, 125-131, 163, 164, 184-185 (185 photograph)
Elderly in prison   192, 195-216, 292-293, 407, 418-420, 448, 464, 468-473
Elections   79, 113, 136, 140-141, 310
        Elections of *capitas*   94-98, 230
Ensemble contre la peine de mort   388
Escapes   119, 120, 137, 225, 247, 314, 336-340, 445
Ethnic relations between prisoners   222-229, 302, 308-313, 417-418
Executions   140, 331, 353, 382-387, 389-390

Families in prison   20, 47, 189-194, 209
Families of prisoners   250-273, 275-289, 291-300
        see also Children of prisoners
Fédération Internationale des Droits de l'Homme (FIDH)   379
Food   44, 47, 49, 56-64 (58 photograph), 88, 93, 99, 112, 121, 122, 155, 162,
        167, 175, 186-187, 228, 229, 230, 231, 232-234, 238, 242, 251, 256,
        257-258, 262, 263, 265, 267, 283, 318, 404, 469, 471
        see also Kitchens
Forces armées rwandaises (FAR) / ex-FAR   23, 25, 140
        ex-FAR prisoners   218-233
France   21, 23, 143
Front Line   309, 354

Gacaca   140, 149, 152, 218, 277, 305, 325, 346, 353, 360-364, 367, 370,
        376-377, 379, 409, 412, 423, 427-428, 437, 443, 472, 477
        Prisoners' *gacaca*   169, 254, 364-366, 400-403, 404-405, 411
Génocidaires   92, 156, 233, 302, 309, 312, 313-317, 332, 340, 355, 397, 451
Genocidal ideology   309, 439, 451

Genocide   11-12, 17-19, 22-25 (24 photograph), 220, 352

Germany   21

Gikondo prison   43, 44, 60, 66, 67, 71, 99, 212, 303-304

Gikongoro   73, 133 (photograph), 264, 356, 472

Gisenyi   231

Gisovu prison   311

Gitagata   175-176

Gitarama   51, 245, 248, 436, 454

Gitarama Central Prison   30, 33, 38-39, 48, 58, 59, 68, 71, 85, 89, 93, 104-105, 117, 132, 135, 151, 152, 160, 164, 166, 167, 170, 174, 182, 183, 187, 190, 197, 201-202, 221, 222, 223-224, 254, 256, 257, 309, 319, 326, 339, 350, 385, 400, 404-405, 416, 468-473

Groupes mobiles   426

Guards   45, 60, 61, 64, 66, 67, 82, 83, 84, 85, 101, 107-112 (109 photograph), 119, 122, 125, 137, 153, 166, 167, 171-172, 213, 221, 227, 228, 231, 233, 234, 239, 240, 242, 243, 244, 247, 248, 250-266 (257 photograph), 272, 281, 292, 337-339

Habyarimana, Juvénal   21, 22, 23, 143, 219, 323

Hatzfeld, Jean   465

Health   53-56, 87, 88, 101, 110, 125, 163, 164

Homosexuality   186-187

Hospitals   53-55, 169

    Hospitals in prison   53-55, 84, 87, 88, 168, 170, 257

Hygiene   32, 47, 49, 53, 78, 83-84, 87, 88, 101, 164, 222

Ibuka   378, 441, 443-444, 448

Igisoro   108, 137-138, 178, 210, 472

Ill-treatment - see Torture

Infiltrés   26, 144-145, 230-231, 232, 397

Ingando   434-448

"Intellectuals"   19, 79, 84, 92, 95, 105, 113, 124, 125, 127, 130, 139, 267, 300, 303, 317, 407, 421-422

Interahamwe   22, 26, 63, 140, 156, 229, 233, 243, 288, 297, 303, 331, 456

International Committee of the Red Cross (ICRC) / Red Cross   43, 47-48, 49, 53, 54, 57, 67, 78, 83, 87, 98, 101, 143, 151, 163, 166, 167, 169, 175, 200, 229, 232, 238, 241, 247, 262, 263, 266, 281, 285, 299, 426, 471

International Criminal Tribunal for Rwanda (ICTR) 140, 144, 343, 358-360,
        378, 379-380, 393, 406, 417-418
Islam - see Muslims

Jehovah's Witnesses 148
Judges 19, 20, 178, 180, 354-357, 358, 360-361, 377, 378, 382, 390, 392,
        433-434, 477

Kabila, Laurent-Désiré 25
Kagame, Paul 26, 79, 130, 140-141, 427
Kanombe 230, 232
Karamira, Froduald 382-385, 387
Karubanda 47, 155, 190, 225-226
Kayibanda, Grégoire 21
Kerry, John 141
Kibungo 233, 319
Kibungo Central Prison 45, 68, 89, 171, 235
Kibungo military prison 226-229
Kibuye 24 (photograph), 124-125, 244
Kibuye Central Prison 319
Kigali 22, 26, 55, 71, 141, 155, 175, 229, 246, 248, 273, 310, 382, 454
Kigali Central Prison 36, 37 (photographs), 41, 42 (photograph), 43, 45, 46,
        51, 55, 56, 58 (photograph), 60, 61, 62, 63, 67, 68, 69 (photograph), 72,
        73, 75, 78, 83, 87, 89, 92, 97, 100, 104, 105, 107, 108, 109 (photograph),
        111-113 (113 photograph), 118, 120, 125, 126, 128, 129, 137,
        138 (photograph), 139, 140, 142, 144, 150, 160, 161, 163 (photograph),
        164, 167, 169, 170, 182, 183, 185 (photograph), 187, 197, 204, 206-208,
        211-212, 250-252, 254, 257 (photograph), 259, 263, 266, 269, 285, 286,
        303, 304, 307 (photograph), 308, 311, 319, 320, 329, 339, 350, 369,
        383-387, 389, 407, 431, 434, 454 (photograph), 463-464,
        476 (photograph)
Kigali Rural 232
Kimironko prison 43, 44, 51, 67, 160, 182, 212, 303-304
Kitchens 33, 40, 43, 45, 52, 58-60, 87, 88, 96, 99, 470

Lake Kivu 12, 13 (photograph)
Laws 176, 182, 218, 309, 351, 354, 360-361, 363, 382, 392-393, 428

Lawyers   19, 70, 355, 356, 359, 370, 382, 391, 392, 397

Letters / Correspondence   48, 105, 111, 191, 261-262, 266, 280, 281, 287,
        293-294, 375, 391, 441, 464

Libraries   129-130, 315

LIPRODHOR   49, 51, 218, 353-354

Local Defence Force   20, 436

Local government officials   19, 70, 71, 129, 130, 294, 305, 312-313, 417

Malaria   54, 203

Mazimhaka, Patrick   130

Médecins sans frontières   38

Mental health / Mental illness   55-56, 336, 442

Military camps   129, 227, 232-233

Military prisoners   119, 217-235, 433

Military prisons   218-221, 226-235, 298-299
        see also Mulindi prison

Ministry of Health   53

Ministry of Interior   50, 61, 101, 121, 215, 253, 304

Ministry of Justice   130, 350, 365, 368, 370, 399, 403, 405
        Minister of Justice   280, 365, 368, 371, 440

Ministry of Labour   458

Minors in prison   72, 85, 128, 155, 160, 173-187 (185 photograph), 197, 319

Misago, Augustin   73, 356

Miyove prison   119, 160, 161-162, 212

Mobutu, Sese Seko   25

Mouvement démocratique républicain (MDR)   382

Mouvement républicain national pour la démocratie et le
        développement (MRND)   22, 323, 391

Mouvement Xaveri   87, 142, 144

Mpanga prison   51, 388

Mugunga   303

Mulindi prison   221, 222, 224, 225, 226, 227, 229-232, 299, 433

Munyagishali, Silas   382-383, 386

Music   106, 125, 131-135, 347

Muslims / Islam   148, 150, 154-155, 161

Myaga   438 (photograph)

National *Gacaca* Service   366, 400

National Prisons Service   428

National Unity and Reconciliation Commission (NURC)   87, 435, 436, 437,
      439, 448

Nsinda prison   32, 48, 51, 56, 58, 62, 63, 67, 70, 74, 85, 97-98, 123, 136, 139,
      171, 197, 206, 214, 222, 223, 235, 319

Ntakirutinka, Charles   73-74

Ntaryamira, Cyprien   22

Nyagatare prison   51

Nyange   24 (photograph)

Nyanza prison   60

Operation Turquoise   23

Parquet - see Prosecutor's office

PCK - see Kigali Central Prison

Penal Reform International (PRI)   48, 49, 101, 116, 361, 362, 364, 436, 465

Pentecostalists   148, 409

Priests   19, 38, 70, 71, 77, 148, 150, 152-153, 154, 313, 409, 417

Prison directors / Deputy directors   19, 55, 59-61, 62-63, 71, 75, 82, 83, 84,
      86, 90-100, 101-107, 108, 113, 117, 120, 131, 136, 137, 142, 154, 169,
      174, 176, 185, 197, 205, 207, 226, 252, 259, 260, 264, 286, 303, 304, 305,
      306, 370, 398, 402, 403, 405, 407, 414, 422

Prison staff   20, 45, 64, 75, 82, 83, 90, 96, 101-111, 116, 125, 312, 343, 407
      see also Guards, Prison directors, Social workers

Prison statistics   18, 36, 38, 48, 49, 51, 56, 85, 101, 102, 160, 174, 197, 228,
      229, 231, 247, 313, 338, 350, 351, 353, 388, 398, 400, 407, 427-428, 431,
      477

Prosecutor / Prosecutor's office (*parquet*)   122, 176-177, 178, 180, 198, 199,
      228, 351, 355, 357-358, 369-370, 375, 382, 398, 401, 402, 403, 413, 414,
      419, 421, 432, 434, 440-441, 442-445, 447, 452, 454-455

Protestants   148, 150, 409

Punishment cells   51, 61, 63, 85, 106, 170, 171, 187, 303-304, 305-306, 337,
      339, 402

Radio   22, 70, 73, 86, 112, 128, 136, 138-146, 165, 231, 272, 310, 359, 377,
        380, 383, 385
        Prisoners' radio   142-146, 226, 452
        Radio Mille Collines   22, 139
        Radio Rwanda   139
Rape   12, 171, 177-179, 183, 186-187, 243, 354
Re-arrests   119, 140, 193, 198-199, 284, 297, 315-316, 333, 340, 369-372, 401,
        426-434, 451, 477
Red Cross - see International Committee of the Red Cross
Refugees   25-26, 78, 182, 220, 266, 303, 322, 330, 334, 351, 406, 416, 432,
        434, 444, 468
Releases   49, 110, 153, 155, 193, 218, 220-221, 247, 311, 319, 320, 323, 325,
        333-336, 350, 357-358, 378, 396-421, 426-448, 449-465, 472, 477
        Releases of elderly prisoners   197-200, 209-210, 212-216
        Releases of minors   176, 185
Religion / Religious communities   125, 132, 147-157, 169, 204, 207, 263, 289,
        318, 336, 354, 389, 401, 408-409, 417, 460, 473
Rilima prison   227, 233, 407
Rugambaje, Lambert   228
Ruhengeri   73, 231, 340
Rwandan Defence Forces   219
Rwandan Patriotic Army (RPA)   25-26, 379-380, 444
        RPA prisoners   218-233
Rwandan Patriotic Front (RPF)   21-23, 25-26, 102, 108, 110, 209, 213, 215,
        308, 310, 314, 325, 350, 379-380, 417, 422-423, 432, 444, 458, 472
Rwandex   32, 47, 52, 86, 117, 127, 134, 137, 155, 191, 225-226

Scouts   87, 155
Searches   63, 102, 105, 110, 111-113 (113 photograph), 129, 213, 258,
        304-305, 337
Seventh Day Adventists   148, 151
Sexual abuse   186-187
Sexual relations   111, 170-172, 186-187
Sibomana, André   38-39, 154
Social workers / Social / Sociale   19, 63-64, 101, 129, 180, 187, 204, 259, 310
Sport   106, 136-137, 165, 178, 185, 222, 230, 384
Straus, Scott   352

Students   19, 125-131, 185

Substitut   198, 357, 358, 371, 375, 414, 433, 443-444, 446

Suicide   336-337

Supreme Court   367, 373, 391, 434

Survivors of the genocide   55, 145, 153, 226, 245, 248, 297, 342, 378, 403,
     409, 427, 436, 437, 438, 441, 443-444, 448, 459-460, 464-465

Tanzania   20, 22, 25, 26, 214, 303, 337, 338, 343, 351, 358, 406

Teachers   19, 70, 92, 95, 125-127, 130, 184, 205, 334, 372, 384

Television   99, 106, 135-136, 230

Theatre   106, 117, 131, 135, 169, 208

Tingi-Tingi   406

Torture / Ill-treatment / Beatings   36, 39, 45, 46, 48, 55, 71, 83, 84, 106, 111,
     166, 190, 196, 200-201, 202, 209, 218, 219, 226, 227, 228, 229, 231,
     232-235, 239-247, 264-265, 268, 292, 303-304, 305, 313, 332, 346, 354,
     374, 392, 431, 435, 436, 439, 440, 468-470

Travail d'intérêt général (TIG) - see Community work

Trials   140, 180, 193, 349-380, 382, 383, 389, 390, 391, 392, 417, 426, 477

Tuberculosis   36, 53, 54, 55, 280, 285

Tutsi prisoners   110, 219, 220, 223-226, 228, 302, 308-313, 365

Twagiramungu, Faustin   140-141, 310

Uganda   20, 21, 75, 102, 214, 310, 312, 338

Uniforms   74-79, 98, 100, 107, 117, 123, 125, 162, 178, 180, 211, 219, 221,
     222, 230, 256, 258, 296, 298, 331-332, 337, 404, 468, 473

United Nations (UN)   23, 38, 343, 358-359

United States of America (USA)   127, 136, 141, 143

Visits   46, 84, 93, 98, 110, 111, 112-113, 140, 153, 155, 166, 167, 169, 178,
     181, 184, 185, 191-193, 199, 201, 207, 208, 210, 213-214, 218, 226, 227,
     229-230, 231, 241-244, 247, 249-274 (257 photograph), 275-289,
     291-300, 315, 317, 319, 320, 332, 334, 343, 400, 404, 410, 436-437, 441,
     442, 443, 463, 469, 471, 473

Women in prison 45, 51, 54, 55-56, 57, 58, 62, 68, 74, 76-79, 85, 86, 88-89, 92, 95, 119, 135, 136, 137, 155, 159-172 (163, 168 photographs), 174, 181, 183-184, 197, 200, 204, 207, 208, 210-213, 279, 288, 306, 319, 385, 442-443, 463

Work 51, 53-54, 58-60, 74, 78, 83-84, 87, 100, 111, 116-125, 162, 165, 186, 204-205, 222, 230, 247-248, 260-261, 314, 331, 339, 388, 404-405, 445, 471-472

Zaire - see Democratic Republic of Congo

The author

Carina Tertsakian is a human rights researcher and campaigner based in London. Since 1987, she has worked for several international non-governmental organisations, including Amnesty International, Human Rights Watch and Global Witness. From 1995 to 2000, she was Amnesty International's researcher on Rwanda. During this period, she visited the country regularly and wrote and published reports on the human rights situation there, as well as on the situation of Rwandan refugees in neighbouring countries. From 2001 to 2005, she worked in the Africa Division of Human Rights Watch, where she researched and reported on human rights developments in Nigeria, Guinea, the Democratic Republic of Congo and Rwanda. Since mid-2005, she has been leading Global Witness's campaign on the links between the exploitation of natural resources and armed conflict in the Democratic Republic of Congo.

In 1999, she translated, updated and wrote a postscript for André Sibomana's book *Gardons espoir pour le Rwanda* (*Hope for Rwanda*), published in the UK by Pluto Press.

Le Château: the lives of prisoners in Rwanda was researched and produced independently, without external funding or support.